Voices in Flight: Daylight Bombing Operations 1939 - 1942

Voices in Flight:
Daylight Bombing
Operations 1939 - 1942

Martin W. Bowman

Pen & Sword
AVIATION

First Published in Great Britain in 2014 by
Pen & Sword Aviation
an imprint of
Pen & Sword Books Ltd
47 Church Street, Barnsley, South Yorkshire S70 2AS

Copyright © Martin W Bowman, 2014
ISBN 9781783831777

Typeset in 10/12pt Palatino
by GMS Enterprises

Printed and bound in England by
CPI Group (UK) Ltd, Croydon, CR0 4YY

Pen & Sword Books Ltd incorporates the Imprints of Pen & Sword
Aviation, Pen & Sword Family History, Pen & Sword Maritime, Pen & Sword
Military, Pen & Sword Discovery, Wharncliffe Local History, Wharncliffe
True Crime, Wharncliffe Transport, Pen & Sword Select, Pen & Sword
Military Classics, Leo Cooper, The Praetorian Press, Remember When,
Seaforth Publishing and Frontline Publishing.

For a complete list of Pen & Sword titles please contact
PEN & SWORD BOOKS LIMITED

47 Church Street, Barnsley, South Yorkshire, S70 2AS, England
E-mail: enquiries@pen-and-sword.co.uk
Website: www.pen-and-sword.co.uk

Contents

Introduction

From the outbreak of the Second World War to the eve of VE Day, the medium bomber crews of 2 Group RAF and 2nd Tactical Air Force flew vital operations over Europe. Here their story is told, in thirteen independent chapters, many of them featuring the airmen and war correspondents who took part. Often the stories run in parallel and sometimes, overlap, because of the nature of these exploits and the aircraft types that entered service and were replaced by newer types as losses mounted and tactics changed. The first chapters concern the 'Blenheim Boys', who more than most suffered appalling losses attacking invasion barges on 'The Blackpool Front', the power stations at Cologne and the largely suicidal 'Blenheim Beats' in the cruel North Sea against enemy shipping in a forlorn attempt to reduce German operations in the east. Recounted also are the 'days of carnage' flying from East Anglia and Malta, 'The Year of the Circus' and the 'Blockade of Brest' when Stirling, Halifax, Wellington and Hampden heavy bombers used in daylight were found wanting and soon switched to attacks at night.

Blenheims too were gradually replaced, by aircraft such as the American-built Douglas Boston and the Lockheed Ventura and the North American B-25 Mitchell and of course, the de Havilland Mosquito, which proved the most successful of all. But the part played by the Boston and the Ventura and to a lesser extent, the B-25 Mitchell, is not overlooked. In 1942-43 these squadrons formed the spearhead of the raids by 2 Group on enemy ports and inland targets and on low-level pinpoint attacks against key targets in occupied Europe. The bringing together of such disparate aircraft culminated in Operation 'Oyster' on Sunday 6th December 1942 when Bostons, Venturas and Mosquitoes bombed the Philips works at Eindhoven in Holland. RAF Bostons, Mitchells and Mosquitoes also helped to provide air cover for the Allied armies in the build-up to D-Day and beyond.

One of the reasons the American daylight bombing offensive from East Anglia ultimately proved so successful was because of the Boeing B-17's combat debut on 90 Squadron RAF against German warships in French harbours and in Scandinavia. Daylight raids using Fortress Is were largely unsuccessful and proved to be a costly experiment but improvements introduced by the RAF crews led to better oxygen systems, greater armament and self-sealing fuel tanks and armoured protection that was sadly lacking when the aircraft left the assembly lines in California. These innovations appeared on the late model B-17s and B-24s sent to the 8th Air Force in East Anglia which, in concert with the RAF by day and largely by night culminated in the 'round the clock bombing' offensive which helped destroy 'Festung Europa' and pave the way for the Allied invasion in June 1944.

Of course no book on RAF daylight raids on occupied Europe would be complete without the involvement of the incomparable Mosquito and the final chapter is largely a retrospective look at the daring daylight pin-point operations in 2nd TAF, which together with the RAF Bostons and Mitchells (and the US 9th Air Force medium bombers) contributed so much to the successful conclusion of the war in Europe.

Martin Bowman
Norwich 2014.

Prologue

Torquay 21/8/40

Dear Daddy,

As this letter will only be read after my death, it may seem a somewhat macabre document, but I do not want you to look on it in that way. I have always had a feeling that our stay on earth, that thing we call 'Life', is but a transistory stage in our development and that the dreaded monosyllable 'Death' ought not to indicate anything to be feared. I have had my fling and must now pass on to the next stage, the consummation of all earthly experience. So don't worry about me; I shall be all right.

I would like to pay tribute to the courage which you and mother have shown, and will continue to show in these tragic times. It is easy to meet an enemy face to face, and to laugh him to scorn, but the unseen enemies Hardship, Anxiety and Despair are very different problems. You have held the family together as few could have done, and I take off my hat to you.

Now for a bit about myself. You know how I hated the idea of War, and that hate will remain with me forever. What has kept me going is the spiritual force to be derived from Music, its reflection of my own feelings, and the power it has to uplift the soul above earthly things. Mark has the same experiences as I have in this, though his medium of encouragement is Poetry. Now I am off to the source of Music, and can fulfil the vague longings of my soul in becoming part of the fountain whence all good comes. I have no belief in a personal God, but I do believe most strongly in a spiritual force which was the source of our being, and which will be our ultimate goal. If there is anything worth fighting for, it is the right to follow our own paths to this goal and to prevent our children from having their souls sterilized by Nazi doctrines. The most horrible aspect of Nazism is its system of education, of driving instead of leading out, and of putting State above all things spiritual. And so I have been fighting.

All I can do now is to voice my faith that this war will end in Victory, and that you will have many years before you in which to resume normal civil life. Good luck to you!

Pilot Officer Michael A. Scott's farewell letter to his father. Pilot Officer Scott RAFVR, B. A. Hons (Oxon), who was from Chester, was the pilot of Blenheim IV V5426 on 110 Squadron on 24 May 1941, which took off from Wattisham at 11.10 for a shipping sweep to Nordeney. He and his

two crewmembers, Pilot Officer Julian Gill RAFVR, aged 32, married, of Teddington, Middlesex and WOp/AG, Sergeant Raymond A. Hewlett RAFVR of Taunton, Somerset, were shot down and killed by Leutnant Karl Rung of 2./JG 52 flying a Bf 109 at 14.30 hours, 120 kilometres NW of Texel after an attack on a convoy off Borkum. Scott was 25 years old when he died. Mr. Scott had three serving sons. Michael's brother Mark was lost at sea in January 1942.

Chapter 1

'Bombers Alone Provide The Means Of Victory'

'The Navy can lose us the war, but only the Air Force can win it. Therefore our supreme effort must be to gain overwhelming mastery in the air. The Fighters are our salvation but the Bombers alone provide the means of victory. We must therefore develop the power to carry an ever-increasing volume of explosives to Germany, so as to pulverize the entire industry and scientific structure on which the war effort and economic life of the enemy depend, while holding him at arm's length from our Island. In no other way at present visible can we hope to overcome the immense military power of Germany...'
Prime Minister Winston Churchill to the War Cabinet on the first anniversary of the outbreak of war.

In the autumn of 1939 and the winter of 1940 operations on land were almost suspended, but the war at sea began in earnest and Bomber Command had a most important part to play in it, though even so, because it was impossible to bomb naval bases, there was still a severe restriction on the use of the bomber as an instrument of naval warfare. The bombers and seaplanes of Coastal Command were mostly engaged in, protecting convoys, but to aircraft of the Bomber Command a more directly offensive role was given. Their immediate and most obvious task was to bomb German surface warships and as a matter of fact Blenheims and Wellingtons went out to bomb units of the German navy on the second day of the war. These ships had been sighted during a reconnaissance flight by a single Blenheim which had left its base within an hour of the declaration of war. Here again, in the war at sea, the power of the bomber against warships was much in dispute and even now the matter has certainly not been tested in all possible circumstances. But Bomber Command began to make the test at once and in doing so learnt much else about the strategy and tactics of war in the air. Enemy ships were the first things to be bombed by the RAF in this war - apart from one accidental bomb on a gun-post in Germany - until the attack on Sylt which followed the German attack on the Orkneys; since these attacks on shipping were the first bombing attacks made by aircraft of the Bomber Command in the war.

The order for the attack on the German fleet on 4 September said definitely that the fleet and the fleet alone was to be bombed. 'There is no alternative target' ran the written instructions. The same precise orders were given in several later attacks; this meant that if a ship was too close to land-against a quay for example - it could not be bombed for fear that the bombs might miss and injure civilians on shore. And so for several months it became the task of our bombers to patrol and reconnoitre the North Sea and the naval bases of north-west Germany in search of warships. Against warships heavily defended by their own massed batteries of anti-aircraft guns, in areas where fighters, warned of the approach of bombers by reports from ships, came out in swarms to meet them, bomber crews had to work out the technique of a new kind of attack, solve new problems of warfare and learn how to add prudence to bravery. Naturally there could be no question of attacking a warship without expecting heavy casualties, but some kinds of attack were found to be quite unnecessarily dangerous and at the same time of little use. For example, it had to he learnt that it was of no use to attack a warship from a very low level; a bomb dropped from under 1,000 feet travels too slow to have much chance of penetrating an armoured deck. And since against warships armour-piercing bombs are used, which are designed to penetrate some way into the ship before they explode, there was the risk that they might bounce off a turret or outwork and so into the sea.

No fighters came out to protect the *Von Scheer*, lying in the Schillig Roads and the other German warships which were attacked on September 4. The danger was from anti-aircraft fire. The attacks were made from a very low level, probably too low to have done more than surface damage to the warships encountered. A Blenheim blew to pieces the *Von Scheer's* catapult, which was used to launch aircraft from the deck of the ship, but no other definite damage was observed. The attack took the *Von Scheer's* crew by complete surprise, but as the bombers flew off the Germans had got to their action stations and a hail of bullets filled the air. The casualties from this attack and from an almost simultaneous attack on a warship at Brünsbuttel were in all two Wellingtons and five Blenheims. The daring and skill of British bomber crews had been proved in this action, but not, as yet, the efficacy of the bomb against warships.

More attacks on warships followed, at first from a low level and then from a high level. On 3 December the advantages of the high-level attack were shown. At 12.20pm on that day twenty-four Wellingtons found two German cruisers and about six smaller craft, probably minelayers, off Heligoland. One of the cruisers - it was probably the *Bremse* or the *Brummer* - was badly damaged and later on she was seen down by the stern and in tow. The Wellingtons mostly attacked from 10,000 feet, but one came down to 7,000 feet and from there dropped bombs which silenced one of the cruiser's anti-aircraft batteries. At these heights the risk from anti-aircraft fire does not seem to have been very great; at any rate only one Wellington was hit and this was brought safely home. But the Germans had warning in time to send up a few fighters, though only one of these made a close attack and then against a Wellington flying apart from the rest. The fighter, a Messerschmitt 109, was shot down into the sea; it was the first fighter shot down by a British bomber in this war.

But the Germans were all the time improving their defences and especially their system of warning; anti-aircraft ships were kept out on the North Sea to send warning of the approach of bombers to fighter stations on land. As many as twenty Messerschmitts and possibly more came out to engage twelve Wellingtons attacking a battleship, a cruiser and three destroyers near Heligoland on 14 December. The weather that day was very bad and low clouds made it impossible for the Wellingtons to attack the warships from the height that had been ordered. The bombers had flown almost at sea-level on the way out and when they reached the warships they were only at about 800 feet, with clouds directly above. At this height effective bombing was impossible and the Wellingtons were exposed to all the guns of the warships; it appears that the enemy used not only anti-aircraft guns but the long-range guns of the ships as well. In the confusion of battle two Wellingtons collided in mid-air and others were seen to be shot down by anti-aircraft fire. One heeled over and with its fabric shot away so that its geodetic structure was exposed it crashed, a skeleton, into the sea.

The fighters, both Messerschmitt 109s and 110s, came up from the Frisian Islands and there was a running fight along the islands. The Messerschmitts made determined attacks from above and from below, but the Wellingtons kept formation and so used their guns in concert, directing ones of fire from their power-operated turrets. This seems to have been the first time that this manoeuvre was used by a large formation of bombers and it was immediately successful; the tactics used on this occasion were often tried again, though they proved more difficult to carry out than one might imagine or had been thought at the beginning of the war. At least three Messerschmitt 110s and two Messerschmitt 109s were shot down; by this time it was growing dark and as the fighters burnt on the surface of the water the sea was lit for miles around. There is some doubt whether or no one bomber was shot down by fighters or by anti-aircraft fire. In all five Wellingtons were lost.

Four days later these tactics were put to a supreme test in a battle between twenty-two Wellingtons and a much greater number of Messerschmitts. It is believed that the Germans were seriously alarmed by the result of the recent battle near Heligoland and in consequence brought back some crack squadrons from the Western Front with what was then the latest German fighter, the two-engined Messerschmitt 110, a fast and heavily armed machine. They were going to make sure of victory in any second battle and, with that curious German habit of confounding their intentions with the fact; they afterwards claimed that they had destroyed fifty-two out of the twenty-two Wellingtons engaged in the fight. Is this sort of thing, one wonders, mere propaganda, or is it a more subtle and interesting symptom of the German mind, an inflexibility in the face of unpleasant facts which goes with the German conviction that their own power is overwhelming?

The Wellingtons were out on armed reconnaissance, to find and bomb

German warships at sea; the German warning system was working well and as the Wellingtons, in four formations, entered the Heligoland Bight they were met by fighters, though not as yet in large numbers. They were not enough to engage the Wellingtons at close range; only one fighter came near and this was immediately shot down. There were no ships in the Bight and so the Wellingtons went on to Wilhelmshaven; as they flew on, more and more fighters came up to meet them. 'They collected like flies,' the leader of the first Wellington formation said, 'waiting to attack us.' The fighters began to close, with the object of breaking up the tightly packed ranks of the bombers.

But as the bombers came over Wilhelmshaven - where there were warships in harbour but too close to the shore to attack with the rules of bombing what they were at that time the ground defences came into action and with the same object as that of the fighters; close-packed bombers make a good target and it was hoped that the ranks would therefore open and allow the fighters to take on the Wellingtons one by one.

The bombers did not budge, but photographed the warships in harbour and bombed four large fleet auxiliaries in the Schillig Roads. As the bombers turned northwards the guns stopped and the watching fighters closed in for the third, the last and the fiercest attack on the still unbroken phalanx. It was like many land battles of the past; if the square held, the battle was won; if it broke, a massed volley of fire would be impossible and each individual could be picked off or pursued one by one. The engagement became desperate as the fighters saw the bombers on their way out and escaping. The Messerschmitt 110s, flown by the most skilful and daring of the Luftwaffe's pilots, attacked at full speed, with all their guns firing as they drove in from each side of the Wellington formations. Against all the converging fire from the tail and front turrets of each Wellington, swinging with swift mechanical ease now to the port and now to the starboard beam, it was the most dangerous method of attack.

Casualties began to mount up on both sides, but they were far heavier on the German side. One bomber alone brought down four enemy fighters; it was attacked continuously for forty minutes. As a gunner said: 'If at any time during the battle we managed to get a fifteen-second rest we were more than grateful.' Of the casualties among the Wellingtons, almost all occurred when, for some reason or other, a bomber was unable to keep up with its section. One such, bomber was eventually forced out of its section and attacked by several fighters at once, until all its guns were put out of action. But in this desperate pass the pilot managed to fly to another section, keep close below it and, under protecting wings, though his bomber was itself defenceless, come safely home.

Yet another defensive manoeuvre was tried during this battle, a manoeuvre which later became part of the recognized tactics for attacks on shipping when enemy fighters were likely to interfere. A bomber was detached from its section and accordingly attacked by a swarm of Messerschmitts. The pilot dived to within a few feet of the sea and skimmed the waves, but two Messerschmitts were still in pursuit. They came too close and the bomber's rear gunner shot both into the sea. Another Messerschmitt took up the chase and its bullets wounded the rear gunner. The second pilot took his place in the rear turret, but found that all the ammunition was spent. A moment later the front gunner was wounded, but the second pilot was again ready, went to the front turret, found plenty of ammunition and used it to good effect. The Messerschmitt fell behind. The reason for this success against heavy odds was demonstrated in a hundred battles later on; it became a recognized procedure for Blenheim pilots to hug the waves when out on a search for shipping. The Messerschmitt prefers to break away from underneath the bomber, but if the bomber is at sea-level it cannot do so. A Blenheim flying in this way was once attacked by three Messerschmitts. At first they tried diving on the bomber from above, but the crew could see the bullets hitting the water and it was quite easy to take evasive action. Then the enemy tried to get under the Blenheim, but there was no room. Then they finally came in at the Blenheim's level, but at a great disadvantage and they were obviously uncomfortable and uncertain whether to risk a dip in the sea or whether to make a half-hearted attack from an unfavourable angle. Eventually they gave up.

The battle of 18 December went on until the Wellingtons were seventy miles from the German coast. The last attack of the fighters was the most desperate; they came in again from the beam at headlong speed. But there was still no breach in the ranks of the bombers and at last the fighters broke off the engagement. It took some time to check all the reports and sum up the results of the battle, but eventually it was probable that eighteen Messerschmitts had been destroyed; twelve of these were seen to fall flaming into the sea. The Germans conceded that two of their fighters had 'landed on the water.' Seven Wellingtons were missing.

From now on the weather got worse and attacks on such small and fleeting targets became almost impossible. Even when ships were icebound in the Heligoland Bight, though these were attacked, the weather made it impossible to see whether any good had been done. Usually, operations proved fruitless, as Larry Donnelly, a WOp/AG on Whitleys, recalled:

'We were told quite early on December 23rd that we would be required for ops. A covering of snow lay on the ground as we prepared for take-off. It was a Saturday and some of the tradesmen had been stood down, so my roommate gave me a hand getting into the turret. He gave me the thumbs up as the Whitley squelched through the slush-covered grass. We were airborne at 1130 hours and climbed away from the airfield. The saving grace of this sortie was that it would be at low level where the temperatures were not too bad, but cold enough in my draughty turret. We crossed the coast at Flamborough Head, our usual place of departure, at 2,000 feet and were able to see quite well despite the slight drizzle. How bloody cold and uninviting the North Sea looked. The pilot gave Fletch and I permission to test our guns and soon tracers and incendiaries burned their way down as we let go. We passed to the north of Heligoland and began our 'creeping line ahead' search pattern. Bick, the pilot, exhorted us to keep our eyes skinned and I diligently scanned behind while the rest of the crew searched ahead. After about 30 minutes in the area north west of Sylt we were alerted to a ship. 'Ship off the starboard bow, heading north.'

The adrenalin began to surge again as Bick turned the aircraft towards it. As we neared the ship it was recognised as a merchantman and up at the sharp end [the crew] were endeavouring to identify the flag flying from its stern. Our feelings were mixed when Enery called, 'It's Swedish, neutral'.

Leaving the ship unmolested we continued our search, but there were no further sightings. We reached our PLE (Prudent Limit of Endurance) and set course for home.'[1]

Bomber Command soon found occasion to work with the Navy in yet another way. With all possible emphasis Hitler announced that he had secret weapon which he could use against the English and which the English could not use against him. To guess what this weapon might be became almost a parlour game and for some time we lived in the atmosphere of the penny dreadful, imagining aerial torpedoes, death-rays and all the more baroque contrivances of Wellsian warfare. But it did seem probable that it would turn out to be some weapon for use against our merchant shipping; presumably Hitler meant that 'the English would not be in a position to use such a weapon against his already blockaded merchant fleet. And so when the magnetic mine came along the general consensus of opinion was that this was indeed the secret weapon. No time was lost in finding measures to defeat it and though at first it did considerable damage and was used without any scruple or respect for the conventions of war, its effect was soon checked. The story of all the measures used to protect shipping against magnetic mines belongs elsewhere, but Bomber Command played a considerable part both in preventing the Germans from using this weapon and eventually in turning the tables against them.

The Germans dropped their mines from aircraft as well as using other means to lay them. They were dropped at night by seaplanes based on the Frisian Islands of Borkum, Nordeney and Sylt and Bomber Command was given the task of keeping up standing patrols over these islands. It was only possible to bomb the seaplanes themselves when they were on the sea. Nevertheless, with bombers overhead it was impossible for the seaplane bases to use their lights and for the seaplanes to take off without serious risk. This simple plan worked very well; night after night the crews came back, after an arduous eight-hour flight and reported quietly that the Germans had been in the dark: all the time they were there. The number of aircraft laying mines in British waters was immediately and greatly reduced. The standing patrols went on through the winter and from time to time the patrolling bombers found something to bomb. Looking through the bare reports of these routine operations one comes on such an expressively restrained phrase as 'Submarine sighted and bombed. Subsidiary task.' At the same time preparations were being made to use the Germans' invention against them when opportunity offered; bombers were being prepared to drop mines from the air.

On 16 March about a dozen enemy aircraft flew over Scapa Flow and attacked two naval ships, unsuccessfully, with incendiary bombs. They also dropped some incendiary bombs on land near Stromness on the largest of the Orkney Islands; a house was demolished and a civilian killed. Three nights later, on the night of 19/20 March, thirty Whitleys and twenty Hampdens made what at that time, with the number of aircraft then at the disposal of Bomber Command, could fairly be described as a heavy raid on the seaplane base on the island of Sylt. The Hampdens and Whitleys were sent, not to bomb only aeroplanes on the water, as in previous patrols of the enemy's seaplane bases, but to bomb the hangars and slipways. For the first time in the war a military objective on land, as a result of the Germans' indiscriminate though admittedly not very extensive bombing of civilian property in the Orkneys, was to be attacked from the air.[2] It was a most welcome respite from the apparent stalemate of the first six months of the war in the air and it is not surprising that the attack should, at the time, have been considered more destructive than in fact it was.

Larry Donnelly recalled: 'Later that day, March 19th, we discovered that we were going to take part in the first bombing raid against a German land target, namely the seaplane base at Hörnum on the Friesian Islands. The change in bombing policy was retaliation for the raid by the Luftwaffe on Scapa Flow in the Orkney Islands on 16 March. The retaliatory raid was to be a 'one off': we would attack no further land targets until the Germans invaded Scandinavia and the Low Countries. We were called to briefing early in the evening, during which we were given the gen on the impending raid. The force of 50 aircraft would be the greatest number of RAF bombers to concentrate on a single German target to date. The atmosphere during briefing was charged with anticipation and excitement at the prospect that we were going to drop bombs instead of those 'bloody leaflets'. The flight over the North Sea went smoothly, but the excitement mounted when 'Nipper' announced over the intercom that we would soon be near the island and the target. He went to the bomb-aiming position in the nose of the aircraft to prepare for the bomb-run from 4,000 feet. The adrenalin flow increased when he reported that he had identified the target and called 'Bomb door open!' We started the bomb-run and the litany commenced: 'Left; left, steady ... ri-ght, steady' as we ran the gauntlet of the flak and searchlight defences. The Whitley lurched as the bombs dropped away. We were now receiving the attentions of the defences, but the skipper kept the aircraft straight and level to enable 'Nipper' to plot the bursts. Some of the flak got uncomfortably close to the tail and I was blinded by the searchlights, so I opened fire down the beams. We got away unscathed from our first bombing sortie. Although the bomb-run had lasted only a few minutes it had seemed much longer. Fletch came on the intercom, reporting that one of our bombers had just transmitted an 'X' signal to base, which, when decoded, read 'The natives are hostile'.[3]

News of the raid was given in the House of Commons while the bombers were still in the air, an unprecedented step which only the long suspense of the months of waiting could have prompted. The attack went on for six hours as the bombers arrived at regular intervals. There was some light anti-aircraft, fire at first and then heavy batteries were brought up as the attack progressed; one aircraft did not return and was thought to have been shot down. Every aspect of the attack was, of course, scrutinized in detail by the staff of Bomber Command and much was learnt from it that proved useful later on. But no targets on the German mainland were attacked until the Germans struck in the West.

Endnotes for Chapter One

1   *The Whitley Boys: 4 Group Bomber Operations 1939-1940*, Air Research Publications.
2   While attacking British ships in Scapa Flow in the Orkney Islands, two nights earlier, German aircraft had dropped bombs on land which killed a civilian (on an airfield) and wounded seven more civilians in a village. The British Government ordered Bomber Command to carry out a reprisal raid on one of the German seaplane bases but only where there was no nearby civilian housing. The seaplane base at Hörnum on the southernmost tip of the island of Sylt was chosen. The Whitleys bombed first, being allocated a 4-hour bombing period; 26 Whitleys claimed to have found the target in clear visibility and to have bombed accurately. The Hampdens followed with a 2-hour bombing period and 15 crews claimed to have bombed accurately. Twenty tons of HE and 1,200 incendiary bombs were dropped. Only one Whitley was lost. This was the biggest operation of the war so far and the first raid on a German land target. Proper photographic reconnaissance was not carried out until 6 April when photographs of poor quality were brought back; no damage could be seen but some *repairs could have been carried out by the Germans in the interval. The Bomber Command War Diaries: An Operational reference book 1939-1945* by Martin Middlebrook and Chris Everitt (Midland Publishing Ltd 1985, 1990, 1995).
3   *The Whitley Boys: 4 Group Bomber Operations 1939-1940*, Air Research Publications.

Chapter 2

The Blackpool Front

'The whole of 'Blackpool Front' as we call the invasion coastline stretching west from Dunkirk, was now in near view. It was an amazing spectacle. Calais docks were on fire. So was the waterfront of Boulogne and glares extended for miles. The whole French coast seemed to be a barrier of flame broken 'only by intense white flashes of exploding bombs and vari-coloured incendiary tracers soaring and circling skywards. Then came the great surging kick on the stick as the bombs left the plane. A second later the bomb aimer was through to me on the 'phones ... 'Bombs gone'. My waiting hand threw open the throttle levers in a flash. The motors thundered out. Hauling back on the stick, kicking at the rudder, we went up in a great banking climb. As we went I stared down and out through the windows. There they were! One, two, three, four vast flashes as my bombs struck. In the light of the last one, just as lightning will suddenly paint a whole landscape, I saw the outline of the jetties in vivid relief. Between them the water boiled with thin black shapes. They were barges flung up-end and fragments turning slowly over and over in the air. Then came a most gigantic crash. We were nearly 2,000 feet up now and well away from the jetties but the whole aircraft pitched over as if a giant blow had struck us underneath. A vivid flash enveloped us and lingered as the sound burst round our ears. It was a blinding white flash like a great sheet of daylight stuck in between the dark. While all hell broke loose round us, I fought like mad to get control of the bomber. But all the time my mind was blankly wondering - half-stunned as I was - what the devil we had hit. Afterwards I learned that the last bomb had struck a group of mines stacked on a jetty waiting to be loaded aboard the mine-layers. Photographs taken the next morning showed two stone jetties blown away to the water's edge; all barges vanished from the inner basins; and devastation over a mile radius!'

Flying Officer (later Squadron Leader) R. S. Gilmour, the pilot of a Blenheim on 18 Squadron, whose target was Ostend.

In May 1940 the airmen of Bomber Command had only a bird's-eye view of the invasion of Holland and Belgium and of the Battle of France when over the battlefield and then a swift return home to wait for the next orders. On 7 May all telephone and telegraphic communications between Holland and the USA were suspended. Three days' later Coastal Command Blenheims on reconnaissance early that morning reported eleven German aircraft crashed on the beach south of the spot where the Amsterdam Canal joins the sea and eleven Junkers on the airfield at The Hague, which was strewn the abandoned parachutes of German troops. The Germans attacked Holland, Belgium and France simultaneously. The Luftwaffe opened attacks on Holland by bombing Schiphol, the barracks at Amsterdam and the anti-aircraft defences nearby. This was soon followed by the descent of parachute troops on key points in and near The Hague, at Delft, Zandvoord, the Hook, Ijmuiden, Eindhoven, Dordrecht and on the Waalhaven airfield near Rotterdam. They succeeded in capturing the aerodrome. By the afternoon of 10 May four major aerodromes in Holland, at Waalhaven, Ypenburg, Ockenburg and Walkenburg were in German hands. The Germans at once began to land troops in large numbers from troop-carrying aircraft. The Royal Air Force immediately gave all the aid it could to the hard-pressed Dutch. Aircraft of Bomber Command were in action within a few hours, but their efforts proved futile. On 15 May at 11.00 am, Holland, overwhelmed, capitulated.

Meanwhile the battle was joined in Belgium and France but the German Blitzkrieg was swift and decisive. On 17 June the French asked for an armistice and the RAF was evacuated from Marseilles on 18 June. The last bombing attack which can really be said to be directly concerned with the Battle of France was made by Blenheims in daylight on 18 June, when armoured fighting vehicles and motor transport were bombed on the roads to Cherbourg. But on 19 June Blenheims were again over France in daylight attacking aerodromes in German hands and the aircraft which were using them. On 21 June, between Maaskuis and Rotterdam, bombers found a hundred or more covered barges, stationary but pointing towards the sea. Each barge was about three hundred feet long and they were tied up in threes. Many similar barges were found on the waterways of' Holland. Day by day more reports of barges came in and at the same time the runways on many aerodromes were being extended, bomb craters filled in and - a sinister sign - Junkers 52s were appearing on them.

On 8 July Blenheims made a daylight attack on barges in Dutch canals; some of the bombers attacked from a height of less than 1,000 feet and their crews saw some of the barges alight and the wreckage of others floating on the water. On the same day a canal south of Furnes in Belgium was reported to be packed with barges over a distance of ten miles. On 11 July large concentrations of barges, tightly packed together were seen on the canal between Dunkirk and Furnes while just south of Furnes there was only a small concentration of barges. Blenheims were now out as often as possible attacking barges in the Dutch and Belgium canals. On 13 July they blew barges to pieces in the Bruges-Ostend Canal and as the main concentration of barges went westwards, or towards the coast, so did the bombing attacks. On 16 July barges in a canal west of Armentieres were bombed and on 18 July Blenheims made a rather heavy attack in daylight on docks and shipping at Boulogne, a port which the Germans might be expected to use for any invasion of Britain.

One evening in July 1940 the British public who tuned into their wireless sets to hear the BBC Home Service were treated to an enthralling account of a raid on the 26,000-ton battle cruiser *Scharnhorst* by a 'Sergeant Air-Observer of an air crew who joined the RAF on 6 February 1939'. 'He has been on active service since the outbreak of war' the announcer continued 'and is regarded as one of the most experienced men in his squadron'. The sinking by the *Scharnhorst* and *Gneisenau* of the *Glorious* with its heavy death toll on 8 June 1940 was one of the most tragic episodes of the Norwegian campaign. In between commerce-raiding in the Atlantic the *Scharnhorst* and her sister ship, the *Gneisenau* (or 'Salmon and Gluckstein' as they were known throughout the Royal Air Force, after a famous London store) took refuge in naval bases where Coastal Command attacked them, either alone or as part of an operation by Bomber Command.[4] On 21 June 1940 the *Scharnhorst* was attacked by Swordfish, Beaufort torpedo aircraft and Hudsons. At least three bombs hit the *Scharnhorst*, one on its stern, another nearly amidships and the third forward on the port side. In this action five aircraft were lost altogether, but the *Scharnhorst* had received sufficient damage to cause her to retire to a floating dock at Kiel. She remained out of action for the rest of the year and did not put to sea again until early in 1941.

Of course, no mention was made in the BBC Home Service radio broadcast of the squadron or even the type of aircraft that the 'Sergeant Air-Observer' served on when the *Scharnhorst* was attacked by Bomber Command on 1 July 1940. In fact it was a Whitley bomber, one of thirteen aloft on that day and one of five that attempted to bomb the huge German ship in the floating dock at Kiel. Instead, he began his broadcast: 'My job is that of air observer, which means that I am navigator, bomb aimer and front gunner. There are five of us in the crew and our routine work is long distance night bombing. We were ready to start as usual on Monday night, but when we reported for final instruction we found that a new job had been arranged. Information had come through that the *Scharnhorst* was in a floating dock at Kiel, for repairs and we were to bomb it. We all had a feeling of general jubilation. We were glad to have the job. When the time came, with the good wishes of those who had to stay behind, our squadron got into the air very quickly. I gave my captain the first course to steer, and soon we were on our way, climbing through heavy, wet cloud. The temperature dropped considerably and was actually below freezing point, but apart from that it looked as though the weather was going to be good to us.

'We crossed over without incident until we reached the enemy coast, when searchlights fingered the sky without finding us. By this time it was a very clear night and we could see water reflections sixty miles away. Visibility was excellent. We flew on over enemy territory, meeting occasional AA fire and searchlights but we ignored them and picked up the part of the eastern coast line we were looking for and with our maps pinpointed our exact position. Then we flew on to our target - the floating dock and the *Scharnhorst*. Everything was very quiet. The estuary was plainly marked and as we approached we spotted the German balloon barrage, but still no ground defences were in action. It was now dead midnight. Just at that moment we saw the AA batteries open up on another of our aircraft that was making its attack. We located the position of the defences and decided how we would go in. We were flying fairly high. When we were in position, I gave the captain the word 'Now sir' and he replied with 'Over she goes' and, shutting off his engine, dived to the attack.

'I directed my line of sight on the floating dock, which stood out sharply in the estuary and gave necessary correction to the captain. Searchlights caught us up in the dive, but we went under the beam. Then I had to put the captain into an almost vertical dive as we came on the target. The *Scharnhorst* couldn't be missed; she stood out so plainly. By this time a curtain of fierce AA fire was floating around us. The defences seemed to be giving everything they had got and I could clearly see tracers of the pom-pom on the deck of the *Scharnhorst* at work. Besides that, the shore batteries and other ships in the harbour were doing their best to blow us out of the sky. We took several heavy jars from exploding shells. The lower part of the starboard tail plane was blown away, the main spar was hit, we got a two-foot hole through the tailplane, which broke a rib and narrowly missed our rudder post and we had another hole a foot wide through the fuselage. The rear gunner said he expected to be launched into space any minute; because he felt sure the turret had been shot away. He gets the worst of the jolts back there and, on pulling out of a dive he swung through a much wider arc. But still everything held together, thanks to the splendid material and fine workmanship that went to the making of our aircraft.

'We came down very low to make sure and when we were dead in line I released a stick of bombs. At that moment, I could only see the ship-gun turrets, masts and control tower. A vast skeet of reddish yellow flame came from the deck and what seemed to be the heart of the *Scharnhorst*, right from the edge of the dock across her. The flashes lit the whole estuary and while we banked to go over the town it seemed as though I was looking up at other ships anchored in the estuary.

'We had finished bombing and went off, pursued by AA fire and then circled for height over the quiet waters of the harbour. While we were doing this, we could see fires breaking out on the dockside, and our own comrades going in, one after the other to do their stuff. We saw their bombs exploding dead in the target area. The fires got bigger and there were a lot of explosions that seemed to come from the middle of the fires until they merged into one vast inferno. One explosion outdid all the others and it was probably either an ammunition dump or oil tanks. When we began to climb we realised the damage that had been done to us, and so, on reaching height, I gave the captain a course for home. But while we were still over the estuary at only about 1,000 feet, a German AA ship opened fire. I turned my front gun and pumped about two hundred rounds at him and he ceased fire.

'We flew on down the enemy coast. The rear gunner was chattering all the time something about the fires. We didn't get what he meant at first, but when we were over the coast we turned the aircraft so that we could have a look and we actually pin-pointed the position, from which we could see it - I don't mean see the glow in the sky, but the actual fire. This distance was eighty-five miles. Then we sent a signal to base, giving our position and telling them that the aircraft was damaged so that they would know where to search for us if anything untoward did happen. That was the last message we were able to send as we flew into a storm which earthed the aerial and the radio went up in smoke.

'Still, damaged as we were, after crossing three hundred and fifty miles of sea, we struck our point only three miles off our beating and came quietly home and made a smooth landing. We were bubbling over with excitement at such a successful night's hunting - a bit tired but pretty certain that the *Scharnhorst* will be unserviceable for many months to come.'

Results were unknown and one Whitley was lost.[5]

Sergeant WOp/AG Mike Henry, his pilot, Flying Officer 'Sandy' Powell and Sergeant 'Rich' Richmond, observer were flown to RAF Wattisham on 19 August to join 110 (Hyderabad) Squadron then under the Command of Wing Commander Laurie Sinclair who had been awarded the George Cross for pulling a WOp/AG from a blazing Blenheim after two of it's bombs had exploded. Wattisham was built before the war and like the majority of early war-time airfields had no runways. Situated on the border of West and East Suffolk, its nearest centres of civilisation were Stowmarket, five miles nor'-west and the county town, Ipswich, about twelve miles to the south-east.

Arriving for the first time on an operational station, a completely different 'atmosphere' was sensed for there was the unmistakable air of competence about the place. The whole unit, from the CO to the lowliest 'erk', was geared to work with near precision, for it was liberally lubricated with team spirit, know-how, sense of mission and a healthy inter-squadron rivalry. It comprised an entity of loyal affiliation: there were the airborne and the chairborne, the fitters, the riggers, the cooks, medics and firemen, drivers, fliers, leaders and followers. There were, of course, the black sheep - there always are - but their presence went unnoticed for responsibility was denied them. The whole 'machine' stood at its mark ready to meet any demand made upon it by its controlling function, Group Headquarters.

'The sister squadrons, 110 and 107, were equipped with Blenheim IV medium bombers. Led by 110, these two squadrons held the distinction of leading the first attack of the war on 4 September, its leader, Flight Lieutenant Doran, earning for himself the first DFC of the war. It should be added that the first sortie, a reconnaissance, was made on 3 September by another 2 Group Blenheim squadron, 139. The second war-time CO of 107 Squadron, Wing Commander Basil Embry, was shot down before I arrived at Wattisham but he turned up like the proverbial bad penny three months later after escaping from enemy-occupied territory. When he stood outside one of the hangars, dressed in a smart lounge suit and a Panama hat, those who didn't know him might have thought 'Just another little man from the ministry or something ... ' But his size belied the dynamic character he really was. I didn't know it then but I was to become a member of 107 Squadron. On four occasions and in 1945, I was to serve under Air Vice-Marshal Embry when he was AOC, No. 2 Group, Brussels.

'Three days after joining the squadron we buzzed round the circuit on an air test lasting fifteen minutes. The following day a battle order was posted and one of the 'A' Flight crews listed was Flying Officer Powell, Sergeant Richmond and Sergeant Henry - we were 'on'. That night, weather permitting, we were to 'dice' beneath the stars and amid other more tangible 'illuminations'.

'The briefing was a new experience and it proved a quietly efficient and nonchalant gathering. I felt excited, apprehensive, eager but a little afraid. I had been told by some cheerful swine that the first and last sortie of a tour were the dangerous ones. There were, thankfully, many exceptions to this observation. Although superstition is normally a woman's prerogative, aircrews had their own special brand. It was, for example, considered an act of suicide to write a farewell letter before charging into the fray.

A large number of pilots, navigators and gunners carried lucky charms (I always carried a steel Shaving mirror in the left breast pocket of my uniform and wore a green silk scarf). 'Lucky' items of clothing would remain unwashed for mouths for fear that its owner might be called upon to fly without it.

'The briefing was thorough in every detail. The target was given first which brought from the assembly a whistled 'pheeeew', a hushed murmur or a deathly hush. Then followed the intelligence reports: known flak concentrations, best place to cross the coast, approach to target, convoy movements across our track etc. The navigation and signals 'kings' had their say as did the 'Met' man (or 'seaweed basher as he was labelled by some). The Station Commander, Group Captain O. R. Gayford (whose service background included many record-breaking, long distance flights), often finished the proceedings with a few well-chosen words terminating with a variation of 'And the best of luck chaps.'

'Our target for that night was the airfield at St Omer, in northern France (the same area where Basil Embry had been nipped out of the sky). Take-off was to be half an hour after midnight. I had plenty to do before returning to the mess for supper. The recoiling portions of my two Brownings (kept in a special gun-cleaning room in the hangar) had to be given the final pull-through and cleaning. I then repaired to the signals section to collect a crate of accumulators for the three pieces of aircraft radio: the R1082 receiver, T1083 transmitter and the TR9 which provided intercommunication between the crew and R/T for the pilot to ground or other aircraft.

'Having completed all our chores, we wandered to the mess for our supper (not, we hoped, our last). Everything was ready; after the last aircraft had landed from air test and the empty bomb trolleys had been parked, a blanket of peace descended over the station, All was still as day turned to dusk and to darkness complete. Take-off wasn't late enough for us to grab some sleep so we played bridge in the mess. This was my first experience of the game but I found it absorbing and time-killing. It also kept my mind off thoughts of shells and bullets and searchlights and wings coming off and flames eating at my backside, of parachutes riddled with holes and other gruesome figments of a fertile imagination.

'About an hour before take-off I wandered with others down to the hangar. We dressed slowly, for to sweat before flying at altitude was asking for frostbite; even in the autumn it was very cold at 20,000 feet. We then boarded the squadron bus, slumped down on the hard, cold seats and were driven off into the darkness. My two pals, Eric and Mac, got off at their respective aircraft, each with a cheerful 'See you at breakfast, Frank.' We always parted with some such expression and didn't consciously set any store on it. But one night Mac didn't utter a word when he left the bus. Eric and I thought it odd and wondered whether he was feeling' a bit off colour. That night his aircraft hit the trees near the airfield when his pilot was going round again and had committed the faux pas of pulling the flaps up too soon. Mac alone survived the crash but his serious injuries kept him in hospital for a long time.

'At each dispersal, three men would leave the 3-tonner and waddle across to their aircraft which stood silently on its hard standing, the ground crew waiting patiently to help them into the machine before going about their various jobs. 'Number 3772' came a voice from outside the truck. This was our aircraft. With my signals satchel, parachute and thermos flasks, I clumped over to the port wing root from where we climbed up onto the wing and into our respective hatches. Sandy and 'Rich' made their way up the port wing and disappeared into the front cockpit.

I dug my boots into the steps built into the fuselage side, lowered myself through the aft hatchway and climbed down the short, fixed ladder inside. The ground crew handed me my gear which I stowed in the appropriate places. Nothing must be loose for there was the danger of fouling the unguarded control cables. It was easy, too, for small objects to disappear beyond reach behind the armour plating aft of the radio and turret. Even my receiver coils were attached to pieces of string for fear that, in the darkness, cold fumbling hands would drop them when they might easily roll to an irretrievable position down in the tail.

'Having shut and bolted the hatch, I killed some of the gloom: by turning on a small glim lamp. Engaging my radio plug in one of the many sockets dangling from the fuselage formers, I flicked the microphone switch on and off. Hearing a lively crackle in the 'phones I knew that the intercom circuit was alive. Looking along the tunnel of the fuselage I could see the pilot and navigator beyond the 'well' (a hollowed-out part of the wing centre section, incorporating the main spar and in which was kept the TR9, the dinghy and other spares). The ever-present smell of petrol, oil and other typical aircraft odours fouled the air.

'Sandy soon had himself strapped securely in his seat and gave the signal to start the engines. The ground crew had already primed the Mercury's by means of a small pump in the undercarriage housing of each nacelle; the trolley-battery operator gave the thumbs up sign. Sandy switched on the ignition and pushed the starter button of first the port and then the starboard engine.

The propellers turned over in a squeaky, laboured sort of way until each engine fired. The silence of the Suffolk countryside was shattered as was the sleep of those in the vicinity. Oily smoke poured back over the quivering tail-plane while the aircraft stood there gently straining against the chocks. When both engines had been run up and cockpit drill had been completed, trimming tabs were neutralised, pitch controls moved to 'fine' and compass set. There was a tap on my hatch. I moved back and opened up; the undercarriage links (made conspicuous with a red but oily flag, they locked the undercarriage to prevent accidental retraction when the aircraft was on the ground. By the same token, they prevented retraction when airborne) and pitot-head covers were thrust into my hands. I slammed the hatch, stowed them and crawled back into the turret.

'All OK in the back?'

'Yes, sir. Intercom OK, links and pitot cover in.'

'What about you, Rich?'

'Fine, can hear you both. Your first course is 064 magnetic.'

'Chocks away' was waved by Sandy and we started to taxi out. At the end of the flarepath we stopped; a final check: lower 15° of flap and wait for the 'green' from the duty controller in the caravan. The Aldis flickered its 'go-ahead'. With engine gills closed we turned into wind, the throttles were moved to the top of the gate and we were rolling. Bouncing slightly over the uneven grass surface we soon lifted off and climbed away into the night. With half a ton of high explosive in the belly of the aircraft, it wasn't a fast rate of climb. In my 'back to the engine' position I saw the single row of flares disappear in the haze. The winking red glow of a flashing beacon pierced the darkness at regular intervals until it, too, was swallowed by the night.

'Our route took us out over the Suffolk coast well to the north of Harwich and its attendant balloon barrage. Climbing steadily to our operational height over the North Sea, we turned onto a southerly course and headed for the French coast. The Dunkirk episode came to mind as we neared those very beaches. Swivelling my turret and looking forward I could see searchlights clawing the sky. As we got nearer, I saw my first flak (from the receiving end that is). It was being hose-piped towards an unseen target well ahead of us. It ascended seemingly slowly as though it were tinsel being carried aloft by playful cherubs. But when we got above it; that multi-coloured stream of tracer whipped by the aircraft at its true and lethal velocity. Another type of flak, 'flaming onions', was squirted at us. Like a string of Christmas-tree decorations they ascended, levelled out at our approximate height and exploded one after another.

'The heavy flak one noticed only when it was close enough to hear and smell and that was close enough, thank you. On a moonlit night their black puffs could easily be (and often were) mistaken for balloons. I think that the most unnerving experience was to look down and watch, hypnotised, the three-foot muzzle flashes of a heavy anti-aircraft battery, then to wait to see how accurate their aim was. ❧

The firing was spasmodic after leaving the coast and as we flew inland it became quieter below and above. Circling for a while, the navigator picked out the target and the aircraft was lined up for the bombing run. The 'Left, left... steady... left a bit... steady...' of the practice bombing days now took on grim reality. We were about to discharge high explosives onto something, someone below. A fleeting thought of horror was suddenly quelled when 'bombs gone' coincided with a fresh burst of hostility from below. Searchlights vied with each other in their groping for victims. A master searchlight stood out more proudly than the others, its violet hue stabbing even further into the heavens.

'Between scanning the sky for night fighters and looking down fascinated at the dark, unfriendly scene below, I wondered how soon it would be before the comparatively frail alloy shell of our aircraft was pierced by hot steel or thrown into sharp relief by a few million candlepower. Having seen our bombs explode in the target area, we wheeled round onto a reciprocal course and headed homewards. We again ran the gauntlet at the coast but were soon out of range. The pyrotechnics ceased and the searchlights flickered out one by one, almost, it seemed, with a frustrated sigh for allowing a fly to slip through their web.

'Still keeping my eyes peeled for signs of air attack, I occasionally got glimpses of tracer and searchlights astern until distance dwarfed them and blackness finally engulfed all signs of enemy activity. There followed a period of elation; a tranquillity I'd never known before but was to experience many, many times. As we approached the Suffolk coast I was feeling positively exuberant. We were practically home and dry but danger still lurked should there be night intruders in the base area.

'It hadn't been a very difficult or dangerous sortie but as an overture to our tour of operations, it had had its moments and over a steaming mug of coffee, these were related in detail to the intelligence officer (10) at de-briefing (interrogation it was then called).

'Four days were to pass before we made our next sortie. Our second venture into hostile air space was to Deauville, a little to the south of Le Havre. It went smoothly enough; no worse, no easier than our first sortie. We landed after that trip at 5 am, so by the time I got my head down the sun was already high.

'At the end of August we were briefed for our third sortie. This time we were Germany-bound. The target was the' north-German port of Emden, at the mouth of the River Ems. The approach from the North Sea meant crossing the Frisian Islands. Those heavily defended bastions, covered by a night-fighter patrol, afforded an effective shield for some of Germany's most vulnerable ports: Wilhelmshaven, Bremerhaven, Hamburg, Cuxhaven and Kiel (as well as, of course, Emden). Because of this, most attacks on them were delivered from an inland direction.

'Our next, the fourth, trip took place on the night of 7/8 September. We had been briefed to attack the docks at Dunkirk. Recce aircraft had brought back photographic evidence of a build-up of invasion barges there and at all the Channel ports (Antwerp, Ostend, Boulogne and Calais, included). The crew bus dropped us off at our aircraft. 'Sandy' made his way up the port wing and into the cockpit, closely followed by 'Rich'. I heaved myself up to the hatch, just behind the turret and lowered myself into the body of the aircraft. Packing my parachute, signals satchel and thermos, I waited at the open hatch for the ground crew to hand me the pitot head cover and the undercarriage links. The former, if not removed, would prevent the airspeed indicator from registering. The links prevented the undercarriage from being retracted - neither desirable. I slammed the hatch cover and crawled into the confines of my turret. Plugging into the intercom system, I told the pilot that the pitot cover and links were stowed. He answered, 'Thanks, all OK in the back?' 'Yes sir, intercom OK.' 'What about you Rich?' 'Fine, can hear you both. Your first course is 064 magnetic.'

'Taxiing out to the flare path, the usual butterfly feeling began to stir in my stomach. Although the target was on the French coast, which meant mat we had no long overland journey, we thought of the warning given at briefing, that light flak at the height we were going to bomb from (between 6,000 and 8,000 feet) would be at its most lethal. We were soon to find out what the night sky over Dunkirk would look like.

'A green light from the Aldis lamp cleared us for take-off. Bumping over the uneven turf; we set course for the Suffolk coast. In my back-to-the-engine position, I saw the single line of flares disappear into the haze. Our route took us across the coast north of Ipswich and Harwich and their attendant balloon barrages as we flew south over the North Sea, there was an ominous glow on the western horizon. This time it wasn't the moon but came from the direction of London, 100 miles to the west.

A Londoner myself, I became anxious for the safety of my parents, relatives and friends but the full realisation of what had happened was not felt until the following morning when the BBC announced that the onslaught against the capital had started. The night-time blitzkrieg had replaced the dog-fights over Kent and the Home Counties; the Battle of Britain had become the Battle of London. When I heard the news, any feelings of guilt I harboured about dropping bombs on others were swiftly replaced by a grim determination to fight back and the ensuing attacks on invasion barges were carried out with an added sense of purpose by all, wherever they lived.

'Eventually we turned due south towards France. The Dunkirk episode came to mind as we approached those very beaches. Swivelling my turret and looking forward I could see the searchlights clawing the sky - one or two master searchlights standing out in contrast, their vivid blue fingers seeking a target. There were other aircraft ahead of us, this becoming obvious when a fierce barrage of light flak joined the searchlights. As we approached this fearsome scene, I felt a mixture of excitement and fear and my imagination began to build frightening pictures until, looking down when finally over target, I became fascinated to watch the flashes from gun batteries - wondering whether they were aimed at us and had they got the right height. Colourful tracer and flaming onions, the latter levelling out at about our altitude and then exploding one by one. The streams of tracer coming from many points and forming a cone nearly was quite terrifying, although when it left the ground it seemed so slow and its wavy trajectory whipped by at its true velocity. We were over the target only a short while, but it seemed an age before we got rid of Our bomb load and turned towards the coast and home. How anybody could survive in that ferocious showing of defence was my upper-most thought - to be repeated every time we bombed a similar target. However, on landing at base we looked all over the aircraft for signs of damage - not a scratch! On our way back from Dunkirk, I noticed an ominous glow in the west, from the direction of London, my home town. At first I thought it might be the moon, but the BBC told us that the Blitzkrieg was replacing the dogfights over Kent and the home counties. The Battle of Britain had been joined by the Battle of London.

'My fifth trip on 8/9 September was to Boulogne. I was not flying with Sandy (who had, incidentally, been promoted to Flight Lieutenant earlier that month) but with Flying Officer Lynch-Blosse. We were briefed to straddle the dock area of Boulogne with our bomb load. I was flying with another crew just for that night. We took off at 19.00 and received the usual reception. The same fascination and fear seeped through my bones. But, again, we came out of that hellish cauldron without a scratch.

On these operations enemy fighters fought clear of their own defences, therefore I sat there without recourse to my machine-gun. Mark you, my eyes were everywhere, with furtive glances at the parachute stowage. Also, radio silence was the order of the night until we reached the East Anglian coast, when we had to get a bearing before crossing it. We had lost one or two aircraft which mistakenly flew up the Thames Estuary and were lost to balloon barrages.[6]

'This was followed by attacks, with my own crew, on Calais (twice), Dunkirk and Boulogne, on 11, 14, 16 and 18 September respectively. On the 14th our take-off for Calais was moved from late evening to early morning - this time we got off the deck at 04.15. We were wrong to assume that the Germans manning the defences were sleeping, for there came up millions worth of Reichsmarks in ammunition and the candle-power must have consumed a few million kilowatts. On the 16th, at 04.00, we took off for Dunkirk. As a matter of interest, the Calais return trip took a little over two hours, while Boulogne was over three hours and the Dunkirk about the same as Calais. So we didn't lose too much beauty sleep.[7]

'The Channel ports, in late 1940, were among the most heavily defended targets I can remember. Hitler's intention of preserving his invasion fleet was made clear for his minions ferociously threw up everything but the kitchen sink. What made matters worse for us was the altitude at which we bad been briefed to attack i.e. between 6,000 and 8,000 feet. At that height, light flak was at its deadliest. It came up like an inverted monsoon of vivid colour; from all directions it poured to· culminate at the apex of a cone of searchlights. They were at the time, some of the most terrifying experiences of my life. 'How any aircraft can survive in that lot,' I thought as we made our bombing run, 'is a miracle.' But, as we found out, the age of miracles was not past and we came through unscathed. Many, of course, didn't and were seen to plummet, flaming pyres, earthwards. Those targets made our first two sorties look like a poor man's Guy Fawkes' night in heavy rain.

'The next on the Channel port 'milk run' was to Boulogne on 18 September (three days after the official climax of the Battle of Britain). The sky over the port was a repeat performance of German anger, if anything a little brighter (contrary to popular belief, one couldn't hear much against the noise of our two engines - except for a very close heavy AA shell burst). Nearly a year later, still in a Blenheim turret, I was part of a daylight 'circus' over Boulogne - we had the comfort of six squadrons of Spitfires and Hurricanes as escort. This operation differed in that the sky was littered with hundreds of dirty black smudges without any useless searchlights. It made a change!'

By 21 September the incessant pounding had put twelve transport ships, four tugs and fifty-one barges out of action. A further nine transport vessels, one tug and one hundred and sixty three barges were damaged. One week later, 214 out of the assembled fleet of 1,918 converted Rhine barges had been temporarily or permanently put out of commission, a serious loss of twelve per cent. This undoubtedly contributed to Hitler's decision to break off the invasion preparations on 12 October. When trips to the Channel ports came to an end the Blenheims began to turn their aircraft noses towards Germany. So that short interlude of colourful enemy aggression over the French Channel ports came to an end. The threatened invasion was called off and we reverted to other targets. I must add that, while we survived those hectic nights over Dunkirk, Calais and Boulogne, we weren't at all sorry to climb higher into the night sky and just remain prey to the heavier flak.'[8]

After a week of September had gone by, barges on the coast seemed to have become an immediate menace again. The greater part of Bomber Command's effort on the night of 7/8 September was directed against barges and shipping in Calais harbour, at Dunkirk and at Ostend. In the early hours of the morning and well on into daylight, Whitleys patrolled the coast between Ostend and Boulogne; sometimes coming down to 500 feet in broad daylight, so urgent was the need for immediate information of the German plans. As the day went on, Blenheims reconnoitred the Channel ports and the ports of the Low Countries; they bombed what barges and ships they could find. But this was only the beginning of a sustained attack on all the ports and harbours of northern France, Belgium and Holland. For many nights in succession Bomber Command sent the greater part of its aircraft, though it still maintained its attacks on targets in Germany, to bomb the barges and destroy the docks and jetties from which an invasion would start.

The attacks went on throughout September, while rumours and threats of the coming invasion went round the world; 15 September was everywhere reported to be the day when the barges would start, but 15 September came and went. Bomber Command did not relax when the advertised day, or any other advertised day, was passed; on the contrary, some of the heaviest attacks on the ports were made towards the end of the month. And the bombing continued into October; on 11 October the Royal Navy joined in and shelled Cherbourg in, the darkness, beginning, at about 3.30 in the morning and going on for an hour or more. Bombers were over the same target at the same time and their crews were astonished by the violence and glare of the Navy's bombardment.

'They didn't know whether it was Christmas or Easter,' a squadron commander said when he described how the German defences reeled under the shock of this sudden blast from the sea; 'the searchlights went quite drunk and waved aimlessly about the sky; the guns went on firing, but goodness knows what at!' From a hundred miles away, the glare was so bright that some crews thought they must have got off course and were perhaps flying towards an air raid on an English town close at hand. It was a spectacular instance of a combined attack by sea and air; no doubt we shall see more such attacks before the war is over.

But at that time combined attack was exceptional, though presumably the method would have been used again and again if invasion had seemed even more imminent. Steadily, at regular intervals, 'Bomber Command went on with the work of disorganizing the ports which front the English coast. For that matter this work has never stopped. Though the barges may be gone, all these harbours are still of use to the Germans for their shipping which creeps along the coast. But though these are now considered comparatively easy targets, no attack on them is ever safe and still less could the attacks of the summer and autumn of 1940 be made with impunity.

The expectation of invasion, the mounting tension, produced its crop of rumour and we meet again that recurrent phenomenon of this war, the production in fantasy of what has long been expected in fact. In America and on the Continent, throughout October and November, it was being said that barges had sailed in September but were smashed by our bombers. In particular, this was said to have happened on 15 September, a date for which invasion had been predicted before. This story at least took more account of inherent probability than most other rumours of this war.

Though it may be difficult to disentangle the work of Bomber Command from that of Fighter Command in preventing any attempt at invasion of Britain, there is little doubt that Bomber Command would play a most important part in repelling any future attempt at invasion. Attacks on a far heavier scale than in the past could - and would - be made on the ports from which the Germans proposed to mount an invasion, on any ships crossing the Channel and on any beaches or ports in Britain where Germans succeeded in landing. Attacks as heavy as any on Germany would be made at much closer range and several times in the twenty-four hours. The invasion might well be over before it started.

Endnotes for Chapter Two

4   They would be attacked 63 times in all in 1941 alone.

5   Early in February 1942, mines laid by 5 Group Hampdens or Manchesters in the Frisian Islands during recent nights, caused some damage when the *Scharnhorst* hit two mines and *Gneisenau*, one. The *Scharnhorst* was more seriously damaged. With speed reduced to twelve knots and shipping a thousand tons of water, she nevertheless managed to limp into Wilhelmshaven. Both the *Scharnhorst* and *Gneisenau* were located in Kiel later. The *Gneisenau* received additional damage between 25 February and 28 February 1942, during bombing raids on the dockyards at Kiel and was never in action again. The Royal Navy got the *Scharnhorst* in the end and she was sunk on Boxing Day 1943, off Norway.

6   Ostend and Boulogne docks were bombed. Five Blenheims (on 40, 101 and 107 Squadrons, with all fifteen aircrew lost) and two Wellingtons on 149 Squadron fell victim to the ferocious flak defences.

7   Unknown to Henry at the time, he had participated in an outstandingly successful raid on the harbour of Dunkirk in the early hours of 16 September. Under a full moon, twenty-six barges were sunk or badly damaged with a further fifty-eight being lightly damaged. Additionally, 500 tons of ammunition was blown up.

8   *Air Gunner* by Mike Henry DFC (Goodall 1997) and *Bristol Blenheim* by Theo Boiten (Crowood1998)

Chapter 3

Blenheim Beats

They found him by a tobacco kiln on Sumas Prairie. The only Englishman on a farm of husky foreigners, he was shaping a pipe for kanikanik out of a reed. It was his seventeenth birthday and he'd been innocent enough to let them know it in the bunk-house. They were tough in the bunk-house - the sweaty Hungarians, Germans and Swedes - tough and careless. So careless that after making one useless complaint about bugs on the walls they took coal-oil and started a fire. Then there were no more bugs on the bunk-house walls because there was no more bunk-house.

Saturday nights they had taken him with them to beat up the town of Chilliwack. At Chilliwack the raw young Englishman had his first illicit drinks and met his first girl. He also trained as an Army cadet and rose to bombardier.

'Mr. Atkinson,' smiled the hairy German by the tobacco kiln, 'we have a present for your seventeenth birthday. Kindly take a walk with us.'

He went with them to a bridge high above a tributary of the Fraser River. Then they lifted him up over the parapet and carelessly dropped him. It was a long way down. Also the water was cold, but that hardly mattered because there was very little water in the tributary of the Fraser River.

So he grew up. They toughened young Bombardier Atkinson on Sumas Prairie.

Work In The Sun from The Fire Was Bright by Leslie Kark, 1943 who instead of 'Attie' Atkinson uses the pseudonym Theodore James 'Roley' Rowlandson.

L. V. E. 'Attie' Atkinson had become a lumberjack in Canada at the age of seventeen. He had had his first illicit drink there and met his first girlfriend. A toughened young man, he had returned to England on the compensation he had received after crushing the little finger of his left hand at work. Back home, the Royal Air Force refused him entry because of a slight cast in his left eye and he took a sedentary job as a probationary clerk at Church House, Dean Street, Westminster, a meeting place for the English clergy and a kind of clerical club. The most exciting day for young Atkinson, probationary clerk, was when he had tea with a Bishop. However, his strabismic eye righted itself and pointed straight in 1936. He was nineteen then and the RAF took him on approval, safeguarding the integrity of the Armed Forces of the Crown by giving him fifty hours' flying at Anstey in

Wiltshire before he was allowed to wear uniform and take the King's Commission. This was known as the throwing-out period. 'Attie' then became an Acting Pilot Officer, 'on probation, under suspicion and in a state of alarm', as he put it. He flew Hawker Harts in his Service training and was then posted to 82 Squadron, which was being formed. At the controls of a peace-time short-nosed Blenheim Acting Pilot Officer 'Attie' Atkinson took part in the first attempted formation flight from the South of England to Scotland. His instruments and wireless failed but caused him little anxiety. He could stay close to his leader. A thin drizzle turned into rain which swept in distorting runnels sideways across the glass in front of him. The leader climbed above the cloud and stayed there till he came down through a gap and the short-nosed Blenheims found themselves over the Firth of Forth. Then he turned back for home and unaware of 'Attie's handicap made again for cloud. Through the blinding mist 'Attie' flew close to the dim shape of the leader's wing-tip, lost him and in the frantic search went into a spin. His Blenheim spun giddily down from 10,000 feet and then, looking round, he saw some cathedral spires. The spires were travelling surprisingly fast and were neither the right way up nor upside-down. They were, in fact, alarmingly horizontal. Acting Pilot Officer Atkinson, on probation, went grey and pulled out. 'So that's where we are,' he said to the observer. 'Durham.'

Thus by the grace of Church House, which had taught him there was only the one cathedral in those parts, he flew down the valleys and got back home.

On Sunday, 3 September 1939 Flying Officer Atkinson was sunning himself on the grass of a brand-new aerodrome. With other pilots he sauntered over at two minutes to eleven to a workmen's canteen, listened to the Prime Minister, Mr. Neville Chamberlain on the wireless. In homes and factories and at other military establishments the length and breadth of Britain, men and women tuned in to the broadcast. Twenty-nine year old Henry Paul Brancker, the manager of the local branch of an insurance company, listened alone in his Manchester flat. Cousin of Air Vice Marshal Sir William Brancker who lost his life in the R101 airship disaster in December 1930, his brawny physique, inherited from a blend of Cornish and Huguenot stock, belied the fact that he had to go his way carefully and asthmatically through school. A RAF Medical Board had already written him off as 'totally unfit for all types of Service flying.'

Shortly after twelve midday 82 Squadron flew to a temporary base further south. As they circled round the aerodrome thecrews saw a thin miniature train of trolleys crawl along the perimeter track. 'Hey, hey,' sighed 'Attie' to his navigator and remarked slowly, 'Real live bombs.' It was still only the white war. Gingerly at first, 'Attie' ferried bombs around the countryside and wondered whether they mightn't fall off and hurt someone. He went on odd sweeps and reconnaissances. On Old Year's Day the aerodrome was feet thick in snow and foggy. 82 Squadron were having a dance that night and Auriol, Atkinson's fiancée was already on the train from London. At noon his CO called him in and said, 'Attie', can you take off in this?' Intending to be respectfully sarcastic, 'Attie' replied that nothing, sir, was simpler. 'Right' said his CO 'Go and do a recco of these positions at Sylt and return to Yorkshire. There's no fog there.' By the aid of money flares on the runway 'Attie' went, did his job and on the way back to Yorkshire thought of Auriol coming up for a New Year's Eve dance to a base far away from Yorkshire. Then his gunner received a signal: 'Return to your own base.' On New Year's Eve 1940 'Attie' danced with his fiancée.

'The real war,' as he called it, started for him on 10 May 1940, with the enemy's breakthrough in the Low Countries. The Germans marched and 82 Squadron went for the bridges. 'Attie' dived down to a thousand feet and then found he was aiming at the wrong bridge. So he stayed at that dangerous level, flying in what he termed 'muck, flak and corruption'. He bombed in the half-light, was hit repeatedly by ground fire and struggled back across the southern North Sea to his East Anglian base, there to make his first operational night landing. A week later he escorted fighters to a landing-field in France, picked up some cheap bottles of champagne in Lille on behalf of 82 Squadron and at base emerged from his Blenheim expecting to be greeted in the mess with huzzas and acclamation. But the wine was not drunk. Or not that night. While 'Attie' was at Lille twelve Blenheims on 82 Squadron had taken off for Gembloux on 17 May. They met fighters at Gembloux and only one came back. So 'Attie' and the remaining crew had little taste for the champagne from Lille. Two days later 82 Squadron were again fully operational. In the sober Squadron history the incident was called the 'Miracle of Gembloux'. By ones and twos, by drays and destroyers, tanks and tugs, some of the lost men of Gembloux returned, reported back to base for further orders and as they came, sipped the champagne intended for a previous occasion.

There were rewarding days over France. Days when the Blenheims were bombing and machine-gunning the massed Germans, eating their way into the heart of France. 'Attie' saw 'tanks crack open, horses pitifully stampeding' lorries tossed high. Once he watched a German airborne at a hundred feet. The enemy had been running when he was caught by the blast of the bombs from a preceding Blenheim. 'Attie' watched him sail up, whole and erect, still pathetically trying to run. A symbol of high-flown Nazism, eventually defeated by natural gravity.

'Attie' was flying one day in a formation of nine when twenty German fighters dived at them out of the sun and shot down three. The remaining six climbed into a cloud, the only cover for miles; it was an uncomfortably small cloud, forcing the Blenheims to do pretty tight turns to keep inside. The' enemy patrolled the circumference, firing at any bomber which skidded out. 'Attie' thought the inner circle routine was becoming a trifle monotonous, when a storm blew up and the Blenheims were able to take a new route.

When the roads of North France were miserable with the processions of refugees distraught from Stuka dive-bombers, 'Attie' and his kind were normally careful to avoid low flying and navigated so that the women below could see the roundels. After dropping his bombs on a German column 'Attie's observer called out, 'Fighter to starboard!' and flung himself down towards his own cabin and his gun. The Blenheim shivered and the next thing 'Attie' saw was his observer rising horizontally by the side of him, without visible means of support. But the shell-blast which delivered the navigator there had also wounded him and after evading the fighter 'Attie' went low to make for the nearest French base and hospital. It was then that he came across the French refugees and considerately climbed again to a thousand feet to show his British markings. Less considerate and more myopic, a French gunner promptly sent up an accurate shell. So thereafter the observer persuaded his captain he would as soon be in an English hospital and his captain decided that charity began in his cockpit and safety at about ten feet. Thereafter the Englishman from Sumas Prairie took a 'rest', a DFC, a handshake from the King, a Squadron-Leadership, a wife and, in a remarkably short space of time, a ticket back to further operations. On 21 Squadron they had whetted his appetite. He was one of the only two pilots left from the whole original Squadron.

Casualties among RAF bombers that attacked by daylight during the Battle of France were very high, so high that eventually only the most urgent targets were bombed in daytime. But the Battle of France had scarcely ended when Blenheims were out over Germany and the Low Countries and northern France in daytime. On 22 June 1940, the day that France signed an armistice with Germany, eighteen Blenheims attacked Merville aerodrome at three o'clock in the afternoon. There was a good deal of cloud to serve as cover. On the next day, 23 June, 26 Blenheims attacked the marshalling yards at Hamm, an objective near Münster and aerodromes in Holland and oil tanks near Amsterdam. Most of these attacks were made singly: During the rest of the month and during July there was scarcely a day when Blenheims were not out, attacking targets either in Germany or in occupied territory. On occasion, some had to abandon, their task for lack of cloud cover, but it is remarkable and has, perhaps not been sufficiently realized, how much daylight bombing Blenheims did in the summer after the Battle of France. The squadrons trained for daylight reconnaissance and bombing had suffered very high casualties; some had retreated and retreated, moved all the staff and stores of their aerodromes backwards and backwards through the crowds of refugees and finally had left France after destroying everything that could not be taken back to England. But they were ready at once to attack the enemy again. Much of their work was the bombing of aerodromes and of barges moving up for the invasion, but, especially in June and July they made a number of daylight attacks on targets in Germany as well. On 27 June twelve Blenheims got as far as Hanover, Bremen, Salzbergen and the Dortmund-Ems Canal; only six aircraft bombed, five at Hanover where oil-storage tanks were hit and set on fire and a tower in the oil refinery collapsed. Thus the German air force was kept busy along the whole coast-line from Norway to the Bay of Biscay; Norway was in the main the business of Coastal Command, but Bomber Command also sent aircraft there at intervals during the summer. Only occasionally and in some attacks on objectives in northern France, did RAF bombers have any fighter escort.

As the Battle of Britain proceeded, daylight squadrons, like the heavier bombers which did their work by night, had to turn to the defence of Britain, chiefly by bombing aerodromes in northern France, but also by attacks on invasion bases. During August there were scarcely any attacks on targets in Germany, but there were as many daylight attacks as possible on Dutch and French aerodromes. In the first ten days of September cloudless weather made daylight bombing impossible, for at this stage of the war the use of cloud cover seems, to have been considered the most satisfactory method of getting through the defences. But on 11 September Blenheims on reconnaissance attacked a convoy off the Belgian coast and, with only one or two exceptions, all the daylight attacks of September were against shipping or barges, either in ports or sailing along the coast. It is improbable that all the shipping attacked in that month was gathered off the coast of France and the Low Countries solely for the invasion of Britain. By then the Germans had probably begun to use coastal shipping to supplement their overworked railways and roads; they certainly made every effort, as time went on, to establish such a sea-route as a cheap and convenient method of transferring plunder from conquered peoples to Germany; and of sending back in return more arms to hold what they had conquered. Tankers have often been sunk carrying oil to the naval bases and aerodromes of north-western France. Towards the end of 1940 the Germans went round a district of northern France collecting every pig they could lay their hands on. They loaded the pigs on to a cargo-boat, a ship of 5,000 tons and sent it off to Germany. But the ship had only just begun to creep cautiously along the French coast when it was sunk. The pigs were washed ashore and there was roast pork for dinner and no doubt gratitude to the RAF in many French homes that day.

In October the daylight attacks on shipping went on; on 3 October a fairly large convoy of merchant ships was bombed off Dunkirk. But a greater variety of targets, including some in Germany, were also attacked that month. On 4 October quite a number of Blenheims were out and though most of them attacked shipping, some penetrated far into Germany. The weather was extraordinary, with thick cloud and sleet over the North Sea and so much ice about - twenty degrees of frost were recorded in one bomber - that some pilots could not see out of their cockpits at all. In fact, there was rather too much cloud cover, but where a gap could be found the bombers' attacks were all the more sudden and effective. Even in the daytime bomber crews must always be ready to fly straight into winter; on one June day in 1940 they ran into sleet over the North Sea.

In November the targets were again miscellaneous, but most of the attacks were lighter, doubtless because the weather was getting more unsuitable and it was not worth sending out many bombers. Only once was there an attack within Germany. In December the attacks were fewer still and Blenheims were able to operate on only six days; most of their targets were in Holland. And in January of 1941 as well, night bombing became increasingly important and day bombing increasingly rare.

Paradoxically enough, it is often more difficult to see the results of bombing by day than by night and this is particularly true when the bomber makes a sudden sortie from cloud cover and quickly takes cover again. Nor is it always easy to see what happens when the bomber approaches and bombs from a very low level. If the bomber is not to be blown up itself, the bombs must have delayed-action fuses and only the rear gunner, looking back from his turret, has much chance of seeing the explosions a dozen or so seconds after the bomber has passed; even then he may be confused by looking back at the target not from above, but from the side and from an aircraft moving very swiftly away. At night the bomber can often circle over the target for the crew to get a leisurely view of the results, but this is hardly ever possible by day; neither bomb flashes nor fires are so easily visible by day as in the darkness and clouds of dust or smoke may conceal the actual, damage done by an explosion. For all these reasons it is as important by day as by night for the crew to get photographs of the bombs bursting and in 1940 the technique of getting such photographs, a more difficult matter than one might think, had not been worked out.

Thus the effect of the many, but seldom heavy, daylight attacks from June to December 1940 are not easy to judge. Often the bomber returned to cloud before results could be observed; often, in particular, a ship was bombed without anyone knowing what had really happened to it. Subsequent reconnaissance can seldom reveal whether a ship has sunk, unless it was in very shallow water; reconnaissance showed that a great many barges in harbour were smashed, though most of the damage was probably done by night. Very naturally, with the small force then in existence and with the urgent need to keep reserves in hand to meet any German invasion of Britain, most of the attacks made in 1940, after the Battle of France was ended, were not made from a very low level; some of them were probably exploratory attacks, designed to test the defences and examine the possibilities of daylight bombing. They certainly proved that daylight bombing was entirely feasible, but they did not, as yet, show how much damage it could do.

In January 1941 there were only a few days when the Blenheims could go out; in February there were more, but none of the attacks could be described as heavy. The most significant development of these two months was that the bombers sometimes went out with a strong fighter escort. On 10 January six Blenheims on 114 Squadron escorted by 72 fighters in the first 'Circus' operation attacked a German ammunition depot in the Forêt de Guines, just to the south of Calais. The attack was made at high noon and in clear weather with nothing but thin, wispy cloud in the sky. With the fighters to guard them there was no attempt to intercept the bombers while they were over the target and the bombs started fires among the enemy's dispersal points on the edge of the forest. None of the Blenheims were lost.

On 6 March 1941 Prime Minister Winston Churchill made a decision that was to have a far-reaching effect on the lives of the crews of the Blenheims in East Anglia. The Battle of the Atlantic was causing a great deal of concern, with the U-boats taking a heavy toll of Allied shipping, so Bomber Command was now to concentrate on naval targets. The role of the Blenheims of 2 Group and the Beauforts, Lockheed Hudsons and Blenheims of Coastal Command was to harass, damage and as far as possible destroy communications between East to West by sea in daylight. Although naval patrol boats were out every night looking for enemy shipping, the Navy could hardly undertake this task in daylight without running an excessive risk from aerial bombardment. German shipping habitually sailed close to the enemy coastline where the Luftwaffe could readily bomb any ships or submarines that attacked its convoys, as they had already demonstrated. The AOC 2 Group, AVM Donald F. 'Butcher' Stevenson, was ordered to see that any enemy ship putting to sea between the Brittany Peninsula and the coast of Norway should be sunk irrespective of the cost, which would prove to be considerable. The manner in which the campaign was to be carried out was to break down the whole length of the enemy coast into 'beats'. The formation of Blenheims would fly at wave-top height to the 'start line', which would be approximately 30 miles from the coast, from where they would fly towards the coast at specified distances apart, dependent on the weather conditions. On reaching a point 3 miles from the coastline they would turn at right-angles and fly for 3 minutes parallel to the coast before turning for home. The order was to sink the first ship sighted, or indeed any ship in the 'beat' area. The Blenheims were to use cloud cover where possible, but they were to attack from a low level and press home the attack against all opposition. Much was to depend on the initiative and judgment of individual pilots, or of the leader of each formation dispatched; the bombers were to sweep the coastal waters of France, Belgium, Holland, Germany, Denmark and to some extent of Norway and they were to attack anything worth attacking.

The Blenheim had hardly been designed for this type of operation, for the only way it could successfully attack a ship was to approach from wave-top height, lift to clear the masts of the ship and either land the bomb on the ship or skim it along the surface of the sea to explode against the vessel's side. Within weeks of the opening of this campaign, enemy convoys were always escorted by heavily armed motor patrol boats, so, with the combined anti-aircraft armament of all the ships in the convoy, the bombers had to fly through an enormous concentration of fire. The attack would only last for a matter of seconds, but all too frequently with fatal results for the bomber crew. Low-level flying is always a risky pastime, demanding absolute concentration on the part of the pilot, while over the sea this becomes even more hazardous in hazy conditions when it is very difficult to judge height above the water. Because low-level flying was to become a major feature of the life of Blenheim crews during that summer, over land it meant keeping as low as the contours of the ground would allow, having to lift over trees, telegraph wires, electricity pylons and so on.

These new operations against German shipping opened on 12 March 1941; it was a long sweep of the Dutch coast. There were no more than occasional patches of cloud to serve as cover and elsewhere there was brilliant sunlight. On this day five Blenheims on 139 Squadron found only one ship to attack, a vessel of about 1,000 tons, which they bombed, losing one aircraft. Two days later Wing Commander Waverley Edward Cameron of 107 Squadron was more fortunate in bombing and sinking a 2,000-ton ship off Norway (Cameron and his crew were lost off the coast of Norway on 6 April). On the 23rd it was the turn of 82 Squadron; they found a convoy of five ships, including a destroyer, off the Ems estuary, which they attacked and claimed to have damaged. The squadron carried out its second shipping sweep the next day when, in attacking another convoy, it lost its first crew in this campaign. These sweeps continued daily. On the 29th, during an attack on a 5,000-ton tanker off Flushing, which was surrounded by six patrol boats, the Blenheim flown by Wing Commander George A. Bartlett DFC was very badly damaged. Bartlett, showing great skill and determination, managed to bring the aircraft home on one engine.

Again and again the conquered people of France, Belgium and Holland waved to the Blenheims, but the crews knew at once when they had crossed into Germany, for then people suddenly began to jump from their bicycles, lie down by the side of the road, or take cover in ditches.

At this stage a new operation, known as the 'Fringe Attack', was introduced. Fighters were given 'Fringe Targets' if no enemy aircraft came up. They were split roughly into three sections: 'Close Encounter' to protect the Blenheims, 'High Wave' to mass for attack at 20,000 feet and 'Withdrawal' to protect the Blenheims on return. Military targets could be found a few miles inland from the enemy coast, which was very convenient, though they were also in the most heavily defended areas. It was now decreed that in order to cause alarm and to embarrass the enemy air defence system' transport columns, vehicles, troops, guns, searchlight emplacements and so on should be attacked from low level. These operations could be either the objective or, having flown a shipping 'beat' and finding nothing to attack; the crews would be directed to cross the coast to bomb any suitable target.

Here is a Blenheim gunner's own account of one attack; at the time he had only recently joined his squadron and the work was new to him; one can see from his story how much of an adventure one of the Blenheim's routine attacks, without any specially exciting incident, must have seemed to him. 'We worked out a plan of attack. If we sighted any ships the leader would head towards them and the others would come up into line abreast, each picking his own target. The method of attack was the usual one - right down on the water and 'jinking' all the way until almost on the ships, then a nice steady course as we climb over the ship and release the bombs. After bombing we would throttle back and allow the others to tuck in again. Our time of take-off was to be 13.30 hours and we were to be bombed up with semi-armour-piercing bombs. We got off without a hitch, dead on time and we had got a few thousand feet up when we arrived at the coast. As soon as we left the coast we got right down on the sea. The weather was very nice and visibility excellent. After about two hours our observer spotted a smudge of smoke on the horizon on our starboard beam; within a minute the shape of a ship appeared and then another and another. We decided to look into things and headed towards them. As we drew nearer we saw that they were four large ships in line astern and a number of smaller ships dispersed around them. There was a flak-ship at either end of the convoy and one in the middle. Fortunately for us, there was a rain-cloud, stretching up from sea-level to about 4,000 feet, near the convoy and we were able to deliver our attack through it.

'The attack was a huge success. Some of the pilots were just a little too eager to get the largest ship and almost collided, but taken all round it was quite a good show and each of the larger ships got bags of attention. About three seconds after we had crossed our ship, the deck near the funnels seemed to go puff in a sheet of red flame and smoke. Flames burst from her right, side down to the water-line. We claimed the ship as a complete 'write-off.' Looking back, I saw another and larger ship on fire and there was a third enveloped in steam and smoke. The convoy had obviously been taken by surprise, because as we went in the reception we got was not up to the usual standard of flak-ships; it warmed up later but that was too late to worry us much. When we had reached a safe distance my pilot throttled back and the others soon zoomed into position. We set a straight course for home, which took us parallel to the enemy coast for part of the way. It would have been better to head out to sea, for some time after our attack we were intercepted by two yellow-nosed Me 109s. The enemy were about 800 yards away on our red beam when I first sighted them. Like us they were flying at sea level. The leading fighter delivered his attack on the red quarter of the rear Blenheim while his friend hung back to watch. The first attack was met by heavy fire from all the Blenheims, but this did not much help the Blenheim under attack, because he was badly hit while the Messerschmitt was still at extreme range; he pulled up and away from the formation and was finished off by the second Messerschmitt. The first Messerschmitt was so eager to get back and finish the job that he made the worst break-away I have ever seen; he showed the whole of his belly and paid the full price for his stupidity. He hit the water only a fraction of a second after the Blenheim.

'The second Messerschmitt stayed with us for another five minutes. He swept across from beam to beam and fired at the formation as a whole; his relative speed was always about 200 mph and his shooting was ineffective, His last attack was suddenly broken off and he went home like a shot. We watched him leave a smoke trail until he was lost to sight.'

Searching the coast, perhaps finding no more ships to attack that day, the crews were able to fly overland as well and harry the German armies of occupation.

'Attie' Atkinson, who had taken command of a flight on 21 Squadron and flew at night to Wilhelmshaven, Hamburg and Hanover, but mainly to Wilhelmshaven, liked the daylight work better than the night, saying that he preferred to work in the sun. He would prove to be one of the most courageous and resourceful leaders in 2 Group. During the spring of 1941 he increased his reputation in the Group for toughness on the job and reticent humour in reporting it. At more than 200 mph at a height of fifty feet; everything on the ground rushes by and yet the Blenheim crews often saw a great deal in momentary glimpses. 'Attie' caught the bleak eye of a very solemn German staff officer watching him from an open touring car. As 'Attie' said afterwards, 'I think we were equally fascinated by the other. In fact the staff officer and his driver were so intent on watching us that they crashed into a tree. I didn't have to use a bullet.' All on its own the staff car was last seen attempting to climb half-way up a fir tree.

Low-level daylight operations in Blenheims against shipping and other heavily defended coastal and inland targets were murderous affairs. Squadrons were turned round in a month, sometimes less. Commanding officers came and went. Such was the mortality rate. On 31 March Blenheims scored their first considerable success; the crews on 82 Squadron reported a very successful attack on a convoy of tankers, well guarded by flak-ships ahead and astern off Le Havre. They were ailing eastward and it was presumed that they were carrying oil to the German submarine bases on the Atlantic coast of France. The Blenheims dived to within 200 feet of the water before they released their bombs. There were two explosions on the first tanker and then a cloud of steam and dirty yellow smoke. Three bombs entered the second tanker just forward of the funnel and first there were jets of steam, then a cloud of steam and then a mass of black smoke. The tail of one of the bombs was thrown into the air 100 feet above one of the Blenheims, The flak-ships turned out of line; the bombers pursued them and machine-gunned their decks. It was all over in two minutes and as the Blenheims flew on their crews looked back and saw that both the tankers were well alight. Some of them watched the smoke until it went down behind the horizon. ✺

On the same day Squadron Leader L. V. E. 'Atty' Atkinson DSO DFC led eight of his crews on 21 Squadron, having been briefed to attack ships off the Dutch Frisian Islands and to open the campaign against 'fringe targets'. 'Attie' found two destroyers. One was bombed from fifty feet, with hits scored on the ship's stern. She slewed round, listing heavily to port as a column of black smoke belched into the sky. Not content with this success, he then led the formation across the islands of the north Dutch coast, saw a German parade, dropped his bombs plumb between the ranks and then chased the regimental cook up a lane. Asked by the Intelligence Officer how he could tell it was a cook, 'Attie' replied soberly that it might have been disguise, but he was wearing a chef's cap and apron. And then his observer commented, 'Dammit, at the height we were flying we could not only tell that it was a cook, we could even tell what the cook was thinking.'

'Attie's report to Intelligence afterwards was typical. 'At Ameland, at about 1400 hours,' he said, 'we sighted what I suppose must have been an after-lunch parade. I alerted my gunner and we sprayed the lot of them. After this, we found a fellow on a gun emplacement, said 'good afternoon' and went on our way.' Their visit had not gone unnoticed, for their presence had attracted a great deal of flak, which, not too surprisingly, accounted for two of the Blenheims.

'Attie' led the first flight to attack a German convoy at low level. It was a perfect April morning with a brittle clear sky as far as the eye could see, and the cold and rather muddy blue of the North Sea was marked with white specks and spume lanes, useful for the navigator's drifts. 'Attie' had been given a fringe target to attack, but on this type of daylight work wide discretion was left to the Section Leader. On that particular April morning the German coast was sighted after a run of two hours sixteen minutes. The automatic camera had been plugged in; rear-gunners put on their helmets and bombs were switched to the 'on' position. Then 'Attie's gunner saw a smudge of smoke on the starboard horizon, fifteen miles to south. They checked the smoke-stain against the broken patches of white cumulus, but there was no doubt - the smoke marked a large German convoy on the move. 'Attie' wheeled the Squadron into position, gave the signal to split formation and open into flights and then he switched into top boost. Ten miles away the ships emerged from 'the haze, plump as partridges. At two thousand yards the Blenheims saw round white mushrooms of steam spewed out by one of the stripy-camouflage flak vessels. They had seen the bombers and the steam whistle was warning the convoy. At one thousand yards the first lines of flak struck out at the bombers, curling over 'Attie's port wing, a shade high. As they closed in at nought feet the Blenheim pilots pressed gun-buttons in their control columns, not that they could do much damage, but to scare the German guns. Their fire became more inaccurate. 'Attie' pulled up from the sea surface, released his bombs and swung over the top of a mast. His rear-gunner fired into the ship in a long burst. Bomb doors sprang-to with a satisfying smack. A few seconds later, out ahead of the convoy, the pilot looked back in time to see his own bombs tear a yellow chunk from the hull of the biggest ship and send it sailing in the air. He watched his boat take fire, list heavily to starboard and throw up great volumes of black and white smoke. Her sister, a German lady of 4,000 tons, was attacked by another of the Blenheims. At one moment she looked as, snug as you please, and the next, nothing but a boiling mass of smoke. A third ship shuddered and caught fire. 'Attie' cruised at gentle speed home across the North Sea, munching a piece of barley sugar. The photograph he brought back with him became a prize ornament in the Group game book.

There were good yarns in the ante-room that evening. A New Zealand observer told how on the way back he was grinning at the plight of a Blenheim which had had its tail shot away and was steering home on its ailerons. 'Then when we landed, 'Taffy' showed me there were exactly four threads of wire, as thin as cotton, left on our own rudder.' It was the cream of farce. He laughed uproariously and had another can of beer.

For this attack 'Attie' was awarded a Bar to the DFC. But he missed the party to celebrate it, flying out instead to Malta. The Mediterranean island has meant many things to its visitors. For St. Paul it meant deliverance from drowning when he was shipwrecked. For Ansaldo, chief keener at each Italian wake, 'Malta has become a huge and unsinkable aircraft-carrier, almost within view of the Italian coast'. For thousands of British peace-time sailors it meant an evening out in the night clubs of Valetta; romantic but tinged with garlic. When 'Attie' came back and was asked for a description of Malta, he said it was 35.40 North, 14.30 East. This was as accurate as anyone could be without being pedantic. Then, conversationally, he added that it was about 1,000 miles from Gibraltar on the west and almost 1,000 miles from Alexandria on the east. During his first stay in Malta Squadron Leader Atkinson DFC* had had command of a flight of Blenheims and led the first attack on a convoy to Tripoli. He personally sank a 4,000-tonner, while others in the flight sank a destroyer. There were four more attacks on convoys and then: he came home, flying all the way from the Bay of Biscay to England on one engine. Sea spray had got in the other. Then 'Attie' was posted back to his own original 82 Squadron. The man from Church House who had joined them as Acting Pilot Officer was, at twenty-six, in command of the Squadron. Some of the men who were now with him had escaped from Gembloux, but most of the faces were new. Wing Commander Atkinson flew again to his familiar base at Luqa, taking his Squadron with him.

Days of playing Patience in the mess, games which stopped when the Marylands came back with news of a target. A lazy, siesta atmosphere, occasionally seared by the sound of bombs whistling down near the Barracca. Lotus-eating dreams disturbed by the high whine of a fighter dropping from the sky. Italian parachutes have a trick of failing to open and sometimes as the Italian airmen came down they were heard to scream. The British air-crews who watched found it even more nerve-racking when they prayed - the sound of the, slew Roman prayer against the swish of the Italian body on its way to pulp. Sometimes they injured their bodies by trying to tear at the parachute rip-cords before they were killed.

As Squadron Commander 'Attie' often went out himself after the ships. Ship-sinking was a matter of gambits. Most frequently the big cargo-boats and even the smaller fry for Rommel would be accompanied by a single Italian destroyer. The Blenheims would fly around, looking for an opening, while the destroyer would frantically circle her charge, sending up showers of spray in an effort to get between the attacking Blenheims and the cargo-boat. The game was hard on both sides, ending sometimes in the loss of both the Italian ships, guardian and ward and sometimes with the loss of the Blenheims.

South of Pantelleria on 22 June, a biggish convoy was sighted and the Blenheims went out. The leader was one of 'Attie's Flight Commanders. Two or three miles away from the ships the leader's port engine was set alight by flak. Had he immediately turned for home the chances are that the whole British attack would have been disrupted. He flew straight on for his ship. But before he reached it his remaining engine also caught fire and cut. His speed was enough to carry him thy short distance and he glided on, aimed his bombs at the ship, took a piece off the funnel and alighted. By the grace of 82 Squadron luck, weeks later 'Attie' received a letter written in an Italian prison camp and starting: 'Dear Sir, - Sorry I shall be late in getting home, but owing to unforeseen circumstances, viz. two engines on fire and one obstructing funnel...' In the same attack on the convoy off Pantelleria was Flight Lieutenant T. J. Watkins. He had been an NCO when 'Attie' first joined 82 Squadron and he was one of the men who escaped after being shot down at Gembloux. Flying just above the water on his way to the ships, Watkins all but had a leg severed by flak. A point-five also came between his legs near the join. There were in addition, as he put it, sundry other scratches. He too flew on, attacked his ship and then passed out. His observer, Sergeant J. S. Sargent, took over, flew the machine back to Luqa and over base Watkins collected himself and landed the Blenheim. 'Attie' picked him out of the cockpit. Watkins was awarded an immediate DSO and Sargent the DFM. Their gunner, Sergeant Eric F. Chandler, was credited with a Fiat CR.42 destroyed which earned him a DFM.

On 24 June 82 Squadron delivered the first low-level attack on Tripoli, with 'Attie' leading. That day, it was said, the Squadron really went to town - Tripoli town - at anything from twenty to nought feet. The Wing Commander and two others bombed a 20,000-ton liner and his gunner saw the whole of the top deck blow off.

Then they went back to base, talked and played Patience.

After returning to East Anglia 'Attie' quickly became dissatisfied with the tactics ordered by Air Vice Marshal Stevenson for the hazardous attacks on shipping. The AOC wanted the attacks made broadside on, but Attie wouldn't have it. He said he wouldn't make beam attacks because (a) the enemy would see you coming miles off and (b) you would then feel the full blast of the ships' fire power. He reckoned that with a Blenheim's own almost total lack of fire power, success must depend upon surprise. This, he contended, could only be achieved in daylight by hugging the waves and attacking the target from astern. He followed these tactics himself and instructed his crews to do likewise. His independence and outspoken attitude always managed to upset those in authority - not least because they knew that more often than not he was right! 'Attie' was eventually posted to a staff job at 2 Group headquarters for his operational 'rest' and there he found the portrait which Eric Kennington, the artist, had painted of him. He examined this idealised creation closely. 'Makes me look like a bloody hero,' he said. It had to be decided where the famous portrait should be hung. 'Better put it in my office instead of me,' he suggested. 'Attie' disliked staff work and the bumph, which went with it and on what he called his 'days off', he would at once speed back to his old squadron. His absences became more and more frequent and one day after a search of 2 Group squadrons had failed to locate him, the civilian police were called in. It was known that he had been drinking more heavily than usual - often the manifestation of long months of excessive operational stress followed by a period of bored inactivity. I believe it was this erratic behaviour which cost him a career in the RAF which could well have taken him to the top. He had the humour, ability, independence of mind and the intellect to get there. Here was one of World War II's true aces. To fly with him was to feel

44

that he and his Blenheim were as one. He was a man of great courage. Without it, he would never have survived two long tours in 2 Group, faced with the cataclysmic losses we endured in those first years of war. In one eleven-month period, 82 Squadron lost seven COs and I can count on the fingers of one hand the crews who survived with me during my time with the unit. This was the environment in which 'Attie' Atkinson made his indelible mark.'[9]

Endnotes for Chapter Three

9   This most memorable character died on 22 March, 1950 leaving his wife and three boys and a girl to carry the family torch. *'Attie' Atkinson 'MAKES ME LOOK LIKE A BLOODY HERO'* by Eric Chandler, a wireless operator-air gunner in 2 Group, quoted in *Thanks For the Memory: Unforgettable Characters In Air Warfare 1939-45* by Laddie Lucas (Stanley Paul 1989).

Chapter 4

Malta Story

Tony Mee, first a Hounslow bank clerk and then a Blenheim rear gunner, has a manner of charming detachment. The first in the Blenheim to observe that she was burning in the starboard wing, he said to the pilot, 'H'm, Bill. Looks to me like your starboard engine's on fire.' The pilot stared round, as astonished at the gunner's tone of voice as at the smoke trail. 'By the sound of your remark,' he said finally, 'anyone would think the bloody kite was mine and not yours.' For a few minutes Blenheim 'L for Leather' continued to fly over the Mediterranean on the port engine alone.
Dinghy! Dinghy! from The Fire Was Bright by Leslie Kark, 1943.

Ten tropicalised Blenheims on 105 Squadron, led by Wing Commander Hughie Idwal Edwards VC DFC arrived at Luqa in the last week of July 1941 to relieve 110 Squadron, one crew landing in neutral Portugal and another having belly-landed at Gibraltar through hydraulics failure. Almost daily the Blenheim crews went out in search of Axis shipping and coastal transports during the next few weeks. By the end of August British Intelligence assessed that 58 per cent of all seaborne supplies intended for the Axis forces in North Africa had been lost at sea. In actuality a record number of eleven merchantmen totalling 35,196 tons were sunk by air attack in the Mediterranean during August and about half the tonnage lost was destroyed by Blenheims. Aircraft losses however, were 12 per cent. Twenty-six crews on 107 Squadron arrived in Malta in the first few weeks of September where they joined forces with 105 Squadron. On the 12th eight crews on 105 and 107 Squadrons found and attacked a large convoy consisting of five heavily armed merchantmen 40 miles North-North-West of Tripoli. The Axis vessels were escorted by seven destroyers and six MC 200 and CR 42 fighters of 23rd Gruppo and they shot down three of the Blenheims into the sea. A fourth, badly shot up, bellied in at Luqa. Only one vessel, a 1,000 ton merchantman, was confirmed sunk.

The crews of two of the Blenheims that were shot down perished but the crew of 'L for Leather', captained by Sergeant Bill Brandwood with Sergeant Jock Miller as observer and Sergeant Tony Mee as WOp/AG manning the twin Brownings, were more fortunate.

This was the crew's twentieth operation. Once before cannon shell had split open their petrol tank and fractured the main spar and on another occasion, during an attack on a convoy of schooners and merchant vessels south of Lampedusa, a ship carrying a gun looking like a howitzer opened up as they passed over and lifted them bodily into the air. Their score in the Mediterranean was already three ships sunk and a fourth shared with two other aircraft and once they had attacked a supply column on the Tripoli-Benghazi road and watched the scared drivers running in all directions into the desert while others took shelter under the lorries. So that they weren't raw for this trip and that was just as well.

They had been briefed at eleven o' clock in the morning by Wing Commander Hughie Edwards. He had thought their target was pretty tough. That morning a reconnaissance machine had counted eighteen merchant vessels and four destroyers, with Macchis escorting them above. Blenheim 'L for Leather' was flying No. 4 in an elongated vic. The pilot's left window was open so that he could keep closer formation and get some air into the machine. Although they were flying in shorts and open shirts the crew felt stifled. They were doing a square search and were on the last leg when they saw on the horizon a line of large ships and Bill Brandwood called out, 'Here we go!'

The Blenheim flew at top boost just above sea level, flying in line abreast with the flight, and at a full five miles away the pilot saw the lines of tracer coming at him from the destroyers. He could see the splash in, the water ahead of, and around, him, and as they got near Tony Mee in the rear turret had an awkward moment as the tracer lines seemed to scissor across him. It was then that Tony looked at the starboard mainplane and made the remark already reported. The smell of burning entered his turret and he informed Bill of that too.

Jock Miller and Tony Mee each took a fire-extinguisher and attempted to dowse the flames coming then from the bomb-well. The radio set was also alight and exuding asphyxiating fumes. Their career in the Fire Service ended when Bill told them that the port engine had cut and gave the order, 'Dinghy! Dinghy!' They wondered what it was going to be like. This is the way they reported their reactions to striking the sea:

Jock, the Observer: Just before coming down I remember wondering how I would take it. I never found out. I suddenly went unconscious. Next thing I knew was that I was in the water with the plane three yards away. Her nose was down and her wings flat on the sea. I looked around for Bill.

Bill, the pilot: I thought I wasn't going to escape. I watched her plunge into the sea and then shut my eyes. I felt a stinging smack on the face from the sheet of water coming at me. It turned me round so that I was facing the armour plating. I felt for the pin of the Sutton harness, which releases you from the straps tying you to the seat. It should lie on the middle of the belly, and you could find it in your sleep. I groped, but it wasn't there. I tried to rise, but couldn't get away from the straps. They were doing their job. I told myself, 'Well, this is it.' Then my hand found the pin just below the shoulders at the back. The straps fell away. I floated up.

Tony, the Rear Gunner: I felt a great pressure on my body. I could hear and see everything inside the .aircraft smashing up in whirling water. The level of the sea was from Bill's sliding hatch to the tail. I was sitting in about two and a half feet of water. I heaved up the dinghy and threw it out, cutting the securing rope with a knife. Jock and Bill had chipped me about this knife. I remember thinking, 'This'll show them.' Curious to think of such a thing at a time like that. There's one other thing, I remember about the crash. It was suddenly cold on my seat.'

Jock Miller was the first to enter the dinghy. He was astonished to watch a flying-boot coming toe first out of the rear gunner's seat. It was followed by Tony Mee, its owner. Jock watched Bill and Tony in the sea, arguing about that flying-boot. Bill wanted him to drop it. Tony clutched if to his breast' and swam with one hand. He behaved as if the war depended on that boot. He said he thought that his spine was hurt and Bill dived down to give him a lift into the dinghy while Jock hauled, at his shoulders. The last tip of 'L for Leather's tail slid into the sea.

Inside the boat the three of them looked at each other. On the western horizon the smoke from the burning convoy was still smearing the sky. From the east the remaining Blenheims came back and waggled their wings to show they knew. For a long while no one spoke. Tony stared at his boot, grinned, threw it overboard and followed it with its mate. Jock was sick eight times, on each occasion turning to the others and saying, 'Excuse me.' Tony had a bad arm and they made a sling for him from the lace 'Of his Mae West. Bill had some of the skin torn off his legs and they were bleeding. Jock, the only one who had kept his watch, looked at it. The hands had stopped dead at 2.25, the moment the sea came in. During the scramble their emergency rations were, lost and sank to the bottom. So they had no water and no food, but at first little doubt that they would be picked up. The afternoon was young.

Clothes were taken off to dry their bodies in the sun. Jock found some cigarettes, but they were wet, and as they dried the paper peeled open. Anyway, the lighter wouldn't work. They dabbed at the blood-stains and lay in the sun.

A dinghy carries a sea: anchor, a kind of drag apparatus composed of ropes and canvas. The three men sat away from the anchor so that the waves broke under the prow. But each spot on which they sat seemed to gather water and Bill took off his shoe to bale out - in the old-fashioned sense. The afternoon wore on and they became hungry, torturing themselves, as hungry men do, by thinking of the dinner they would be having back at Malta.

The sun went down and they reassured each other that there was no doubt they would get picked up. After all, the rest of the flight had seen them and as much as told them so. The three men said it again and again. They would get picked up, all right. But nothing came and then it was too dark for anything to come. They settled down for the night, huddling together for warmth. One or other of them dozed off for a few minutes at a time. Hours were spent staring down at darting fish of strange shape, their scales glinting in the moonlight. Tony was no kind of a navigator, but he knew three stars, members of the Plough. He had picked them out as a child and remained intimate with them as he grew up. They were there over the Mediterranean watching him as he floated on a bit of rubber in the middle of the sea. About midnight the men heard the noises of aircraft and argued whether they should let off one of their two distress signals to draw attention. But Bill was captain and he refused, wisely. The time to fire a distress signal is when there was a reasonable chance of its being of some use.

Throughout the night they got colder and stiffer, constantly trying different angles for their legs. They saw the faint yellow of the false dawn, then dark again and then the real dawn - a red glow, a yellow burst and the sun suddenly up. The men in the dinghy thought they heard voices, but they were seagulls calling to each other. Flying fish, blue, silver-blue and green, darted out of the water to catch the sun on their bodies and disappear. A vast turtle paddled up and both parties looked at each other hungrily. And then, only some twenty yards away, they saw a series of dorsal fins. Dolphins. One of the fins came towards the dinghy and vanished below the water. The men splashed madly and once again Tony got ready his knife. At ten minutes to eight in the morning a black oblong, like an old square-sail, was seen in the distance. Tony flashed it with a mirror, and Bill got a flare ready. They paddled towards it at about half a knot until they knew that the vertical oblong was the conning tower of a submarine. Bill fired the flare and the thirteen white stars climbed. a hundred feet into the cloudless sky.

They strained their eyes for signs of nationality. And then they were weak enough to have cried with disappointment. They saw a sailor in a green shirt on the conning tower, and another in a red shirt on the hull. Bill said, 'Damn! They're Eyeties' and thought what a villainous couple they looked. Jock tied his secret navigation papers to Tony's clasp-knife and they hung it over the side to drop as soon as they were certain. Despondently Bill shouted, 'Are you British?' A Yorkshire voice answered them, 'Yes' and then, as an afterthought, 'Good show, lads.' The men of the dinghy did not tell the men of the submarine what they had thought of their looks or their shirts. They weren't looking much like an inspection themselves.

They saw the name - *Utmost* - and were taken down the hatch for a double breakfast each. They were put in bunks, cuts were stitched and they dreamed about food. The men of the Utmost put them ashore and they drank together.

That was the day Air Ministry received the signal: *'From HQ Malta. Crew of missing Blenheim rescued safe by naval unit today.'*

Chapter 5

'The Year of the Circus'

Circus: RAF bombing operation strongly escorted by fighters to lure German fighters into combat.

In East Anglia on 3 April 1941 Wing Commander Christopher Grant Hill DFC took command of 18 Squadron in place of Wing Commander A. C. H. Sharpe (who took up a position at the Air Ministry) and moved it to Oulton, near the market town of Aylsham. A decision had been made by Bomber Command that No 2 Group must adopt a much more aggressive role and there were to be no more night operations. On 11 April Blenheims on 105 Squadron flew the last 2 Group night operation, bombing targets at Cologne, Bremerhaven and Brest. Attacks from now on were to be made at low level on enemy shipping close to the enemy coast, these shipping lanes from Norway to the Bay of Biscay being split into 'beats'. Crews would either be detailed to look exclusively for shipping or, on occasions, when no shipping was sighted, to cross the coast to look for and bomb suitable targets. Also, low-level attacks on industrial or military targets on the Continent, sometimes using cloud for cover. Later (during May) crews were allocated a further task, to operate in formation at heights of about 10,000 feet with fighter escort. These operations, known as 'Circuses', were to be flown with the primary objective of persuading the fighters of the Luftwaffe to attack us so that they could be engaged and destroyed by our escorting fighters. Similar operations, known as 'Ramrods', were also to be flown where the target, rather than ourselves, acting as the 'sacrificial lamb' was the primary objective.

Ted Sismore, a Blenheim navigator who later flew on Mosquitoes and ended the war as a Squadron Leader with the DSO and DFC, recalls: '2 Group from 1940 into 1942 was the light bomber group in Bomber Command and was used for a wide variety of things that the medium bombers, the Wellingtons, Whitleys and Stirlings, didn't do. In my tour in the Blenheim we started doing medium-level night bombing, we then did low-level anti-shipping anywhere down the coast from Denmark to Western France. We then did some night low-level on specific targets, mostly ports, canals close to the coast. Then we did the 'Circuses' where we had the fighter escort. We attacked targets usually near the coast because British fighters at that time were relatively short-range. We occasionally pulled up the enemy and were attacked once or twice by Me 109s.

'We did hit the sea one night in a Blenheim, off the entrance to the Kiel Canal. It was a misty, foggy night. We were looking for a ship that was reputedly in the Canal and as we turned away from this very flat country we hit the water and bounced off. It transpired later we'd lost one propeller blade and we'd bent back the other five. We came back with the aeroplane vibrating badly and we set off to fly down along the Frisian Islands, really expecting that we would have to make a landing or ditching. The guns were too active, so we said we would risk the North Sea. We set off for home. I had plotted a position in the middle of the sea and I said, 'If we get past there, we'll ditch and Air Sea Rescue can pick us up in the morning.' But we came all the way back. We got to the airfield, but because we were making such a strange noise they turned all the lights out. The RT we had at the time, the old TR9, was notoriously inefficient and it took us some time to persuade them to put the lights on. Eventually we got them and landed back at base successfully.

'The great thing about low flying was that it was always the aim to be as low as you could with safety, because it protected you from the guns; and from radar. It was exciting to be down among the trees, but the pilot had to be looking a long way ahead to see what he had to do next. Over Holland and the North German plain you could get very low indeed. Further inland, with the hills, not quite so low. You did see everything that was going on. We were navigating then with a map. Church steeples were great navigation aids at low level. If you had a map with churches on, the easiest way to navigate was by steeple. You could also see people - you could see cars, trucks, horses and carts. In hilly country we literally flew past someone's front door and as we flew past I looked across over the wingtip and a man opened the door. I was looking him straight in the eye at about 40 feet. On one occasion in the flat country of Northern Germany we were flying very low across some open fields with very few trees and there was a farmer with his horse and cart coming towards us. We were down deliberately low; I doubt if 10 or 20 feet would be an exaggeration. As we got close the horse reared up and threw the man off the cart before we went over. We were that close to people. Low flying in itself was not dangerous. We were flying in a Blenheim, cruising at 180 mph. That's slow - you've got time to see trees, even high-tension cables. I've known people clip the target by being a few feet too low, but that was unusual. Occasionally somebody came back with a piece of tree.

'Now night low level was different. That really was dangerous if you got a bit too low and people sometimes did. We had one night when we were attacking shipping in the Channel at full moon. One Blenheim came back and landed and the pilot asked us to come and look at it. 'What happened?' we said. 'Well, I saw a ship so I bombed it and hit it;' he said. 'I pulled up over the mast and I dropped down the other side. There was another ship that he hadn't seen; so I went through his mast' When we got out to the aeroplane we found that the propeller hadn't hit the mast, but the engine had collected a piece of wood that was burning gently against the cylinders.'

The year 1941 would become known as 'the year of the Circus'. It was the aim to entice enemy fighters into the air and destroy them over France - perhaps with as few as a 'box' of six Blenheims (the bait) and 103 British fighters from as many as nine squadrons (the hunters). The Blenheims were not only bait as they also had a bombing target in the range of the fighter cover. The campaign actually began on 12 March, when one of the other squadrons in the Group patrolling a shipping 'beat' along the Dutch coast, sighted a ship of about 1,000 tons, which they bombed. The 'Circus' operation was not without some problems: a tight formation with no straggling; straight and level bombing on the leader; fighters and bombers being exactly at the right spot on the right time; and sorting out friendly fighters from enemy aircraft. Flying at 10,000 feet in broad daylight and attracting heavy flak, the Blenheims were wallowing around in the thinner air, far short of their best performance, wanting the enemy to come and attack but dependent on friendly fighters, which had limited range, to stop them. By 12 April the Blenheims had flown 315 sorties and 121 ships had been attacked, of which six were believed to have been sunk and eight damaged, with the loss of nine aircraft and their crews.

On 19 April three crews on 18 Squadron, led by Squadron Leader Hugh John Norman Lindsaye, found a 7,000-ton freighter with a destroyer escort that was belching out what must have seemed to the attackers to be an impenetrable wall of flak. Undeterred, they ploughed in, delivering their attack from mast height and gaining hits on the freighter, which was soon listing and was firmly believed to have been sunk. On 15 April Wing Commander Hill and his crew were lost without trace during another shipping strike. Wing Commander G. C. O. Key took over command of 18 Squadron on the 23rd.

On 24 April a new and if possible, even more dangerous tactic was introduced for the crews of 2 Group, known officially as Channel Stop', although those involved gave it a less complimentary title. The object of this particular exercise was to close the Straits of Dover to enemy shipping during daylight, leaving the motor torpedo boats of the Royal Navy to carry out the same exercise at night. The Blenheim squadrons would, in turn, be based at RAF Manston; as soon as shipping was sighted they would take off and attack, accompanied by an escort of Spitfires or Hurricanes.

The first aircraft to be committed to this task was a flight on 101 Squadron, which waited at Manston for a report on shipping movements. This information was supplied by fighters patrolling the Straits, who became known as 'Jim Crows'. On 28 April word came that there were some enemy trawlers off Calais and three of the Blenheims set off in pursuit with their escort. During the attack one of the Blenheims was shot down by the frightening firepower from the ship, though their escort drove off an enemy fighter that tried to intervene. The crews on 101 Squadron continued their role with varying degrees of success and casualties; for example, on 3 May, while attacking a small convoy off Boulogne, two of the three crews were lost to flak. On 9 May, no doubt to the relief of those who had survived, the crews flew their Blenheims back to their base at West Raynham, 'Channel Stop' being postponed, but only for a while.

Not content with the variety of tasks to which the Blenheim squadrons had been committed, on 26 April six crews on 21 Squadron, led by the indomitable Squadron Leader Atkinson, flew out to Malta to study the feasibility of operating from that beleaguered island. The previous day was momentous for the crews on 18 Squadron, one of the crews finding a large merchant ship of at least 7,000 tons with an escort of motor patrol boats. A hit was scored on the ship, which caused an enormous explosion, while two of the escort vessels were bombed, a hit being claimed on one of them.

On 26 April six crews on 21 Squadron sought a convoy of three 4,000-tonners, eight smaller ships and three flak ships, which between them were able to put up a murderous hail of flak. Wing Commander George Bartlett DFC, leading the attack, was fatally hit, crashing into the sea. He was followed almost immediately by the aircraft piloted by Sergeant Cyril Francis Spouge, both crews being killed. The same day twelve Blenheims on 82 Squadron carried out a sweep off Norway, where they attacked three cargo ships, while other crews were flying 'fringe beats' with varying degrees of success. Pilot Officer Ralph Eric Tallis and his crew bombed and machine gunned five Bf 110s on an airfield west of Sand, destroying one and damaging the others. He was joined by Sergeant Inman and his crew and together they successfully survived a 16-minute battle with three 109s.[10]

During the month one particularly successful shipping strike was carried out by Squadron Leader Hugh Lindsaye, who found and attacked a 7,000-ton enemy vessel, gaining a direct hit and leaving it with a 35-degree list. Sadly, a few days later, on the 30th, he was flying a Blenheim locally on a test flight when the aircraft crashed, killing him and Flying Officer Frank Holmes. While we were saddened by the losses on operations, the impact was even greater when they died as the result of an accident.'

In England on 3 May 18 Squadron moved, temporarily, to a new airstrip at Portreath near Redruth on the north coast of Cornwall. On the 5th 17 Blenheims on 105 Squadron left for Lossiemouth on detachment to attack shipping off the coast of Norway, where supplies of iron ore were being convoyed to Germany. On 8 May six Blenheims, operating in pairs, made the first successful attack when the first pair, flown by Wing Commander Arnold Louis Christian, who was twice Mentioned in Despatches, and Pilot Officer J. Buckley, found 20 ships forming up at the entrance to Hvs Fiord. During a low-level dive on a steamer, Christian's Blenheim was hit by flak and he was last seen two miles off the Norwegian coast with the port engine burning furiously. Flight Sergeant Harold Frederick Hancock, his observer and Sergeant George Wade, the WOp/AG, also perished. Buckley probably destroyed a merchant ship and he managed to return to Lossiemouth. The other pairs returned without sighting any ships. The loss of Christian, his skill, sense of fun, dry humour and superb airmanship, was a huge blow to the squadron that he had rapidly transformed to efficient daylight low-level operations. Just two days later, 26-year-old Wing Commander Hughie Edwards, an Australian of Welsh ancestry, replaced him.

At Horsham St. Faith Wing Commander Edmund Nelson, on taking command of 139 Squadron, with no experience of operational flying, found that the squadron had suffered from the losses of aircrew and had few experienced crews. However, there was one sergeant pilot who had almost completed his operational tour, so it was from this lowly officer that Nelson obtained most of his knowledge for his new command.

On 11 May 107 Squadron, commanded by Wing Commander Laurence Victor Elliott Petley, a square-jawed, pensive and unassuming man known as 'Petters', arrived at Great Massingham from Leuchars, Scotland, where they had been based temporarily since March, attached to Coastal Command flying shipping sorties. Although they had attacked two U-boats during April and had distinguished themselves in several shipping strikes and convoy escorts, the squadron had lost two COs, Wing Commanders J. W. Duggan, on 21 January 1941 and Waverley Cameron, on 6 April.

No sooner had the Blenheim crews touched down and found their billets, in houses and country homes in the village, than they were on their way again, this time on a shipping strike off Heligoland on 13 May. Twelve aircraft were detailed to attack and they flew across the North Sea in line abreast, led superbly by leading navigator Sergeant John Colin 'Polly' Wilson RNZAF. Two Blenheims returned early with mechanical problems, but the remaining aircraft went in at 200-400 feet and dropped almost 4 tons of bombs smack on the target. The attack was achieved with complete surprise and the Blenheims were safely away before the Luftwaffe could intervene. A congratulatory telegram arrived the same day from the AOC: 'Well done 107 Squadron - Stevenson'.

On 21 May 107 Squadron once more went after shipping at Heligoland. The Blenheims roared in at 50 feet, the prevailing good visibility unfortunately ensuring that there could be no element of surprise. As the formation drew level with the coast the gunners opened up in an attempt to swamp the enemy defences, but they were immediately enveloped by bursts of heavy flak. Flight Sergeant Kenneth Wolstenholme's Blenheim was hit and he left the scene as fast as he could with one engine on fire and 'Polly' Wilson dead at his position. Another Blenheim was forced to ditch and would almost certainly have been picked up by the Germans if Sergeant Roy Ralston, the pilot of another Blenheim, had not turned back, climbed to 1,500 feet and sent out a distress signal in plain language, giving the position of the ditched crew who by now had taken to their dinghy (except Flight Sergeant Douglas John Robert Craig, who drowned). They were rescued by ASR and Ralston was awarded the DFM for his action.[11] Wolstenholme (who became world famous after the war as a BBC sports commentator) made it back to Great Massingham and 'Polly' Wilson was laid to rest in the lovely country churchyard at Little Massingham.

Shipping sweeps continued on 22 May, but 105 Squadron made only one attack, in poor visibility, on a 1,000-tonner, without results. However, a sweep on the 25th proved more rewarding. Three aircraft attacked two 6,000-ton and one 4,000-ton merchant ships and hits were observed on all three. Twenty miles away and only 3 minutes later, another 4,000-tonner was attacked by another crew, but without visible result. Intense light flak was met during all attacks and north of Texel Pilot Officer George Eric Joseph Rushbrooke's Blenheim was hit. Although apparently undamaged, they were last seen flying toward Ameland.[12]

Eight aircraft had been briefed for the shipping attacks and a further three joined five of 18 Squadron in an attack on Nordeney. The formation was met by intense heavy and light flak when within 3 miles of the town and the leader turned away to assess the situation, only to be set upon by two Bf 109s. One aircraft lost an engine and dropped behind, but the attacks were beaten off successfully. Later three more 109s appeared, but the formation held close together and only one Blenheim, of 18 Squadron, was lost, the gunner of another being killed. One of the 109s was damaged.

Charles Patterson, a young pilot, was posted at the end of April, to 114 Squadron. Blenheims had gone back on daylight again and they were being used on low-level shipping strikes. Blenheims were totally vulnerable once intercepted by fighters but I was incredibly fortunate in that, instead of being thrown straight into the deep end by being posted to Norfolk to do standard, routine daylight bombing operations, I was posted to the one squadron in 2 Group that had been detached to Scotland to cover the North Sea and the Scandinavian coast. Opposition there was on a very much lower scale.

'My first operations were low-level daylight and dusk reconnaissance of the Norwegian coast and a few convoy escorts. In June I was sent out to look for the pocket battleship *Lützow*, which was known to be steaming up the Norwegian coast towards Bergen. It was the time of the midnight sun and I was flying down the Norwegian coast virtually within sight of the cliffs. Staring forward into the gloom I thought that I only had another minute of my patrol to go and I had escaped without finding anything. Then suddenly I saw in front of me an enormous area of white. It was the bow wave of the *Lützow*, whose enormous and terrifying looking superstructure suddenly loomed into view, steaming at about 30 knots. I was practically on top of it. This bloody battleship was only 10,000 tons but, when viewed from 300 feet and flying straight at it, looked about 40,000 tons. It was the most terrifying thing I had ever seen. I gave one horrified glance and swung away to starboard and opened the throttles. Amazingly they never opened fire. I sent my radio message and 114 Squadron and a Beaufort Squadron went out to attack it. (Subsequently, a torpedo from one of the Beauforts hit the *Lützow*; it limped into Bergen and did not come out again for a year.)'

The England and Middlesex cricketer, Pilot Officer W. J. 'Bill' Edrich from Norfolk, his observer, Vic Phipps - a Londoner - and his WOp/AG, Ernie Hope - a Lancastrian - had been posted to 107 Squadron at Great Massingham in Norfolk on 21 May. Hope was a friend and associate from their days at the OTU at Upwood in Cambridgeshire. Edrich had always wanted to fly; he felt that he was best qualified to undergo training for aircrew; and that this would be the fullest contribution he could make in the war: At Christmas in 1939 he was still awaiting call-up at home with his family in Norfolk. He did have to exercise a little subterfuge to gain his wings. A friend had told him that the quickest route into aircrew was to join the RAF Physical Training Branch and then re-muster. He was posted to Uxbridge where one of his instructors was his Middlesex captain, Walter Robins. It was a lucky reunion and there was a friendly game of cricket to seal it. After the match Robins asked Edrich to let him know if he had any requests. 'Yes,' said Bill,' I want a transfer to aircrew.' Within forty-eight hours he was enrolled in the first of a series of courses. Twelve months later, after flying training at Cranwell, at the end of which he was commissioned and operational training on Blenheims at Upwood, Edrich was posted to 2 Group, Bomber Command.

An extract from one Fighter Intelligence report after a raid on the Cherbourg docks on 6 June presented an eloquent image of the low-flying quests. 'The sea-coloured camouflage on the top surface of the Blenheims was so effective that the first we saw of them as they flew out from the target was their wakes on the water.' The perils of these daylight attacks, judged to be among the most dangerous of the war, claimed casualties on a horrendous scale. Brian Edrich, who also served in the RAF, described the skills required by his brother and fellow pilots. The low-level raids on enemy convoys in the North Sea and English Channel were carried out often at mast height, between 10 feet and 20 feet. The convoys were escorted by flak (anti-aircraft) ships, which could zero in on the bombers with their heavy and light guns. 'The Blenheims attacked the ships by coming straight at them just lifting over the top and then releasing their bombs into the sides of the vessels. At the speed they came in - around 250 mph - they were fairly easy targets,' explained the younger Edrich. The hazards were heightened by the lack of manoeuvrability of the slow and cumbersome Blenheim bombers, which had been developed from civilian aircraft. Evasion tactics had to be learned by bitter experience. Once over the first few trips pilots had a better chance of survival. Sadly, many did not progress so far and were killed in their initial operations. Bill Edrich was never deflated by apparently insuperable odds, in war, or in cricket. 'Billy boy: we'd follow you anywhere,' was the compliment of one Canadian flier.

Hope regarded Edrich as an inspirational figure.' Bill was a great man and he flew his aircraft in the same cavalier spirit as he played his cricket,' he said. Edrich was Hope's best man at his wedding in June 1942. None of his cricket achievements, Edrich commented later; could ever approach the drama, endeavours and comradeship of his wartime campaign. 'In four months in 1941 I experienced the heights and depths of emotions - supreme elation like the effects of good wine and profound remorse at losing so many fine friends,' he said. Losses had got so bad that the mood among the air crews, while determined, became grim, so much so that at Massingham one evening Flying Officer Ewels observed that after a particularly hazardous operation 'the Wing Commander and other 107 Squadron pilots in the mess sat for a long time in silence and then quietly got out notepaper and wrote out their wills. Not long afterwards all were gone.'

On 6 June Winston Churchill, with the Chief of the Air Staff and accompanied by other members of the Government, visited West Raynham on 6 June and Blenheim crews in 2 Group were assembled there to meet him. 'Churchill, wearing a light grey suit and carrying an unlighted cigar' remembers Bill Edrich, 'mounted a set of servicing steps and addressed us. He began by reminding us that 48,000 civilians had been killed in air raids on Britain in the previous months and that his promise that the RAF would retaliate by day and night had not yet been fulfilled. He had come personally, he said, to explain the importance of the special tasks we would be undertaking in the next few weeks, when our operations were likely to have a major impact on the course of the war. He then gave us some unpalatable facts. German intervention in the Middle East was turning the war against us in that theatre. 'Germany must be forced to move her fighters westwards', he told us. We would attack targets in the west which Germany would have to defend and sometimes to lure the Luftwaffe into the air; we would be escorted by large numbers of fighters. Our purpose would be to relieve pressure on other fronts and to ease the stranglehold on our life-lines. 'I am relying on you', said Churchill.

'This eve-of-battle appeal from the Prime Minister certainly did something for our morale. But sitting in the cockpit of my Blenheim next morning with the engines ticking over, waiting for the signal to take part with eight other crews in a raid on a heavily defended convoy en route from Hamburg to Rotterdam I dare not analyse my feelings. I had been impatient to make a start and so I knew had Vic and Ernie. We had been flying together for three months and we needed something to show for it. But these impulses evaporated as the moment approached and I was left with the uncomfortable knowledge that I was just another freshman pilot on the threshold of a new experience, setting off into the unknown. Some of the old hands on the squadron had teased us by exaggerating the dangers. Others, partly perhaps to reassure themselves, dismissed 'ops' as a 'piece of cake'. I was apprehensive and yet in a curious way I was also elated. There was only one way of finding out the truth about what layout there beyond the Channel and the North Sea and about oneself. I was about to find out.

'In the little cottage attached to the nursery gardens on the edge of our grass satellite airfield, which was all the squadron boasted as a headquarters, we had learned that a large and heavily defended enemy convoy, on its way from Hamburg to Rotterdam, was moving down the Dutch coast. There were two big ships in the convoy, both carrying important war cargoes, according to our Intelligence and these would be our primary targets. Nine crews were briefed to attack in three 'vics' of three. I was flying No. 3 to the leader, Squadron Leader Peter Simmons DFC. He was at the other end of the scale - on the last trip of his second tour.

'At last Peter Simmons gave the signal and we began to roll forward. Vic Phipps was sitting beside me for take-off with Ernie Hope behind me in the fuselage. Peter did a circuit of the airfield to give us time to form up and we headed for the coast at 500 feet, dropping down to 30 feet over the sea. Then our way was barred by a white screen of fleecy cloud, stretching from about 600 feet right down to the water and I wondered if Simmons would turn back. The density looked likely to break up all but the closest formations, but I guessed that the volatile Simmons would not want his last trip to be abortive and I tucked in even closer. At the same time I noticed that No.2 in the formation, on Simmons's right, was above and a little behind. He wouldn't last long in a fighter attack. And he would almost certainly lose us in that cloud. I hadn't had time to get to know the pilot of this aircraft, but I had exchanged a few words with the navigator. He and I were due to play cricket for the squadron against the village team that afternoon: If we got back all right.

'Peter held his course, climbing almost imperceptibly. We were still below 100 feet. Then we were enmeshed in cotton-wool cloud, flying entirely on instruments. I had no experience of cloud formation flying, it was something one just didn't practice and I was frightened. Did Peter really mean to press on? I had to trust not only my own altimeter, but Peter's as well and I was terrified of flying into the sea. I edged in closer than ever, determined not to lose contact. All I could see was a dark smudge in the cloud which was Peter's wing-tip. Several times I nearly gave up. But for twenty minutes I hung on, concentrating more fiercely than ever before in my life. Then quite suddenly the cloud thinned. I could see the whole of Peter's Blenheim from wing-tip to wing-tip and a moment later we were through the cloud and visibility was about two miles. I followed Peter back to wave-top level and we flew so low that the surface of the sea was rippled by our slipstream. There was no sign of our No.2. We assumed he had turned back. There was no sign, either, of our other two formations of three and it looked as though Peter and I would be attacking alone. I knew this would not deter Peter. Two minutes later I heard Vic, who had moved down into the perspex nose after take-off, shout over the intercom. 'There they are!' Strung out in front of me like beads, about two miles distant and slightly to the north, I could see the silhouettes of about a dozen ships. This was it!

'We stayed at low level until we were about a mile off. Then, as Peter zoomed up to 250 feet, I broke formation and did the same, pulling in the full boost lever to give me maximum speed - about 240 knots - for the attack. Two big merchantmen stood out from all the others, one in the centre of the convoy and the other near the rear. I estimated them as between 5,000 and 6,000 tons. Typically, Peter went hurtling after the one in the centre. I went for the one at the rear. But I' thought mine looked slightly the larger of the two. A five-starred rocket floated up from one of the ships, challenging our identity. Then the ship's guns opened up. I was bearing down on the rear merchantman in a shallow dive, skidding and jinking to put the gunners off their aim. But the fire was horribly accurate.

'Then I spotted a flak-ship having a go at us three hundred yards to port. My front gun was fixed and I couldn't bring that to bear. 'Ernie, look after that Flak-ship!' I heard the clatter of his guns above the engine noise and glancing to the left I saw that he was right on target. But we were flying now through a terrific barrage from the ship we were attacking and as the tracer squirted up towards me my instinct was to duck.' 'We were enmeshed in this cotton-wool cloud, flying entirely on instruments' said Edrich. 'I had no experience of cloud formation flying. I was frightened. Several times I nearly gave up. But for twenty minutes, I hung on, concentrating more fiercely than ever before in my life.' Suddenly the clouds thinned and soon the convoy appeared in their sights. Two big merchant ships stood out from all the others; one in the centre of the convoy and the other near the rear. Edrich bore down on the latter ship, jinking and rolling to distract the defending gunners. They were now flying through an intense barrage. 'I experienced an extraordinary feeling of claustrophobia, trapped in the goldfish bowl of the cockpit', wrote Edrich, in a personal account in the family's papers 'feeling that if any of those rising balls of light hit the windscreen my whole world would disappear in some abrupt feat of legerdemain. I pressed on my own gun button, letting the tracer hose all over the ship and after seven or eight seconds of this I felt that if the gunners weren't dead at least they would be taking cover. But all this was subsidiary to my main obsession, to time my run so as to sling my bombs into the hull of the ship.

'The superstructure was floating up towards me at terrific rate and I shouted to Vic, 'Now!' Vic pulled the contact across the switches and we dropped our four 250lb bombs almost simultaneously. I held on until I was sure they'd gone. The deck of the merchantman filled my windscreen and I thought we must hit her. For some reason the Blenheim was hanging awkwardly to the left. I pulled back viciously on the stick and at once she responded and with a prayer of thankfulness I zoomed upwards, just in time to clear the masts. ''Get down!' My climb had taken us up to 800 feet and Vic, fearing fighters, was shouting at me to get back on the water. I pushed the nose forward hurriedly, weaving as I did so to avoid the flak, still flying northwards. After a minute or so of this I judged we were out of range and I turned to port and set course for home. As we turned we looked back at our ship. She was labouring under a billowing cloud of flames and smoke, an almost exact replica of the ship attacked by Peter, which was listing as well. Vic was jumping up and down in his seat, but I knew that Ernie, back in the turret, was the only one who could have seen the bombs fall, I called him on the intercom but there was no reply. 'Vic, see if Ernie's all right'. Vic's reply silenced my fears. 'He's in the turret and he's moving'.

'According to the book I should have looked for Peter and formated on him again, but we had split up for the actual attack and it might have taken some time. I decided that the curtain of cloud we had passed through on the way out would make an ideal refuge and soon I was back on instruments at 800 feet. Ernie then left his guns and called me up. 'Did you see the bombs hit?' I asked. 'Yes - two just undershot, but the other two must have hit'. 'You didn't actually see them?' 'There were only two splashes on the water. And you saw the ship'. Just then I glanced at my altimeter and was horrified to see that while talking to Ernie I had allowed my concentration to wander and we were right down to nought feet. I felt sick with fear and self-disgust and I yanked back the stick and pulled up to 500 feet. 'What the hell's happening'?' 'It's OK now. We were bloody close to the water'. In the same instant the engines spluttered and coughed. I couldn't believe it. We still had more than a hundred miles of water ahead of us. But within seconds both engines picked up again. The trouble must have been caused by some momentary hiatus in the petrol feed, through suddenly pushing the nose forward after a steep climb.

'When we landed back at Great Massingham we found that quite a lot of the rudder had been shot away, which explained the way we had hung to the left just after the attack. But the Blenheim would take a lot of punishment and I was learning to have tremendous faith in the aircraft I was flying, V5529. I was never quite so happy in any other machine. At the interrogation which followed, Peter's crew and mine were able to corroborate our respective claims. For leading this highly successful attack on his last trip, Peter was awarded a bar to his DFC. We learned now of the experience of the other seven crews - or anyway, of five of them. They had run into patches of dense fog and had turned back. Even though they had not been in action, one aircraft was missing from the other two vics. Edrich's No 2 survived the attack but he saw his No. 3 flown by Sergeant Francis S. B. Knox plunging towards the sea with his port wing a blazing torch. And of [Sergeant Harry Frederick Fordham, Simmons's No 2] nothing more was heard or seen. I re-lived that ghastly moment when I had so nearly flown into the sea through faulty instrument flying and I wondered if that was what had happened to the missing two. They were as inexperienced at that sort of flying as I was. Their absence threw a damper on the exaltation we felt at our own success. I thought, though, that we had made a positive response to Churchill's appeal.'[13]

The same afternoon Edrich played cricket for the squadron against a local village team - quite a contrast, although typical of the strange existence of all operational aircrew, one minute in the thick of battle then back to the comforts of their base with a trip to the local or whatever took the individual's fancy. 'Restful relaxation' wrote Edrich 'came from our visits to the Crown Hotel in Fakenham, about eight miles from Little Massingham, near West Raynham. There were three attractive young daughters of the proprietors, 'Pop' and Mrs. Myers, who were nicknamed 'The Crown Jewels'. The girls played records and we danced and when closing time came the police turned a blind eye. 'Within ten days of Churchill's visit' continues Edrich '107 Squadron was involved in the 'Circus' type of operations, the combined bomber-fighter sweeps which he had envisaged to force the Germans to disperse their air strength. Compared to the tensions of unescorted low-level flying in close formation over the sea, against shipping and other perimeter targets, which was our normal occupation, 'Circuses' were almost fun'.

June had begun badly with four frustrating missions, none of which were completed due to the weather and the Met Officer bore the brunt of the crews' frustrations. Then on 15 June Wing Commander Hughie Edwards, CO of 105 Squadron, led six crews on a shipping sweep, when they found a convoy of eight merchant ships off Den Haag. Edwards carried out a successful attack on a 4,000-ton merchantman, Sergeant Jackson bombing another large ship. (A squadron of ten E-boats was seen and avoided by most of the formation, but Flying Officer Peter H. Watts, on his first operation with the Squadron, mistook the heavily armed and manoeuvrable craft for merchant shipping. He went in low and although he hit one, he was shot down in flames. On 1 July Edwards was awarded the DFC for this daring low-level operation.) Twenty-three year old Flight Sergeant Arthur Guseford on 110 Squadron, who was shot down by Unteroffizier Barein of I./JGl in a Bf 109F on 15 June and another Blenheim, were lost on shipping beats. Next day, Beats 7 and 10 resulted in the loss of two more Blenheims. Off Borkum during an attack on a Squealer 24-year old Sergeant Evered Arthur Reginald Rex Leavers DFM on 21 Squadron hit the ship's mast and he cart-wheeled into the North Sea. Sergeant Ian Overheu DFM RNZAF and Sergeant Joseph William Howell Phelps died with him. Leavers was due to marry his fiancée Peggy Stanton on his next leave. Pilot Officers Ian Watson and Ernest Keith Aires, who had cheated death on 25 May, were lost when they were shot down by flak from a German convoy off the Hook of Holland. WOp/AG Sergeant Tom Dean was the third member of the 18 Squadron crew.

By the beginning of June 1941 the Blenheims had already destroyed 83 ships, severely damaged or disabled 18 others and done a varying amount of damage to another 54. All this had been done without any fighter escort and without any reliance on cloud cover, which the Blenheims used only when it happened to be there. They had also attacked many targets on land. At first such attacks were incidental to the drive against shipping and even when the crews were briefed for a raid on a land target they were often instructed to bomb shipping by preference if they sighted any on the way out. In this way they discovered that the low-level approach was as effective over the land as over the water and in consequence objectives on land were sometimes made the primary target. At first they mostly bombed objectives near the coast of Holland, or on the German Frisian Islands, for the farther they went inland the greater the danger. Even as early as 27 April Blenheims had penetrated as far as a power station to the west of Osnabrück and just north of the Ruhr, about 100 miles from the German coast, in all a journey there and back of about 700 miles. The Blenheims had some cloud cover and swooped out of it to drop their bombs on the power station from a low level; they observed a good deal or damage, clouds of smoke and fragments of masonry thrown into the air. But this was unusual and could only have been done when the weather was just right and the clouds suitably disposed. The more usual attack, which could be made without waiting for everything to be favourable, was on the fringe of the enemy's coast. Thus on the afternoon of 13 May a squadron of Blenheims made a surprise attack on the naval base of Heligoland. The Blenheims flew in low over the island in line abreast and bore down on their targets before the defences had time to open up. The bombers had taken off soon after midday and had flown over a calm and grey sea, with clouds of the same grey above them. 'It gave us the feeling,' one pilot said, 'of flying in a ball of space without any horizon.' The navigator in the aircraft leading the squadron did his work well and took the bombers straight to Heligoland. It is easy to miss an island only one and a half miles long and six hundred yards wide.

The first thing the crew saw were the island gulls and then out of the haze loomed the red cliffs of Heligoland. The crew could see their targets perfectly; the only difference they noticed from the photographs in the Ops Room was that there were no white rings or arrows to mark them out. Not until the whole of the squadron was over the island were the bombs dropped and then they all went down at once. The bombs fell just where they were meant to. Dust and debris filled the air and over the town itself there was a black fog of smoke through which an oblong of orange flame was beginning to emerge. Just as one Blenheim had left the island and was taking violent evasive action at almost sea-level, its port airs crew struck the water and the bomber was covered by a whirling mass of white foam. It needed all the pilot's strength to drag back the control column. The Blenheim lifted, but' a few seconds later the port engine caught fire. In the cockpit of every aircraft are dozens of knobs and switches; but the Blenheim pilot found the fire-extinguisher button at trigger-speed. In no time the fire was out. When it hit the sea the Blenheim was turned right round by the impact and now it was heading again for the island. A steep bank and once more it was making for the west. The port airscrew was badly bent, but the pilot kept the aircraft fairly level. Then a small and well-armed convoy appeared out of the mist; the ships' guns were at once trained on the bomber, but it was away before they could do any harm.

Before long the Blenheim crew were sending out their first distress signal: 'May have to land in sea.' Next the damaged and useless port airs crew fell off. This was some relief to the pilot, who now no longer had to counter-act the effect of its bent blades with his rudder bar. But the other engine was vibrating so badly that he could make no height. So long as the bomber stayed in the air there were two courses open to the pilot: he could either give the engine extra boost and risk tearing it to bits, or jog along dropping all, the time. 'I decided to take a chance on the engine holding together,' the pilot said, 'and as I slowly climbed we sent out another message: 'SOS. May be forced to come down in sea without further message.'

The bomber was now about forty miles from the English coast. Soon, through the early evening mist, the crew saw cliffs ahead half-silhouetted 'against the sun. Presently the crew were so near to the shore that even if the remaining engine had failed they would have had only a mile or two to paddle in their dinghy. But it did not fail. They crossed the coast and made for their aerodrome. They found that their undercarriage was damaged and would not come down, so they strapped themselves in, opened the escape hatches, jettisoned the last of their petrol - and the Blenheim came down to make a safe belly landing. When the crew reported to the Duty Pilot he said, 'Lucky for you there were no thunderstorms about. You might have been frightened.'

As the months went by and the bomber crews gained confidence and experience, the attacks became heavier, more daring and more destructive. Reviewing the campaign, Air Marshal Sir Richard Peirse, who was then Commander-in-Chief of Bomber Command, issued an order of the day in which he described how 'The success of these attacks lies in the daring and resolution which, have gone to their making. In the absence of cloud cover or of fighter protection the formidable defences of the enemy have been overborne by fine airman ship and high courage. To the captains and crews I say 'Well done.'

Much of June was a little of an anti-climax, for several operations were abandoned through the lack of the cloud cover so necessary for the survival of the poorly armed Blenheims. On Thursday 27 June ten crews on 107 Squadron were ordered to fly to Swanton Morley for a special briefing where they and ten crews on 105, were told that they would carry out a low-level attack in daylight on the docks at Bremen the following day. This meant flying over the German mainland for some 105 miles, far beyond the range of fighter protection. The formation was to be led by Wing Commander Laurence Petley, but when it was time for takeoff at 0430 'Petters' was unable to start his starboard engine. The remaining 19 aircraft took off on time, so it fell to the lot of Pilot Officer Bill Edrich, flying his 11th operation, to take over the lead. They had been flying for some time when Petley, having persuaded his faulty engine to start, caught up with them and took over the lead, much to the relief of Edrich. When they reached a point opposite Cuxhaven they saw a large enemy convoy, which opened up on them, so the essential element of surprise had been lost. Reluctantly, therefore, Petley turned round and brought the formation back home. Hughie Edwards, at the head of the 105 formation, said afterwards that having got so far he thought they might have gone on. Command thought so too, as Bill Edrich explains:

'After landing back at Massingham we went straight over to the cottage that housed our tiny ops room and headquarters and there the adjutant, Tony Richardson RAFVR was standing with the telephone in his hand. He called out to 'Petters', 'Sir, the AOC's on the line.' We were all feeling pretty glum and the chatter that normally succeeds an operation was absent. All eyes were watching 'Petters' as he took the receiver. We saw his face blanch and tauten with anger and humiliation as he listened to the voice that we ourselves couldn't hear. In the silent ops room we were watching our leader being accused of cowardice and we knew that in Stevenson's mind we were all tainted with it. Watching 'Petters' and remembering how nearly the leadership had fallen to me, I wondered again what I would have done and I saw myself, like 'Petters' arraigned before the entire squadron by a contemptuous AOC.

'If that's what you think,' we heard 'Petters' say; 'we'll do the whole bloody show again this afternoon.'

'We didn't doubt that he meant it. And we didn't doubt that Stevenson was capable of sending us. The political pressures he was being subjected to, six days after Hitler's attack on Russia, must have been enormous. We hung around to hear our fate, but when it came through it was an anti-climax. We were to fly up to Driffield, a bomber station in Yorkshire, that afternoon and await orders.'

Petley led nine crews to Driffield but was ordered not to fly on the subsequent operation. 107 Squadron was informed that six Halifax bombers, the first ever to operate, were to bomb Kiel the following morning as a diversion and seven Blenheims on 107 Squadron were to mount a low-level raid on the Luftwaffe base at Westerland on the island of Sylt. The news was received in silence, for Sylt was renowned for its formidable defences. The Station Commander at Driffield did his best to boost morale, claiming that it was no accident that the raid was timed for midday Sunday 'when the German fighter pilots, creatures of habit, will be enjoying a pre-lunch lager'. This inspired planning was invalidated when the operation was delayed for 24 hours, until 1000 hours on Monday 30 June. The seven Blenheims, led by a New Zealander, Squadron Leader 'Zeke' Murray, took off at 10 o'clock that morning, leaving Petley and one unserviceable Blenheim behind and headed out over the North Sea to Sylt where they were to draw off the fighters from the Halifax raid.

Edrich recalled: 'We flew at extremely low level for the entire North Sea crossing, a distance of 360 miles, relying on dead reckoning and on what drifts the navigators could get from the wave-tops. I was No.3 to 'Zeke' in the leading vic of three, with a box of four behind us and the long crossing at low altitude demanded intense concentration. Several times I felt my back stiffen up, but it was impossible to relax. At length, straight ahead of us, we could make out the coastline of Sylt, flat and featureless, a bleak panorama of lonely sand dunes. So far we had not been seen. As we lifted over the sand dunes we saw that we were crossing the narrow extremity of the island 10 miles south of the central bulk. Soon we were over the sea again, between island and mainland and as 'Zeke' altered course to the north we followed. At once the gun flashes began sparking off at us, to the left from the island and to the right from the mainland and straight ahead from the causeway which connects the two. I have seen paintings of naval battles, with gun flashes, illuminating the scene and the water being thrown up on all sides by shell bursts, but never have I seen such an inferno of fire-power as was directed at us in the next few minutes. We not only had to fly through this hail of metal: we had to fly through the plumes of water too.

'I shut my mind to everything and concentrated on 'Zeke's' port wing-tip to my right. In close formation we might present a better target, but I knew that the heavier guns would have difficulty in ranging on us at low level. And all my experience had convinced me that to lose formation over the target was fatal. We began to switch into line abreast for our bombing run. Our bombs had eleven-second delay fuses and we all wanted to be clear of the target before they went off. Over my right shoulder I caught a glimpse of a Blenheim from the box of four behind us. It was flying higher than the rest of us and for a moment it looked like a wild duck that has just been hit and is about to drop. When I looked again seconds later it was gone.

'We crossed the causeway but I was hardly aware of it; seven of us had begun the bombing run. There were four of us left. I turned to port in the direction of the airfield and once over the island the flak thinned out a little. I knew where the airfield was, but. I couldn't pick out a single pin-point. We were so disorientated from the pasting we had received and the whole picture was so much more complex and confused than those strikingly clear 'stills' we'd seen at briefing that we simply dropped our bombs on the most likely looking building and hared out. to sea as fast as we could. That was how it was. You can call it indiscriminate bombing if you like.

'Now we strove to get back into tight formation before the fighter attack that we knew must come. I knew in my mind's eye where 'Zeke' was and soon I slid back into position to his left. I saw another Blenheim zoom erratically into the No. 2 position and then I saw a fourth Blenheim to port and astern, intent on catching us up. Soon we were in a box of four, flying low so as to show nothing but our top camouflage to any pursuing fighter. No one seemed to be chasing us. Four of us, at least, had got away with it. When we were 100 miles from Sylt I lit a cigarette and relaxed. Then I heard a shout from Ernie, 'Snappers!'

'I had forgotten the fighters at Terschelling, on the Frisian Islands. Four of them, Bf 109s, were hurrying up towards us from the south. 'Zeke' coolly turned our formation northwards, drawing the fighters further away from their base. We knew their range was limited. But the Bf 109s hung on. 'Zeke's' gunner took control of the voice radio to direct the fire-power of the four Blenheims and we prepared to put into practice the tactics we had rehearsed so often. The principle was that when bombers are being attacked by fighters of superior speed, the best defence is to turn into the direction of attack, thus making it difficult for the fighters to get a good stern view.

'We tried this as the Germans began their attack, but they didn't fall for it. Two of them took up position to the port rear, two to the starboard rear. As the port pair attacked with cannon and machine-gun and we turned left to make them miss and overshoot, the starboard pair automatically fastened on our stern. 'Bandit port five o'clock, half a mile. Hold it... Hold it... Fire!' The Blenheim juddered as Ernie opened up and we sniffed the rank stench of cordite. Ahead of me I could see the water bubbling and foaming as the bullets from the '109 churned up the sea. Had it not been for 'Zeke's' gunner and his clear and timely directions we would never have survived that first attack, let alone those that followed. We couldn't match the fire-power of the '109s, but four Blenheim turrets firing simultaneously, switching rapidly from target to target, kept the German pilots at arm's length.

'Every now and then I could see spluttering little spurts on the metal surfaces of the other Blenheims where hits were being scored. I guessed the same thing was happening to us. One cannon shell burst with a little pink explosion on the rear of 'Zeke's' port engine nacelle. It left a jagged hole and as I watched the fluid streaming down the fuselage and spraying off the tail I knew his port inner petrol tank had been hit. 'My guns have packed up!' It was Ernie Hope from the turret. Soon, in all four Blenheims, the guns were either jammed or out of ammunition. With four badly mauled aircraft, greatly reducing our ability to manoeuvre, we were left with evasion as our only hope.

'Mercifully three of the '109s were giving up the chase and turning back for Terschelling. But the fourth was coming in for the kill, The German pilot was approaching from the port rear and we could not shake him off. Reassured by the absence of answering fire, he came in closer and closer. We were sitting ducks. Yet still he did not fire. As he overtook us he banked above me and I looked straight up into his face. His look of exasperation was unmistakable. He too had run out of ammunition. With a shrug of the shoulders he turned away and headed south.'[14] David Brocklehurst, a friend of later years, was given another version of the escape. Edrich said that the German pilot had flown around him twice and when, flying alongside, they had waved at each other. The German raised his thumb to concede his failure and flew off home. A glance at Bill's severely damaged aircraft, spinning desperately in the skies, convinced him that his enemy would soon plunge into the seas and oblivion.

'I called up 'Zeke' to tell him about his petrol tank and to suggest that he switch off his port engine. This reduced his speed to 130 mph, but the rest of us closed in and escorted him back to the Yorkshire coast. Nothing was ever more welcome than the sight of Flamborough Head. I suggested that in view of the damage we had all sustained we should land singly, instead of in our usual formation, with 'Zeke' going in first. Both 'Zeke' and the second Blenheim crash-landed, but the remaining two of us landed normally. Soon we were grouped around one of the crashed aircraft, talking excitedly about the trip.

'While we were doing so a lone Blenheim, obviously in trouble, staggered over the field. It was one of the three missing aircraft, piloted by a sergeant pilot named Leven. We had lost two aircraft on the run in and one of them had slewed into Leven, chewing up his ailerons and his flaps on one side.

Somehow Leven had recovered and escaped into cloud; his was very probably the aircraft I had seen lurching like an injured bird. He had kept the Blenheim straight and level by holding the aileron control in the vertical instead of the horizontal position, but it had been such a strain that he had borrowed a leather belt from his navigator and strapped up the controls. He had then skipped from cloud to cloud and eventually came back to Driffield. He received an immediate award of a DFM. 'Are all your trips like this?' asked the highly impressed bomber crews based at Driffield.

'Most of them', we said laconically.'[15]

Edrich was badly shaken. The faces of the ground crew were almost as grim as the returning airmen. 'We thought you'd had it sir' one man told Edrich. Another thought that he was looking at a ghost. Edrich removed his tattered England sweater, which he had worn on his first test match three years before. He never failed to wear it while flying - it was his lucky mascot - and drank a reviving beer. There was a pleasing assignation to complete the day. Bill had a rendezvous with a handsome village girl that evening.

When, on the evening of 3 July, crews in East Anglia went to bed, Bremen had already been scheduled as the target for the morrow. Operation 'Wreckage', as it was code-named, would be led by Wing Commander Hughie Edwards, who had followed behind Petley to the same target ten days earlier. As usual sleep was difficult, probably more so given the nature of the difficult and dangerous operation. Flight Lieutenant Tony Richardson RAVR, 107 Squadron adjutant at Massingham had already witnessed too many such days and nights at close hand. His was the painful duty to write to the bereaved relatives of his brother officers and men who never returned. He later dedicated a poem, *Night Before Bremen*, to his CO and the crews of 107 Squadron, who would fly the 'Wreckage' operation.

At least one man relished the thought. Irishman Warrant Officer Samuel Joseph Magee, the legendary 107 Squadron Armament Officer, had persuaded Petley to let him go along as an extra gunner aboard one of the Blenheims. During low-level raids by German intruders at Wattisham, while everyone else took cover, Magee had calmly set up his .303 Vickers Gas Operated with its wooden butt and special trigger and had blasted away at incoming Dorniers and Junkers 88. Off duty Magee ran a 180-hp Wolseley around the narrow country lanes at alarming speeds, on seemingly inexhaustible supplies of petrol.

On the morning of 4 July Magee joined Flight Lieutenant Wellburn and his observer, Sergeant David Arthur Dupree and Sergeant Allan Ernest Routley, air gunner and together they boarded V6193, one of six 107 Squadron Blenheims taking part. Magee entered the almost dark compartment aft of the bomb well armed with his beloved VGO and several magazines containing 100% tracer. He settled on to the uncomfortably small ledge behind the bomb well camera hatch so he could see through the small perspex panel in the centre of the door, which he would remove just before the target and hurl a 40lb GP bomb through it before blasting away with his VGO!

Edwards took off at 0521 hours from Swanton Morley and led nine Blenheims into the clear blue Norfolk sky. It was his 36th operation of the war.

His observer, Pilot Officer Alastair Stewart Ramsay and his gunner, Sergeant G. D. P. Quinn, settled down to their tasks and the crew kept their eyes peeled for the six crews of 107 Squadron led by Petley, who would be joining them after take-off from Massingham. However, mist and fog, which was to dog the first 100 miles of the operation, shielded them from view as the formation droned low over the sea, maintaining radio silence. Edwards could see his two wingmen but little else. Meanwhile, diversions were in progress: Wing Commander Ralph George Hurst was leading five crews of 226 Squadron to bomb gun emplacements on Nordeney and six Blenheims of 21 Squadron were flying a 'Circus', with the customary fighter escort, to the Chocques Chemical Works. Hurst's Blenheim, hit by flak, literally blew up.

When the 'Wreckage' Blenheims finally made landfall at the German coast, one sub-flight of three aircraft of 107 Squadron was no longer with them; Squadron Leader 'Zeke' Murray and Flying Officer Charney[16] had returned to Massingham with mechanical problems, while a third had aborted when Flight Lieutenant Jones, the pilot, became ill. The remaining twelve tightened up formation and pressed on.

Just before 0730 hours the formation was sighted by a coastal convoy near Nordeney, but Edwards pressed on. As the formation crossed into Germany a few miles south of Cuxhaven, people working in the fields, mistaking the low-level bombers for German aircraft, stopped and looked up to wave. Still at a height of between 50 and 100 feet, Edwards turned the formation south towards Bremen. The attack, timed for 0800 hours, was to be made in a 1½ mile-wide line-abreast formation, the aircraft spaced 100-200 yards apart and flying at tree-top height. Edwards and his crews weaved between the barrage balloons hoisted to 50 feet above the port and braved the tremendous ack-ack fire that greeted their arrival. As Edwards was to recall later: 'As we rightly assumed, the flak and balloons split up the formation and it became every man for himself. The flak was terrific and frightening. It was bursting all around me for ten minutes. There was a distinct smell of cordite in the air. I was flying so low that I flew through telephone and telegraph wires.'

About 20 shells found their mark on Edwards's Blenheim and Quinn was hit in the knee by shrapnel. Behind them two 105 Squadron machines were shot out of the sky; Sergeant William Angus MacKillop's Blenheim was hit by flak and crashed on to a factory, Sergeants Eric Gordon Nethercott and George Frederick Entwhistle dying with him, while Flying Officer Michael Montgomery Lambert's aircraft was last seen by other crews heading away from Bremen, burning fiercely, later to crash, killing Lambert, Sergeant Reginald Copeland and Sergeant Frederick William Rodney Charles.

107 Squadron also lost two Blenheims. Petley was shot down by flak in the target area, killing him, his observer, Flight Lieutenant Raymond Arthur Bailey DFC and Sergeant Wilfred Marshall Harris, air gunner. The Blenheim piloted by Flight Lieutenant F. Wellburn was also shot down by flak and crashed in the target area. Sergeant David Arthur Dupree, Sergeant Allan Ernest Routley and Warrant Officer Magee, the latter no doubt firing to the end, died in the crash, but Wellburn survived to be taken prisoner.[17]

All the aircraft were damaged. After the target Edwards proceeded to circle

Bremen and strafed a stationary train that had opened up on them, before leading the formation out of Germany at low level. He recalled, 'I had great pleasure in using up the ammunition from my one front gun, which silenced the opposition.'

Edwards, his aircraft minus part of the port wing, the port aileron badly damaged; a cannon shell in the radio rack and a length of telegraph wire wrapped round the tail wheel and trailing behind, headed for Bremerhaven and Wilhelmshaven. More flak rose to greet them at Bremerhaven until finally the coastline at Heligoland came into view and the Blenheims dived down to sea level again. The battered formation flew north of the Frisians for a short time and then headed westwards for East Anglia. At Swanton Morley Sergeant W. H. A. Jackson had to belly-land with the observer and gunner wounded. Edwards brought his ailing bomber home and put down safely at Swanton Morley, where Quinn had to be lifted out of the aircraft with a Coles crane. Although four crews were lost, successful attacks had been made on the docks, factories, a timber yard and railways and great damage was caused to the tankers and transports that were loaded with vital supplies. Operation 'Wreckage' received considerable publicity and congratulations were sent from the C-in-C Bomber Command and the Chief of Air Staff, Sir Charles Portal, downwards. ACM Stevenson sent a telegram that read, 'This low-flying raid, so gallantly carried out, deep into Germany, without the support of fighters, will always rank high in the history of the Royal Air Force.' One Sergeant even had to broadcast his impression of the raid on the BBC Home Service.

An immediate signal from the C-in-C Bomber Command, Sir Richard Peirse, read: 'YOUR ATTACK THIS MORNING HAS BEEN A GREAT CONTRIBUTION TO THE DAY OFFENSIVE NOW BEING FOUGHT. IT WILL REMAIN AN OUTSTANDING EXAMPLE OF DASH AND INITIATIVE. I SEND YOU AND YOUR CAPTAINS AND CREWS MY WARMEST CONGRATULATIONS AND THE ADMIRATION OF THE COMMAND'.

Amid all the bravura, at Massingham Adjutant Flight Lieutenant Anthony Richardson quietly sat down and penned letters of condolence to the relatives of the crews lost on the raid. After the war the gifted Richardson would write Wingless Victory, the story of Basil Embry, his CO when at Wattisham earlier in the war. Bill Edrich, who returned from leave, had read the reports of the raid in the newspapers. 'When I got back to Little Massingham, the mess that had always been so full of life and personality was silent and empty. 'I'm afraid there's no one from the squadron here,' said the Mess Sergeant. 'We lost nearly all the officers on the Bremen raid. Those who are left have moved over to West Raynham.' He promised to lay on some transport and I went to my room to collect my things.'

On 7 July 101 Squadron converted to Wellingtons and transferred to 3 Group. Two days later 88 Squadron joined 2 Group at Swanton Morley. At this time the other Blenheim squadrons operating from the UK were: 110 Squadron at Wattisham (226 Squadron had joined 2 Group at Wattisham in May); 18 at Oulton (which sent a detachment to Malta in October and saw out the rest of the war in the Mediterranean theatre); 105 (detached to Lossiemouth as well as Malta); 21 at Watton; 82 at Bodney (which also sent a detachment to Malta); 139 at Horsham St. Faith; 107 at Great Massingham; and 114 at Leuchars (attached to 18 Group Coastal Command).

On 21 July Edwards was awarded the VC for courage and leadership displayed on the Bremen operation. He thus became only the second Australian to receive this award (the first having been awarded to Lieutenant F. H. McNamara of the RFC during the First World War).[18] By this time 105 Squadron was in Malta for operations in the Mediterranean. At the end of August Edwards was posted to AHQ Malta and was replaced by Wing Commander Donald William Scivier RAAF of 107 Squadron. Scivier was in action on his first day, but on 22 September his aircraft collided with another Blenheim and crashed into the sea after his tail fell off. There were no survivors. Five days later the last sortie was flown. On 28 September the surviving squadron members sailed home in a cruiser.

After 'Wreckage' 107 Squadron needed to be reformed before it could participate in further raids. Bill Edrich, now with the rank of Flight Lieutenant (a double promotion only six weeks after first becoming operational), still had a serviceable Blenheim and a full crew, so they were loaned to 21 Squadron, where in fact they stayed. Edrich was promoted to Squadron Leader (he had gone from Pilot Officer to Squadron Leader in 19 days) and flew the rest of his ops on 21 Squadron.

Meanwhile, at West Raynham, 107 Squadron took shape again after its mauling. On 6 July Wing Commander Arthur Frank Calvert Booth took command; previously he had been a Squadron Leader with 105 Squadron under Hughie Edwards. However, senior rank was certainly no protection. Within a week of his new posting, on 12 July, he was killed during an anti-shipping strike. The new CO was Wing Commander Frazer Apsley 'Bunny' Harte DFC SAAF, who was killed in action on 9 October 1941 leading the squadron in Malta. In fact, 2 Group lost six wing commanders in one week. One of them was Wing Commander Thomas Noel 'Tim' Partridge DFC, CO of 18 Squadron, who piloted one of four Blenheims that were shot down by flak, on 16 July, when 36 Blenheims on 18, 21 and 139 Squadrons carried out a low-level daylight raid on the docks at Rotterdam. Wing Commander P. F. 'Tom' Webster, commanding 21 Squadron, who led the first wave, was rested and replaced by Wing Commander John C. Kercher.

On the afternoon of 16 July a strong force of Blenheims swept low across the fields of Holland to attack enemy ships concentrated in the docks at Rotterdam. As they passed overhead people in the towns and countryside recognized the blue-and-red roundels of the RAF and waved encouragement; they, may well have noticed the symbolic V-formation in which the bombers were flying. In two waves the Blenheims passed over the chimneys of Rotterdam and then, each wave in line abreast so that no bomber would be over the target when the delayed-action bombs of another bomber exploded, they made for the ships packed close in the docks. An air gunner, who afterwards broadcast his description of the attack, said: 'We bombed at 4.55 in the afternoon. As we flashed across the docks the observer singled out a ship for us to attack. Going for a target like that is like partridge-shooting. When the covey gets up you know immediately which is 'your' bird. In the same way we knew 'our' ship; it had a bulky black hull and one funnel. We nipped across the quayside buildings and from mast-high let our load drop. She was a medium-sized ship - I should guess about 4,000 tons. I could feel the bomb doors swinging to; and we were away over towards the town... Off to the left the first wave of attackers had left many ships burning... On our way out I could see great pillars of smoke rising and then, underneath me, I saw what the Germans had done to Rotterdam. The centre of the town was flat-level acres where once there were great and fine buildings.'

Many ships were destroyed that afternoon and others were hit and severely damaged. Warehouses and dock equipment were smashed and burnt and our crews turned their guns on everything German they could find. It was clear from the reports of all the crews that the attack had gone according to plan; it had been well timed and the enemy were given no chance to get their defences going. 'There was but slight opposition from anti-aircraft guns and though twelve Me 110s were seen to take off from an aerodrome it was too late for them to engage the attacking force.

In the middle of July, the day of reckoning that Charles Patterson knew must come finally arrived. 'We had to leave Scotland and the comparative safety of the Norwegian coast and rejoin 2 Group in Norfolk for daylight bomber operations. Virtually every operation from now on meant being shot at in some way or other in broad daylight. We flew down to West Raynham in formation. Wing Commander George L. B. 'Bok' Hull DFC, our South African Squadron commander, a veteran from 1940 and the most marvellous CO, was absolutely thrilled that we were going back to 2 Group proper where he would be able to head his squadron into the thick of things. I could not help being caught up in the excitement, even though I was very nervous of what was to come. I was also, in a way, exhilarated. From the moment we landed the whole tempo became more highly charged. We arrived to find that our station commander was the famous, ineffable and unique Paddy Bandon, Group Captain, the Earl of Bandon, whose personality and achievements were a legend. Behind his always cheerful and friendly exterior was a man of extraordinary sympathy, kindness and tolerance. His task was to maintain morale amongst very young, mostly inexperienced, raw and terrified crews during this period of appalling casualties. He was a teamwork leader, wonderful at getting people of conflicting personalities to work together.

'That summer the King and Queen paid a visit to the station in the middle of an intense operational period. Lord Bandon was a friend of the King and he had been at Sandringham, which was nearby, staying the night and duck shooting. At 8 o'clock in the morning on the way to London the King and Queen paid a visit. I was a Flight Commander at the time (I went from Pilot Officer to Squadron Leader in six weeks due to the casualties) and each Flight Commander had to take first the King and then the Queen and present their flight to them, all lined up in the crew room, one flight down one side, one flight down the other. We had all been very strictly briefed that the only thing we said when the King or Queen offered us their hand was 'How do you do Sir' or 'How do you do Ma'am' and nothing else. If they asked you a question, you answered it.

'I brought the Queen up the line, presenting each one by name and she took each one by the hand and looked up at these young chaps - none of us was more than 22 - looked up at each one as much as to say 'I think you're wonderful'. Then to my horror one young Yorkshire Sergeant air gunner, a tall raw bone youth, was so overcome that he seized the Queen's hand with both of his and said, 'I am so pleased to meet Your Majesty'. I nearly passed out. I thought I'd had it now, but all she did was put her other hand on top of his and say, 'No more pleased than I am to meet you, Sergeant, I assure you.' That absolutely made his day, he was on cloud nine. A week later he was dead.

'I also had the unexpected and completely new experience of finding myself billeted in Weasenham Hall, which belonged to the Earls of Leicester, the Coke family, which had been turned into a mess for us. To my amazement I found myself a Flight Lieutenant overnight, having only done about twelve operations. A state of affairs had been reached where any officer pilot who completed about ten operations was virtually automatically a Flight Lieutenant. Anyone who could get through 15 was a Squadron Leader. This situation most certainly never existed at any other time during the war. 'Bok' Hull was keen and ready to start operating. The very day after we arrived I had to move the whole of my flight to Bodney, a satellite airfield about 8 miles away and have it ready for operations the next morning. It was a standard 'Circus', a formation of Blenheims going out with Fighter Command on a fighter sweep across the Channel at medium level, about 10,000 feet. Our target was a power station near Rouen. It was regarded as a fairly safe form of operation, but it was made clear that there would inevitably be a great deal of heavy flak, which is what one encountered from 8,000 feet upwards. I had no idea what it would look like, although I was told there would be a lot of black puffs. The main thing that was impressed upon me was to keep formation and follow the Squadron commander in his evasive action, which would be gentle weaves and turns towards the target. I must follow him and keep them going straight and level when he said 'straight and level'. The moment bombs were gone the Squadron commander would swing away and resume evasive action.

'I led a 'Vic' of three and formated under the Squadron commander's tail. It was a glorious, sunny day, necessary of course for a 'Circus' - you could not do it with cloud. The whole thing was a sort of daze. I just did not know what would happen when the flak started. I genuinely had no confidence that I would be able to take it. On the other hand, the thing in my head was that it just had to be done. There was no way out. I suppose my training and instincts were subconsciously operating even though I was not aware of it.

'We circled over Dungeness and out of the corner of my eye I saw a sight that raised my spirits to a remarkable degree. Down below, against a bank of cumulus cloud, I could see an enormous swarm of what looked like gnats, silhouetted against this cloud, racing across and climbing in a great upward sweep. This was 11 Group's Hurricanes coming up to provide our escort. They joined and took up close positions all around us; one could see the pilots in their cockpits. Of course, it gave a wonderful sense of security, although it was no security whatsoever against flak.'I felt quite good but crossing the enemy coast had a sinister connotation, then I seemed to just live from minute to minute, longing for the target to come up, dreading the flak. We carried on straight and level. Still nothing happened, then my navigator said, 'we must be getting to the target fairly soon.' Sure enough, the Squadron commander started gentle evasive action and then the dreaded moment arrived. There was a thud and the aircraft shook. My first sight of the famous black puffs produced an irresistible longing to just turn and run, but I couldn't. I was in the middle of the box. I had my orders. I just had to carry on.

'The puffs got nearer. The thuds got more severe. I actually saw the orange flash in the puffs of smoke, but I didn't feel too bad while the Squadron commander was still doing this gentle evasive action, weaving slowly and gently to port or starboard with a climb or with a loss of height. Then we had to straighten up and go straight and level. I just sat there, frozen at the controls, waiting for the whole aeroplane to disappear into oblivion, but we went on and on and still we were surviving. The longer it went on the more I thought with just a bit more to go that'll be when we get it. I don't know how, but I carried on, on this long straight and narrow run, which never seemed to end. At last, the leading navigator gave the signal for 'Bombs gone!' In a Blenheim the bombs opened the doors with their own weight.

'Every now and then some of the thuds were extremely close, but we were still in one piece. Then to my unforgettable relief, Wing Commander Hull turned away and we were all able to swing away. I was so exhilarated that I had got through and done it that I really did not think much about the dangers that might occur on the way back. The fighters were all around us and we returned across the Channel. At the English coast the fighters fell away and we flew on at 8-10,000 feet back to Norfolk. Hull gave the order to break formation and then we all landed. I'd actually done it. I did a few more 'Circuses' like that and managed to get through them, but I still had not done a low-level daylight.

'On Blenheims we lived day to day, each governed by what the bomb load was, your fate designated on the notice board at Weasenham Hall. If you had instantaneous fuses in the bomb load, it meant that you were going on a 'Circus' at medium level. If it was semi-armour-piercing (SAP) 11-second delay, it meant a low-level shipping attack. Then you simply turned away from the notice board and assumed that your own death warrant had been signed.'

On 23 July Blenheims on 18 and 139 Squadrons carried out a sweep off the Dutch coast without success. As they were turning for home, led by 23-year-old Squadron Leader D. J. A. Roe, the youngest officer of the rank in the RAF, whose father was an MT Sergeant on his squadron, Bf 110s of 5./ZG76 appeared, damaging every Blenheim and shooting down two. Sergeant Peter D. Baker and Sergeant William M. G. Dunham RCAF fell victim to a combination of attacks by Oberleutnant Hotari Schmude, Oberfeldwebel Leschnik and Feldwebel Schmidt. A third Blenheim, piloted by Sergeant Wood, severely damaged in the attacks, limped back to Horsham St. Faith, where it was crash-landed by Wood. He and his observer Sergeant Johnson were severely injured. Worse, six crews on 21 Squadron based at Manston attacked a 4,000-ton tanker escorted by four flak ships and three Blenheims were shot down.

On 24 July 36 Blenheims on 139, 18, 107, 226 and 114 Squadrons flew 'Circus' operations to cause a diversion for the bombers attempting to stop the 'Channel Dash' by the *Scharnhorst* and *Gneisenau*. On 30 July 12 crews on 18 and 82 Squadrons, led by Squadron Leader Roe, were briefed to attack shipping in the Kiel Canal, making use of cloud cover, which, as so often happened, petered out before they reached the target. However, the operation was anything but uneventful, crews on 18 Squadron attacking a ship in convoy off Heligoland with the loss of Sergeant H. D. Cue and crew who were taken prisoner. The 82 Squadron Blenheims seriously damaged three ships in another convoy with the loss of two aircraft. 139 Squadron fared even worse, losing four Blenheims to Bf 110s of ZG76. So ended July, during which 39 crews failed to return.

On 2 August Charles Patterson saw the dreaded SAP. 'There was nothing I could do about it. Then I got my first experience of flying across the North Sea, at low level, in formation. I was one of a 'Vic' of three going to do a beat along the Frisian Islands. Apart from flying over to Norway, this was the first time I experienced the sensation of flying very low over the sea in broad daylight, little knowing that it was to be an experience that was to become so familiar over the years ahead. It is difficult to describe the sensation, really. You were literally racing across the surface of the sea. The concentration required to do this and formate at the same time kept the mind fully occupied, but still at the back of one's mind was the dread of when one would have to turn on to the actual shipping beat and whether one would actually find a convoy.

'We raced on and when we reached the Frisian Islands we turned to port and ran along the northern shores of Ameland towards Borkum. Suddenly, the leader said something on the TR9. Alan Griffith, my gunner, assured me on his intercom that it was a call of 'Snappers', which meant that fighters were coming to intercept us. I looked everywhere and couldn't see any. Suddenly, the leader climbed. Fortunately, there was a thin belt of cloud, enough in the leader's opinion to conceal us. He climbed and I tried to follow, but I soon lost him in the cloud. Now the operation would have to be abandoned and we would drop down out of the cloud when out of range of the German fighters. I decided to take a peek below: on the port side from a thousand feet, as plain and as clear as anything, was Ameland. I just don't know what came over me, but I was suddenly seized with the idea that to go home without dropping my bombs on anything was wrong. Against all the training and against all my own views and principles, I decided to use the thousand feet to get up speed, charge down and race across the island at full throttle in the hope of seeing something that might be worth bombing.

'So, without consulting my crew, I just told them I was going to do it. I put the Blenheim into a dive, pulled the Plus 9 boost and went down to the sea in a fast shallow dive. I should think that the aeroplane was doing about 260 on the clock when I got down to sea level. The island came racing toward me at an alarming speed and before I knew where I was I was racing up over sand dunes. There in front of me were four enormous long barrels, 4.7mm AA guns, pointing to the sky, surrounded by a lot of sand bags and a lot of German soldiers. I pressed the tit and dropped the bombs. I saw a lot of steely blue flashes around the ground, which I realised was machine-gun fire. Turning to starboard I raced down to the beach to get out to sea again. There were a lot of young naked men, presumably German soldiers, having a swim. Alan Griffith raked them left and right with machine-gun fire. As we raced out to sea he told me that there was a great deal of blood and so on. I thought he'd done very well. So did he. I now look back on it with revulsion). Then he called out that there were terrific flashes and a lot of smoke. Something had been hit.

'When I landed Group Captain Bandon was waiting to greet me. His face was wreathed in smiles. Apparently, the Squadron leader had seen me dive down and cross the coast and he saw, following my bombing, a tremendous flash and smoke up to 1,500 feet. It was evident that the detonation of these bombs had touched off their ammunition dump! Being very young and inexperienced this was the first time in my life I'd ever done anything that appeared to be individually rather successful.

'Two days later, on 4 August, I was sent out on a shipping beat in the Heligoland Bight. I had to lead two Sergeants who'd never been on operations before. One was only 19 and I don't think the other one was more than about 20. My morale was lifted by the previous attack so I was not quite as frightened as I ought to have been. It was a cloudy day, grey and rather sinister. As we turned south we entered a rain storm and visibility came down. We emerged and quite suddenly, there, 2 miles slap in front, was what looked like an 8,000-ton merchant ship, surrounded, to my horror, by twelve flak ships as escort. And we were racing toward it!

'I got very low down on the sea and started to open the throttles. The two Sergeants, whose formation-keeping up to now was poor, weaved around, obviously panic-stricken by the sight of this convoy. One was at about 200 feet and the other at about 100 feet, one each side of me. The whole tactical essence of low-level attack on ships was to keep right down on the sea so that the enemy did not see you until the last minute. If you were over 20 feet you could be seen over the horizon from the deck of the ships. To my final horror, a mile out the leading flak ship flashed an order signal for me to identify myself. There was a lot of cloud above and I made a sudden decision to lead the two Sergeants into it, try to drop out and attack again from about 800 feet.

'When we came out all I could see was grey sea. We never found the convoy again. I set course for home, bombing a 'Squealer', a little vessel a few miles out to sea used as an observation post for anti-shipping Blenheims. I was crestfallen because although I could put a perfectly genuine tactical reason forward for having turned away, I knew in my own heart that I'd funked it. I was not so much worried about what the Group Captain and the AOC, 'Butcher' Stevenson, of whom we all lived in dread, would say; I was more worried by the fact that I knew the real reason. However, the explanation was accepted and I heard no more. Then I realised that I had got to try to live with it and cope next time. All my elation was gone. I went out again two days later, leading another shipping beat up the Dutch coast, low level, but fortunately nothing was sighted.

'Then something fundamentally changed my whole operational career and indeed my whole life. We got wind that there was a major operation to be laid on and as time went by the more alarming became the rumours. We understood that it was to be a major effort involving all the Blenheims in 2 Group. We did a lot of low-level formation practice. We had a new Squadron commander, Wing Commander John Nicol, who arrived with no previous operational experience, to take over from Wing Commander Howe, who fell out of the first floor window of Weasenham Hall after a party and was in hospital in Cambridge - not a very gallant accident for such a gallant man. The operation was to be led by 114 Squadron and Nicol had never operated before. This seemed very strange to us, but he had a wonderful navigator to go with him. Flight Lieutenant Tommy Baker DFM, Howe's navigator, was an ex-Halton boy who became a very great friend of mine and whom I admired tremendously. Meanwhile, low-level practices went on.'

During August squadrons in 2 Group were directed to carry out a period of intensive training in low-level flying, which caused much speculation among the aircrew, who wondered what was to be their target.

'On Friday 10 August' continues Charles Patterson, 'Nicol and I were taken into the operations room. I was to be deputy leader and we were to look at the target and see what this operation was to be. It had been rumoured that it was to be a factory outside Paris, which, without fighter escort, sounded terrifying enough. I'll never forget the sight that met my eyes. On a table in the centre of the ops room a huge map had been laid out and there, leading absolutely straight, was a red tape from Orford Ness, across the North Sea, right through Holland and right down to Cologne. At first I just did not believe that this was the target. I assumed it referred to something else. Then I realised it did not. The truth, the reality, dawned on me. I was going to have to take part in a low-level daylight attack on Cologne - with no fighter escort - in Blenheims. It was no use panicking so I listened to the briefing and the instructions I was given. The target was not Cologne itself, but the Knapsack power station, which the Group Captain said was the biggest in Europe. I was shown a photograph. It had eight chimneys on one side and four on the other (known in Germany as the 'twelve apostles'). We were to fly between these chimneys, then turn round and come back again. Of course I couldn't communicate what the target was to anybody else. I had to carry this secret about with me for two days. The chances of surviving an operation like this were negligible. How could I, a fundamental coward who'd managed to skate past it up to now, make myself do this operation? The next two days were spent wrestling with myself as to how I was to do it. The only thing to do was to stop worrying and to say to myself, 'You're not coming back. You've just got to go. You're caught in this situation.' The alternative was to funk it and not go at all. Of the two this seemed the more impossible, so I just resigned myself to the fact that I was not coming back. Curiously, this rid me of uncertainty and made it easier. Then came the early morning of 12 August when we were to go. I had a pretty poor night's sleep the night before. When I woke at 6.30 I suddenly remembered that this was the Sunday morning when I was just not going to come back. I was still saying, well, it's got to be.

'The operation was very comprehensively planned. Thirty-six aircraft were to attack Knapsack in six formations of six aircraft each. Everything was being done to mislead and divert the enemy fighter force, with diversionary bombing attacks in France and northern Germany.'

August 12th. Grouse shooting began in Scotland. Beaters were out on the moors. The Blenheim formation was to fly to Cologne. There they would split into two forces to make simultaneous attacks on the Quadrath and Knapsack power stations. It would be Bomber Command's largest force it had so far used against Germany in daytime. The object of the attack was to reduce Germany's output in the industrial district round Cologne by attacking the Knapsack and Quadrath power stations which lie in open and arid country between Cologne and Aachen. Both these stations were of a newly developed type which burned soft peaty brown coal or lignite; the use of lignite for electric power was a recent discovery, the result of intensive research. The power stations stood beside the open workings where the brown coal, which was just below the surface of the ground, was mined. The Goldenburg plant at Knapsack was the largest steam-power plant in Europe, with nearly twice the capacity of the Battersea power station and it supplied electricity for a huge grid and transformer system. The Fortuna plant at Quadrath was slightly smaller, but it was being enlarged even before the war; it served the Troisdorf explosives factory as well as many industries in Cologne and in the district of Bergheim. Another and perhaps equally important purpose of the attack was to rouse the Germans to the danger that their industries in the West might be raided in the daytime; it was thought likely that this would make them reinforce their defences in the West with fighters detached from the Russian front.

The 56 Blenheim crews who would have the central role in this historic low-level daylight operation entered their respective operations rooms on the morning of 12 August rooms and their eyes were drawn to the large map of Western Europe on the wall, with the proposed routes and targets displayed. Being human beings, with a desire to survive, their reactions must have varied considerably, though if they felt fear they would have made sure it was not evident to their colleagues. At Watton the briefing was attended by the 18 crews of Force 1 (12 on 21 Squadron and six on 82 Squadron), none of whom had probably heard of Quadrath, but they would certainly recognise on the map the city of Cologne nearby. (The huge Knapsack power station was the largest steam generator in Europe, producing 600,000W; the Quadrath station produced 200,000W and their destruction would significantly affect war production.) The aircrew listened intently to their station commander, Group Captain Laurie F. Sinclair. The aircraft were detailed to fly in three boxes of six aircraft (each split into two vics of three), led by Wing Commander John O. C. Kercher (lead box) with Bill Edrich (port box) and Squadron Leader H. J. 'Jack' Meakin of 82 Squadron (starboard box). At the same time 38 crews of Force 2 (comprising 18, 107, 114 and 139 Squadrons), led by Wing Commander James L. Nicol, CO of 114 Squadron were briefed for their attack on Knapsack.

Ernie Hope later recorded: 'We were keyed up when we went into the briefing room at 0645 and the Station Commander's opening remarks did nothing to lessen the tension. He started off by saying, 'You are going on the biggest and most ambitious operation ever undertaken by the RAF.' Then he told us what it was. Cologne - in daylight - 150-odd miles across Germany at tree-top height and then - the power house. Our orders were to destroy our objectives at all costs. We were given the course to follow, the rendezvous with other squadrons of bombers and the rendezvous with fighters. We were given the parting point for the fighters and the moment at which certain flights would peel off the formation for the attack on the second power house and then - in formation across Germany.'

'In the operations room all the crews in the Squadron realised what the target was' recalled Charles Patterson. 'Hardened though some of them were, there was the gasp of disbelief, even from the most hardened ones. Unlike me, they had not had the opportunity to prepare themselves. It was the only time that I saw some of my fellow aircrew, including my own gunner, who was a pretty imperturbable type, literally grey and shaking. Curiously enough, seeing all the others looking so alarmed rather bolstered me a bit.'

The Prime Minister would follow the operation with keen interest. Cologne was a way of helping the Russians. It must go through - at all costs. 'At all costs' became a theme song. Gunners scrambled round the Signals Officer; navigators wielded their dividers, protractors and parallel rules. Somebody said, 'What a trip!' And got the reply, 'Yes, but Christ, what a target!'

Each Force would be escorted as far as Doel, just inside the Belgian border, by six Whirlwind fighters of 263 Squadron and three squadrons of Spitfires would provide withdrawal support from Walsoorden onwards. The operation would also involve four Fortress Is of 90 Squadron, two of whom would make a high-level attack on Cologne, another De Kooy airfield and the other Emden, while a 5 Group 'Circus' involving six Hampdens on 106 Squadron and six on 44 Squadron and several squadrons of Spitfires and Hurricanes, would make attacks on Gosnay power station and St Omer-Longuenesse aerodrome respectively.[19]

Ernie Hope takes up the story: 'While pilots and observers were getting all they could from the weather man, we rear gunners gathered round the Signals Officer for identification signs, then hurried out to get ready. Someone said 'What a trip!' and got the answer, 'Yes, but what a target! Knapsack, we were told, was the biggest steam power plant in Europe, producing hundreds of thousands of kilowatts to supply a vital industrial area. If we got it, it would be as good as getting hold of a dozen large factories. One of the pilots on the raid was in civil life a mains engineer for the County of London Electricity Supply. He came away rubbing his hands and explained to us that, with turbines setting up about 3,000 revolutions a minute, blades were likely to fly off in all directions at astronomical speeds, smashing everything and everyone as they went.'

Bill Edrich recalls that it had been hoped, by synchronising the two attacks, to confuse the enemy. As one of the leaders of Force 1, he flew low over a fairly choppy sea to the mouth of the Scheldt, following a series of dog-legs on the way to the target, hoping that the enemy would not guess their intentions. 'Flattened low on the water, tucked in as close as I dared to the leader' he recalled, 'I felt an exhilaration that swamped all other emotions. Low flying did not bother me. I loved it: It gave me an illusion of speed and security. Two hundred knots may not be much by 'sound barrier' standards: but with the sea racing by 30 feet below it seems incredibly fast.' As they flew across Holland, pulling over trees and church spires, people everywhere waved them on. Crews looked down at fields planted out in the pattern of the Dutch flag. The bombers had soared over the flat countryside, pulling over the tall trees and church spires. They were given an ecstatic welcome by Dutch farm-workers looking upwards to see RAF roundels on the aircraft flying low over their fields for the first time. 'It was great to watch them waving joyously to us as we sped over' said Edrich, Harvesting was in progress, as the corn ripened in the glorious weather. The landscape and the activity were reminders of other happier times on the farmlands of his native Norfolk.

'We took off at about 0800' recalls Charles Patterson 'and I formed up closely on Wing Commander Nicol, setting off for Orford Ness. We rendezvoused on time and came down to low level over the North Sea.' Down to the water went the Blenheims. With a normal flying speed of 120 mph slower than the average German fighters, they had 300 miles of enemy territory to cross before they returned to water again. The sea was choppy and the wing of bombers flew in a spread stream of low vics, with the Whirlwinds weaving above in the sun. 'Although we thought we were going to certain death' continues Patterson, 'perhaps it was the scale, the element of the adventure, the actual flying, but somehow one was not as panicky as expected. I had always wondered what enemy territory looked like. In fact, everything looked so normal that in some way it was actually reassuring. We flew down the Schelde estuary, south of Woensdrecht airfield and into the heath land of Holland, all of it new to me. At any moment we expected enemy fighters. We went on, mile after mile, not a cloud in the sky and still no fighters. I asked my navigator, 'How long?'

'Not long now,' he said.'

As they turned into the estuary of the Scheldt the men in the bombers scanned their field of vision for German fighters. They saw only two Dutchmen in a fishing vessel gaping up at them. Soon the Whirlwind escort peeled off and the Blenheim rear-gunners watched their curious high tails disappear in the direction of England. The bombers were alone. The guns of the Blenheims were mostly silent while the bombers flew below the height of church spires and windmill-tops and the harvesters waved. No. 2 to the leader Wing Commander Nicol was 'A for Apple' piloted by Flight Lieutenant Charles St. J. Phelps, a pilot of thirty-five operations. In his own country before the war the farmers knew him as a stylish young point-to-point rider. Then, one raw November day in 1939, young Aircraftman (Second Class) Charles St. John Phelps was full of the joy of the spring to come as he swept into Canford depot in Middlesex. He had gloves, a trilby hat and a general air of expectancy. He was 'going for a pilot'. For twelve grinding months Phelps learned about things he'd never imagined and then - November 1940. Pilot Officer St. John Phelps was at the controls of brand-new Blenheim 'A for Apple', escorting convoys up the East Coast; moonlight trips over Denmark and Norway.

At a crossroad 'A-Apple's gunner spotted an obese German in SS uniform. He was enjoying himself in the sunshine, thumbs in belt, basking. The sergeant

Gunner had no compunction in getting him in his reflector sight, allowed something for deflection and, almost nothing for bullet trail and rolled him into the ditch with a whiff from his Brownings. As the formation neared the German frontier crews noticed that people were no longer waving, they just watched. In Germany itself people scuttled off to their shelters. It was the war's first major daylight invasion of the Fatherland. Still there were no fighters, and suspense in the Blenheims was high but three Blenheims were lost to flak.[20]

Seventeen Blenheims left the formation and headed for the subsidiary power plant at Quadrath. There were seven minutes left for the target. Bill Edrich remembers: 'We had practised our attack many times over a power station at St. Neots and now we prepared to put it into effect. With four 250lb, 11-second-delay bombs each, we had to clear the target in fairly quick time. My box of six was going in last. At St. Neots we had got everyone across the target in less than three seconds. Could we manage it now?

'There's the target - dead ahead,' called out Edrich's navigator, Vic Phipps.

'The tall chimneys of the power station stood out ominously, forcing us up to 400 feet and more. The three sections were stepped up slightly from front to rear. There was some light flak coming up from the target area, but otherwise we were unopposed - we had achieved complete surprise. Kercher and Meakin flew their formations in like regiments, directly in front of us and slightly below. All we had to do was to keep our position.

'We were well past the target when the first bombs went off. Rear-facing cameras in each Blenheim were recording our results. But we could see that the attack had been successful. The core of the power station was in flames when the first bombs went off.'

In his rear turret Ernie Hope the 21-year-old Blenheim gunner did not know that they were over the target until he saw the power-house chimneys above: four on one side, eight on the other. 'Then Vic Phipps called out 'Bombs gone!' and as I felt the doors swinging to, Bill Edrich yelled 'Machine gun!' I fired bursts in all directions as we turned away to starboard. Three miles off I had a good view of the place. We had used delayed-action bombs and banks of black smoke and scalding steam were gushing out. Debris was rocketing into the air and I thought of those turbine blades ricocheting around the building.' Ernie Hope reported many direct hits and photographs taken by rear-facing cameras later confirmed the finding.

All seventeen aircraft of Force 1 dropped their bombs within the target area. They all came off the target unscathed, then drove off some Bf 109 fighters that approached them before, purely by chance, the Blenheims crossed a Luftwaffe airfield near Antwerp. They machine gunned some Bf 109s on the ground and shot one down that was taking off. Still unopposed, they flew into a heavy thunderstorm near the Scheldt estuary, which broke up the formation and caused the loss of a Blenheim. On clearing the storm Edrich was joined by several other Blenheims and together they sped across the shallows and mudflats of the estuary towards their rendezvous with the Spitfires. It was then that they experienced their most serious opposition, partly from intensive fire from coastal batteries and even more seriously from huge flocks of ducks and geese rising from their nesting grounds. 'Birds seemed to be shooting past us in all directions and it was easily the most frightening part of the whole trip,' said Edrich.

Wing Commander James Nicol leading Force 2, the last flight to bomb the Knapsack power station was in a particularly good position to observe the success of the attack. 'Over Germany' he said, 'we flew below the level of the trees. My observer called me up when we were seven minutes from the target and at that moment another squadron of Blenheims crossed our path. They were on their way to the other power station. The air seemed alive with British bombers. We were nearly there when my rear gunner cried 'Tally-ho! Fighter to port.' I felt the aircraft jar twice and saw cannon shells hitting the port wing. I told my flight to take evasive action. Then the flak became intense. I could see it bursting among bombers in front of me and I looked on the ground to see where it came from. I saw flashes from a gun emplacement and went straight for it. We passed about three feet over the gun and I saw a soldier in a trench hit by a stream of bullets. The gun ceased fire. On the R/T Charles Patterson heard Nicol say, 'Turn to starboard.'

The pilot on 'Apple's right missed the turn and the remaining Blenheims had to pull over him. He throttled back and joined in at the rear. As he climbed the hill of Knapsack, Phelps saw in the distance the spires of Cologne Cathedral, and then he was occupied in escaping the high-tension cables of the Braunweiler Grid system. The fat yawning condensers were attractive, but the Pilots had been briefed not to waste their bombs in them. Instead they soared down the lane of twelve chimneys, ignoring two Messerschmitts circling above. Observers pulled back release levers and short delay bombs banged open the spring-loaded doors.

'As I turned slightly' continues Charles Patterson 'there, up on top of a long, long slope about 3 miles away was this enormous industrial complex. I realised that this was Knapsack. I thought, well, we've just got to go on now and there'll be a big bang. We had to climb a bit to avoid the increasing maze of electricity pylons and cables. Then the chimneys came into view, until they were coming right at us. Wing Commander Nicol swung in between the chimneys and I followed him. I became enveloped in mist and steam. I was in it now. There was nothing I could do except concentrate on flying the aeroplane properly. We had been told not to release our bombs on the attractive-looking water coolers but to keep them for the actual power house at the far end. We flew on down between these chimneys. As we did so I saw again a lot of blue flashes, which would be machine-gun fire, but I was past caring about that now. At the far end I could see the great turbine house and the steam and the smoke and everything. I pressed the tit and let the bombs go. As I did so, Nicol just ahead of me, swerved sharply to starboard and I did the same. I realised that he was about to fly into a chimney, which he just missed. Then, out the other side, a lot more blue flashes and sparks and tracer. We dived down to the ground. Nicol was there. He'd survived. I formed up on him. We raced away across the cables again down past the other side of the power station. We started to turn to starboard to fly on the course for the Dutch coast and then to my amazement all of the other five members of the formation emerged safely and formed up with us. We set off on the journey home.'

Nicol recalled: 'You couldn't miss the target. There were the twelve chimneys - a row of four and a parallel of eight-standing dark against the sky. The sun was to our port bow. There were smoke and flames coming from the plant, so we climbed to attack; the flames were fifty feet high and the smoke too thick to let us bomb accurately from any lower. Inside the buildings we could see the sullen red glow of explosions under the smoke. I flew straight between the chimneys. I was watching my observer's elbow as he pulled back the release lever and then I heard him call, 'Bombs gone.' I did a steep turn over a belt of trees down into a sandstone quarry to get away from the flak. I should think we went about thirty feet below the level of the ground. As we came up there was a great deal of crackling in the earphones and I couldn't quite catch something my rear gunner said. But then I heard him repeat it; it was 'Fighter again' and at the same moment a piece of my port wing fell away. I heard no more from my rear gunner and it must have been then that he was wounded. I tried more evasive action. A bullet came in behind my head and another smacked the armour-plating at my back. My observer said that he could see a stream of bullets coming between his legs. I turned to the right to give the fighter a more difficult angle of fire and this seemed to work; he sprayed the air below us. While we twisted about I hit the top of a telegraph post and chipped the airscrew. I could see that the yellow tips were uneven as they turned and the note of the airscrew's roar was a little different. But this didn't seem to affect our flying. There was a film of oil over my perspex; I didn't see a church spire and my observer told me of it just in time to let me miss it. I banked sharply and caught the tip of my wing in a tree. Once more we were lucky and we managed to catch up with the others.

'The worst of the attack was over then, but I have never known anything so welcome as the squadrons of British fighters which came out to meet us. They staved off the attacks of more Messerschmitts and then I had time to think of my rear gunner. I tried to call him up and then he passed me a note which he'd written on his knee pad. 'Please get there quickly. Bleeding badly,' he said. I gave the observer a bandage and he crept through to the gunner. We flew on back in an interval between two storms and I made straight for base. Our undercarriage had been damaged and would not go down; the observer had to hold the rear gunner while we made a belly landing.'

Nicol had flown lower than the rest. Phelps watched him out of the corner of his eye and involuntarily drew back. He saw that ahead of Nicol, at the end of the lane of high chimneys, there stood a hidden obstruction. The Wing Commander's Blenheim disappeared in the brown smoke of the plant and then miraculously banked over and missed the trap. Rear flights had received more attention from awakening fighters. The leader of the last vic saw cannon shell hitting the root of his port wing; he sawed up and down, took skidding turns and continued on. Ahead he saw light flak among the forward flights. Detecting the gun-flashes on the ground, the pilot flew at the emplacement. He passed three feet over the artillery while his gunner silenced its fire and felled a soldier. While the first bombs were exploding and rocking the plant, succeeding waves of Blenheims climbed to 800 feet to escape the blast. In turbines that had been setting up 3,000 revolutions a minute it is likely that broken blades were hurtling off at astronomical speeds, doing as much damage as the bombs themselves. Phelps looked back and saw debris appear to hang in the sky while weighty sections of building climbed leisurely up. The mission was successful; the worst 'would be to come. Meantime 'A for Apple' machine-gunned a goods train.

Charles Patterson had settled down in formation. 'Another chap formated on me. The whole formation got together. On to Holland we went. No interception yet. Then we flew into a rain storm and for a wonderful moment I thought we were going to get cloud cover, but it was only a shower and we emerged shortly afterwards into the brilliant sun again and no cloud above us. On and on past little villages and hamlets, occasionally an individual diving into a ditch beneath us. Just before we got to the Dutch border, we flew over a baronial German mansion. In the garden, beside a cedar tree, I just got a glimpse of a table with a large white table cloth, all laid out for lunch and a group of people standing around it. As we whizzed over the top my gunner let fly and it broke up the party. He felt that any rich Germans who were living like that while the war was on deserved it.

'On across Holland, now it suddenly seemed to me that we were going to make it. Nothing was going to happen after all, but it's always when that psychological moment comes that you're brought down to earth. Ahead of us, just as we were coming up to the Schelde estuary, black dots appeared. For a moment my navigator thought that they might be Spitfires that had come out to escort us home, but of course they were not. They were not Whirlwinds either, which had escorted us out and were due to escort us back. Nicol called out 'Snappers!' Before I knew where I was, I was flying on straight into these Messerschmitts, which were circling around about a thousand feet above us

'Nicol told us to close in tight. He led us right down on to the water, sparkling in the sun, not more than 10, 15, occasionally perhaps 20 feet below. I got as tight into him as I could, with my wing-tip practically inside his. I knew this was life or death. It took all the flying concentration and skill I possessed to do it, which drove out most of the fear of the fighters. The others closed in. Then Nicol handed over to the leading gunner, Pilot Officer Morton, a very experienced second tour man. He directed the formation because the gunners, looking back, could all see the fighters coming into attack. He had to decide when it was the right moment to open fire and when to take evasive action. Then I heard the rattle of machine-gun fire and realised that our guns were firing. Every now and then the water was ripped with white froth from the cannon shells of these 109s. On one turn, out of the corner of one eye, I caught a glimpse of a 109 right in front peeling off from the attack. It was so close that I could see the pilot in the cockpit, let alone the black crosses and the yellow nose of the 109. My reaction was simply one of interest in seeing a 109 so close. We all knew that the only safety was out to sea and out of range of these 109s. Would we make it? After each attack we just had to crouch down and prepare for the next. This carried on all the way up the Schelde. Yet we seemed to survive them. Then, unbelievably, the islands to each side of us suddenly ceased and we were in the open sea. We'd hardly gone any distance when the leading gunner told us over the R/T that the fighters had broken off the attack.

I suppose they were running out of ammunition. Still, we didn't feel it was all over yet.'

Back over slag-heaps, derricks, grimy industrial structures, heathy country and then through a Dutch rain-storm. Slowly the Blenheim air-crews gained the feeling that they would get back home. And then after some trees and a wide expanse of water Phelps saw what at first he thought was a cloud of birds but materialised into a cloud of Messerschmitts. He turned left and right, heard his own guns stuttering, watched cannon shells rip into the water between the bombers and then a few feet above his cockpit saw the black crosses of a Messerschmitt as it peeled off.

'The first reaction of realising that one had survived was a sort of numbness' concludes Charles Patterson. 'The leading Blenheim climbed gently to about 600 feet and I realised that we had survived. We'd made it. It was just marvellous, happy relief, sheer joy, flying back across the North Sea. Then the cliffs came up - England. We were back. There was a general opinion that we'd all hit the target and reports came in that we'd got away with it, but by the afternoon word got round that we had lost 12 of the 36 and that several others had been badly shot up and crash-landed. Two Blenheims, which had navigated the Whirlwind fighters out to escort us home, had also both been shot down. This was very tragic and a terrible waste.'

Force One had lost two Blenheims and Force Two, eight Blenheims. V5725 on 139 Squadron flown by Sergeant Harry Ingleby RCAF was shot down by flak over the target and crashed at Berrenrath; all three crew were killed. A few moments later Z7448, also on 139 Squadron and flown by Sergeant G. Coast, crashed at Hucheln; he had probably been hit by flak over the target. Coast and his observer, Pilot Officer K. J. Mackintosh, survived and were taken prisoner, while Sergeant Dennis A. Wilson, WOp/AG, was killed. Nearing the Dutch coast Pilot Officer Malcolm Thomas Kershaw Walkden's Blenheim on 18 Squadron hit high-tension cables, which sheared off the tail; the aircraft crashed in the mouth of the Scheldt with no survivors. Pilot Officer James 'Jim' Wilmot Corfield on 21 Squadron also hit high-tension cables in the Dutch coast area on the way back and crashed into the sea off Texel; he died together with Pilot Officer Arthur Lionel Alfred Williams and Pilot Officer Maurice Williams, WOp/AG.

The Blenheim flown by New Zealander Flight Lieutenant George A. Herbert on 139 Squadron was damaged by light flak over the target and at 1318 was finished off by Oberleutnant Adolf Galland of Stab./JG26, his 77th victory. It crashed into the mouth of the Scheldt, killing all three crew. Two minutes later Z7281 on 114 Squadron flown by Sergeant Douglas J. Wheatley was set upon by Oberleutnant Kurt Ruppert in a Bf 109 of III./JG26, who shot it down in flames. The Blenheim hit the sea off Flushing and there were no survivors. At 1328 Oberleutnant Baron Freiherr Hubertus von Holtey of Stab./JG26 in a Bf 109E shot down the Blenheim flown by Squadron Leader A. F. H. Mills RCAF who ditched in the sea south of Flushing. All three crew were taken prisoner.[21]

The twelve Blenheims that were lost represented 15.4% of the force. This would have been acceptable had the damage to the power stations reported by the aircrews been confirmed by later reconnaissance, but they were both soon back in commission again. 'It had been a thrilling trip to take part in and although we had achieved it large measure of success, it was a heavy price to pay,' commented Bill Edrich.

One bomber brought back five Dutch ducks. A pilot officer took the tip off an airs crew on a telegraph post. A draughty hole in a front window was stopped by the gallant observer firmly placing his bottom in it to keep out the draught. Not every self-sacrificing action gets a decoration. That day the Blenheim aircrews had a late lunch in the mess. 'Then, of course, the inevitable relaxation' adds Charles Patterson. 'We were all to go to Norwich, the whole group, for a party and a beat-up. We all met up and drank away. All great excitement, great fun. We felt very heroic and wonderful. We thought, 'This is it, we've done it.' We forgot there was any future. For the rest of my operational career I found that the way to make myself overcome my fear was to tell myself that I was not coming back and just accept the fact. That is the way I personally conquered fear. I don't think that all my fellow aircrew thought quite as I did. How we conquered our own individual fear was not a thing we ever talked about, however intimate or friendly we were.

Two days later Wing Commander Nicol and Wing Commander Kercher and the leaders of the sections were summoned to receive the personal congratulations of the Chief of the Air Staff, Sir Charles Portal. The leaders of the three formations of 18 were each awarded the DSO, Edrich, along with other leaders of the boxes of six aircraft, were awarded the DFC.[22]

'Nicol was awarded an immediate DSO for leading the Knapsack raid' says Charles Patterson. 'However, it had been taken for granted before we took off that if he got back he would get a VC; it caused a considerable disappointment. About a week later Wing Commander Nicol went out on his next trip and never came back.[23] At the end of his first tour Charles Phelps took a course on how to be an Instructor and reported to his new unit wearing a DFC. On its next raid 'A for Apple' was piloted by a new captain. The bomber did not return.

'In the summer of 1941' adds Charles Patterson 'the casualty rate on Blenheims in 2 Group was such that statistically you could not survive more than seven to ten ops, but you had to do 30. As already mentioned, anyone who did seven trips was promoted to Flight Lieutenant and on average anyone who'd done about 15 was a Squadron Leader. Due to the fact that I'd survived for so long, I suddenly found myself made a Squadron Leader, when only six or seven weeks before I'd been a Pilot Officer and I had a flight to command. The tremendous privilege of commanding these men when I was only 21 seemed to me the most wonderful, worthwhile job in the world. The rest of my tour consisted of one or two shipping beats and a number of 'Circuses'. To be taken off it, to be sent on a rest, on 10 October 1941, came as a terrible blow. It wasn't because I wanted to go on fighting. It was because I wanted to go on commanding the flight. After a course at Upavon, for the next ten months I was an instructor. Just before Christmas my spirits were suddenly lifted when I was told to my astonishment that a DFC had come through for me and a DFM for Alan Griffith. I've never been quite sure about whether I deserved the DFC except that I can always say anyone who got through a tour on Blenheims in 1941 could feel that he'd reasonably deserved it for surviving it.'[24]

Bryan Stevens, Bill Edrich's old Norfolk cricket friend, remembered the tremendous ovation received by the newly-honoured Edrich at Lord's a few weeks after the Cologne raid. Edrich was a member of a Lord's XI opposed to an Army team. Stevens was then serving in the Royal Corps of Signals and stationed in Whitehall prior to being posted to the Middle East. By careful negotiation with his colleagues he was able to arrange time off to coincide with cricket occasions in London, There was a big crowd, approaching 10,000 and we had a great day's cricket. Bill was soon in the picture, dismissing the first Army batsman with a good slip catch and then taking a couple of wickets. The crowd rose to Bill when he came out to bat He was cheered all the way out to the wicket'. The salutations were rudely halted by a certain Army sergeant running at full tilt to take a catch in front of the pavilion. Edrich had scored only four. 'Bill was brilliantly caught by Sergeant-Instructor Denis Compton.' Compton had already scored a century: his alertness deprived the spectators of another batting feast.

In later years Dennis Compton, in reference to Edrich's driving, would tell his friend, 'Just remember, Bill, you're not flying your aeroplane.' Edrich drove a succession of cars just as furiously as he flew his Blenheim. He affected his more nervous passengers in much the same manner as he scared the wits of a chimney sweep on one flying jaunt. The Edrich family by this time had moved to Lillingstone Dayrell in Buckinghamshire. One of Bill's customary actions, on his safe return from an operation, was to dip his wings in salute to his family. His elder brother, Eric, said: 'Bill would rush out and say: 'Bill's here.' There was a small valley leading up to our house. Bill would circle round and you could actually look down on him and watch the plane zoom up to the houses.

On one occasion, to Edrich's immense relief, a suicidal operation to Brest to attack the German warship *Prinz Eugen* was aborted soon after take-off. An elated Bill returned home from the airfield at Portreath in Cornwall. He signalled his arrival with an aerobatics extravaganza. To Amos Clark, the village chimney sweep, this presented an imminent threat of disintegrating chimneys; he was poised on a ladder, working on one of them, there was no warning, just an eerie rush of air as Bill's aircraft careered over the roof-tops. The terrified Amos vowed he would never go up a chimney again. 'Blast these young devils, always playing about,' he said.

On 18 August, 88 Squadron, which on 1 August had moved from Swanton Morley to Attlebridge, received 19 Blenheim Mk IVs from 105 Squadron for anti-shipping operations off the Dutch coast. Results were poor, however and were little better on 21 August when cloud obscured the chemical works at Chocques; crews dropped their bombs on factories and railway junctions near St. Omer instead. Shipping was again the target on 26 August when 21, 82 and 88 Squadrons all suffered loss. Worst hit was 82 Squadron, which lost four Blenheims to Bf 109s of 2. and 3./JG52. Nine crews on 88 Squadron took part. Squadron Leader Alan Lynn, the CO and Flight Lieutenant Alexander caught a 4,000-ton motor vessel travelling in convoy, which they attacked, scoring direct hits. The vessel was aflame and dead in the water as the Blenheims sped away. Pilot Officer George Ballantyne Dunn's Blenheim was hit by flak and exploded as it hit the water; Dunn, his observer, Pilot Officer John Reginald Arthur Jones and Flight Sergeant Basil Douglas Davies were killed. When 27-year old Welshman, Pilot Officer Tudor G. Edwards' Blenheim was attacked by two Bf 110s, 25-year old Flight Sergeant Frank Tweedale of Allerton, Liverpool, kept the Luftwaffe at bay while his pilot jettisoned the bomb load and the crew made it back safely.

On 27 August Edrich, who was then in charge of 21 Squadron as Wing Commander Kercher the CO went on leave, was informed that he was to supply six aircraft for a low-level strike on the docks at Rotterdam on 28 August. Reconnaissance had shown that the Germans were once again assembling many ships in Rotterdam to carry war materials and food along the coasts of the occupied countries. The order further specified that Edrich was not to fly. Twenty-one year old Flight Lieutenant Richard Ashton 'Dick' Shuttleworth, whose promotion to acting Squadron Leader would come through on the day of the raid, was to lead. He had married his fiancée Honor only two weeks' earlier. 'I didn't think Dick had had anything like enough experience to lead the squadron on so dangerous a raid' recalled Edrich. 'I was worried too about the raid's whole conception. The tactics to be employed were far too much a repetition of Tom Webster's successful raid of six weeks earlier. This time the Germans would surely be ready for us:' Edrich was so concerned that he requested to be allowed to lead the operation instead of Shuttleworth, a request that was turned down. 'There was nothing for it but to throw everything into making the raid a success. But when the six Blenheims took off from Watton the following afternoon I was deeply anxious about the outcome.'

The first attempt, just after 1440, was recalled at 1530. At around 1720 18 crews on 21, 88, 110 and 226 Squadrons were successful, though 'F-Freddie' on 226 Squadron crashed on take-off at Wattisham. Spitfire IIa's on 19 Squadron at Coltishall and 152 at Swanton Morley which provided fighter escort were picked up and the formation flew to a point four miles south of Oostvoorm, where they would turn to their second point five miles south of Waalhaven where the three boxes of aircraft would come into line abreast and speed in at roof-top height. The formation made landfall at the Dutch coast, but as soon as they reached the mouth of the Nieuwe Waterweg, the canal that links Rotterdam to the sea, destroyers and anti-aircraft batteries threw up a terrific barrage of flak. As soon as they were clear of the flak they came under attack from enemy fighters. One Messerschmitt 109F pierced the screen of Spitfires to engage a Blenheim, but was immediately chased away. The Blenheims flew on, hugging the ground all the way to the docks. Their arrival was greeted with a hail of light machine gun and flak fire as they swept across Rotterdam at roof-top height in line abreast. The Spitfires, meanwhile, had climbed to 1,500 feet to provide top cover while the Blenheims went in over the docks at between twenty and fifty feet and hurled their bombs into shipping and construction yards. They were met by a hail of light anti-aircraft shells and machine-gun bullets - there was even rifle-fire from the ground.

Two of the Blenheims made for a large ship in the south-west end of Maashaven. Nineteen-year-old Flight Lieutenant Mayer Henry Richard 'Dickie' Namias of Knightsbridge, London on 88 Squadron spectacularly sank a 10,000-tonner when one of his bombs bounced from the dockside and hit under the stern of the ship, which exploded and sank. Squadron Leader Alan Lynn caught a 5,000-ton vessel, while Flight Lieutenant Stewart bombed a 4,000-ton ship, which he missed. Stewart then turned to the shipyards, but was attacked by a trio of Bf 109s of 6./JG53. His gunner, Flight Sergeant Mills, was wounded and the aircraft was badly damaged. 21 Squadron hit two large ships and dock buildings. One Blenheim, with an engine knocked out by gun-fire, fell behind its formation. The pilot of another Blenheim saw this and kept company with the damaged bomber; two Spitfires then joined up to make all safe. But the attack was not made without losses. In all, seven Blenheims failed to return. Sergeant Kenneth Hayes and Pilot Officer W. L. MacDonald were shot down by Leutnant Hans Müller of 6./JG53 in a Bf 109F. None of Hayes' crew survived but MacDonald and his WOp/AG survived and they were taken prisoner. Two Blenheims on 226 Squadron joined three on 110 Squadron and made a run on shipping at just 20 feet. Pilot Officer F. M. V. Johnstone on 226 Squadron flew so low that he crashed headlong into a warehouse on the north-west corner of Maashaven and exploded into a ball of fire. Incredibly, Johnstone and his two crew survived and were taken prisoner. The demise of this Blenheim had been seen by other crews and was confirmed four days later by photographic reconnaissance. The western side of a long warehouse building was seen to be severely damaged by fire; the warehouse was exactly where the Blenheim had been seen to crash. An 88 Squadron Blenheim crewed by Pilot Officer Tudor Edwards, Pilot Officer Fred A. Letchford and Flight Sergeant Frank Tweedale, who had returned after the brush with Bf 110s two days earlier, were shot down and killed, as were 23-year old Canadian Flight Lieutenant James O. Alexander and crew. One of two flak victims was the Blenheim flown by Dick Shuttleworth, which crashed in Scheurpolder. After the attack the Blenheims joined up with their escorts, now reinforced with a dozen Spitfires of 266 Squadron.

Dick Shuttleworth died later in the Wilhelmina Hospital in Amsterdam. Edrich's premonition had been confirmed. 'Only two Blenheims got back and one of them was very badly shot up, with the rear-gunner wounded. Among the four pilots shot down was Dick Shuttleworth. Also among the missing was Canadian Frankie Orme. I had laid on nine late suppers in the Officer's Mess, but only one Officer got back. His supper remained uneaten. Late that evening I was having a brandy in the Mess and trying to pull myself together when the squadron Adjutant reminded me that Dick Shuttleworth's wife was staying at the Crown Hotel in Watton. Would I go and break the news to her? I said I would if he would come with me, anyway as far as the hotel foyer. There followed one of the saddest nights of my life. Honor was very brave. She had already sensed that something was wrong and was packing her bags when I entered the room. She asked me if I would drive her to Dick's parents, who lived at Wroxham, just the other side of Norwich and this I did. At about two o'clock that morning I found myself ringing the door-bell of the house. As soon as Dick's father saw me he knew what had happened. Mrs Shuttleworth senior took charge of Dick's wife and I watched while Mr. Shuttleworth poured two large whiskies. 'You probably need this' he said, 'as much as I do.'

'It was a bleak and lonely drive back to Watton. Next day I discovered why they hadn't let me go on the raid. I had been posted to 2 Group Headquarters. My tour of operations was over. After that last tragic raid I think it was just as well for me that I was given a rest at that time. Apart from one week's leave I had been flying on operations virtually the entire summer and I was one of the few to survive.'

Edrich had earned his rest. Apart from one week's leave, he had been flying for virtually the entire summer and he was one of the few airmen to survive. 'In the 'here today, gone tomorrow' atmosphere of squadron life in wartime, parties were a necessary antidote to the neuroses of anxiety and depression. These parties were largely stag. Women certainly came into our lives, but few lasting attachments were made. The real buttress to morale came from mess life and the feeling that if the other fellow could take it so could you. When there were losses we closed our ranks.

'Another source of strength was regimental pride. We were 107 Squadron, the daylight boys; yet our fiercest rivalries were not with the heavy bomber crews or the fighter squadrons, but with the other Blenheim squadrons who were doing the same job as ourselves. Each squadron wanted to be top squadron and during Guest Nights the rivalry came very near the physical. Every month one Station in the Group would hold a Guest Night to which the other Stations would be invited and the horseplay sometimes got out of hand. I remember finishing up one night at the bottom of a High Cockalorum scrum - a massed pick-a-battle between squadron and squadron - and the neck injury I received was still giving me trouble nine years later.'[25]

In a minute to the Chief of Air Staff on 29 August, Churchill, obviously perturbed by the losses sustained in the operation, wrote: 'The loss of seven Blenheims out of 17 in the daylight attack on merchant shipping and docks at Rotterdam is most severe...While I greatly admire the bravery of the pilots, I do not want them pressed too hard. Easier targets giving a high damage return compared to casualties may be more often selected.' The following day he drafted a message to the crews: 'The devotion and gallantry of the attacks on Rotterdam and other objectives are beyond all praise. The Charge of the Light Brigade is eclipsed in brightness by these almost daily deeds of fame.' The comparison with the unfortunate Charge of the Light Brigade may well have been appropriate, but was hardly encouraging to those taking part. During August the loss rate was as high as 30%. Of 77 Blenheims that attacked shipping, 23 were lost, while of 480 sorties flown, 36 failed to return. Coupled with their losses in Malta, it was a very demanding and fateful period for 2 Group.

The anti-shipping role and shipping 'beat' patrols of 2 Group Blenheims were coming to an end by September, but not before they inflicted a terrible penalty on the crews taking part.[26] On 17 September ten Blenheims on 139 Squadron flew a 'Circus', their target being the Grand Quevilly power station near Rouen, on which they claimed three direct hits. They too came under attack from enemy fighters, one of the Blenheims being damaged while the Spitfire escort claimed to have shot down four of the 109s for the loss of four of their own. On 82 Squadron meanwhile, Pilot Officer Courteney John Harper (an Argentine) and crew failed to return from an attack on Mazingarbe power station and chemical complex. Three days later, on 20 September, in an attempt to confuse the enemy defences, 'Circuses' were directed at three different targets. Three Blenheims on 18 Squadron went to the marshalling yards at Hazebrouck, nine on 82 and 114 Squadrons to the shipyards at Rouen, while Hampdens bombed Mazingarbe. On the same day, at a much lower level, 'shipping beats' were flown off the Dutch coast by 22 Blenheims on 18, 139 and 226 Squadrons, Spitfires on 66 and 152 Squadrons flying escort. Twelve Blenheims flew straight into an enemy convoy of fourteen ships and attacked it. The crews on 18 Squadron found a motor ship and a tanker, which they seriously damaged for the loss of Sergeant John M. Nickleson RCAF and his crew who were shot down in flames.

Meanwhile, off the Hook of Holland the crews on 226 Squadron found a convoy of 14 ships flying protective balloons, which they attacked, setting fire to four of them and breaking the back of another. Twenty-year old Sergeant James Cecil Valentine Colmer's Blenheim was destroyed in one of the bomb bursts. Following his attack, the aircraft flown by Flight Lieutenant 'Dickie' Namias was hit in the starboard engine by fire from a flak ship; yet despite this he dropped his bombs before ditching in the sea. All the crew died. Another Blenheim, piloted by Flight Lieutenant 'Digger' Wheeler, an incredibly tough New Zealander who had been a sheep rancher in the Argentine, was also hit in one engine and although he twice bounced off the sea, he somehow managed to bring his aircraft and his crew home safely. The search for a target by the crews on 139 Squadron had been fruitless.

On the 21st 'Circuses' were flown by six Blenheims on 18 Squadron, whose target was the power station at Bethune and six on 139 Squadron, who unloaded their bombs on the power station at Gosnay. On the 27th the last 'Circuses' of the month were flown by 110, 226 and 114 Squadrons when the new FW 190 was encountered for the first time. In October the last shipping 'beats' were flown by Blenheims in the UK, the Air Staff at last having concluded that the aircraft was just not suitable for this role. (Anti-shipping operations were taken over by Hurricane fighter bombers on 402, 605 and 607 Squadrons.)

During October the most successful 'Circus' flown took place on the 12th. It was directed at the docks at Boulogne and involved 24 aircraft on 21, 110 and 226 Squadrons. Elsewhere on the same day three or four ships in a convoy off Den Haag were hit and 82 Squadron found a convoy of seven merchantmen protected by three flak ships eight miles off the Dutch coast between Ijmuiden and Scheveningen. Led by Squadron Leader Jack Meakin, the aircraft swept into the attack, scoring a direct hit on a 5,000-ton tanker and leaving a freighter on fire. The flak was, as always, fierce; one severely damaged Blenheim ditched in the sea close to the convoy, another plunged into the sea with the loss of all on board, while a third, more fortunate, having lost an airscrew, somehow managed to stagger back to base.

Next day, 13 October, the Blenheims were out on another 'Circus', this time once more to the Mazingarbe ammonia production works. On 15 October Wing Commander Vernon Stanley Butler DFC led a formation of 226 Squadron Blenheims to Le Havre harbour. In a clear blue sky the CO began his bombing run 8 miles from the docks, making the aircraft an ideal target for the anti-aircraft gunners, who not unnaturally responded not only with enthusiasm but also accuracy, literally shooting two of the bombers out of the sky. The escorting fighters, meanwhile, found themselves doing battle with Bf 109s. Butler led the remains of his formation down to low level and they made good their escape, though the aircrew undoubtedly could not forgive their leader for taking them on a ridiculously long bombing run.[27] Altogether 160 Blenheims and 480 airmen in 2 Group were lost between 24 March and 31 October 1941. This figure does not include aircraft that crashed on their return to the UK or the crippling losses by the squadrons detached to operate from Malta.

On 17 December AVM A. Lees replaced AVM Stevenson at Group HQ; Stevenson was posted overseas and later commanded the RAF in Burma. On his departure, he said: 'Since February 17th I have watched with admiration the courage, determination and war efficiency displayed by squadron commanders, flight commanders, leaders and crews. These fulfilled the highest traditions of the service and were maintained throughout the vigorous day offensive against the enemy. Many hundreds of thousands of tons of Axis shipping, both here and in the Mediterranean, have been sunk and damaged, while such daylight raids as Bremen, Cologne and Rotterdam already have their place in the history of the air war...'

The Blenheim's unsuitability for daylight operations was self-evident by the end of 1941 and on 27 December they took part in one last big daylight raid before being switched to night intruding. Operation 'Archery', the first combined Army-Navy-Air Force operations raid of the war was mounted against the German iron-ore convoy assembly base at Vaagsö on the Norwegian coast between Bergen and Trondheim. Five hundred and twenty-five Army Commandos were landed on the island by Royal Navy assault craft and successfully overpowered the German garrison in a sharp engagement, suffering only light casualties. In support of this raid, 404 Squadron RCAF dispatched two fighter Blenheims from Sumburgh on the Shetland Islands to cover the landing, while Bomber Command contributed nineteen Blenheim and ten Hampden sorties.

As a diversionary tactic, six Blenheim crews on 110 Squadron at Lossiemouth carried out a shipping sweep off the coast near Stavanger with the aim of drawing off German fighters from the Commando raid. Five of the Blenheims found a convoy off Egero and four attacked but two Blenheims fell victim to flak and the other two were destroyed by Bf 109s of I/JG77 from an airstrip at Herdla just north of Bergen. Seven Hampdens on 50 Squadron were sent to lay a smoke-screen at Vaagsö but two were shot down, most likely by shore defences. The three other Hampdens bombed a German gun position covering the approaches to Vaagsö.

Thirteen crews on 114 Squadron led by 24 year old Wing Commander John

Fraser Grant Jenkins DFC meanwhile, had taken off from Lossiemouth to attack the airstrip, built on a rock headland north-south, in an effort to prevent German fighters intervening in the Commando landing. Jenkins' navigator was 31-year old Flying Officer Paul Brancker, who on the day that war was declared had sat alone in his Manchester flat listening to Chamberlain's speech on the wireless. Despite being written off by the RAF Medical Board as being 'totally unfit for all types of Service flying' he had been accepted and on a cold, grey evening on 8 November 1940 - good for duck-shooting but little else - was releasing bombs on the German U-boat base at Lorient. As he peered at the distant searchlights of France he had thought, 'Here goes. I'm in the war.' Since that November day he flew about forty times against the enemy. He once got hit in the ankle over Ostend. Coming back he gingerly felt his foot and his hand touched a fragment of shell sticking two inches out through the leather of his flying boot. That was a night operation. It was more dangerous but he preferred daylight. 'I'm so big and in my night flying clothes I can't move or breathe so well.' Ever since his asthma days he was conscious of the importance of breathing well. On one squally February night, when many pilots had to turn back from an attack on Wilhelmshaven, Brancker navigated his pilot on and successfully bombed through an intense barrage. There were some daylight operations too taken into account when he earned his DFC. Nothing spectacular but showing his quality.

'Jenks' Jenkins and Brancker knew about the 'show' before Christmas. Brancker had spent long hours poring over charts, familiarizing himself with every surface of that tangle of fjords and hills. Christmas Day 114 Squadron spent in the North, seeking by practice to find from which height they could best drop bombs on runways without their bouncing off. A bounce might have meant the loss of the Blenheims, failure of an operation, more lives lost at Vaagsö. They played on Christmas Day with heights and speed, finally deciding to bomb flying as slowly as the Blenheims could without stalling. They knew that this meant increased dangers from flak. On a Saturday morning word came through that Vaagsö was 'on'. The Squadron took off from Lossiemouth and flew through heavy snow showers low over the North Sea for 360 miles. Sixty miles away Paul Brancker saw the snowy-capped Norwegian hills and wondered how against that background he could pick out one rock on the map from another. 'Jenks' and Brancker were excellent in the circumstances, flying at 15 to 20 feet above the sea for three hours. Near the coast an old man in a rowing-boat rested his oars, looked up and waved. And they noticed on a tiny island a small boy swiftly climb a fence and run on. German noises crackled over the radio telephone. Herdla knew they were coming.

Jenkins led the formation inland further south than the target and flew low level still over land, turning and coming down a fjord to attack the target at just after midday on the way out to the North Sea. Brancker did well to find such a small target which consisted of a single runway with two rows of railway sleepers side by side, suitable only for fighter aircraft. The Blenheims flew over the perimeter at hangar height spread out in vics of three in order to bomb the whole length of the runway, which had to be carried out from 250 feet for accuracy on such a small target but also in order that the 11-second delay bombs would dig into the sleepers - any lower and the bombs might have skidded off into the sea before exploding. Three 109s were in the circuit at about 1,000 feet, probably waiting to land and refuel and one was starting to move down the airstrip, presumably to intercept the Blenheims, his slipstream stirring a visible white wake in the snow. The Blenheims bombed and watched the spurts of snow as the bombs dug into the snow-covered sleepers. As the bombs sent up towers of snow the 109 taxiing-off flew into the bomb burst and crater. Flight Sergeant Charles Henry Gray DFM, Jenkins' rear gunner called out 'He's gone bang into our bomb hole! 'He said it' Paul Brancker repeated 'as though we owned the thing.' A moment later nothing could be seen of the Messerschmitt but a forlorn tail jutting like an angry tumour from the snow. Hits were scored on the operations room and hangars, a workshop truck was riddled with bullets and several ground crew were killed and injured. Crumbly snow again rose high, now stained and capped by black smoke. Light flak opened up and all the Blenheim air gunners took great delight in machine-gunning large numbers of personnel running for shelter. One Blenheim which might have been hit by flak slid into the aircraft alongside and they dived vertically into the sea with no hope of survivors. Having achieved their objective, the Commandos were subsequently taken off the island by the Royal Navy. The raid was regarded as a great success, but once more the Blenheim bomber crews had paid a heavy price.

Paul Brancker's long hours of night study - without the solace of a pipe or a cigarette because he happened not to smoke - were immeasurably justified. His added knowledge was written down in note form into the bound volume on the mantelpiece of his bedroom with three other volumes - Motley's *Dutch Republic*, Aldous Huxley's *Ends & Means* and a book of essays by Joad. The bound volume was in the navigator's own handwriting - his passport to navigation. This fat book contained the gist of more than a year's hard labour. On the right of the fireplace was a huge picture of a girl, half nude, put there by his batman. He changed it once a month and never said a word about why he did. Probably he did it for someone in the last war. The pictures just appeared. Neither 'Jenks' nor Brancker had the heart to stop him. Their batman's fingers had never run through the pages of the navigator's volume. If they had he would possibly have revised his mental sketch of Brancker's character. The very variety of the lecture notes contained appals the lay mind - from terminal velocities to polyconic projections and from azimuth to isobars.

In recognition of his leadership on the Herdla raid, Jenkins received the DSO. For his superb navigation Paul Brancker received the DFC. For when the war was over, the man once described as 'the man with the largest nose and about the most loveable personality in the daylight Bomber Group' had a curious ambition. Despite his great accumulation of flying knowledge gained since the days when he first took a five-bob joy ride, Brancker's object was not to go flying. Nor was it to return to the academic and impersonal insurance business, which because of its actuarial concern with calculations he found not unlike the paper side of navigation. He felt that in the Air Force he had learned how to meet and enjoy people. After the war he intended to run a hotel. All his plans were laid but like so many others, he never lived to see them through. Paul Brancker failed to return from a night intruder raid on Soesterberg airfield in Blenheim 'N-Nuts' piloted by 'Jenks' Jenkins on 27 March 1942. At first it was believed that he and 'Jenks' and Flight Sergeant Gray were prisoners. Rumours went around. 'It was impossible to think of him as dead.' Then the truth came in a signal from the Red Cross, via the Air Ministry.

Paul Brancker's hotel would probably have been a good hotel and rather friendly. Perhaps the Daylight Bomber men, greying now and mellowed, would have stayed there sometimes and talked about old days in the Squadron, about Paddy and Mike and the rickety bus over from the flights and the parties in the long white room and Rotterdam, Ijmuiden and Herdla.

Endnotes for Chapter Five

10   Flight Lieutenant Tallis DFC was lost on 29 April when 82 Squadron dispatched 15 aircraft in a sweep off Norway. Pilot Officer David White also failed to return.

11   Wing Commander Joseph Roy George Ralston, DSO* AFC DFM was born in Manchester on 12 January 1915, Ralston enlisted in the RAF as a Halton Aircraft Apprentice on 9 September 1930 and was trained as a metal rigger, graduating three years later and being posted as an AC1 (Aircraftman 1st Class) to Hornchurch, to service 54 Squadron's Bristol Bulldog fighters. Four years later he was accepted for pilot training at Hamble and later, Brize Norton. He gained his wings as a Sergeant pilot on 15 December 1937. In May 1938 he joined 108 Squadron at Bassingbourn, flying Hawker Hinds and, later, Bristol Blenheims, but on 8 April 1940 his squadron and 104 Squadron were used to form 13 OTU at Bicester and he became an instructor on Blenheims. Just four months later, however, came his opportunity to join the sharp end of operations when, on 18 August 1940, he was posted to 107 Squadron at Wattisham, a Blenheim IV bomber unit in 2 Group. Only five days later Roy Ralston flew his first operational sortie. His crew were Sergeant John 'Jackie' Brown DFM (WOp/AG) and Sergeant Syd Clayton, born in Lancashire in March 1916 and they were destined to fly 42 sorties together before Brown was killed during a low-level attack on a German convoy off the Norwegian coast on 18 April 1941. Thereafter Ralston and his navigator, Clayton during three years, completed 78 sorties together. Promoted to Flight Sergeant, then Warrant Officer, Ralston remained on 107 Squadron when it moved to Great Massingham on 12 May 1941. In December 1941 he was commissioned as a Pilot Officer and posted to instructional duties at 17 OTU, Upwood. His rest from operations lasted only until 22 May 1942, when he joined 105 Squadron at Horsham St. Faith equipped with Mosquito bombers. Ralston was rejoined by Syd Clayton. On 1 April 1943 they flew their last sortie together. It was Syd Clayton's 100th operation as a navigator and Ralston's 83rd sortie. Clayton received an immediate award of a DSO to add to his DFC and DFM and then left to begin pilot training. He made his first solo flight as pilot of a Mosquito in LR535 on 31 May 1944 and was posted to 464 Squadron RAAF in 140 Wing, 2nd Tactical Air Force at Thorney Island. He flew the first of 46 operational trips on the night of 26 August 1944; an attack on rail and road transport, using flares to illuminate targets. Clayton returned to Lancashire after the war and initially opened a hotel in Morecambe for eight years, before taking over some newsagent shops. In 1971 he became a Civil Servant after selling his newsagent's business, but died at his home in November 1976 in tragic circumstances. Roy Ralston meanwhile, received a Bar to his DSO. Ralston was appointed OC 1655 Mosquito Training Unit (MTU) at Marham. In August 1944 he joined the staff of 8 Group HQ at Castle Hill House, Huntingdon as Group Training Inspector for the PFF. On 1 March 1945 he was given command of 139 Squadron operating Mosquitoes at Upwood. Ralston flew eight trips to take his operational tally 91 before the end of the war in May 1945. At the end of the war Ralston was listed for a permanent commission but a medical examination revealed that he had TB and he was invalided out of the RAF in 1946. Wing Commander Ralston DSO* DFC DFM AFC died on 8 October 1996.

12 Rushbrooke and his two crew were killed.

13 Quoted in *Blenheim Strike* by Theo Boiten (ARP 1995).

14 Identified by Theo Boiten as Oberleutnant Karl-Heinz Leesmann, CO of 1./JG 52, who was the last of his unit to return to base at Bergen/Alkmaar after the prolonged fight with the Blenheims. Leesmann claimed two Blenheims shot down of Edrich's formation - confirmed by the German High Command as his 21st and 22nd victories! But all British aircraft returned to base. Leesmann was awarded the Knight's Cross after this battle. See *Blenheim Strike* by Theo Boiten (ARP 1995).

15 Quoted in *Blenheim Strike* by Theo Boiten (ARP 1995).

16 Squadron Leader Frederick Richard Howard Charney DFC was KIA on 12 September 1941 on 105 Squadron.

17 Dupree, Routley and Magee were buried on 7 July in the Hollefriedhot cemetery, but in 1945 were exhumed for reburial at Becklingen War Cemetery, Soltau, where all the other crews were buried after the raid.

18 On 28 July Pilot Officer Alastair Stewart Ramsey was awarded the DFC, Sergeant Quinn was awarded a bar to his DFM and Sergeants Jackson, J. A. Purves and W. N. Williams were each awarded the DFM for their part in the raid. Ramsey was KIA on 1 August 1941.

19 Hampdens and Fortresses were to confuse the defenders by making diversionary attacks, not only elsewhere in Germany but also in France and Holland. The plan worked well and German fighters, because of conflicting messages between observation posts and headquarters, were sent scurrying between Emden and Cologne, between Gosnay in France and De Kooy in Holland. The Hampdens, which went deep into the Pas de Calais with a strong escort of fighters, drew off over 150 Messerschmitts stationed in this area. At the same time the Blenheims were on their way to Germany. They were guided as far as the mouth of the Scheldt by squadrons of Whirlwind fighters. Without their escort the Blenheims flew very low over Holland, waved on by many people in fields and streets.

20 T2437 of 82 Squadron, piloted by 18-year-old Pilot Officer Graham C. Rolland was hit by flak and crashed at Strijensas, near the Moerdijk bridge at 1210. He and his two crew, Pilot Officers Hugh M. Clark and Sergeant Ernest Bainbridge were killed. V6423 on 18 Squadron, which was being flown by Pilot Officer G. H. Hill, crashed at Diest, Belgium. All three crew survived and were taken prisoner. V7451 on 21 Squadron, piloted by Pilot Officer Jim Langston, was hit by a burst of flak, which knocked rear-gunner Sergeant Ken Attew out of his turret before the aircraft crashed at Potz, near the target. Langstone and Sergeant Dave Roberts, observer, survived and were taken prisoner.

21 Among the withdrawal forces, Spitfire P8446 on 152 Squadron was shot down at 1312 by the Luftwaffe Flakabteilung 43/XI near Biervliet and pilot George White was killed. Two minutes later the same battery shot down P6793 on 19 Squadron; the pilot belly-landed near Breskens and was taken to hospital. Two Blenheims on 226 Squadron, navigating as fighter leaders, were lost. At 1253 V5859, piloted by Flight Lieutenant Gwilym I. Lewis was hit by flak and crashed near Philippine in Zeeuws-Vlaanderen, Belgium. Lewis, Flight Sergeant Neville Cardell, observer and Flight Sergeant Jack Woods, WOp/AG, were killed. At Katwijk at 1245 the Flakalarm was sounded, pilots of I./JG 1 climbed into their Bf 109s and took off in the direction of Zeeuws-Vlaanderen, while at the same time Bf 109Es of JG 26 took off from Wevelgem and Woensdrecht. As the returning aircraft approached, the flak guns opened up, only breaking off their barrage when Unteroffizier Zick of I./JG 1 dived his Bf 109E on to the tail of Z7352 piloted by Flight Lieutenant Hugh S. Young and dispatched it with a burst of gunfire. The Blenheim crashed at 1300 hours in the mouth of the Scheldt with no survivors.

22 Extracts from the recommendations for his award read: 'This officer had the difficult task of bringing his formation in to attack the main power station immediately after the leading box had attacked. This needed fine judgement as it was imperative that the target should be bombed from as low an altitude as possible. He had to delay his attack in order to avoid his formation being destroyed by explosions from the delay action bombs of the previous boxes, This required coolness and courage ... Squadron Leader Edrich led his formation in at exactly the right height and time, all aircraft dropping the bombs in the centre of the target area. By carrying out his orders with the greatest exactitude and determination, he must be given credit for a large part of the success of the attack.

23   On 19 August Wing Commander Nicol DSO, Flight Sergeant Edward T. W. Jones, observer and Flying Officer Herbert J. Madden DFC were all killed when their Blenheim was shot down by a Bf 110 of 5./ZG76 near Vlieland.

24   Charles Patterson went on to complete two tours of daylight operations on Mosquitoes. He was awarded the DSO early in 1944.

25   In 1943 Edrich was one of eight RAF officers sent on a course, lasting sixteen weeks, to the Army Staff College at Camberley, having been pronounced unfit for flying duties. He was subsequently employed on RAF Group operations at Wallingford in Berkshire. His round-the-clock duties were to help in the preparations for D-Day and the invasion of Europe.

26   On 6 September 88 Squadron moved on detachment to Manston in Kent to take part in 'Channel Stop' operations. (Further detachments, to Long Kesh in January-February 1942, Abbotsinch in May and Ford in July 1942, were made before the whole Squadron moved from Attlebridge to Oulton, Norfolk in September 1942.)

27   Wing Commander Butler was KIA on 8 March 1942.

Chapter 6

The Blockade Of Brest

That night we were just making an ordinary night attack on Brest harbour. We'd been there before, and we knew roughly what to expect. There was a bright moon when we got near the place, and the flak - the anti-aircraft fire - was coming up in much the usual sort of way. There were curtains of fire here and there, cones of fire over the more important spots and searchlights wandering all over the place.

It was pretty cold, but you expect it to be cold at the height at which we were flying. Then suddenly the port engine stopped. My observer, who was in the nose of the aircraft, switched on the inter-communication telephone and asked:

'What's happened?'

'Port engine stopped,' I told him. Then, just as I said it, most of the noise died out of the aeroplane and I said: 'Gosh, starboard engine stopped, too.'

'Well, here we go,' said the observer.

And that was all you could say about it. Both engines had iced up and stopped and we were gliding, without any power, slowly downwards.

I was not particularly worried at first. Engines do sometimes ice up and stop, and when you come down into warmer air, with any luck they pick up again. My only worry was to travel as slowly as possible, so that the glide would last as long as possible. The observer and I had a chat about it and decided that, as we were already over Brest, we might as well have a smack at the target, even without any engines. The flak had died away for the moment, so we started out first run in. By then we had lost about a thousand feet in height.

We made a run across the target area, but we couldn't see the exact target we wanted, so we came round again and started another run, a few hundred feet lower. And we kept on doing that, a bit lower each time, for what seemed about ten years - although really our whole glide lasted for less than a quarter of an hour.

By this time, of course, the German gunners knew we were there, and now and then they seemed to have a pretty good idea exactly where we were. There was one particularly nasty burst of flak all round us when we were about half-way down, and it shook the aircraft a bit, but we weren't hit. Every now and then a searchlight picked us up and I had to take avoiding action to get out of it. I didn't want to do that more than I could help, because every time I did it we lost a little more height, and shortened the length of the glide. Once I called to the air gunner to ask him if everything was all right.

'Sure,' he said. 'May I shoot out some of these searchlights?' But I couldn't let him do that for fear of giving our position away completely. He was disappointed, and every now and then he, came on the 'phone and said hopefully: 'There's a searchlight on us now, sir.'

By the time we were down to about 4,000 feet, still without any engines, things began to look rather nasty. We were still gliding, and still making our runs over the target area, with the observer doing his best to get the primary target into his bomb-sight - and, of course, we were still losing height. To add to our worries, another Blenheim high above us, without the slightest idea that we were below, was dropping flares and lighting the place up.

When we had lost another thousand feet, we ran slap into the middle of trouble. The flak came up like a hailstorm going the wrong way. But even then, by a stroke of luck nothing hit us.

A little lower, however, our luck broke. The port wing stopped an explosive shell, which tore a hole two feet square in it. I called to the observer to get rid of the bombs on something useful, because we hadn't got enough height to go round again. The observer released the bombs and they fell near the entrance to the Port Militaire - and still we were gliding downwards.

By now we were so low that we could see almost everything on the ground and in the harbour. I took one quick look over the side, but one look was enough. The tracer fire was coming up so quickly at us that I had to rely on the observer to direct me through the various streams of it. I had no time to watch it myself. The gunner got the dinghy ready in case we came down in the water, and he afterwards swore that he could see the black shapes of men by the guns on the ground, but I think it was probably the gun emplacements that he saw. Right over the middle of the harbour, at just about 1,000 feet, we were caught in a strong blue searchlight-and almost simultaneously both our engines picked up again.

I raced out of the harbour, through even more violent flak, fortunately without being hit again, for at first the aircraft refused to climb.

All the way home I had to keep the control wheel hard over to the right, to hold the damaged wing up, and several times the observer had to come back to help me hang on to the wheel, the pull was so heavy. We made for the nearest aerodrome in England, where they did everything they could to help us down. But directly I lowered the undercarriage the aircraft started to drop out of the sky like a brick.

The only thing to do was to land fast, so the crew braced themselves on the straps, opened all the hatches, and we came in just 60 mph faster than the Blenheim's usual landing speed. Luckily the undercarriage was undamaged and we landed safely.

Just one thing more. That aircraft is now in service again. the engineers worked on it night and day and, thanks to them, within three days I flew it back to my own aerodrome.

Raid On Brest by A Pilot Officer.

The Royal Navy had to mobilize a great force to catch the *Bismarck* because she might have destroyed whole convoys if she were left on the high seas. And when the battle-cruisers *Scharnhorst* and *Gneisenau* got out into the Atlantic, at the beginning of 1941, they sank about twenty merchant ships, a serious loss when added to the ships sunk by U-boats or long-range bombers. It was almost impossible to sink a capital ship with bombs and therefore torpedoes must be dropped if warships are to be finally disposed of by air attack alone. When the cruisers were in dry dock there was no more point in torpedoing them than in dropping a torpedo on a factory. When the cruisers were from time to time moored to a jetty, usually by the torpedo-boat station in the Rade Abri, they were completely protected from torpedoes by anti-torpedo booms and nets. So they had to be attacked by bombs and this meant that they had to be attacked from a

Above: Sergeant WOp/AG Mike Henry on the crew of Flying Officer 'Sandy' Powell and Sergeant 'Rich' Richmond, observer on 110 (Hyderabad) Squadron at RAF Wattisham.

Below: Twenty-seven-year old Wing Commander James 'Nick' Nicol, hunting off duty from Upwood in July 1941. Later that month Nicol, a pre-war regular, was posted to command 114 Squadron, being awarded a DSO for leading Strike Force 2 on the Cologne raid of 12 August 1941, his first operation. One week after the Cologne raid, a complete vic of three 114 Squadron Blenheims that Nicol was leading were shot down by three Bf 110s of II/ZG76 during a shipping strike off Vlieland. There were no survivors. (Pip Wray via Theo Boiten)

Above: Squadron Leader L. V. E. 'Attie' Atkinson DSO DFC* (Portrait by Eric Kennington)

Below: Wing Commander Hughie Idwal Edwards, an Australian of Welsh ancestry, commanded 105 Squadron in 1941. On 1 July Edwards was awarded the DFC for a low-level operation on 15 June when he led six crews in an attack on a convoy of eight merchant ships off Den Haag. On 21 July Edwards was awarded the Victoria Cross for courage and leadership displayed on Operation 'Wreckage' on 4 July when Bremen was attacked.

Blenheim IVs on 13 OTU (FV-) and a (XJ-) machine in formation.

When eleven Blenheims IVs carried out a shipping strike off the Dutch coast between The Hague and Ijmuiden on 7 July 1941 no less than eight 250lb bombs struck the *Delaware,* a Danish merchantman. Of these only two exploded and caused little damage. Four Danish sailors were killed in the blast and one was injured but the vessel sailed on under her own steam. One Blenheim was shot down by flak in the Scheldt Estuary and three others were shot down either by flak or by enemy fighters during a convoy attack off Scheveningen. Two crew members were taken prisoner; the rest were killed. No ships were sunk or heavily damaged during this strike. (RAF)

Bottom Left: Blenheim IV V6020 flown by Wing Commander Laurence Petley, the 107 Squadron, CO which was lost in the target area at Bremen on 4 July 1941 on Operation 'Wreckage'. Petley and his six crew were killed.

Off Borkum on 16 June 1941 during an attack on a 'Squealer' 24-year old Sergeant Evered Arthur Reginald Rex Leavers DFM of Dunkirk, Nottingham the pilot of Blenheim IV V6034 YH-D on 21 Squadron hit the ship's mast and he cart-wheeled into the North Sea. 23-year old Sergeant Ian Overheu DFM RNZAF and Sergeant Joseph William Howell Phelps died with him. Leavers was due to marry his fiancée Peggy Stanton on his his next leave.

The smiles on the faces on 114 Squadron aircrew at West Raynham on 12 February 1942 conceal the unsuccessful attempts to bomb the German warships in the 'Channel Dash'. Left to right are Kendrick; John Newberry; Wing Commander John F. G. Jenkins DSO DFC, 114 Squadron CO; King; Flying Officer Henry Paul Brancker DFC* and Flight Sergeant C. H. Gray DFM. *(Mrs. Vera Sherring)*

Below: Engine fitters and armourers working on a Blenheim IV at its dispersal.

A Blenheim of 21 Squadron, returned from an operation. Flight Lieutenant Howard Waples DFC (KIA 23 June 1941) in flying kit; acting Squadron CO, Squadron Leader Doug Cooper, with a plaster on his face; Group Captain Laurie Sinclair, Station Commander, RAF Watton with hands in pockets, back to camera; and Flying Officer Tonks, Intelligence Officer, without a cap beside the aircraft, next to Flying Officer Duncan, 21 Squadron MO and Squadron Leader Buckler, facing camera. Note the single VGO .303 inch machine gun which was replaced by a twin Browning .303 inch machine gun installation in the turret in the winter of 1941. *(Wartime Watton Museum)*

Wreckage of Blenheim L9248 on 57 Squadron in France in 1940. The squadron operated Blenheim Is and IVs, from March 1938 until November 1940.

107 Squadron pilots and their crews, May-June 1941, posed before the camera in the garden of the Dixon-Spains' house at Little Massingham, which at that time served as the 107 Squadron Officers' Mess. The pilots are in the back row, their observers (middle) and air gunners (front). Back row: U/k Flight Sergeant pilot; Flying Officer Dudenay; Flight Lieutenant F. Wellburn (PoW 4 July 1941); Squadron Leader Peter Simmons; Wing Commander Laurence Petley, CO; Squadron Leader 'Zeke' Murray RNZAF; Pilot Officer Bill Edrich; Flying Officer Maurice Viner Redfern-Smith and an u/k Flight Sergeant pilot. Other ranks identified are: in front of Wellburn his observer, Sergeant David Arthur Dupree and his air gunner, Sergeant Allan Ernest Routley (both KIA 4 July 1941, Bremen); in front of Petley, Flight Lieutenant Raymond Arthur Bailey DFC and Sergeant Wilfred Marshall Harris, air gunner (all three KIA 4 July 1941, Bremen); in front of Edrich, Sergeant Vic Phipps, observer and Sergeant Ernest Hope, air gunner; and in front of Redfern-Smith, Sergeant John Alfred Rudkin, observer and Sergeant Kenneth Thomas Noakes (all KIA 22/23 June 1941, Dunkirk). (Mrs Vera Sherring)

Blenheim IV V5580 YH-X on 21 Squadron at Watton, Norfolk, which went MIA on an anti-shipping strike in 'Beat 8' on 21 October 1941 with 29-year old Flight Lieutenant Frederick C. Powles DFC of Harrow, Middlesex and crew. The aircraft hit the sea with its propellers and ditched off Terschelling killing Powles, 21-year old Sergeant John D. Life RAFVR, observer and Flight Sergeant Simon J. Williams, WOp/AG.

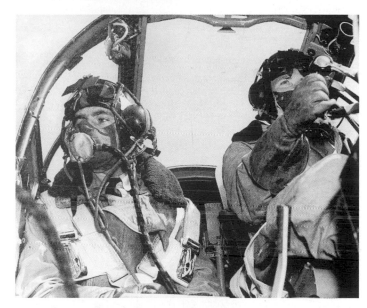

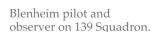

Blenheim pilot and observer on 139 Squadron.

A replacement fuel tank is loaded into position during repairs to a damaged Blenheim IV on 110 Squadron at Wattisham in June 1940.

Rear view of Herdla aerodrome in Norway during the joint raid on the German iron-ore convoy assembly base at Vaagsö on the Norwegian coast between Bergen and Trondheim on 27 December 1941 when Blenheims took part in Operation 'Archery', the first combined Army-Navy-Air Force operations raid of the war. It was one last big daylight raid before Blenheims were switched to night intruding.

On 12 August 1941 56 Blenheims, split into two forces, attacked the Quadrath and Knapsack power stations at Cologne. Four Blenheims on 139 Squadron, three on 18 and one each on 21, 82 and 114, plus two Blenheims on 226 Squadron, which were used as fighter navigators for the Spitfire withdrawal support, and four Spitfires, failed to return. *(Wartime Watton Museum)*

Blenheim IV GB-X on 105 Squadron flying at low-level over the North Sea on an anti-shipping strike. Low-level flying was to become a major feature of the life of Blenheim crews during the summer of 1941. Always a risky pastime, demanding absolute concentration on the part of the pilot, this became even more hazardous while over the sea in hazy conditions when it was very difficult to judge height above the water. Anti-shipping 'beats' during March-May 1941 continued to show scant reward for the high losses suffered.

Blenheim IV R3600 on 110 (Hyderabad) Squadron at RAF Wattisham, Suffolk which went MIA on an anti-shipping strike ('Beat 7') on 6 May 1941. Flight Lieutenant Edward N. Steel (24, of Wellington, New Zealand), Flight Sergeant Ronald A. Freestone, observer and Sergeant Joseph D. Bramall, WOp/AG were killed when the aircraft hit the sea off the Dutch coast. The squadron operated Blenheim Is and IVs, from August 1938 to February 1942.

Three Blenheim IVs in flight over East Anglia.

The Ventura carried a crew of five and was armed with two fixed 0.50 calibre guns and two depressible 0.303 inch guns in the nose, two or four 0.303 inch guns in a dorsal turret and two 0.303 inch guns in the ventral position firing aft. The bomb load was four 250lb and three 500lb bombs. *(Wartime Walton Museum)*

Venturas on 21 Squadron at Methwold on 26 May 1943. Note the Boulton Paul Type C Mk.IV dorsal gun turret with two 0.303 in machine guns. Sixty-five Ventura Mk Is and 71 Mk IIs were delivered to 2 Group. Thirty-one Venturas failed to return from operations; nine were written off with severe battle damage and eight were lost in flying accidents. *(RAF Museum)*

Smiling Boston aircrew on 226 Squadron gather around their maps for a photo call by *Illustrated* magazine after a briefing at Swanton Morley in April 1942.

The cockpit of a Boston showing the sideways opening canopy.

Boston III OM-U on 107 Squadron banking over the Norfolk countryside. *(via Nigel Buswell)*

Above: Mitchell IIs FV905/'S for Stalingrad', FW130/'A' and FW128/'H' on 226 Squadron in May 1944. *(via A. S. Thomas)*

Right: Bombing up North American Mitchell FL196/'J' on 22 Squadron. *(137/149 Wing Assoc)*

Below: Mitchell II FV914 VO-A on 98 Squadron dropping its bomb load over northern France on 19 April 1944. This aircraft was SOC on 5 June 1947. *(IWM)*

Mitchells on 180 Squadron en route to their target.
(*Smith-Carrington via Theo Boiten*)

great height; a bomb dropped from anything under 10,000 feet or so would not have enough momentum-mass multiplied by velocity to penetrate the armour of the ships. And the *Scharnhorst* and *Gneisenau* are the most heavily armoured ships in the German navy. Calibre of guns has been sacrificed to weight of armour-plating; their biggest guns are only of 11-inch calibre, but their decks have 6-inch plating, their turrets 12-inch plating and amidships there is a belt of 12- to 13-inch plating. Attack from a great height means, of course, that many bombs will miss for one that hits the ships; the better protected the ships are, the larger in all probability the proportion of misses to hits.

Brest was extraordinarily well protected, so much so that even if the ships had not been hit at all the RAF would have been, doing useful work by keeping, as they did, several squadrons of day and night fighters round Brest instead of on the Eastern front or in the Mediterranean and something like 200 anti-aircraft guns in the harbour when they were just as urgently needed elsewhere. The *Scharnhorst* and *Gneisenau* themselves are well armed against air attacks and, their own guns have often been used against our bombers; they each have fourteen 4.1 anti-aircraft guns and sixteen 37-millimetre anti-aircraft guns. To make things yet more difficult, the ships were camouflaged with extraordinary care. They lay under a kind of tent, which tied them to the dry docks or to a jetty and as a further precaution the Germans habitually used a smoke screen which, when it had been working for some time, eventually covered the whole harbour with an impenetrable cloud. Thus it often became of urgent importance to get air attacks in quickly and to get all the bombs down as soon as possible, before the long trails of smoke, streaming across the port, had spread and merged into a dense fog.

At first the *Scharnhorst* and *Gneisenau* were not engaged in commerce raiding; they were supporting the invasion of Norway. Between them they sank the aircraft carrier *Glorious* whose Gladiators had so magnificently given fighter protection to the British troops at Narvik. This was on 7 June 1940; on 21 June the *Scharnhorst* was found by Sunderlands and bombed by Hudsons and Beauforts of Coastal Command. She was hit three times and had to be sent back to Kiel for repairs, where she was again attacked by Whitleys and Hampdens on 1/2 July 1940. One of the Hampdens attacking the *Scharnhorst* was flown by 21-year old Flying Officer Guy Penrose Gibson on 83 Squadron, who dropped the first 2,000lb SAP bomb of the war. Although well-known to the public, principally for his outstanding leadership of 617 Squadron's attacks on the German dams on the night of 16/17 May 1943 Gibson flew a total of 177 operational sorties before his death in action in a Mosquito on 19 September 1944 - 76 of these on bombers and the remainder on fighters. Gibson released the 2,000lb SAP bomb on the sixth shallow dive-bombing attempt but the bomb overshot the *Scharnhorst* and exploded in the town of Kiel. The navigator in the aircraft which claimed to have hit the ship recalled. 'I directed my line of sight on the floating dock,' he said, 'which stood out sharply in the estuary. Searchlights caught us in the dive, but we went under the beam. Then I put the captain into dive as we came on the target. The *Scharnhorst* couldn't be missed; she stood out so plainly ... I could clearly see tracers coming from the pom-pom on the deck of the *Scharnhorst*.' After describing the damage inflicted a few seconds later on the aircraft by AA fire - it included a hole two foot square in the tail-plane - he went on: 'We came down very low to make sure and when we were dead in line I released a stick of bombs. A vast shoot of reddish-yellow flame came from the deck.' Ten people were killed in Kiel on this night. A Whitley on 58 Squadron at Linton-On-Ouse and a Hampden on 83 Squadron at Scampton crashed in the target area with no survivors from both crews. As a result of this raid the *Scharnhorst* was not fit for the open sea until the winter of 1941. Then she went out into the Atlantic with the *Gneisenau*. Both ships went to Brest to refit in March 1941 and the first attack on them there was made on the night of 30/31 March. They were joined at the beginning of June 1941 by the cruiser *Prinz Eugen*, which had accompanied the Bismarck across the Atlantic and had fled to Brest to escape the Bismarck's fate.

From the end of March 1941 four thousand tons of the heaviest armour-piercing bombs, of general-purpose bombs, both very large and of normal size and of incendiaries, were poured into Brest. The main object was to hit the ships with the armour-piercing bombs, but it was also a good thing to damage repair shops and to make Brest naval base as uninhabitable as possible. On the night of 1/2 July 1941, a force of 52 Wellingtons attacked the dry dock (the No. 8 dry, dock) in which the *Prinz Eugen* was then lying. Bomb bursts, with fire and smoke, were observed round this dock, but a hit on the ship was not positively claimed at the time. Later there were several reports that the *Prinz Eugen* was hit by two bombs and damaged by a third which fell close to the hull of the ship. One bomb was said to have fallen down the funnel of the ship and to have done serious internal damage; there were many casualties among the crew. There were also reports of more hits on the *Prinz Eugen* during attacks made in October and November 1941. Though it cannot be known for certain how much damage she sustained, what is certain is that the *Prinz Eugen* was unable to move until 12 February 1942 from a most dangerous harbour.

On 22 July 1941 the *Scharnhorst* left Brest to make a trial run, southwards along the coast of France. On 23 July a reconnaissance aircraft found her moored to a break-water in the harbour of La Pallice, 240 miles south of Brest. That evening, while it was still daylight; a formation of six Stirlings made the first of a succession of attacks against the two battle-cruisers. Enemy fighters had already been dispatched to the south to protect the *Scharnhorst*; the Stirlings, without any fighters to protect them, had to fight their way through to bomb. One Stirling was gliding in to bomb from about 8,000 feet when six Messerschmitt 109s came up to attack. One flew out of the sun and the pilot of the Stirling dived so that his rear gunner could get a better aim. The Messerschmitt plunged below the Stirling and climbed again; the Stirling's rear gunner fired two bursts and the Messerschmitt turned over and dived into the sea. Then came a second Messerschmitt. The rear gunner thought that this time he must have killed the pilot; the Messerschmitt dived towards the sea with its guns still firing. Just above the waves it fluttered, then burst into flames and pancaked into the water. At this the remaining four Messerschmitts kept their distance, firing only occasional bursts, but the rear gunner of another Stirling fired at them and saw a flash from one of them where his bullets went home. The four Messerschmitts turned about and made off, while the first Stirling continued its shallow dive over the *Scharnhorst*. The bomb aimer released a very heavy armour-piercing bomb and the rear gunner saw the flash of its explosion and black smoke on the stern of the ship. One of the Stirlings was lost and a few hours later, an hour or two after midnight, thirty Whitleys attacked the harbour of La Pallice. A rain of flares lit up the docks and a constant succession of high-explosive bombs and incendiaries, which started large fires made La Pallice a far from comfortable haven for the *Scharnhorst* but again, no bombs hit the battle cruiser.

It was on 23 July, on 35 Squadron at Linton-on-Ouse that Pilot Officer Richard C. Rivaz's pilot, Braddles, sent for him. The 31 year old tail gunner had volunteered for the RAF one evening in August 1940 and had found that he was too old for pilot training. 'I've some news for you, Riv' he said. 'We're on a daylight raid tomorrow and you're flying with me.'

'Good show!' I replied. 'D'you know where we're going?'

'No, not definitely but we're after the *Scharnhorst*. She's left Brest and gone south, but I've not been told where yet. We load up here and go down to Stanton Harcourt sometime this evening and set off from there tomorrow. I don't, know any details yet. We'll air-test as soon as I've made out the crew lists: I'm leaving all the gunnery side in your hands. There are nine of us going from here and we're leading.'

Operation 'Sunrise' was planned to launch a surprise attack on 24 July against the *Scharnhorst* and *Gneisenau* in Brest harbour using a mixed force of approximately 150 medium and heavy bombers. Three Spitfire squadrons were to escort the second wave of the attacking force, two more following later to deal with enemy fighters that managed to refuel and rejoin the battle. At the last minute *Scharnhorst* moved to La Rochelle, 200 miles south and 100 bombers were detailed to attack this target. In the hope that they would draw up German fighters prematurely, three Fortresses were to bomb from 30,000 feet while 18 Hampdens, escorted by three squadrons of Spitfires with long-range fuel tanks, would also help the process of 'drawing-up' of the enemy fighters, leaving the main bombing force of 79 Wellingtons from 1 and 3 Groups to attack unescorted. Fifteen Halifaxes - nine on 35 Squadron and six on 76 Squadron - were to carry out an entirely unescorted raid on the *Scharnhorst* at La Pallice.[28] After leaving Stanton Harcourt the formation would fly out via Lizard Point and then across to a position fifty miles west of Ushant, while maintaining a height of 1,000 feet or less to avoid detection by enemy radar. From there they would fly direct to the target, intending to bomb from 19,000 feet, but as events turned out, it was ultimately carried out form 15,000 feet[29]

'There was plenty to do that morning and afternoon' continues Richard Rivaz on 35 Squadron. 'In fact, until we moved at about nine pm guns had to be harmonized, ammunition checked, turrets and guns tested; all the usual routine jobs before an operational trip; only even more so.

'I suppose a daylight raid is the ambition of most gunners. It is the time when the gunner really comes into his own and really has a chance to prove himself. It is his chance and he will be of some real importance and use. On so many night' trips he sees nothing except a dark curtain around him, with probably some stars showing; he will probably see searchlights and flashes of exploding shells, but he is powerless to do anything against these. His job so often is one of complete inactivity: of cold and discomfort when all he can do is to sit and stare and be ready; ready for something that time and again never happens. But on a day raid it would be different! The whole crew would rely on him for safety: the safety of the crew and the aeroplane would be, to a great extent, in his hands. To me a daylight raid was more or less an unknown quantity and something of a mystery. It was a new experience and an experience I did not want to miss. I knew quite a lot about night bombing and what to expect: I knew the sound and feel' and even the smell of flak. I had seen hundreds of searchlights. I had seen storms and ice, bright moonlit, nights, arid nights black with clouds: I had seen bright sunsets and dawns breaking, but I had not been over enemy country by day. I had my usual bouts of 'stage fright'; my usual qualms and that dull feeling in my stomach which with me always goes hand in glove with any operational trip, but nevertheless, I was glad to be going, glad of a new experience and I had a feeling of excitement and almost pleasurable anticipation.

'As this was to be a day raid and not a routine night trip we had a picked crew. There were Braddles; Blake, second pilot; Nick, navigator; Jerry, wireless operator; Wheeler, engineer and I chose a Canadian - Berry - as front gunner.[30]

'I was in the tail. Blake was a young Sergeant pilot and a Somersetshire man. He had been in one or two night raids; but, like the rest of us, this was his first day raid and he was very thrilled at the prospect of going. Nick, who had recently been commissioned, was twenty years of age and one of the best navigators we had: 'he was very keen and really knew his job and he had done over forty trips. Jerry was another very experienced man and about the same age as Nick: he, too, was very keen and seemed to take a real pleasure in everything he did. I chose Berry because of his keenness to fly. He had not done an operational trip as yet, but I felt confident that I could rely on him. He had been with us for about a month and was waiting to be crewed up. I think he was very disappointed at not being put on crew sooner. His one ambition was to fly operationally and I felt quite happy about having him in the nose of our aeroplane.

'We did our air-test at about eleven o'clock and Braddles was well satisfied with everything. It was one of those hot July days with a slight breeze and very clear visibility and it was a real pleasure to be flying. The ground below 'showed clear and neat, like some intricate patchwork quilt made up of an infinite number of shades and different materials. I thought also that it looked rather like some gigantic jig-saw puzzle; each field or wood or village being a piece in the puzzle and all fitting perfectly together. It consisted of thousands of pieces, which did not make a picture, but rather some abstract design and a masterpiece in pattern and colour. The cornfields were ripening and were a lovely golden brown and newly-cut hayfields showed clearly the marks of the mower. On some hayfields the cutting was not finished and there were square and rectangular shapes in the middle where the grass was still standing. No two fields were the same shape and very few were the same colour; woods and trees showed in dark patches and dots and all appeared perfectly flat. There was no indication of any undulation or roughness: all seemed smooth and neat and rather unreal. Roads twisted .about as pale, thin streaks and rivers looked like pieces of fine ribbon or threads of silk curling about, yet fitting in perfectly with the pattern. Houses and cottages were like tiny, perfectly made models nestling amongst the trees and woods.

'There were some light fleecy clouds between us and the' ground which threw dark shadows across the pattern below us. Our own shadow was racing across the ground like a little demon: leaping across hedges and houses and trees alike, sometimes disappearing when it crossed the cloud shadows and then reappearing again on the other side. The whole scene was fresh and clean and ever-changing and one at which I could never tire of looking. There was no sign of discord: the puzzle was complete and no piece was missing. I had very little to do in my turret once I had satisfied myself that everything was as it should be and soon I gave myself up to the beauty below me; a beauty of ever-changing colours and of calm and peace. Although we were up there not for pleasure and not for seeking beauty, but in preparation for our task on the morrow, when we might suffer and probably cause suffering to others, yet I drove the thought from my mind as something unfit for our present surroundings and thought only of the present and the far future. The near future and its final issue were too uncertain for prolonged thought while the far future was sufficiently far off and remote to allow of tranquil and pleasurable thoughts. 'I had been on too many bombing raids and known danger much too close to allow myself to think beforehand of what could and might happen. The thought was ever-present but by now I could control my feelings to a certain extent and keep thoughts of dangers that I knew about at the back of my mind. Nevertheless, the thoughts were still there, but under control: my motto was 'Sufficient unto the day.'

'As we came down, gradually losing height while approaching the aerodrome the illusion of the unreality of the ground gradually disappeared and objects began to take their natural forms. Trees began to look like trees and houses looked as though they were inhabited. Details began to appear and people could be seen quite clearly. As we came in to land the ground seemed to rush by more quickly and one really had an idea of the speed at which one was travelling despite the fact that it was considerably reduced for landing. We passed over the edge of the aerodrome at about a hundred feet and from the tail I could see objects rushing by. There were some workmen on there and I saw them stop and look up. We were losing height all the time and once over the, runway the pilot closed the throttles and we sank down in our forward rush over the' concrete below us. As we touched the ground there was a screaming sound from the tyres on the concrete and the runway rushed away from the tail faster than I had ever seen any road move before me in a car. The tail wheel was bouncing up and down and I was being bumped in my turret. We came to a standstill in a remarkably short distance and turned off to the right to taxi to our parking-place. The ground crew were waiting for us, anxious for our report on the aeroplane's behaviour. Armourers came to me to ask how the turret behaved. I was well satisfied and told them so. Other aircraft were landing from their air-test and we saw some of them coming in. We watched them for a few minutes, although we could see them landing any day, for there is always something fascinating about seeing a heavy aeroplane land. Some made perfect landings and ran smoothly over the runways once their wheels touched the ground, while others were not so good and bounced up into the air and down again and rose several more times until they were going too slowly to leave the ground any more. Each time an aeroplane landed and the wheels touched the ground a wave of blue smoke was left behind. This was caused by the rubber burning from the sudden friction when the tyres first touched the ground at a speed of about a hundred mph. The wear on those tyres, strong as they are, must be terrific.

'During lunch there was no talk of the coming raid, although it was probably the main thought at the back of most of our minds. I know it was with me! We all knew that the success of the raid - and our own lives - depended to a large extent on absolute secrecy and to a certain extent, on our keeping our mouths shut. In the afternoon I went out to our aircraft and watched her being bombed up. It was the first time I had seen any heavy armour-piercing bombs at close quarters. They were long, evil-looking brutes, thinner than the ordinary bomb and really looking as though they were capable of enormous damage. To the armourers this was an everyday job; a job requiring considerable skill, but one at which they were expert through constant practice and thorough training. Sometimes when they had finished they would chalk messages on the bombs, such as *To Hitler from me* or *Love and Kisses to Jerry* or something similar. Sometimes an aeroplane would not be ready for bombing, for some reason or other, until shortly before take-off time, which might not be until late at night or in the early hours of the morning-yet the armourers would carry, out this job as cheerfully and thoroughly as though they had just come on duty, although they would probably have been waiting for hours. Occasionally an aeroplane, would not take off at all, owing to trouble at the last moment and the bomb load would have to be removed. 'this is a long and tiring business, particularly in the dark and means collecting the bomb trolleys and winches for lowering the bombs on to the trolleys: it means getting a tractor to tow the trolleys back to the bomb dump; altogether entails probably well over an hour's work yet the only feeling of discontent that I have ever seen the armourers show is that there would be so many less bombs to drop on Germany that night!

'The armourers inside our aeroplane were winding the bombs into their racks by means of winches, which sounded like enlarged fishing reels or grandfather clocks being wound. Other armourers below were steadying the bombs and shouting directions to those inside. It seemed to me a complicated business, with much shouting from those outside to those inside, mingled with many and by their repetition, monotonous, swear words. But the job was completed without a hitch in a remarkably short time. As I looked at the bombs lying side by side in their racks, only waiting for Nick to press the button to release them, I wondered if they would find their mark. Accurate bombing from a high level is much more difficult than people realize. In order to bomb accurately, the aeroplane has to fly absolutely straight and be quite level during the time the navigator is sighting his target - which is the 'run-up' - and until after the bombs have gone. Any slight inaccuracy of flying, such as a turn off course of even one degree just as the bomb-aimer is about to release the bombs, might throw them hundreds of feet off their mark. If the nose of the aeroplane drops or rises the slightest bit the bombs will fall well short of or far beyond, their aiming-point. Often during the run-up one is being shot at from the ground and shells burst all around the aeroplane. Sometimes the bursts are so close that the aircraft is blown many feet by the blast: sometimes she is blown on her side and almost out of control and is made to stall and fall into a spin or a dive until she can be righted. If any of these things should happen just as the bomb aimer is about to release the bombs, they may fall as much as a mile or more away from where they were intended to drop.

'Even if the opposition is not near enough to be felt, the bomb-aimer and pilot have to have perfect cooperation and understanding. The bomb-aimer lies in the nose of the aeroplane, where his bomb-sight is set so that he can see the ground through his sight immediately in front and below him. He will have to release the bombs well before the aeroplane is over the target; as they will have the forward motion of the aircraft as well as their own drop. Bombs of varying shapes and weights will have their own peculiarities of drop for which allowances have to be made: the height and speed of the aeroplane at the time of dropping the bombs have to be set on the sight; also the direction and velocity of the wind. It can be seen that bomb-aiming is a very difficult business and one that requires a great deal of skill and practice on the part of the bomb-aimer. I went round to the tail to have another look at my turret and guns and I wondered if I should have to use them.

'We arrived at Stanton Harcourt just as it was getting dusk and had several miles to drive to the Mess, where they had supper ready for us. I saw several people there whom I knew and had not seen for some time but I did not stay up talking long, as we had to be up early next morning and had to be fresh. There was not room for us all to sleep in the Mess, so there were beds put ready for us in the Roman Catholic chapel as it was apparently the only available space they had. We did not know until the following morning that we had been. Sleeping in a chapel and I hope we did not desecrate it: had we known I don't know whether we would have been more subdued, as we were in high spirits and there was considerable horseplay and ragging.

'We were wakened next morning at five o'clock. There was a thick white mist which completely obscured objects thirty yards away and it considerably damped my spirits. Everyone said it was heat mist and would clear when the sun got stronger but it looked pretty hopeless at the moment and I thought it might hang about for hours. Briefing was at seven o'clock and we were due to take off at ten-thirty. Briefing was less formal than usual, as we were in a make-shift hut so unlike our own briefing-room, with its walls hung with maps and charts and photographs but the Colonel was there and in his usual good form despite the early hour, The Colonel was our intelligence officer. Actually, he had been up all night collecting the latest information and weather reports and working with the CO and Navigation Officer on our route.

'The Scharnhorst was our target and she was lying at La Pallice - which is the harbour to La Rochelle, about 250 miles south of Brest and in the Bay of Biscay. We were shown photographs of the harbour, which was easily recognizable as there was: an island quite 'Close to it. The Scharnhorst was lying alongside what looked like a sea wall or large breakwater running some way out to sea. We had to drop our bombs from fifteen thousand feet, to allow them to have their full power of penetration. The Scharnhorst has vast thicknesses of armour-plating on her decks and an ordinary bomb would have little or no effect: certainly it would not sink it, although it might do a certain amount of superficial damage. It is necessary for an armour-piercing bomb to be dropped from a great height, in order that it may reach its terminal velocity and so have the necessary power behind it to pierce the thickness of armour before exploding. There are only two ways of sinking a ship as heavily armoured as the Scharnhorst either torpedoes or heavy armour-piercing bombs. She would be very difficult to hit, lying as she was by herself and would appear very small at 15,000 feet: actually she would look about the size of the small lead ships that children have. Her importance to the Germans was pointed out to us by the Colonel, particularly her importance to them in blockading our supplies crossing the Atlantic. It was essential that she should be kept out of commission or sunk. She was a very difficult target and we had to make every effort to hit her: the raid was timed to take place to coincide with plans made for another attack that same day on the *Gneisenau* which was still lying at Brest. The Colonel told us all he could about the organization of both raids.

'The mist was clearing as we came out after briefing and we could see the sky a soft blue. The ground was still blurred and indistinct, but the mist was definitely dispersing: it was evidently going to be another very hot day and I wondered what I should wear. Obviously it would be sweltering in the aeroplane at low level, but probably rather cold when we got to 15,000 feet. I decided to wear my full flying-suit, but with less on underneath. I would rather be too hot than too cold. If you are too cold you can't concentrate and altogether feel thoroughly miserable; while if you are too hot all you do is to sweat but you can still think. Granted, both extremes are unpleasant but still I would rather be too hot. Definitely we should need to concentrate very hard indeed. We did not know for certain how much opposition we should meet but it would be considerable and there were sure to be some fighters. After briefing was over we still had more than two hours to take-off time. I had left my parachute and flying-kit in the aeroplane, so there was no need to cart anything about with me.

'Braddles went off with the CO and I called together all the gunners to have a final discussion of plans and make certain everything was as it should be. We were all in good spirits and keyed up for what was to come: we should probably have to do more than just sit this time! Now that we knew more about the target and where it was, we could go' more thoroughly into the details of out plans. There was some coffee and sandwiches for us at nine o'clock and we stood about in groups in the sunshine as we ate and drank, discussing the job before us. We drifted gradually into groups consisting of our crews. Blake told us of an aunt of his who lived about fifty miles from La Rochelle: he said that if he had to bail out, he would try to escape there. This seemed an excellent plan and we begged him not to forget his pals.

'It was turning into a glorious morning-as we moved out to our aeroplanes. The sun was already hot and as it shone on the perspex of the turrets and cabins of the aeroplanes they sparkled and gleamed like so many lights twinkling. The fabric and metal of the aircraft were hot to the touch. Yes, it was a perfect day; a day to be bathing in the sea or lazing about in the country and it did not seem to fit in at all with bombing and violence. It was a day for peace and laughing and happiness. Not that we were unhappy! We weren't! At least nobody looked unhappy. We had been selected for an important raid and an experience that very few people were privileged to have. There would be dangers, yes but so many things really worth doing were dangerous to a certain extent. Motor-car racing is dangerous up to a point; yet it is a good sport and those taking part in it do not think of the danger part of it; at least, not while they are racing. Danger is a thing of the imagination more than of actual fact: in one's mind one can imagine countless things that could and might happen but they very rarely do happen! When danger does come upon one it is usually so sudden and very often when one is least expecting it, that one has not the time to be frightened. The racing motorist does not think of what would happen if he burst a tyre at a hundred miles an hour while he is driving and even if he does, the thought does not stay with him for long. He may think about it beforehand and make plans accordingly, but he only thinks of it as a possible contingency and one that he must guard against. The thought, if he allows it to stay with him for long, may cause him considerable worry and strain, but this is merely 'stage fright'. If he does actually burst a tyre, he is so occupied as to have no time for feat. So in the air: it is all the endless things that might happen that scare me and give me that horrible 'sinking feeling' yet when, danger has been really close I have usually been too occupied to be frightened.

'As I stood by our aeroplane I was excited at the prospect of a new experience but that numb feeling at the bottom of my chest and the dryness in my throat, came back as I started to get into my flying-kit: Somehow, dressing in flying clothing seemed to me to be symbolical of dangers and death. As I slowly and methodically dressed I cursed my imagination and myself for being a fool as all the stories I had heard of the more unpleasant side of flying and aerial warfare raced through my mind. I looked at the others and wondered if they were feeling the same.

'Braddles was talking to the CO and the Colonel - who was prodding him in the chest with the stem of his pipe and grinning his cherubic grin. Nick and Jerry were' smoking cigarettes and joking. Blake was being helped into his 'Mae West' by one of the ground crew. Wheeler was looking up at one of the engines as though he were talking to it and Berry was standing beside me already fully clothed. They all looked perfectly normal and I suppose I looked the same. I remember having exactly the same feeling while standing outside the headmaster's study at school waiting for a probable beating. I was not frightened, unless you can call 'stage fright' being frightened. I was more apprehensive. If anyone had come to me and said 'may I go instead of you?' I would have said 'No!' without hesitation, even if I had been in the position to say otherwise.

'By the time I was fully clothed I was wet through to my tunic with perspiration and was beginning to think I was a bit of a fool to wear so many clothes but I consoled myself with the thought that I would probably be glad of them at fifteen thousand feet!

'Braddles climbed into the aeroplane, followed by Wheeler and Blake. The CO and the Colonel, after wishing us luck, had moved off to say good-bye to the other crews. I intended to wait until the last moment before getting in, as it was cooler outside than in the aeroplane. I heard one of the ground crew call up to Braddles, who was in his pilot's seat; 'Contact port outer.' Almost immediately the airscrew blades of the port outer engine began to turn slowly and then burst into life. It was followed in turn by the port inner engine then the starboard outer and finally the starboard inner engine, I stood behind the engines so as to get the draught from their slip-stream; I turned my face towards them with my head lifted and felt the cool air fanning my skin and I stood there for several seconds taking deep breaths. Jerry scrambled in, as excited as a schoolboy at an outing. Nick followed him, with his satchel full of maps and he was closely followed by Berry. I followed suit.

'The heat in my turret was stifling and the sweat was soon pouring off me. I fastened my helmet as lightly as possible and plugged in the intercom. Braddles was asking Wheeler about the engine temperatures. However slow and deliberate Wheeler might appear on the ground, when he was in the air and on the job his reactions always seemed to be instantaneous. He seemed to be .anticipating Braddles' question, because he answered immediately, I had noticed the same thing on many other occasions. His replies were always quite definite, too: I have known Braddles say to him - 'Are you sure?' and he would always reply 'Quite sure, sir.' And he was always right!

'No wonder Braddles used to insist on having Wheeler in his crew. He once said to me; 'Riv' old boy, there are two people I insist on having with me and they are you and Wheeler!'

'As Braddles ran up the engines, clouds of dust were thrown up by the slipstream, completely obscuring my vision, When the engines were running, normally again, I signalled to an armourer who was standing near to dust the. Outside of my perspex for me. As he was finishing rubbing it over we started to move. He walked a few steps with us, still polishing and then gave a cheery wave of his hand and a grin and rejoined his pals.

'When we moved on to the runway preparatory to take-off, I saw the usual group of people standing watching us set out. The group was larger than usual. I recognized the CO and the Colonel; but there were several whom I did not know. The tail shook and vibrated as the engines roared and I could feel the aircraft straining ready to leap forward. The runway raced beneath me faster and faster and appeared to drop away lower and lower and its place was taken by fields below me: I looked back and saw the next aircraft already in position and that, too, started to move down the runway. I was feeling perfectly normal now and quite impersonal and seemed to be working from outside myself. I was not an individual any longer, but part of a team.

'Braddles set course straight away and we climbed gently. He called through to me and asked me if I could see any of the others and I told him that numbers two and three were airborne and that I could just see number four on the runway. I spent the next half-hour of the trip reporting to Braddles on the movements of the formation.

'Number two was the first to come into position on our right. The pilot's name was Johnny and I could see him sitting with one hand on the control column and the other on the throttles. He would be tired before the trip was over, as formation flying needs a lot of concentration. The leader is all right, as he simply has to fly on a straight course but those formating on him have to make continual corrections in their flying, as no two aeroplanes can fly exactly alike. No aeroplane can fly absolutely straight and level for long: there are continual atmospheric changes which affect its flight and cause it to drop and rise and turn a degree or two every so often.

'Johnny was one of those large, quiet and absolutely unshakable men. His tail gunner told me that he was always the same and completely calm, no matter what happened. On one occasion when a shell burst particularly close behind the tail and tore a large chunk out of the tail plane, the gunner reported it through to Johnny who said in a casual way: 'Has it burst yet?' The gunner replied that it had whereupon Johnny said: 'You're not dead yet, are you?

'No.'

'Well, what are you worrying about, then?' But he said it in such a way as to make the gunner feel quite confident and happy. Most gunners get very attached to their pilots and I know this one worshipped Johnny. Incidentally, Johnny thought the world of his gunner.

'The other aircraft, one by one, came into position. We flew in three separate formations of three aircraft each, with our own aeroplane leading and one on either side of us and slightly behind. There was another group of three about two hundred yards on our starboard and behind with another three in a corresponding position on our port. As I looked at the aircraft behind me I thought they seemed like some impersonal monsters and it was strange to think that they each contained seven-men; seven individuals, each with his own life and each capable of deep feeling. We were all bent on the same object: all out to destroy a ship that was a menace to civilization. We would do all in our power to prevent that ship from doing the job for which it was intended. While I watched the other aeroplanes I wondered how those people would be feeling and of what they would be thinking. The pilots and navigators, I knew, would be too busy to let their thoughts wander, but the other people would not have much to do yet. The gunners would be sitting in their turrets as I was looking about them and probably talking occasionally to their pilots or other members of their crews and they would be chewing gum or sucking barley sugar. Some, I believe, knew they would not return. One gunner I was told about afterwards had given full instructions as to what he wanted done with his body. He had his head blown off by a cannon shell! I was talking to him a few minutes before we went to our aeroplanes: he was cheerful and appeared quite unconcerned and might almost have been setting out on a flight across England only.[31]

'I once had the feeling that I should not return and it was like a nightmare that lasted all day. We were detailed for some target in the Ruhr and as soon as, I knew in the morning that we were flying that night I had the most horrible feeling I had ever experienced, which got worse as the day went on. It was far worse, than the usual 'stage fright' I always get and it was with me all day, increasing in intensity. I can't describe what I felt or experienced, as it had no concrete form but it was a feeling of utter helplessness and depression and was with me in everything I did: it occupied my whole mind and try as I would, I could not shake it from me.

'When we went to do our air-test in the morning there was some trouble with one of the engines and we had to wait until later. When we eventually got down just before lunch it was found that one of the radiators was leaking and it had to be changed. That afternoon I played tennis, hoping to clear my mind by means of some hard exercise, but the depression still persisted and I found I could not concentrate on the game, try as I would: I would throw up the ball for service and between throwing it and hitting it my mind would go through torment. So it went on all through the day and until I got into my turret that evening. I thought that maybe when I got into the aeroplane I should feel all right but no, the feeling was still there. When the engines were running I tested the illuminated sight. It would not function, although it had been perfectly all right when I had tried it in the morning, so I called through to Braddles to tell him. I tried another bulb, but that would not work either. An armourer was sent speeding for a new part, which was fitted and the sight was OK. We started to taxi out to the take-off point and on the way, further technical trouble started, so we went back to have it seen to. It was found that it was too long a job to be ready in time, so we were ordered to stay on the ground. We were detailed to fly again two nights later and that time I felt perfectly normal.

'The sun was beating down on to my turret and the sweat was running freely out of me: my face was wet and my clothes were sticking to my body. The sky was absolutely cloudless; the mist had cleared and I could see for miles. I could see every detail of the ground below. We were over country I knew very well, having motored over it many times and I was thrilled when we passed over landmarks I recognized. Most of these landmarks brought back memories of holidays; of people I was with, or of people I was going to see. I began thinking of those people and I realized with a shock how many I had lost touch with since the war began. Some, no doubt, were continuing as they always had done, with the routine of their lives altered very little by the war: some like myself would be fighting and others I knew had been killed. Some people who were fighting were rather revelling in it and probably having a jolly sight better time than they did in peace-time; some would be fighting because they had to and others because they felt they ought to.

'I was glad for many of those who were not fighting and I hoped that they would never have to. Some people are too gentle and ordered in their lives to fight or be concerned in fighting and I hoped that those people would never see violence or bloodshed. I thought of my old grandmother, who lived through the bombing of London and died after the worst of it was over. I don't think she was ever really frightened and I think she was proud to know that she was in the war in her beloved London and was holding her own. She once told me that she found the raids inconvenient, but said she slept better when the guns were firing. Nothing would induce her to move, even when the flat above her was gutted by a fire bomb. That is the spirit which will never be broken and the spirit that the Nazis can never understand! My grandmother loved a fight and she was always quarrelling with her nurses. On one occasion when she was ill and in bed the nurse who was attending her dropped a tray, whereupon my grandmother quite rightly screamed. The nurse bent over her and said 'Poor old thing!' This infuriated my grandmother so much that she said without a moment's hesitation: 'I may be poor; I grant you I am old but I am not a THING! You are dismissed!'

'We were over the hilly and more broken country of the west counties and some of the higher hills were only a few hundred feet below us. The rivers, looking invitingly cool, were sparkling in the bright sunlight as they wound about the valleys, sometimes hidden by the woods and trees. I had fished some of these rivers and I tried to see if I could recognize any of the stretches I had actually visited. We crossed over Dartmoor with its great expanse of heath and rock and bog. The surface of the hills made them look less ferocious than they really are. I could see the sheep and ponies grazing peacefully in the sunshine and quite oblivious of our scrutiny. These rugged expanses of hill and rock seemed much less awe-inspiring and more approachable as we sped a few hundred feet above their tops. I felt I wanted to get out and walk for miles as far as I could see. Those moorland hills seemed to be calling out to me to join them.

'The tors looked almost neatly placed on the highest tops of the moors, instead of being great rugged hunks of granite. Actually, the beauty and charm and magic of those moors was diminished as their size decreased. Viewed from above, they were gentler, more subdued and less wild than they really are. The streams were like pale blue threads trickling through the valleys and down the slopes: the grey stone cottages seemed if anything even more isolated and lonely than they actually are, as I could 'see the miles of empty moorland surrounding them. I had been on Dartmoor and had seen her under all her variety of moods and changes but this was the first time that I had seen her from above. Her beauty from here was quite new to me: she seemed more gentle and more easy to know and I felt I ought to be reintroduced. I had camped on Dartmoor just over a year before and it looked as though we were going to pass very close to our camp site now: I was getting excited as I recognized parts of the moor that, I knew very well. We were very near the spot where we had pitched our tent and I was getting more and more thrilled: I forgot all, about the mission that we were / on and it was like meeting an old friend whom one had not seen for a long time. Yes there was the actual spot where our tent had been pitched! There was the stream where we had got our water; the old dead tree we had used for firewood the stone wall over which we had had to climb to reach our tent and countless other little familiar things that were like friends. I felt I wanted to get out and renew my, acquaintance with them all: they seemed part of a different life somehow. A lot had happened to me since then far more than I had ever thought would happen and I would not have missed any of it. I used to read with envy about the adventures of' other people and wonder if ever I should see any real excitement.

'We left Tavistock on our right and could just see some ruins in Plymouth on our left. Although the tail gunner sits with his back towards the direction of travel, if he sees something on his left-hand side, he refers to it as being on the right or starboard. This saves any form of confusion and the pilot 'knows that if 'his gunner reports, let us say, a fighter on the starboard, it is on the right-hand side of the aeroplane and not the gunner's right hand: The sky is divided into areas around the aeroplane - each area occupying an angle of forty-five degrees and they are referred to in naval terms. Thus, 'starboard bow' would be somewhere ahead but on the right 'port quarter' would be somewhere behind but on the left and port or starboard beam would be on the left or right-hand side.

'We crossed the coast and flew almost parallel with it for some distance. The sea was a lovely blue and very calm. Near the shore it was extraordinarily clear and I could see light patches below the water where there was sand and dark patches where there were rocks and seaweed. There were many people bathing and they might have been watching us. When they read about the raid next day, or heard about it on the wireless, they would probably remember us and tell their friends that they had seen a formation of bombers going over. If they guessed we were on a raid when we passed over; perhaps they would wish us luck.

'As we moved farther away from the coast I could no longer see any people. I missed those people bathing and walking along the beaches: although they were all strangers and probably I should never see them again, yet they were part of England that was getting farther away and that would soon be out of sight. I felt slightly homesick as the coastline got thinner and less distinct. I called through to Braddles and told him that I was going to test my guns and he told me to carry on. I pointed the guns downward and pressed the firing button. There was slight vibration as the guns fired and a few seconds later I could see, splashes in the sea as the bullets hit the water. I felt comforted at this power in front of me. If I should have to use it I would have to be cool and think quickly but I had the necessary power and the knowledge to use it and the rest was up to me.

'I heard Berry ask if he should test his guns and shortly afterwards I heard him say 'My guns are OK Captain!'

'Our shadows sped across the sea below, keeping us company all the way. We were flying south and I called through to Berry and told him to keep a careful look-out and to beware of attacks from out of the sun. A fighter will very often attack from the glare of the sun, if he can and it is very necessary to keep a close watch in that direction. When we reached the Bay of Biscay there were a lot of small fishing-boats about. Some looked like steam trawlers while others had sails, some of which were brightly coloured. They were a lovely sight in the bright sunshine, with their colours standing out vividly against the blue background of the sea. I wondered if they were French or German but whichever they were, they looked very picturesque and peaceful. They were probably wondering far more who we were and where we were going! I hoped none of them were carrying wireless transmission sets.

'Just as we entered the Bay we saw an open boat crammed with men; obviously a shipwrecked crew. They waved frantically to us as we passed over the top of them, but there was nothing we could do then except note their position: on no account could we use our wireless and risk giving our own position away thereby jeopardizing our chances of reaching our objective undetected. My heart went out to those men, as I knew to a certain extent what they must be suffering. They must have been overjoyed when they saw us approaching and felt that surely they would get some help and their dismay must have been awful when they saw us pass by without apparently noticing them. I wondered how long they had been in that boat and how much water they had left. They might have been there for days or even weeks. I have often thought about them since and wondered if they were ever picked up: they were about fifty miles from the coast and there was no sign of any other Shipping near them at the time. I had no idea of their nationality, but I imagined them to be British.

'As we climbed, the French coast could just be seen away out on our port side. Occasionally it would disappear as the coastline withdrew into bays. I thought how different that stretch of coast must be to what it was a few years before. It was no longer the playground of the rich and the holiday-makers but the hiding-place of fighters which might come at us at any moment!

'The coast and the sky above us had to be watched very carefully by us, as the direction from which we might expect to be attacked. We were having to be very alert now, as we were well within the range of enemy fighters and I could no longer afford to let my mind wander allowing thoughts to drift idly through my mind. My job now was to defend our aeroplane: I was its ears and if necessary, its sting! My job was just beginning. I could afford to be idle up to now, but now I must be on the watch: I must concentrate alert and ready for instant action. At any moment a fighter might dive down at us out of the sun, undetected by those in front.

'I could sense the tension throughout the whole crew. No longer was there any idle chatter, remarking on things' we had seen, or things of little importance but a silence to be broken only by a remark vital to the job in hand. Each man was looking, searching intently in the direction most convenient to his position in the aeroplane. The silence was broken by Nick exclaiming, 'I can see a ship ahead. She looks like a cruiser!'

'Braddles swore. It would mean that as soon as we were spotted our position, course and even height would be signalled all along the coast even if it had not been done already by one of the trawlers over which we had passed! Our alertness and the concentration in our search was if anything intensified when we heard Nick's report. Within a few minutes the ship opened fire on us and I saw puffs of smoke appear in amongst the formation as if from nowhere. I immediately called through to Braddles to tell him but almost before I had finished speaking there was a salvo right underneath! We could hear the shells bursting with their dull thuds very close to us and at the same time the aeroplane would lurch as it was buffeted by the blast. They had got our range and height accurately straight away and for the next few minutes we had to fly through the barrage around us.

'The sky was getting thick with the smoke from bursting shells and several times I could smell the acrid stink of burnt explosives as we flew through the fumes. More shells were bursting all the time and I could see their yellow flashes followed instantly by grey puffs as they spread themselves across the sky. Sometimes they would burst just beside or underneath the aeroplane, which would heel over or appear to jump up several feet: sometimes there would be a string of grey puffs just beside us, dark at first, but getting lighter, which would rush by and by broken up as Johnny or some other aeroplane flew through them or sometimes they would continue rushing past just above or below the aeroplanes and be joined by more of the devilish little clouds. Occasionally I actually saw the shell on its upward flight, looking, like a silver streak soaring upwards, which would suddenly stop and give place to a grey puff. It was never alone; always surrounded and followed by others. Those near us could be heard and felt and sometimes even smelt: the muffled thud of the explosions was rather like the noise a brick might make as it hit the water when dropped down a deep well.

'Nobody spoke. We were too intent controlling our emotions. I sat perfectly still in my turret, watching fascinated this fury about me and wishing it would stop! It was too close for my comfort and peace of mind; it only needed a shell to burst a few feet nearer to us than those were doing already and we should, be blown from the sky.

'When we passed over the ship I was able to see her. How small she looked - just like a toy - to be sending up so many shells! It seemed strange to think that there were men - our enemies - below, working furiously in the hot sunshine to fire and reload the guns. Probably they would be cursing the sudden intrusion and wondering what it was all about. The ship was taking no chances, either and obviously she thought she might be our target for she was zigzagging about all over the surface of the water. She was safe, however, as we were after bigger fry!32

'When we got out of range of her guns the barrage ceased and we continued on our way as before. No one had been shot down or seriously damaged, as far as I could see. We were still in formation and were flying as though nothing untoward had happened. The sky was absolutely clear except for a grey haze behind us where the smoke from the shells still lingered as a reminder of the interruption a few moments before. The ship had finished her snaking and had settled down to a straight course, as I could see from the wake she left behind her.

'Another fifteen minutes'll see us there,' said Nick down the intercom.

'Keep a very careful look-out, everybody!' said Braddles.

'We were nearer the French coast now and I could just distinguish the fields and woods. I should have liked to be able to look longer at the coast, as this was the first time I had flown near France in the day time but I had to search the sky above, below and all around me. My eyes ached, staring and straining into, the dazzling blue of the sky. If there were fighters about we should soon see them, as we were very near our destination.

Berry suddenly said one word - 'Fighters!' down the intercom. Whether he intended the effect to be dramatic I don't know: probably not! Nevertheless, the word sounded distinctly dramatic coming as it did through the intercom. In his Canadian accent after a silence of ten minutes and it was followed a few seconds later by, 'They're away out on our port beam!'

'They were too far round for me to see them but in a few seconds I saw three more, flying in formation several miles away and well above us. They were not closing in, but were flying from the port quarter round to the starboard quarter and I gave their position and range to Braddles.

'There are some more climbing up,' Berry said.

'Evidently they did not intend to attack until they were up in full force: they seemed to be sizing us up and wondering how formidable a target we should be. Well they were soon to find out! More fighters were still climbing up to join those already up there. I could see three formations of three, which were shortly joined by six more. They were all about three miles away and showed no, signs of coming in yet. Berry said he could see about twelve more from the nose which were flying across our track and all several miles away. Still they did not come in to attack. Evidently they did not consider themselves strong enough even yet. Johnny had closed right in to us, with his wing tip only a few feet from our tail; and it was the same with number three. They came close in for mutual support, as the nearer they flew to us the better we should be able to protect ourselves by the combined fire from our turrets. Braddles was flying very well and the others were able to formate perfectly. Any hope we had had of carrying out a surprise attack had been forestalled, probably by the cruiser we had flown over a quarter of an hour before. They were waiting for us with their fighters and their guns and we should have to fight our way in and out again. More fighters were in the sky and still they seemed content to wait.

'We were within a few minutes of the target and Nick said he could see it clearly. The rest of the formation got into position ready to drop their bombs. I sat keyed up, waiting for what should come, Sitting waiting to, be attacked was a great strain. When were they going to come at us? We continued on, ever nearer the target and the fighters flew around us about two, miles away. I waited, ready.

'Suddenly the tell-tale puffs of smoke appeared! There were dozens of them and all around us and as we moved, fresh ones followed us. I was not watching out for the shell bursts, though I could see them and feel them and hear them all the time; I looking around for fighters watching those I could see and searching the sky for fresh ones. The sky behind us was getting thick with the fumes and smoke of shell bursts. They were firing all they had got right at us and as hard as they could. The thirty guns from the *Scharnhorst* were blazing away, supported by many more from the shore. The crump of the shells around and below us was incessant and many times I was blown hard against the side of my turret or off the seat yet I hardly noticed the barrage: I was waiting to be attacked, waiting to defend our aeroplane from the fighters that were ever increasing in numbers and were flying around us and above us, yet had not as yet started their assault. The sky was getting very thick with smoke and it was difficult to see. I no longer had a clear, unobstructed view around me: it was rather like looking through a fog or a thick haze, with fresh clouds appearing continuously.

'Jerry and Blake had gone back into the fuselage to man the beam guns, which were situated two on either side and about half way along the fuselage. They were standing there looking out and waiting for attacks. Suddenly the fighters seemed to be amongst us! Diving, climbing and twisting amongst us! For the moment our aeroplane was left alone and those behind us were getting the brunt of the attacks. The fighters were in amongst the flak bursts, which died down considerably when they started their attacks. I saw one burst into flames, roll over on its back and dive down towards the Sea, leaving a trail of black smoke behind it. Almost at the same time I saw one of our own aeroplanes diving down with smoke pouring .from two of its engines and with three fighters on its tail. I could not tell which one it was or who, was in it and I did not dare to watch it for long as I could not keep my eyes fixed in One place for more than a few seconds: I was continually looking around me, turning my turret first one way and then the other and peering through the Clouds, now in parts looking like storm clouds and all the time increasing. All the time .Johnny was near us, following our every move, I saw two fighters diving on his tail from above. One of them continued on its dive past his tail with smoke belching from it!

'Through all the medley and the noise of shell bursts around us I heard Nick giving direction to Braddles in his bombing run-up: he sounded entirely oblivious to the hell let loose around him and only conscious of the target below him. As I heard him giving his directions of 'lefts', 'rights' and 'steadys', I could feel the aeroplane turn and check as Braddles made the corrections. 'Bombs gone!' he finally said and then, almost immediately I got a wizard sight.

'All the time I was waiting and wondering why we were not being attacked: I almost wished we were, as I could do something then. As it was, all I could do was to sit and watch and wait for our turn and watch our aeroplanes being shot at! Under normal conditions I should have been absorbed and scared by the flak bursting so frequently and so near us. The crumps underneath, behind and on either side of us, seemed to follow one another almost without pause. Several times I felt the jar and thud as splinters hit us and tore through the fuselage and tail, yet only part of my mind registered and realized the fact. I could do nothing about it anyway. I could only sit and watch and hope that we should get no fatal hits. My mind was absorbed with the fighters and wondering when they were going to attack. I could do something with them that was what I was there for. I was there to fight back but I could not fight unless they first came at us. That was what was getting me down, watching them, waiting and unable to do anything.

'Almost as soon as Nick said 'Bombs Gone' I saw a fighter diving down on us. I immediately called through to Braddles: 'Fighter diving down port quarter up!'

'I started giving him directions for turning and at the same time I elevated my guns to meet the attack. As we turned, the fighter passed over the top of us and disappeared from my range of vision.

'As soon as I lost sight of this one, I saw another one climbing up at us and again I called through to Braddles:

'Fighter starboard quarter down!'

'The fighter started firing at us almost as soon as I spotted' it and I saw the flashes from his guns and the tracers streaking past us. He was using cannon and was really out of range of my machine-guns. However, I opened fire, hoping to put him off, as I had plenty of ammunition and could afford to use it. He came steadily in, firing in bursts and I replied with my guns: he still came in, getting nearer and still I fired back. I could hear and feel his shells and bullets striking the fuselage just behind me and still he came in, ever nearer. I felt no antagonism, but was calm yet determined to shoot him down. I felt as a boxer or a duellist might feel, pitting his skill against that of his opponent. 'Why hasn't he gone down?' I kept thinking 'surely I must be hitting him?' yet he was still able to hit back and his tracers still kept streaming past me!' And why haven't I been hit?' I thought, as he still kept closing in. We were twisting about the sky and he was following us, shooting all the time.

'I had no feeling of fright, only of amazement that I had not shot him down, as we seemed to have been shooting at each other for so long. I was also amazed that I had not been hit, as the bullets and cannon shells were pouring all around me continuously. Perhaps I had been hit and did not know it. I would look around afterwards.

'Out of the corner of my eye I saw part of the tail plane ripped away by a cannon shell and almost at the same time the fighter rolled over on his back and went into a spin! I felt a vast feeling of relief surge through me as I called through to Braddles and said, 'I've got him!'

'The whole combat seemed to have gone on for a very long time, although really it could have lasted only for a few seconds. I began to feel very scared. I was too intent while we were being attacked, to feel at all frightened but now that there was a lull from activity against us for a few seconds, I felt my heart pounding against my chest and my, throat and mouth felt dry. Outwardly I was perfectly calm though and ready for further attacks.

'Almost as soon as I said 'I've got him' I heard Blake calling:

'Jerry has been hit, sir.'

'Is he bad?' Braddles asked.

'Yes sir, I think so. I'm doing all I can.'

'All around us the shells were bursting and the air was even blacker with smoke now like great dark clouds through which we were flying. Bombers and fighters were flying and twisting amongst it.

'I saw another Halifax diving down with smoke pouring from it and two more fighters diving to their doom, one in flames and the other obviously out of control. I could see another Halifax with three fighters close behind its tail.

'My turret was thick with cordite fumes, which were making me cough.

'I think he's dead, sir' Blake said.

'Fighters were all around now, but none were actually attacking us. We were getting away from the flak and the air was becoming clearer. Two fighters were chasing us from behind but they were not firing at us yet and were not within range.

'Where is he hit?' Braddles asked.

'In the chest' Blake answered. 'I can't see any other marks.'

'Jerry was standing by his guns watching out for fighters when he was hit. He was jumping up and down in his excitement, as he had just seen a fighter crash into the sea in flames. Suddenly he turned round and looked at Blake with a surprised expression on his face and slowly sank down and rolled over ... dead.[33]

'The fighters who were chasing us gave up and I saw them turn away: they had probably had enough for one day and did not want to get taken too far from their base. Two of my guns had jammed and were out of action: I had noticed they had stopped, as soon as I had ceased firing, but I had decided not to touch them while there was a chance of being attacked again at any moment but to wait until I had more breathing space. I still had two more guns working and I felt confident of them in an emergency.

'Now that there were no fighters within about half a mile of me, I had a look at the stopped guns. One I was able to put right quite easily and I fired a short burst to make certain that it was working but the other one I should have to dismantle when 'we were well clear of the target.

'Johnny was fairly close behind us and on our starboard, with another Halifax slightly behind him but those were all I could see at the moment. The second one I noticed had white smoke belching from behind one of his engines which 'meant that one of his radiators had gone and that very soon that engine would stop. However, he could carry on with three engines quite well.

'The area we had just left was thick with what looked like dark ugly clouds consisting of smoke fumes hanging like a pall over the target, where twenty minutes before there had been bright blue sky. It seemed to be hanging there in mourning for the dead.

'As I watched this dark and dreary mass behind us I saw two more Halifaxes appear: we were making for sea level or rather, about a thousand feet above it and they were doing the same.

'How many Halifaxes can you see from the tail?' Braddles asked.

'I can see three altogether; our number two and two others some way behind' I replied.

'Let me know if you see any more.'

We were still within sight of the French coast and I kept a look out chiefly in that direction.

'How are you feeling, front gunner?' I asked.

'I'm feeling fine sir. How about you?'

'I'm OK' I replied.

'I'm going to fly well clear of the coast navigator' I heard Braddles say to Nick.

'I looked round at the tall plane that had been hit: there was a large ragged hole there and the fabric where it had been ripped away was flapping behind like streamers. I saw that the hole was in the starboard elevator and that the whole structure was badly damaged.

'I called through to Braddles to tell him about it and' he sent Wheeler back to have a look. Wheeler reported that it was OK and he also said that the fuselage round by the tail was full' of holes. I knew it must be so, as I had heard and felt the pullets and cannon shells hitting and tearing into it. Braddles asked him how the engines were and he replied that one was running very hot and that it would probably pack up pretty soon. He also said that one of the tanks must be badly damaged, as it was neatly empty. We had a good two hours' flying before reaching our own coast, so our position did not look too good. What further damage had been done we could not tell but we were still flying, which was the main thing, anyway.

'I felt very depressed. All the excitement I had felt while I was in combat had died down and reaction had set in. Jerry was lying dead just behind me and I was thinking of him all the time: I remembered how cheerful and happy and how much alive he had always seemed and how he had always been smiling and laughing. Less than half an hour ago he had been alive not thinking of himself; only that our trip should be a success and now he was dead; killed by a fighter he never even saw. I had shot down the fighter that killed Jerry, but too late not before Jerry had been killed.

'I turned and looked through the glass panel behind my back and saw him lying on the floor with his helmet still on and his oxygen mask over his face. Blake had folded his hands across his chest. I remembered how I had seen him before how he had sprung into the aeroplane laughing and so full of life and spirit and I felt very miserable as I saw him lying there dead and so still. I thought of his mother and how she would feel: it is those who are left behind who have to suffer.

'Blake was sitting beside Jerry with his head between his hands and he looked about all in, poor chap. I suggested to Braddles that he might go forward now, as we were well away from the target so he called him. Blake said he thought he had something in his eye. Actually there was a tiny shell splinter embedded there. We discovered later that he had three other wounds as well two bullet wounds in his leg and a shell splinter in his shoulder but he said he knew nothing about them and did not even know he had been hit until after he had got out of the aeroplane. He said his leg felt a bit stiff! We were silent for some time. Reaction from our activity had set in and I think we all felt rather miserable. The silence was broken by Berry's Canadian accent: 'Say, Captain; is there a lavatory aboard this ship?' The tension was broken for me then, as I saw the unconscious humour of his remark and I was able to laugh particularly when Braddles said that he had not heard; and asked him to repeat it.

'We had lost sight of the French coast and were flying about a thousand feet above the sea calm and blue and a vast contrast to the grimness we had left behind. The sun was beating into my turret and once again I was conscious of the heat.

'I felt suffocated in my turret, which still stank with the burnt cordite fumes and I would have given anything to be able to stand in a cool breeze. I felt very cramped, too and would have loved to get out and stretch. However, I would have to stay where I was, as it was not safe to leave my turret even for a minute: at any moment more fighters might come at us from the shore, only just beyond the horizon on our starboard. Reports would have been sent all along the coast that we were returning and even now fighters were probably looking for us. We would not be safe until we reached the shelter of our own shore, still about an hour and a half away.

'There were not so many ships and boats about .now, as we were considerably farther out to sea than we had been on our outward journey. Those we did see seemed to have lost much of the beauty they had had before.

'D'you know where we are navigator?' Braddles asked Nick.

'Not exactly, sir but I think we're all right. I can't be certain though, without the wireless.'

'How are we off for petrol, Wheeler?'

'About another hour and a half, sir.'

'We'll make for the Cornish coast' Braddles decided. I'll land at --!'

'This bucked me up quite a lot, as it was quite near my home and with any luck I should be able to get there that night. I felt I wanted to go home but we were still a long way away. I was very tired.

'Johnny was flying in close formation to us again: he had all his four engines running and I could not see any sign of damage to his machine. Once he flew right over, the top of us and I imagine he was having a close look to see how much damage we had sustained. The other aircraft had dropped back, about a mile behind. I told Braddles this and he asked me to let him know if it dropped back any farther. Johnny was evidently worrying about him, too, as he turned around arid flew alongside. I reported this to Braddles, who said we would continue on as we were, as Johnny seemed to be OK we would have only just enough petrol to get back as it was and he could not afford to lose any distance by turning round. Johnny and the other aeroplane were flying together and there was nothing we could do by flying with them so we continued on alone.

'I watched our shadow on the water now all alone and I missed seeing Johnny just behind us: he had seemed so secure and steady. I could still see him and the other aircraft behind us, but they were gradually losing distance.

'We were running into some low, misty cloud which in a way was an advantage, as it would shield us from possible fighter attacks. It looked like a sea mist or fog and seemed to be right down on the water. When we ran into it I lost sight of the aeroplanes behind us. The mist was in patches and we kept flying through it and into bright sunshine again alternately. When we came out of it I could see a film of moisture on the tail plane and on the perspex round my turret. It was quite a relief flying through this mist, as the sun for a short time ceased to blaze down on me and I felt almost cool. This misty cloud did not last for long and once again we flew into clear, cloudless sky. The sun beating down on to the sea below and behind us sent up a dazzling, shimmering brightness which burnt my eyes. I looked at my watch and saw that we had about another forty-five minutes to go before reaching our coast.

'Nick gave Braddles a change of course which meant that we must have been at a point somewhere west of Brest and were making a turn to starboard to bring us to the Cornish coast. After we turned, the sun was no longer right behind us, which I found a relief but slightly on our starboard.

'There was no sign of shipping or land, only a vast expanse of sea below us, calm and clear and blue, disappearing into a misty horizon. It would be the same sea beating against the shores of Cornwall, a coast I knew and loved well.

'Unpleasant and uncomfortable thoughts began passing through my mind. I imagined what would happen if Nick was wrong in his navigation if the course he had given Braddles would not take us to the Cornish coast, but past Land's End and up the Irish Sea. We might pass right clear of the west coast and run out of petrol without ever seeing land! Or Wheeler might be wrong ill his calculations of our petrol supply and we might have even less than he thought and run out just as land came in sight! Or the petrol gauges might be wrong and even at this moment the tanks might be nearly dry and the engines sucking their last few gallons

'I drove these thoughts from my mind as being unnecessarily foolish and weak. Nevertheless, they were unpleasant while they lasted.

'How is the petrol, Wheeler?' Braddles asked.

'About another forty-five minutes sir,' Wheeler told him.

'What is our ETA at the coast, Navigator?' Braddles asked again.

'Another thirty minutes should see us there,' Nick answered.

'As soon as we hit the coast, give me a course for --' Braddles said.

'We certainly had not much petrol to spare. The aircraft was flying quite steadily and the engine that Wheeler had his doubts about was still functioning though it was losing a lot of power.

'I think I can see some land' I heard Berry say from the nose, sometime later.

'Pray God he's right!' I thought and began to feel more cheerful.

'With land in sight we should soon be back and an unpleasant day would be just another memory.

'There was no sign of the other aircraft: I had not seen anything of them since we got into the misty clouds. I hoped they were all right. They had probably changed course before we had: one of them was sure to have wireless, in which case they would know exactly where they were.

'I peered on either side of me, looking for the land but I could not see far enough forward. It must have been quite close, as I heard Braddles say to Nick, 'Can you get a pin-point yet, navigator?'

'We must have been a bit too far west, for in a moment I heard Nick give a course bringing us farther east.

'At last, by leaning forward, I was just able to see the coast some miles away on my right. What a glorious sight it was! I thought that I had never been so pleased to see the shore. It was even better than when returning home at night, as I was able to see it showing clearly in detail in the sunlight whereas at night usually all one can see is a thin, pale streak.

'Our journey was nearly over and I was just beginning to realize how tired and exhausted I really was. The past few hours had been a great strain owing to the need for constant concentration and also that uncertainty all the time of wondering if we should make it.

'As we crossed the coast and I was able to look down into the rocks and wonderfully clear sea below, a wave of happiness and relief surged over me. This was home and looking at its best, alive and, clear and clean. We passed the rocky coast and over the short green turf and scrubby trees above the cliffs. Then cattle and sheep were grazing as I had seen them six hours earlier. We crossed the valleys with their rocky streams, the hills criss-crossed with their stone walls over the woods and the little villages all so quiet and peaceful and unhurried. This was home and England, a sight one has to lose and be away from to fully appreciate and enjoy.

'The ambulance came alongside after we landed and 1 stayed in my turret until Jerry had been lifted from the aeroplane. I had seen him jump in so cheerfully and happily and 1 felt I could not bear to see him carried out dead.

'There was a group of people round our 'plane as we got out and one of them said to me, 'Who was he; the tail gunner?'

'No' I replied. 'I'm the tail gunner.'

'We were not the only Halifax to land there; there were four of us altogether. We had parked next to one and 1 saw that the tail turret had been nearly blown away. Medical orderlies were still trying to extricate the gunner.

'1 felt very weak and sat down on the grass. Someone offered me a cigarette. I said I would smoke my pipe.

'After we had been interrogated and had had a meal and some drinks, I hired a car and drove home, taking Nick with me.'

Four Halifaxes were lost and all the remainder damaged.[34] All crews, except one whose bombs had hung-up, had succeeded in delivering an attack - but only one claimed a direct hit. Five direct hits had actually been scored, but three were by armour-piercing bombs that passed right through the *Scharnhorst*, each leaving only a small hole; the remaining two did explode, but caused only minor damage. A contemporary account said: 'In the act of bombing, the bomber crews took photographs of the cruisers, which were then each in dry dock, side by side. It was a very clear day, methods of aerial photography had by this time been improved and the photographs came out extremely clear, They showed the bursting of the bombs in a continuous succession of pictures, the first with the characteristic thick mushroom of smoke that rises immediately after the bomb has burst and the rest with the smoke streaming upwards, higher and higher in each successive photograph. Armour-piercing bombs produce so much smoke and there was so much in the photographs, that at first the photographic-interpretation officers had to determine whether by any chance some of it came from the smoke screen. But it soon became obvious that nothing but smoke from bombs could have produced this particular effect, at first the mushrooms and then the pillars of smoke getting higher and higher. The smoke may well have hidden the effect of some of the bombs and more damage may well have been done than is visible in the photographs. But the following is at any rate quite certain. One heavy bomb fell between the starboard side of the stern of the *Gneisenau* and the side of the dry dock in which she lay. The explosion may be expected to have damaged the ship's steering gear, the shafts of the propellers and the propellers themselves. Fragments of the heavily cased armour-piercing bomb may well have penetrated the side of the ship, for the distance between the ship and the side of the dock was only some twenty or thirty feet and an explosion in this confined space would be very destructive. Similarly another bomb fell between the port side of the stern of the *Scharnhorst* and the side of the dock in which she lay, with the same probable effects. It is almost certain, though the confusion of smoke precludes absolute certainty, that a heavy bomb fell amidships and penetrated the deck of the *Scharnhorst*. The gates of the two docks were closed, at the time of the attack; both gates slide into a recess between the docks when they are open; this recess had a direct hit and it was reasonable to suppose that the ships could not be removed until the damage was put right. All round the ships other bombs had fallen and these must have done considerable damage to the docks and quite possibly to the ships themselves. The submarine pens behind the seaplane base to the west of the dry docks were also heavily bombed during the attack; the photographs showed that they had received one certain and two almost certain hits. Buildings, possibly workshops, behind the submarine pens had been laid flat.'

The Germans decided that *Scharnhorst* should return at once for the better repair facilities and flak cover at Brest and she sailed that night with much water inside the ship (reports vary between 3,000 and 7,000 tons of water). This operation was, therefore, a major success in that it ensured that this powerful warship was forced to stay in harbour for a further prolonged period, four months being required for repairs.[35]

Six hits were claimed on the *Gneisenau* but could not be confirmed. The German fighter opposition was stronger and more prolonged than expected and ten Wellingtons and two Hampdens were lost to fighter attack or flak.[36] A contemporary account saw the attack on Brest somewhat differently and somewhat spectacularly:

'On 24 July, two hours after midday, Bomber Command began the heaviest daylight attack which the RAF had yet made since the outbreak of war. Three targets, hundreds of miles apart, were attacked according to plan - that is, with complete punctuality, with an absolute co-ordination of tactics and with unhurried determination in the face of all the German defences. Blenheims were out in force to make a diversion by attacking the port of Cherbourg, where they hit and set on fire a whale-oil ship and damaged the harbour. The main weight of the attack was against Brest; it was led by a formation of Fortress I aircraft of the Bomber Command. These arrived over Brest at a fantastic height, scarcely visible and scarcely audible to anyone on the ground; in all probability the rising scream, of their bombs was the first and the only sign that the Fortresses were there. In the icy cold, with frost and rime a quarter of an inch thick on all the windows, the crews looked down on Brest in the summer sunlight below and it seemed, as one of the pilots said, 'no bigger than your thumb.' They could see no individual houses, but occasionally there was a flash of light, as though from a tiny mirror, where the sun was glancing on windows or on small patches of water. A heavy load of American bombs was aimed at the minute ship below. It seemed an almost impossible time before the flashes of the bombs were seen, but when at last they came, even from that height they were impressive. A sudden attack from such a great height must have done much to confuse the enemy fighters and before they could be ready to meet it a tight formation of Hampdens had swept in far below the Fortresses. And the Hampdens had come with a guard of Spitfires, which had scarcely ever gone so far before and for which the Germans were probably quite unready. Certainly the Messerschmitts which came up to intercept the Hampdens were quite unable to check the ferocity of the attack; the Hampdens approached their targets, bombed and darted away to leave room for a procession of Wellingtons that followed. The Fortresses were still overhead and, as the Hampdens bombed, the Fortress crews saw a star cluster of flashes round the *Gneisenau*.

'Without a pause the Wellingtons attacked and fought their way through. 'It was a marvellous sight' a pilot said 'to see bombers ahead of us and bombers behind us in the sunshine, with the fighters wheeling overhead. All the little ships in the harbour were scuttling out to sea as we came in, with frightened traits of white foam behind them.' In all there were seven direct hits, all with heavy armour-piercing bombs, on the *Gneisenau*. A flight commander described how a bomb from one of the aircraft he was commanding hit the ship. 'The ship was perfectly plain,' he said, 'and one of, our bombs hit it. Whether it was camouflaged or not, it looked just like a battle-cruiser to me and all its guns seemed to be going at once.' Such a success was not got without losses or without desperate fighting. Even while the anti-aircraft barrage from Brest was at its height Messerschmitt 109s made to intercept the Hampdens. But the Hampdens shot down at least three of the enemy and probably one more. One Hampden and one Messerschmitt opened fire at the same moment. The Messerschmitt turned over on its, back but went on firing and hit the Hampden's wireless set and the inner port tank. But the Messerschmitt went down in a steep dive and the Hampden's bullets followed it; it tried to pull up at 1,000 feet, failed and hit the ground on the coast. The crew of one bomber saw a Hampden falling towards the sea and at the very same moment a Messerschmitt falling north of Brest and bursting into flames on the ground. The Wellingtons had as hard a battle. One was fiercely attacked by two Messerschmitt 109Fs; it destroyed one and badly damaged the other. Yet another Messerschmitt fell like a stone after an engagement with a Wellington and as it fell the Wellington's rear gunner fired 150 rounds straight into its belly. It hit the ground and exploded. It was after this attack that, as I have described before, a Wellington caught fire and landed in England with so much of its fabric burnt away that it was almost a skeleton.

'The *Scharnhorst* at La Pallice was attacked by Halifaxes; they had no fighter escort and had to meet as much opposition as the Stirlings on the day before. They fought back and bombed with precision and the crew of one Halifax marked a direct hit on the deck of the battle-cruiser and afterwards saw a pillar of black smoke rise 1,000 feet. The fighters which had accompanied the bombers to Brest shot down at least twelve Messerschmitts; the bombers themselves, both at Brest and La Pallice, shot down twenty-one, probably destroyed seven more and damaged nine others.

'Within a short while the *Scharnhorst* was back at Brest and there she remained, together with the *Gneisenau* and *Prinz Eugen*, until 12 February 1942. But there were indications towards the end of December 1941 that the ships, though repeatedly hit during night attacks between July and the end of the year, were getting ready to come out again. Further abortive attempts were made to sink the German warships holed up in Brest and though black smoke was reported rising from the *Gneisenau*, the ships remained afloat.'

On 35 Squadron at Linton-on-Ouse one morning early in December Flight Lieutenant Richard C. Rivaz was in Leonard Cheshire's office for his usual morning visit. Rivaz had been Cheshire's tail gunner on 102 Squadron and was with him on the night of 12/13 November 1940 when Cheshire had been awarded the DSO for bringing his very badly damaged Whitley home to Driffield. The first thing Cheshire said to Rivaz was: 'I've got news for you, Revs.'

'What is it? Don't tell me you're posted.'

'No, nothing like that: There's to be daylight in the near future.'

'Are you flying?' I asked him quickly. 'If so I'm coming with you.'

'I'm afraid not Revs. At least, that's the verdict at the moment. I shall try and work it though. The Wing Commander is flying and wants you with him.'

'I wish to goodness you were going, Leonard!'

'So do I 'Revs' but there we are.'

'As you say 'there we are'! D'you know where were going?'

'Leonard pointed to the map and put his finger on Brest. 'But for God's sake, not a word,' he added. 'Only the Wing Commander, you and I know the target and it must be kept dark.'

Rivaz went up to see Wing Commander 'Robby' Robinson. Basil Vernon Robinson was a pre-war pilot, born in Gateshead in 1912 and initially commissioned in the RAF in 1933. He quickly distinguished himself playing Rugby as a wing three-quarter for the RAF and his home county XVs and by April 1938 had been promoted to Flight Lieutenant. By 1941 he had risen to Squadron Leader and been awarded a DFC in July of that year during an operational tour on 78 Squadron. An ebullient character, with a distinctly unorthodox approach to certain RAF customs and procedures, his trademark was a generously proportioned ginger bushy moustache. Robinson had joined 35 Squadron in late 1941, at Linton-on-Ouse.

'We've got to keep this show as quiet as we can,' the Wing Commander went on. 'I propose to have a meeting of all the flying crews this, morning and tell them all I can but it is essential there is no talking about it afterwards. We've got about another nine days and we'll spend all the time in formation flying and practice bombing!'

'Leonard has told me the news, sir.' I said to him.

'I don't know much more than you do yet, Riv,' he replied' but we've got to get in bags of training, Who shall we take as front gunner?'

'I don't know, sir: I'll think it over and let you know.'

'The weather was good - cold and clear with the ground frozen hard - and we got busy right away. There were to be forty bombers on the job altogether and we were, supplying six of them, with Robby leading. During the days before the actual raid we practised every day: we practised flying in formation and bombing in formation and we got really good. I thought it might be a good scheme for the rear gunners to fly with the main perspex panel taken out of their turrets and I took the panel out of mine to try the idea. The first time I tested it we did not go above two thousand feet and I was delighted with the scheme. It meant that we should have a perfectly clear view behind as there was nothing to obstruct our vision; the entire front of the turret being exposed to the outside air. But the next time I flew in the open turret we were at 15,000 feet and a temperature of -30 degrees centigrade! Although we were only up at that height for an hour, I thought I had got frostbite. The cold beating in was agonizing and I felt thoroughly miserable and decided then and there that we should not fly with the turrets open!

'I enjoyed those days of training and practice. The weather was perfect and every day was brilliantly clear. We usually flew at fifteen thousand feet, which was the height at which we intended to operate. The ground from that height appears very unreal; rather like a beautifully painted large-scale map. Sometimes we left vapour trails behind us which looked like great spiral, horizontal columns of white smoke swirling in our wake: there were always four of them, one from each engine and they completely obscured the aircraft formating behind us, as would a thick fog. Sometimes these great swirling, spiral trails followed us the whole time we were up at that height and at other times they would cease for a few miles as suddenly as they had started and then gush forth again. They were a nuisance when we were in formation, as they left the aeroplanes behind us enveloped in their swirling fog.

'I chose Dick as our front gunner. I had never flown with him before, but I knew him to be sound. We had Freddy as our navigator, Joe as our wireless operator, Tom as our engineer and Peter as second pilot. Robby seemed very pleased with his crew and we were certainly happy with him.

'The raid was detailed for 18 December and the formation had reached a high standard of flying. On the night before the raid I had a bad bout of 'stage fright'. As I lay in bed my imagination got the better of me for a bit and ran riot. All sorts of nightmarish horrors raced through my mind as I lay bathed in perspiration, despite the cold winter night. I saw fighters coming at us unmercifully from all directions; my turret was out of action, with me in it unable to fight back: I saw myself trapped in my turret with flames around me and unable to conquer them: I heard and saw shells bursting about me, tearing through the aircraft and my turret: I saw myself having to land on the sea: all these and many other horrors were with me as I lay in the dark, trying to sleep. Very weak and foolish, no doubt, but there I was while I was at the mercy of my imagination. Nor was I free from imaginings when I was asleep, as that night I dreamt I was taken prisoner!

'We were to take off at ten o'clock and all the crews met in the crew room before it was light to hear a final discussion of plans. We had been briefed the previous evening, so we knew what was expected of us. The *Scharnhorst*, *Gneisenau* and *Prinz Eugen* were all lying in Brest harbour and we were shown photographs and large-scale diagrams, as well as a coloured chalk drawing on the blackboard giving their exact positions. I knew most of these drawings by heart, having been to Brest before at night. Brest is a very well defended target and of course during the time the ships were there the defences were very much increased. It was pretty evident that we should be in for a hot time. We were to have a strong fighter escort, which was a considerable comfort. Altogether, there were forty bombers, consisting of sixteen Stirlings, fourteen Halifaxes and ten Manchesters. The Stirlings were to lead the way in, followed by the Halifaxes, who in turn would be followed by the Manchesters.

'There was a thick white frost when we went out to our aeroplanes and it was still freezing hard. The ground crew were waiting for us, muffled in greatcoats, scarves and Balaclava helmets. Some of them were beating their arms across their chests and stamping their feet, trying to get warm. Our aeroplane was gleaming white with frost, which glistened as the rays of the sun - just appearing above the horizon - glanced across it. The perspex round my turret was caked with an opaque white brine, which re-formed almost as soon as I wiped it away. I used a rag soaked in petrol, but even this froze almost at once and it was obvious that I should have to wait for the frost to clear itself when we climbed to a drier atmosphere. Some airmen were standing on the wings and tail plane, sweeping away with brooms the frost, which fell to the ground like fine powdered snow. The sun showing just above the hills in the distance was throwing its silver rays horizontally across the ground and casting elongated and grotesque shadows from the aeroplanes. The ground shone and sparkled, crisp and clean: it was a perfect English morning.

'The Station Commander drove up with the AOC, who had come to see us off. They stopped and talked with us for a few minutes and then wished us luck and moved off to the other aeroplanes.

'It was time to start up, so we got in and I pushed and struggled my way to my turret, where there was no room to spare. Shortly after we were airborne my perspex cleared itself of the frost and I was able to see out quite distinctly. Wilkie was formating on our starboard and Willie on our port. Wilkie was a tall, dark-haired, loose-limbed fellow and the first impression a stranger might have of, him could be that he was a rather irresponsible, carefree and vague individual. But on closer acquaintance it would be seen that he had one of the kindest, gentlest and most sympathetic and thoughtful natures any man could possess. Curiously enough, he was carrying the same gunner that Johnny had had on our previous daylight raid.

'I have flown with Wilkie on two operational trips, so I know all his sterling qualities. He has the knack of inspiring confidence in every member of his crew. I certainly look back on the trips I did with him, which were to Brest and Wilhelmshaven, with very happy memories. When flying he is always perfectly calm and I cannot imagine anything disturbing him. Each time I reported back to him searchlights behind our tail, or flak bursts particularly near the tail, or fighters in the distance, ne replied with one word - 'Right' - spoken in a long-drawn-out way and in a manner to make you feel that all was right.

'A good captain can inspire confidence and well-being in his crew by his manner and by the way he speaks or replies. I have flown with some excellent captains and I know! A good crew is like a happy family, all working together, thinking together and in an emergency acting together and for each other.

'Willie was a young sergeant pilot and one with whom I had always wanted to fly, but had never had the opportunity. He was a first class pilot, but very modest, shy and unobtrusive.

'Robby, Wilkie and Willie had been flying together in formation for the past nine days and they knew each other's ways of flying perfectly.

'Shortly after Wilkie and Willie formated on us, I saw our second formation of three come up and take- up their position about three hundred yards behind us. We climbed steadily, still circling the aerodrome, which appeared smaller and smaller and less distinct. In the distance I could see six more Halifaxes coming towards us and as they came nearer I saw four more appear out of the blue. We still continued to climb and circle, while the others, in their turn, took up their positions in our rear.

'When we reached ten thousand feet we set course in a south-westerly direction and once again I watched and enjoyed the ever-changing panorama below us. The sun was slightly to my right and almost enveloped Wilkie's aeroplane in its brilliance. I was well dressed to meet the cold, but all my clothes made movement in my turret well-nigh impossible. I sat with my hands on the control column, moving the turret every few minutes to prevent it freezing. We crossed the Welsh mountains - looking rather like the relief maps you see in schools - and made our way towards Lundy Island where we were to meet the Stirlings and Manchesters. The Stirlings had arrived there a few minutes before we did and the Manchesters appeared as we formated behind the Stirlings.

'So we set course for Brest along, formidable line of determined might on that cold, clear December morning. There was very little cloud about and I watched Lundy Island - looking rather lonely - fade into the background of blue and then the rugged coast of Cornwall stretched away on either side, 15,000 feet below. I was within a few miles of my home; and I looked longingly down on this shore that I know so well and wondered what was happening there.

'It did not take long to pass over this narrow stretch of land and we were soon over the sea again well on the way towards our objective. Our own land was gradually disappearing and getting farther away as the enemy got nearer. As the French coast came in sight to those in front, I asked Robby if he could see any fighters.

'Yes, plenty, but I can't see what they are yet.'

'Well, we shall soon see,' I thought and I hoped they were our escort. There would be no difficulty in sighting our target, as the sea stretched clear and blue below us, with only occasional wisps of fleecy cloud.

As was previously arranged, Wilkie dropped behind and below us; Willie behind and below him; and the same with the other three, as we neared the target. This was the formation we intended to bomb from and it would allow each of us to bomb the target with a greater degree of accuracy. I looked along the line bobbing up and down behind us, as I had seen them so many times on our practice flights

'As we neared the target the guns opened on us: They had been concentrating on the Stirlings and now that we were getting within range, they started on us!

It was as I had expected and experienced before; just as noisy, uncomfortable and unpleasant. The first few shells went above us and to starboard but they soon corrected this and we flew through and into the puffs which a split second before had been destructive, white hot, ragged chunks of steel. As I looked down the line I saw the shells bursting around each of the aeroplanes. Sometimes a shell seemed to burst right on one of them and I knew that only a split second and a question of feet had saved it from complete destruction. Once Willie was blown on to his side and almost on to his back and for a horrible moment I thought he was going down, as he swung right out, shuddered on his side and more shells burst around him. However, he recovered in some miraculous manner and resumed his place in the formation as though nothing had happened.

'There were no fighters near us; our escort was seeing to that but I could see them flying around in pairs some distance off. Once or twice I saw a scrap, but they were too far away for me to see much. I kept my turret moving continually, looking around me ready for the odd Jerry that might sneak through our screen.

'I heard Robby say 'Bomb doors open!' and knew that he would have sighted the target and would be preparing for the bombing 'run-up'. Shells were bursting around us incessantly, causing our aeroplane to shudder and lurch. I saw the bomb doors open in the other aircraft down the line. We were all ready to drop our load.

'The barrage seemed to be increasing in intensity; as though those below were determined we should never drop our bombs. They hoped to turn us back; make us waver or have us down but I knew that nothing would make Robby take any evasive action until after he had dropped his bombs. We had not been practising for the past nine days and come all this way for nothing! The shells kept screaming and bursting around us as we went, six formidable monsters ready to pounce on our prey. Freddy had got the ships in his sights and was giving his 'lefts' and 'rights' and 'steady' and finally, 'Bombs gone! Each aircraft in turn released its bombs and I saw them start their journey down. As they left their racks they seemed to hover for a second and then drop rapidly, gradually pointing their noses to the ground. While I watched the weight of bombs on their downward drop, Robby called to me: 'See if you can spot where they fall, Riv.'

'I leant forward, peering down and as I watched I was hurled hard against the side of my turret while the aeroplane shuddered and rocked on its side, losing height rapidly. At the same time there was a crash like a breaking plate-glass window as shrapnel tore through my turret, ripping open the sleeve of my flying coat and tunic. I did not know if a piece had gone through me or not! I felt no pain, so imagined I had escaped.

'The aeroplane was steady now but was gradually losing height. Wilkie and Willie had taken up their positions again on either side and kept close to us. Black smoke was belching past the tail from both port engines. 'I called through and told Robby, who said - "Yes, they're on fire.' 'Would nothing upset the man?' I wondered. The shells were still at us, mingling their smoke with the smoke from our engines.

'I think the fires are dying down,' I heard Freddy say. The smoke was certainly less dense and I began to think that there might be hope for us yet. That first sight of black dirty smoke rushing past my turret had seemed final, somehow. It does not take long for fire to spread in the air and I knew the flames might gradually be getting nearer the wing tanks.

'Yes, the smoke and sparks had ceased to gush out so fearfully and had thinned down to a faint grey, which at last disappeared altogether. Both engines had stopped and we were listing hard to starboard. The port wing had taken the brunt of the shock as the shell burst: it must have burst just in front of the wing, hurtling splinters through both engines. The shells had ceased and Brest was disappearing behind us. Wilkie and Willie were still with us, like faithful dogs following their weary master home.

'Send out an SOS. We're coming down in the sea!'

'Time seemed to stand still as I heard Robby say this to Joe. It was as though a death sentence had been passed on me. So my nightmare of the previous night was coming true, after all! I felt empty inside. God! I had done this before; I knew what it was like.

'Can't you make it, sir?' I called through to Robby.

'No. I'm afraid you're in for another ducking, Riv old boy.'

'How much longer sir?'

'Ten more minutes.'

'Ten more minutes! What then? Was this to be the end, after all? I knew no Halifax had as yet landed on the sea and got away with it. How should we fare? As we hit the water, would it be the end? Or would we float for days, getting weaker all the time?

'What would happen? Ten more minutes, less now. Oh, hell!'

'This won't do! We were still alive and there might be hope. Yes, there was always a chance! We were still alive and we were clear of Brest! That was what really mattered.

'Five more minutes now! There was silence down the intercom except for Joe's tapping on the Morse key as he methodically sent out SOS's.

'Stand by for ditching!'

'I hurriedly left my turret and went forward. My actions were mechanical. I knew what to do: 'Mae West' inflated, boots tightly strapped, flying clothing fastened, helmet on and also securely fastened these things I looked to as I made my way forward, pushing and squeezing my way past the tail wheel leg, through the rear bulkhead door and so to the centre of the fuselage. As I passed by the side fuselage windows I looked down at the sea, so calm and blue yet as hard as concrete to hit. I opened the rear escape hatch in the roof, ready for a hasty exit. Freddy and Dick were already in the fuselage and they were followed by Joe, Sam and Peter. All exchanged what were intended to be reassuring smiles. Freddy and I lay on the floor with our feet braced against the main spar and the others were farther forward on the beds. So we waited; for what?

'As I lay looking up at the blue sky through the open hatch above my head, my thoughts raced, tumbling over each other. What would happen? I knew all the hazards of a sea-landing, chancy at the best of times but with two engines on the same side gone, more than doubly so. I heard the engines throttle back and prepared myself for the shock; body braced; muscles tense. We glided silently for a few seconds; seconds that seemed like minutes. There was a deafening crash; a rush of icy water as we were hurled forward and then, oh, joy! We were floating!

Ten minutes which seemed like a lifetime were over. I climbed out of the rear escape hatch at the same time as Robby came out of the forward one. As he poked his head out he greeted me with an enormous belch which seemed to relieve his feelings somewhat.

'Nice work, sir,' I said, referring to his ditching, not his belch.

'Well we made it OK. Everyone all right?' he asked.

'By this time we were all standing clustered on the wing, watching the dinghy slowly opening. Oh, glorious sight! The yellow dinghy unfolding and inflating in the sunshine ready to receive us.

'Wilkie and Willie were circling round us and we were waving up at them and laughing - yes, laughing. We were gay and happy and had every cause to be. The odds had been more against than for us; by now we might have been dead; crushed and mangled by the broken, twisted aeroplane: or struggling in the darkness with our lungs full of water as the aeroplane sank below the surface to the bottom, never to be seen again.

'The dinghy was ready for us; big and round and secure: it was more than twice the size of the last one I had been in. We pushed it off the wing and stepped gingerly in; all excepting Robby, who still stood on the wing waving .his arms wildly to the circling aircraft.

'Anyone want anything from inside?' he asked. 'I'm going to have a look at her.'

'He climbed on to the top of the fuselage, took a deep breath and lowered himself inside. I wished he would stop fooling about and come and join us: I was scared stiff that the aeroplane would sink with him inside it. After a bit he reappeared and sat on the hatch with his legs dangling inside, 'She's filling up,' he said, 'What about getting in the dinghy, sir?' I asked.

'No hurry yet, Riv. I'm going back in a moment to try and find my pipe.'

'Well you can't very well call your CO a bloody fool, even if you think he is one!

'He took another deep breath and disappeared once more. The aeroplane was more than half full of water and I thought in danger of sinking at any moment. After what seemed an uncomfortably long time; Robby appeared without his pipe and at last joined us. As he got in there was a nasty hissing sound just behind me and I looked round to see a jagged hole from which the air was rapidly escaping. There were some large wooden stoppers handy for just such an emergency and I hurriedly screwed one in. The dinghy had rubbed hard against a damaged bit of the wing which had caused the trouble. We shoved her off from the wing and floated some yards away from the aircraft.

'Well, Riv what do we do now?' Robby asked. 'You ought to know as you've done this sort of thing before.'

'We don't do anything. We just sit!'

'Has anyone got a pack of cards?'

'There might be one in here,' Freddy said. He was undoing a large canvas satchel.

'It did not contain any cards, however but was full of tinned food, distress signals, first-aid kit, cigarettes and matches. The cigarettes were passed round and we lit up.

'Anyone hungry, or shall we wait?' Robby asked.

'We decided to wait, in case we should really need the food later. We had a drink of water each, though, as we were feeling a little dry after swallowing so much of the salt sea.

'Wilkie was still circling us. He had climbed up to a few thousand feet and was obviously wirelessing our position and calling for help. It was a comforting sight, seeing him there and knowing that we were not alone or forgotten. Already the vast air-sea rescue service would be busy sending out search planes and informing any ships in our vicinity.

'Willie had disappeared and had presumably returned to base. We watched Wilkie for some time in silence. I was profoundly thankful and curiously at peace and happy, thinking how different this was to the last time I had been floating in a dinghy. The sea was quite calm, with only a slight swell which caused us to rise up and down with a regular rhythmical movement rather like a swing after it has died down and is just swaying to and fro.

'My arse is wet,' Robby said, after a long silence. 'Let's see if we can get the inside of this dinghy dry.'

'We were sitting round the edge with our feet in the middle and the water kept lapping over the side, washing against our bottoms, which was distinctly uncomfortable. There were several inches of water in the bottom of the dinghy. We tried scooping it up, but had nothing effective with which to do it so soaked it up with our gloves and scarves, which were wet anyway. By working fairly hard this way we were able to keep the inside reasonably dry.

'Wilkie had evidently done all he could for he came down and skimmed a few feet over the sea right by us and flew off out of sight. I felt rather lonely after he had gone and missed the sound of his engines. While he was flying around us we seemed to have some definite contact with our own country and I felt, that at any rate someone knew where we were. He had stayed with us for half an hour and I wondered how long it would be before we saw someone else besides ourselves.

'We were alone, except for our Halifax floating a few yards away from us. She was a pathetic sight, lying there so helpless and impotent; gradually getting lower in the water and looking as though she might go down at any moment. Her wings were awash, with the wake lapping against the sides of the fuselage. I looked at my turret, with the guns showing just above the water. It seemed strange to think that not so long before I had been sitting in that turret looking down on the sea on which we were now floating. The nose of the aeroplane dropped lower in the sea: she rolled slowly over on her side, raising her scarred port wing majestically to the sky and gradually disappeared, leaving only a swirl of water to mark her grave. We were silent for some time and I think all of us felt rather sad. We were alone now, surrounded by the vast expanse of the slowly moving sea.

'Does anyone know a song?' Robby asked, after a bit and without waiting for a reply, he started on the tune of the *'Volga Boatmen'*.

'On the whole, we were a very cheerful party. Our chances of being picked up were fairly good, as it was definitely known that we were on the sea and our position fixed. Only some extraordinary bad luck - such as the dinghy sinking;

some sudden storm or fog-could prevent us from being saved. I don't think the thought of being picked up by an enemy ship occurred to us, although we were considerably nearer to the French coast than to our own. Once or twice as I looked at the rolling mass of blue about us my heart seemed to miss a boat as I foresaw several days of floating, unseen by any searchers but these pangs were only momentary and for the most part I felt reasonably cheerful.

'I sat with Robby on one side of me and Joe on the other. Freddy was opposite me with Dick and Sam and Peter on either side of him. 'How are you feeling, Freddy?' I asked. 'You're looking a bit green!'

'I'm feeling a bit green' he replied and suiting his actions to his words, was sick over the side. This apparently was too much for Dick, as he did likewise. This created some slight diversion for us, as we offered sundry advice all round!

'I could do with a drink!' Robby said.

'I've got a flask of rum.'

'Come on, Riv out with it! Let's have a swig.'

'No! Let's wait until we see some help and then celebrate.'

'Good idea.'

'So we sat, sometimes talking, sometimes silent; for the most part cheerful and all the time looking around and listening for the help that should come. We began reckoning how long it would take for a rescue boat to arrive and what sort of a boat or ship they would send for us.

'Robby said to me - 'Could you see the bombs burst, Riv?' 'No sir. There was so much smoke around the ships that I couldn't be certain. It looked to me as though they were on fire.'

'I got a wizard sight,' Freddy declared. 'I swear the bombs dropped right across the ships. They must have been hit!'

'Good show.'

'What time does it get dark?' Sam asked, after a bit.

'About five o'clock. Why?'

'I was just wondering how much longer we'd got before dark, that was all.'

'Oh we've got another hour or two yet.'

'I can hear an aeroplane!' Peter suddenly said. 'Yes, there it is. Look!'

'It's a Lysander' someone announced.

'Where's that flask Riv?'

'Hold on, sir. Let's make certain first.'

'The Lysander was approaching, flying on a zigzag course about five hundred feet up and making more or less in our direction.

'Get the pistol ready, Freddy!' Robby said.

'Don't fire it too soon,' I suggested. 'Wait until it comes a bit closer.'

'It was getting steadily nearer and we all watched it anxiously. When it was about half a mile away, Freddy fired the Very pistol. The signal must have been seen, for the Lysander immediately turned in our direction and flew over us, flashing an answering light. I passed my flask to Robby and we drank to the Lysander circling above us. One stage towards our rescue was over and I hoped the next would be as easy. The Lysander flew round and round us for about an hour and then, without any warning, turned off out of sight.

'Oh hell! What's happening now? Surely it can't be getting low in petrol and leaving us?'

'We waited anxiously, watching the spot where it had disappeared and in a few minutes we saw it reappear again and come towards us. It circled us once more; fired a Very cartridge and then went off again in the same direction as before, only to reappear again, firing another cartridge. It repeated that performance several times and the reason was obvious: it had seen a ship and was guiding it towards us. Presently three dots appeared on the horizon and gradually took the shape of boats. Our joy and relief were terrific and we waved to the Lysander and shouted and sang until the ships drew alongside. There was a motor launch escorted by two motor torpedo-boats. The motor launch threw us a line and hauled us alongside.

'Hop in Riv' Robby said.

'Hop's about the right word, sir. I think I've broken my foot.

'You bloody fool! Why the hell didn't you say so before?'

'Well there wasn't much point, was there?'

'We were hauled aboard and once more I took off wet clothes in front of a roaring stove. Rum and cigarettes were pressed on us and we felt very much at home and content. The skipper was a marvellous host and he waited on us and fussed round us continuously. Robby was lamenting the fate of his favourite pipe, now at the bottom of the sea and the skipper said: 'My dear chap! I've the very thing for you. It hasn't been smoked and I don't like it; anyway. It's yours!' Robby took it gratefully and lit up.

'What about the news?' the skipper said at six o'clock.

'A strong force of our bombers attacked Brest in daylight today' we heard.

'Looking back, I remember an evening of dozing, smoking, talking and drinking rum. It was an evening of content and complete happiness and one I shall always remember. The skipper and his crew talked to us, asking innumerable questions. We fixed up future meetings and the whole evening went far too quickly! 'We were taken off to hospital when we got ashore, much to Robby's disgust. He wanted a party and protested at some length but without the desired result. We arrived back at our unit late the following night and were met by half the squadron who turned up at the railway station to welcome us. I was supported between Freddy and Joe.

'A few days after Christmas the squadron was detailed to go again to Brest. Robby had a new gunner in my place. I was merely a spectator and I felt rather out of it. As I stood, leaning on my crutches, watching the crews pile into the transport to take them to their aeroplanes, Robby said to me - 'I wish you were coming with us, Riv!'

'So do I sir.'[37]

Shortly after a total of ten decorations were awarded to various participating air crew, including Wing Commander Robinson who received a DSO [38] while Richard Rivaz was awarded the DFC.[39] Five other crews - four of them Stirlings - failed to return. One of the Stirling crews was captured and there were no survivors on the other three bombers. A fifth Stirling returned damaged and a 97 Squadron Manchester crashed at Coningsby on return to take the Squadron's losses to two. The night following 19 Whitleys tried without success to hit the warships at anchor in Brest harbour.

On 12 February 1942 the *Gneisenau*, *Scharnhorst* and the *Prinz Eugen* passed up the English Channel. There had been a fair number of night attacks on Brest between 18 December, when the last considerable daylight attack was made and 12 February, but there was never a night of really clear weather and bright moonlight, when the bombers could be reasonably certain of damaging the ships. The, bad weather of the winter of 1941/1942, which interfered with the strategic bombing of Germany, made equally difficult the effective blockade of Brest and for the first time the warships could be repaired, at any rate well enough for a brief voyage along the coast, before new damage could be done to them. The Germans moved the ships out on a dark and moonless night when there was every reason to expect low cloud over the Channel next day; the weather, as so often, did what they wanted it to do - Hitler's weather seems to be at least as remarkable as Queen Victoria's - and they got their low cloud.

The *Scharnhorst*, the *Gneisenau* and the *Prinz Eugen* were seen by a Spitfire pilot when near Boulogne, soon after eleven o'clock on the morning of 12 February, which was rather late in the day. There is reason to suppose that we had expected them to come out soon, but not to, go through the Channel; Coastal. Command might have sunk them with torpedo bombers if they had sailed out to the Atlantic with a view to getting round by the North of Scotland. As a result, new plans had to be quickly made to supplement what Coastal Command and the Fleet Air Arm could do in the circumstances and Bomber Command had to send out between two and three hundred bombers of all types in the hope of hitting and delaying the ships, The weather made this an almost impossible task, for the cloud base over the Channel and along the coast of the Low Countries was usually at about 300 feet; Armour-piercing bombs dropped from such a height would not penetrate the decks and might well bounce off into the sea; general-purpose bombs would only damage un-essential parts of the superstructure; if the bombers went higher, to give their bombs momentum, the warships would be invisible. The Germans had regrouped their fighters where they could best protect the warships and sent all of them up to keep continuous patrol overhead. The low cloud made it almost impossible for our fighters to engage the enemy, for in the low vault between sea and cloud they could not get room to manoeuvre for the attack. On the other hand, the bombers were particularly vulnerable in the same confined space. They had to make their steady bombing run very low over the cruisers, with flak-ships, destroyers and E-boats sending up a hail of light anti-aircraft fire; they could not get away from the Messerschmitts except by going back into cloud and so running the risk of losing the warships altogether. Thus at the moment when a Manchester sighted the warships it was only 300 feet above the sea and there were two Messerschmitts on its tail. The rear end of the fuselage, the tail-plane and the rudders were riddled with bullets from the Messerschmitts and with fragments of light anti-aircraft shells from the ships; the rear gunner was seriously wounded. Accurate bombing was certainly difficult in such circumstances.

In such weather there could be no question of attack by massed formations of bombers; every attack was delivered separately. A Wellington set out with a formation of other Wellingtons, but soon got separated in cloud. Near the place where the pilot expected to find the warships he saw a Stirling and tried to formate on it before going down to attack. But when the time came to dive through the cloud he lost the Stirling in the descent. Anti-aircraft fire came up through the clouds and a shell fragment hit the underside of the pilot's arm-rest and wounded him in the right arm. He went on down and when he came out of the cloud there were the *Gneisenau* and the *Prinz Eugen*, about a mile and a half apart. The ships were steaming all out and raising a great wake behind them. There appeared to be no other bombers about and all the guns of the warship and their escort seemed to be aiming at the Wellington. It was hit again and the top of the cockpit over the pilot's head was knocked right off. An oil pipe was cut and oil spurted all over the navigator.

The Wellington had not broken cloud in the best place for aiming, so the pilot climbed, dived again - this was what is called a 'dummy dive,' designed, like the 'dummy run,' as a test of aim - climbed again and then tore down at 300 mph on to the *Prinz Eugen*. Her decks seemed to shoot up to meet the Wellington; they grew larger every second. The guns went on; the front gunner found himself leaning to one side of his turret, but had time to reflect that he would be no safer thus than if he sat square in the middle. He raked the decks of the cruiser as the Wellington came down and at 400 feet the bomb aimer let the bombs go. The pilot tried to pull out of the dive, but the control would not answer at once and he thought he would go straight into the sea. With both arms and feet braced against the instrument panel he tugged at the control column; the bomber's nose only came up when it was a foot or two from the sea. The pilot made for the cloud. Looking back, the rear gunner and the second pilot saw the bombs burst just under the bows of the *Prinz Eugen*; they may have done some damage. The Wellington shot straight into the clouds and went home.

Inevitably a good many crews could not find the warships at all. A Hampden pilot flew straight to the Dutch coast to check his position. The clouds were so thick that he crossed the coast at only 300 feet without seeing it. The pilot turned and when out to sea again he found that if he flew lower still he and his crew could see for about 200 yards along the surface of the water. For more than an hour he flew up and down over the area where the warships were reported to be, but it would have been sheer good luck to find them so and the Hampden had at last to return.

The weather, in fact, amounted to a huge smoke screen for the warships; if this had not been so they would not have been there and Bomber Command had to accept the fact as a necessary condition of the whole operation. It had to be a search through a labyrinth of cloud, with rain or sleet drawing a vertical curtain in front of the pilots as effectively as the clouds hid everything below. In places there were three distinct layers of cloud, all impossible to see through.

Only very occasionally was high-level bombing possible, but at about three o'clock the crews of three Wellingtons flying at 8,000 feet found the ships by seeing their wake through a gap in the clouds; all three bombed, but the clouds closed again before anyone could see where the bombs burst. Ten minutes later a Wellington had to bomb from 150 feet and, with the cloud base only about a hundred feet higher, the pilot of another Wellington thought it better, because his bombs might prove ineffective when dropped from such a height to circle and shadow the warships for some twenty minutes and so get 'fixes' and enable other forces to find the enemy. Later there was another chance for high-level bombing. Blenheims were flying at over 10,000 feet when the clouds parted for a moment and the ships were seen below, steaming north-east with their escort in three lines. In the brief interval the gunner of one Blenheim saw a bomb burst either on or just short of one of the warships.

Very probably the bombers did not do so much damage as the smaller number of torpedo-carrying aircraft which found the warships, but they may well have done something towards keeping the warships for some time in a German port. There were too many reports of the warships being well in their bomb-sights for no hits to have been obtained. The news that the warships had got through the Channel, coming as it did at the same time as the news of the fall of Singapore, had a very depressing effect and a good many people seemed to take it as proof that the bombing of Brest was ineffective. But Mr Churchill surprised everybody by disclosing that the Admiralty was relieved to have the cruisers out of Brest and that in his opinion also the situation in the Atlantic was' relieved by their departure. If the cruisers had come out into the Atlantic that would certainly have meant that our bombing of Brest had ceased to take effect, though it would not have meant that Bomber Command had wasted its time; even if the battle-cruisers had been battle-worthy after nearly a year, they would still have been blockaded for nearly a year. But this did not happen; on the contrary, the Germans had probably concluded that there was no chance of their getting the warships properly repaired in such an ·inferno as Brest had become. Mr Churchill also pointed out that by the time the warships were finally repaired in some German port, if our bombing should allow this to happen, the British and American navies would have received powerful reinforcement.

The total casualties in all the attacks on Brest made between March 1941 and February 1942, by Coastal as well as by Bomber Command, amounted to 43 aircraft and 247 men. To these losses must be added the 20 bombers, 15 of Bomber and five of Coastal Command, the six Swordfish of the Fleet Air Arm and the 16 fighters lost in the attack on the warships after they had left Brest. It was not long before the *Scharnhorst* and *Gneisenau* were found again; they were both undergoing repairs in Kiel at the end of February. The *Prinz Eugen* ended up with the *Tirpitz* in Trondheim Fjord.

Kiel was accordingly bombed. On 25 February the weather was fair and the *Gneisenau's* depot ship - either the liner *Monte Olivia* or a ship of the same class - was set on fire and burnt out. Both the *Scharnhorst* and the *Gneisenau* may have been damaged on the same night; both were certainly hit during one or more of our attacks on Kiel that spring. The *Gneisenau* left Kiel at the end of March or the beginning of April and went to the Polish port of Gdynia; she was photographed there in June 1942. All her turrets were then being dismantled. The 'A' for'ard turret had been completely removed and was seen lying on the dockside. The 'B' for'ard turret and the 'Y' aft turret were partly dismantled; a floating crane was working over it. Thirty feet of the forecastle deck had been removed.

There was some reason to think that the Germans might have decided to write the *Gneisenau* off altogether and not only because Gdynia, unlike Kiel, is a port where major repairs cannot be made to capital ships. Possibly the guns were going to be removed and used for some other purpose. But whatever might be going to happen, the work of dismantling was evidence of very severe damage. Even if the *Gneisenau* was eventually going to fight again it would not be for a long time. Up till July of 1942 the *Scharnhorst* had not left Kiel; there were other reasons besides this to support that she had incurred fresh damage after her removal from Brest to Kiel.

So ended, most opportunely for the opening of the campaign of 1942, one of the major diversions from strategic bombing which Bomber Command had to undertake. It was a dull and apparently unrewarding campaign, which made everyone except the experts and the Admiralty grumble. But it did its work and that work had strategic consequences which were not easily understood at the time. I said at the beginning of this chapter that the Germans probably intended to use their fleet, not to challenge the power of the British fleet, as in the last war, but for commerce raiding. One expects such commerce raiding to be done by single ships, or by capital ships supported by lesser ships. But there was always a chance that our convoys might have been attacked by the German fleet operating as a whole and commerce raiding on such a scale would have been a most serious threat. Bomber Command's work at Brest and Kiel not only immobilized two capital ships, but kept the German navy from joining up. In consequence the *Bismarck* was more easily sunk, because she had to operate with only one cruiser for support. The *Tirpitz* is now in much the same position and so far the Germans have not shown any sign of being willing to run the risks with her that they took with the *Bismarck*.

Endnotes for Chapter Six

28 As a diversion for the Brest raid, 36 Blenheims in several waves and all escorted by Spitfires, attacked Cherbourg docks with good bombing results but no German fighters appeared. All the Blenheims returned safely.

29 *Handley Page Halifax: From Hell to Victory and Beyond* by K. A. Merrick (Chevron Publishing, 2009).

30 Sergeant Wallace Llewellyn Berry RCAF was KIA on 14/15 August 1941 on the operation on Magdeburg when he was flying as tail gunner on Pilot Officer Ronald Lisle's crew. All the crew were killed.

31 Sergeant Peter George Bolton.

32 It was a German destroyer which was passing near the Isle d' Yeu and believing itself about to be attacked began evasive action and opened fire. However, as soon as it was realized that it was not the target it radioed the course and size of the formation to the shore facilities.

33 This is possibly Pilot Officer Harold Walter Stone DFM. He and Sergeant Peter George Bolton are the only two members on 35 Squadron who were killed on 24 July other than the four on Flight Sergeant Godwin's crew. Another clue is that Richard Rivaz referred to the sergeants on his crew by their surname and his fellow officers by their Christian names, i.e. 'Nick' and 'Gerry'.

34 L9512/U on 35 Squadron was hit by flak and was finished off by a Bf 109 and left to crash in the sea, just north of the Ile de Ré. Flight Sergeant S. D. Greaves and his crew all survived as PoWs. 76 Squadron lost three: L9494 was first hit by flak then finished off by a Bf 109, Squadron Leader W. Williams ditching it near La Rochelle, the crew being rescued by a French fishing boat only to be made PoWs; Pilot Officer Joseph F. P. J. McKenna's L9517 was shot down by flak and also crashed off La Rochelle, killing all on board; Flight Lieutenant Austin Ellerker Lewin's L9529 was shot down by fighters near Vendee at l'Aiguillon-sur-Mer. Lewin and four of the crew were killed; three men were taken prisoner. Flight Sergeant Clarence Arthur Godwin's L9527/M, seriously damaged by flak, was attacked by three Bf 109s over the town of Angles, where it went down in

a slow spiral with smoke coming from one or two of its engines. Only two parachutes emerged before the Halifax crashed 15 km (9.32 miles) from the town of Lucon. One Halifax on 35 Squadron landed safely but was so badly damaged it was written-off as Damaged Beyond Repair (DBR). Five more were damaged to the extent that they required approximately three weeks to repair, while two others were damaged to a lesser degree. The remaining two suffered only superficial damage.

35 *The Bomber Command War Diaries* by Martin Middlebrook and Chris Everitt. (Midland Publishing Ltd 1985, 1990, 1995).

36 *The Bomber Command War Diaries* by Martin Middlebrook and Chris Everitt. (Midland Publishing Ltd 1985, 1990, 1995).

37 *Tail Gunner* by Flight Lieutenant R. C. Rivaz DFC (Jarrold's Publishers London Ltd).

38 Robinson was awarded a bar to his DFC for bringing his badly damaged Halifax home alone on the night of 18/19 November 1942 when the target was Turin. On 1 May 1943 Robinson was promoted to Group Captain and he was appointed commander of RAF Graveley. Station commanders were severely restricted by higher authority from undertaking operations, being rationed to two or three sorties per month at most. Robinson, typically, selected particularly tough targets for his few trips and on the night of 23/24 August 1943 the target was Berlin. He personally briefed Graveley's crews and then took a scratch crew out on 35 Squadron in a Halifax. Of the 719 bombers dispatched to Berlin that night - 117 of these PFF aircraft - 56 failed to return, including two 'Station Masters': Group Captain A. H. Willetts at Oakington and Group Captain Basil Vernon Robinson DSO DFC* AFC.

39 Flight Lieutenant R. C. Rivaz DFC was killed on 13 October 1945 when the Liberator VI transport he was flying in crashed on takeoff at Melsbroek in Belgium. The Liberator which was piloted by Flight Lieutenant Peter Green, was carrying a crew of five and 26 passengers; members of the RAMC including 223 Field Ambulance, a dentist and a member of the catering corps. It was found that the aircraft had been incorrectly loaded. The 37-year old Rivaz was buried in Brussels Town Cemetery. At the time of his death he was researching another book, on RAF Transport Command.

Chapter 7

Boeing Boys In Blue

The new Fortress I aircraft of Bomber Command were used as the spearhead of the big daylight assault on the German warships at Brest on the afternoon of July 24, 1941. The Fortress Is, as the Boeing B-17Cs are called in the RAF, flew far above the rest of the attacking force where they would be unlikely to be hit by the anti-aircraft guns of Brest.

The advantages of a bomber which can fly at above 30,000 feet are obvious. To intercept a Fortress, fighters would either have to climb to this great height, by which time the bomber would have gone many miles on its course, or the enemy would have to maintain fighter patrols, which is always an expensive procedure. On the first occasion that a Fortress was intercepted, which was not until August 15, 1941, it was by a standing patrol. This was after another daylight attack on Brest, this time by Fortresses alone. Flying at a great height, but not at their full ceiling, the bombers crossed the Channel. The weather was such that one of the bombers left vapour trails behind it and it is probable that these were seen by the enemy before the Fortresses reached Brest. Near Brest one of the Fortresses got separated from the rest of the detachment; it swerved to the left of a large patch of cloud while the others swerved to the right. After that it flew on, attacked and returned by itself. Three minutes after the Fortress had bombed, two fighters were seen coming out from light cloud about 1,000 feet below the Fortress and slightly to starboard. They were joined almost at once by five Messerschmitt 109Fs; all the fighters appeared to come from the same quarter of the sky. Their arrival was so prompt that it was obvious they had come from a standing patrol, almost certainly sent up when the vapour trails were first seen over the sea.

The fighters made many attacks from both sides and from dead astern. Two of the Fortress's gunners and the wireless operator were severely wounded. In spite of his wounds, the wireless operator continued to signal to his base. The captain swung the bomber quickly from side to side and dived, now fast, now slow. Down came all the fighters after him, firing all the while. The Fortress's No. 4 petrol tank was punctured and the crew thought the engine had caught fire; as one of them said, 'There seemed to be no part of the bomber which was not hit.' One of the fighters passed in front of the Fortress as it dived and at once the observer fired at it. Then, when the fight had gone on for twenty minutes, the Fortress reached a low patch of cloud and all the enemy fighters broke away. Black smoke was now pouring from the bomber.

As soon as the fighters had left, the fighting controller, wounded himself in hand and leg, made to reach the other wounded men. But to do this he would have had to walk along a gangway which leads from the pilot's cabin to the rear. The gangway was covered with a tangled mass of wires and cables and the guide-ropes alongside it had been shot away. The bomb doors, damaged in the battle, were wide open and the gangway was now a narrow bridge over empty air and sea. To cross this was no task for a wounded man and the fire controller had to be held back. The observer then tried to get across, but half-way over he found that a slip was almost certain; he went back for his parachute and tried again, but this time his parachute was caught and entangled in the wreckage. He had to give up.

When the Fortress reached the English coast the captain, who still thought that his No. 4 engine might be alight, made for the nearest aerodrome. With flaps out of action, tail tabs shot away, bomb doors wide open, tail wheels stuck half up and half down, brakes not working, only one aileron any good and a scarcely controllable rudder, the captain had to land on a small and unfamiliar aerodrome. With his second pilot doing everything he could to help, he made his landing.

This was one of the few occasions when things went wrong with a Fortress. In other attacks it showed how useful a weapon of war it was. Thus on July 26, only two days after the first operation of the Fortresses in the attack on Brest, a Fortress made a reconnaissance flight over Germany and dropped a heavy load of bombs on the port of Emden in daylight. Photographs taken from the aircraft at the time showed the accuracy of the American automatic bomb sight. The bombs burst among industrial buildings; curiously enough very close to an area of devastation where one of our largest bombs had exploded in a previous attack. On August 2 another armed reconnaissance took a Fortress to Kiel. It was evident that its bombs were dropped without warning, for neither fighters nor anti-aircraft guns resisted the attack. Even from .the great height at which the Fortress was flying, the crew saw much smoke welling up after the explosion of the bombs.

Apart from the safety which great height gives to the bomber, it is a considerable advantage to drop bombs such a distance if they can be accurately aimed. When they reach the ground they will be travelling at something near their terminal velocity, at a speed of between six and seven hundred miles an hour. They will then be almost as deadly as shells from the largest naval guns. Two factors make it possible to aim accurately from such a height: the automatic bomb sight and the clearness of the atmosphere. In the tropopause, the region two or three miles thick between the air near the earth and the stratosphere, there is no dust or smoke and it is too cold for there to be any water vapour. If, of course, there is thick cloud below, the clearness of the upper air will be of no advantage, so that Fortresses are likely to be most useful in periods of clear weather and during summer. It may be noticed that during the winter of 1941 and 1942 Fortresses have worked in the Mediterranean and Middle East rather than over Germany.

The Fortress I is doubtless only the first of many high-flying bombers to come in the future, even in the near future. But to get even so far as the Fortress I is a remarkable achievement, of engineering and many of the most difficult problems of high altitude flying have already been solved in its construction. It could not, for example, fly so high if it were not for the turbo-exhaust supercharger fitted to each engine. While the normal supercharger obtains its drive from the engine, the turbo supercharger is driven by exhaust gases controlled by the waste-gate filter in the exhaust pipe. This makes it possible to drive the supercharger at the speed required and to maintain the efficiency of the engine at high altitudes. Or again, fuel has a tendency to boil at great heights and this may cause vapour locks. A new type of pump has overcome this difficulty.'

The care and the choice of crews flying at such heights has needed as much research as the making of the Fortress itself. Cold and thin air would very soon destroy life if *proper precautions were not taken. Lack of oxygen affects the brain before anything else, makes the judgment defective and induces a spurious self-confidence. All mental processes are slowed down, so that a navigator, for example, will find that he cannot do even the simplest sums. The vision is dimmed, the arms and legs feel weak, the hands and feet feel cold and air-sickness is very common. The heart beats more rapidly and one is apt to become dizzy. Fortress crews are trained in a pressure-chamber where the pressure of the air is reduced to the pressure at 30,000 feet or more, in fact to a quarter of its density at sea-level. In the chamber the crews are taught to be conscious all the time of their oxygen apparatus and of how they are using it; everyone is told to let himself become unconscious at least once.*

But even so not many are fit to endure the hard training and even harder work of flying in a Fortress. There is great individual variation in susceptibility to the difference, at high altitudes, between the pressure of the nitrogen in the air and the pressure of nitrogen in the blood. The lower pressure in the air may induce the nitrogen in the blood to come out and form bubbles in the vessels and tissues which may tear the tissues and block the vessels. Young and thin men are, on the whole, least susceptible to this reaction; fat men are not encouraged to fly in Fortresses. Divers and men who work in caissons suffer from the same complaint, which is known as 'decompression sickness,' or 'Bends'; the milder symptoms are an itching of the skin, pain in the limbs, especially in the shoulders and knees, abdominal pain, sweating, cold and dizziness and troublesome coughing. At a great height men may also suffer from stomach ache, because gas distends the gut when the pressure of the outside air is reduced.

Fortresses are flown by picked and highly trained men who have so mastered the technique of high-altitude flying that they feel no serious discomfort in the air or afterwards. Indeed, many of them appear to have enjoyed, the experience of flying at so great a height; they have described the new world into which the Fortresses took them. As the captain of one of the Fortresses said in a broadcast: 'I don't want to dwell on physical discomforts, because flying in the sub stratosphere has great compensations.' It appears that flying at a great height gives the airman a sense of power and almost of exaltation. He can see the curve of the earth and the colour of everything below him is richer and more intense than in the normal world. The sea, as the Fortresses cross the Channel, is a deep sapphire-blue and the sky where it meets the sea is of as brilliant a colour. Conversely, the sky above is less than normally blue. When Captains Stevens and Anderson, of the United States Army, reached a height of 17.31 miles (72,395 feet), the highest that anyone has yet reached, they found the sky pitch-black. Even at the height at which the Fortress usually flies there is a kind of twilight above, as though night were just about to fall. The reason for this is that it is the air which makes the sky blue; at 30,000 feet there is more air below than above. In good weather the crews can see farther than 150 miles; they often saw on the horizon the shores of France a good half-hour's flying distance away. But where there is no land there seems to be no horizon, no distinction between sea and sky and it is like flying in a ball of space.

The cold is intense, for until the stratosphere, the region between ten and thirty miles above the surface of the earth, is reached, the temperature gets steadily less. Oddly enough, at that point the temperature no longer varies, except that the air is warmer over the Poles and colder over the Equator. The Fortress crews often had to fly with their windows open, for white frost almost invariably formed on the perspex to a depth of a quarter of an inch. Walking in their warm flying clothes to the aircraft the crews naturally sweated on a hot summer day; the sweat froze on them before they had been many minutes in the air. The film of perspiration on the hands froze solid and made the fingers hurt.

The attacks by Fortresses were an extremely interesting experiment, with promise of much more to come...

'One lease-lend day in 1941' wrote Leslie Kark, a British PRO [40] the first Boeing Flying Fortress arrived at a new aerodrome in the Daylight Bomber Group in England'. The British Purchasing Commission had taken up an offer by the United States Government of 20 Boeing B-17Cs with the necessary personnel to instruct and assist in bringing the aircraft into RAF service as the Fortress I. [41] The need for operational aircraft for daylight operations by the RAF was so great that despite the Americans' suggestion that the aircraft be used only for training until a more fully developed type was available for operational flying; it was decided to modify the B-17Cs to an operational standard. The first Fortress I to arrive flew the Atlantic Ferry Route on 14 April with Major Walsh USAAC, who was to head the American advisory personnel, at the controls. AN521 crossed the Atlantic in the then record time of 8 hours and 26 minutes, but for security reasons the news was not released. It was intended that the Fortress would equip 21 Squadron but as this would mean taking a first-line squadron off operations, on 7 May 90 Squadron was officially reformed at Watton in Norfolk under the command of 2 Group, whose headquarters was at Huntingdon. No. 2 Group was unique in RAF Bomber Command in that it specialized in daylight bombing.

On 5 May a group of bemused young airmen had arrived at the bleak Norfolk airfield at Watton to be confronted with the Boeing B-17C Model 299T; an aircraft they had never seen before and one which they were to fly in broad daylight and at high altitude. Most of the men were veterans of RAF night bombing or low-level daylight operations and recent graduates of a rigorous de-compression test (which consisted of 'climbing' at 3,000 feet/minute to 35,000 feet and remaining there for 5 hours) at Farnborough. Sergeant Tim (Mick) Wood, an Australian, had recently completed seven Wellington operations on 115 Squadron at RAF Marham. 'I was on the land in Australia jackerooing when the war threatened. I always wanted to fly and could never afford it, so 1939 came and the chance to get it for free.' Nineteen-year-old Sergeant (later Air Commodore) Tom Imrie DFM was already a veteran of 34 operations as a WOp/AG (wireless operator-air gunner) on Whitley bombers on 51 Squadron at Dishforth, Yorkshire. Roy Boast (later Group Captain CBE DFC) a navigator, had previously flown on Whitleys and, more recently, the Halifax. He had 'foolishly' volunteered to go to Farnborough for a day's high altitude test 'to get a night in London' only to find himself posted to 90 Squadron forthwith. Like many other old hands on 90 Squadron he yearned for a return to night 'ops'.

The B-17C possessed an impressive top speed of 325 mph at around 29,000 feet and could cruise at 230 mph at 30,000 feet. These speeds were only achievable because the lack of armour plate (which was only installed in the tail behind the waist positions) and power operated gun turrets, meant there was no excess weight. Nevertheless, the B-17C was considered well armed, with one or two .30-inch nose and six .50-inch pannier-fed guns (two in the waist, two in a ventral cupola and two in the dorsal position). The B-17C's range was poor and only American bombs, up to 1,000lb, could be carried. The top secret Norden precision bomb sight, developed by the US Navy and able to place a bomb in 'a pickle barrel' had been deleted and replaced by the Sperry sight. Depending on one's point of view, it was either a very bad bomb sight ('one needed a bloody big barrel') or an excellent device but limited because it was only calibrated for automatic operation to 25,000 feet and bomb aimers had to 'guestimate' by feeding in pre-set calculations supplied by Sperrys at higher altitudes.

'Everyone who could climbed over the Fortress, looking at the ash-trays and the built-in thermos coffee-jugs and generally marvelling at the comfort' wrote Leslie Kark. 'Princess Margaret, an early visitor, did not fail to point out to her mother 'the pretty carpets'. The system of fire was not as it is now. These were virtually civil aircraft, designed some years back and rushed to us by an America eager to help in every way she could. The newer armaments would come, but meanwhile here was the turbo super-charger, which enabled the aircraft to fly in the sub-stratosphere and the precision automatic bomb-sight (claimed to 'drop a bomb in a barrel') before whose canvassed secrecy we stood in awe.' When the bomb-sight was unveiled, Kark 'marvelled at the human ingenuity which could deal with so many gauges, needles, buttons, knobs and switches'. 'And then, by contrast, we marvelled that so simple an instrument could on its own perform the task, without aid for lateral control from the pilot, of flying the Fortress to the aiming point and releasing the bombs itself. The new bomb-sight needed months of special training of bomb aimers. To place it in the hands of even a normally learned navigator, the Wing Commander of the Squadron explained, would be like giving a scientific instrument into the eager hands of a child.'

The squadron CO, Wing Commander J. MacDougall, or 'Mad Mac' as he was known, had previously commanded 110 Squadron (Blenheims) at Wattisham. He was Anglo-Argentinean by birth, often appeared pompous and airmen recall he wanted everything done 'at the double' which was probably a result of his earlier time in the army.

'Intense training began' wrote Leslie Kark 'and essential modifications were brought in, causing headaches at Group Headquarters which gave rise to the popular song *Boeings, Boeings, they'll ne'er fly like Blenheims for me*, to the tune of *Bring back, oh bring back my bonnie to me*. When the Fortresses were few there was inevitable difficulty in recognition and fighters were occasionally suspicious. Once when flying high over the coast I observed rather anxiously that two Spitfires were coming menacingly close. We fired recognition cartridges, but they persisted, A German aircraft, we did not know at the time, was reported in the neighbourhood. A Spitfire made a mock attack and I noticed with gratitude that others in the Fortress appeared equally scared. The observer opened the starboard window and gave the Spitfire pilots a rude sign, but still they came on. The Germans, after all, would also know the rude sign. And then the observer took his Aldis lamp and signalled in Morse. The meaning of the message escaped me, but with intense relief I saw our fighters disappear. 'And what,' I asked the observer, 'did you signal?' 'Kindly ---- off,' he answered. Few Germans, I thought, would be likely to know this idiomatic English phrase.

'Fortress air-crews had to be specially selected for the task of flying at about seven miles high, for even of fit men few are able to withstand the absence of pressure. All were subjected to the pressure-chamber, in which work the Squadron 'Doc' took unholy delight in literally taking the wind out of his subjects.' Flying Officer Antony J. Barwood (later Group Captain Barwood OBE) was posted to 90 Squadron in May to deal with the problems of high altitude flying. The young medical officer had been sent to Farnborough where he had been exposed to a routine 'bends test' in the decompression chamber. The Fortress was expected to fly at heights well in excess of 30,000 feet, an altitude not achieved by operational RAF bombers (except for the pressurized experimental Wellington Mk.V/VI). Tony Barwood recalls:

'I was still very young but much older than most of the aircrew. Later, my job became selection of aircrew at Polebrook where we operated a mobile pressure chamber, which could take six men to a simulated 35,000 feet, driven by a Coventry Victor single-cylinder engine. Crews were young, keen and declared fit to fly B-17Cs after they had passed the decompression test. I always flew with them on their first training sortie. Wing Commander Noel Singer, Senior Air Staff Officer to the AOC, Air Marshal Peirce at 2 Group HQ, came to Polebrook to fly in a B-17. I said he had to be bends-tested first. He didn't pass and was not allowed to fly. Squadron Leader Edgar Bright (another aviation medicine specialist who retired as Air Commodore Bright AFC) came in as Station SMO at Polebrook and did some of the training. Before each sortie we always checked every crew's oxygen supply to make sure that the cylinders were correctly filled and the regulators at each crew position were fully functional. We also briefed the crews on oxygen systems and clothing and attended operation debriefings to see if there had been any problems.'

'For my grim interest' recalled Leslie Kark '[Tony Barwood] placed me with another volunteer in the pressure-chamber and then took us up to 35,000 feet, when he switched off my companion's oxygen and told him to count aloud. At ten I borrowed his silver pencil and at eighteen he passed out. Oxygen was switched on again and he continued counting 'fourteen, fifteen, sixteen...' as though he had never been 'out'. Nor could he recall lending me his pencil. 'The serious work continued...'

On 7 May AN521 - now called 'K-King' - was flown to Burtonwood near Liverpool by Major Walsh with Roy Boast. That same day AN534 arrived at Watton to become the squadron's first Fortress I. On 11 May Major Mike Walsh, accompanied by Tom Imrie and others, flew AN529 to Watton from Burtonwood. The only incident occurred when the 2nd pilot forgot to lock the throttles and the Fortress began heading for the barrage balloons over Liverpool. Next day flying training was started from Watton's satellite airfield at Bodney. It proved a very short sojourn, lasting only two days, for the undulating grass runways proved most unsuitable for Fortress training. On 13 May Australian pilot, Flight Sergeant Mick Wood, made his first Fortress flight on conversion to type in AN534 with Captain Connolly USAAC and followed it on 14 May with an intercom test in AN529, again with Captain Connolly. Wood and the other pilots also received instruction from Major Walsh and Lieutenant Bradley, son of US General Omar Bradley. Altogether, the Air Corps provided five experienced airmen while other American advisors included Franklyn Joseph, an expert on the Sperry 01 bombsight; a number of Boeing representatives including Bob Crawford and Tex O' Camb - an expert on Wright Cyclones and superchargers and Air Corps reservist who joined the RAF as a flight lieutenant on condition that he could transfer to the USAAC if America entered the war.

On 15 May Fortress training flights continued, this time from Great Massingham, a satellite of RAF West Raynham, while Fortresses went for overhaul at West Raynham. Despite the constant upheaval, training was beginning to pay dividends and Wing Commander MacDougall chose Mick Wood as his second pilot and Tom Imrie became one of his gunners.

There were many problems with the oxygen and intercom systems which needed sorting out before the aircraft could be operated at altitude. 'We started with American Oxygen system, Λ8 individually controlled regulators and BLB re-breather bag masks with hand-held carbon granule microphones. The regulators seized up, the masks froze and the microphones became progressively more useless above 15,000 feet as they depended on air density to excite the carbon granules within the diaphragm of the microphone. We then changed to British Mk VIII oxygen regulators and Type 'E' masks with an incorporated electromagnetic microphone, which also required amplified changes in the aircraft. The masks still froze and were modified with an additional valve. I covered the diaphragm on the microphone with a French letter to prevent it freezing. An oxygen economiser, which had been invented by Professor - later Sir - Brian Matthews KBE, was introduced. It stored the oxygen flowing through the regulator while the user was not breathing in, which is only about one-third of the breathing cycle. The original economisers were hand-made by 'metal bashers' within the Royal Aircraft Establishment and at the Physiology Laboratory, as the IAM then was. They effectively reduced the weight of oxygen cylinders which the aircraft had to carry by 50% and produced a more effective oxygen system. The final change was to a Mk 10 regulator controlled centrally by the captain delivering oxygen to each crew position.'

The bitter cold at altitude was made far worse by the aircraft having to fly with all four of the rear fuselage blisters off so that high air blast affected all the rear crew, rendering effective flying clothing of vital importance. At first we used electrically heated one-piece suits made by Seibe-Gorman with electrically heated gloves and boots. The suits restricted movement which was so essential for the gunners and were bulky and not very reliable. In August the 'Taylor' suit became available, again one-piece but much more easily donned, with an electrically heated lining, glove lining and socks. These were used with fleecy-lined flying boots and soft leather gauntlets. The suit also provided built-in flotation. It was reliable and much easier to move in.' There were technical problems to contend with, too. Tom Imrie recalls: 'We had constant engine oil problems caused by the pressure differences. The oxygen system and the intercom were bad. Armament was prehistoric with free-mounted .5s in the waist and one .300 in the nose. Ammunition was contained in heavy 50 lb containers and it was a hell of a struggle trying to lift them onto the mountings at 30,000 feet+. The guns jumped around all over the place and hose-piped on the free mountings. Often they didn't fire. They iced up at altitude and we had to wash them in petrol. The windscreens iced up too and eventually had to be double-glazed.'

By 26 May four crews had converted successfully to the Fortress and now there were five on squadron strength. Training took on a new importance with regular cross country, bombing and altitude flights being made throughout East Anglia and, on occasions, further afield.

'We moved about so much we hardly ever had time to unpack, but morale always remained high. At West Raynham we shared the station with two Blenheim squadrons which at that time had suffered high losses in attacks on the Channel ports. Imrie for one was finding the transition from night operations to very high altitude daylight operations 'terrifying'. 'It was nerve wracking flying in broad daylight and on one test flight over Cornwall on 4 June we even got the B-17 up to 41,000 feet. We could see the earth's curvature and the sky had turned a dark purple colour instead of blue. However, there were welcome features which were absent on RAF aircraft. On one occasion, at Abingdon, we were visited by HRH King George VI and Queen Elizabeth and the two princesses. The young Princess Elizabeth enquired about the incongruous dark grey carpets throughout and thermos flasks on the bulkhead. These were a left over from the Fortress's early role on long over-water operations when crew comfort was important.'

Tony Barwood adds: 'My first training sortie was to be a routine training flight from West Raynham on the afternoon of 22 June. I was fully briefed and kitted out by Squadron Leader David Alan Hope Robson MB CHB, the Station Medical Officer as West Raynham and himself a pilot. The flight was delayed as Flight Lieutenant William K. Steward (later Air Vice-Marshal CBE DFC, Commander of the RAF Institute of Aviation Medicine) and a test pilot, Flight Lieutenant John Bernard William Humpherson DFC, were on the way from Farnborough to gain experience of a Fortress sortie so I was turned off. The Fort, AN522 'J-Johnny' was flown by Flying Officer John Charles 'Mike' Hawley with Lieutenant Jim Bradley as Instructor pilot. At high altitude the aircraft hit some cumulo nimbus at around 30,000 feet over Catterick, Yorkshire and broke up. Steward was trapped in the tail section which broke away from the fuselage. It fell 12,000 feet but he managed to bail out at about 3,000 feet. He was the only survivor.'[42]

During 27-29 June MacDougall and his available crews flew to Polebrook, their new permanent home near Peterborough. Much of the base was still under construction and crews, used to pre-war brick-built barracks at other bases, were taken aback to find themselves billeted in highly uncomfortable wooden huts little better than the leaky Nissens with their iron stoves used on other bases. The airfield tended to flood but at least the concrete runway was a vast improvement over grass. Tom Imrie recalled: 'I think RAF Polebrook must have been put together fairly quickly as during the summer of 1941, when there were-frequent thunderstorms, the camp roads - particularly in the area of Squadron Headquarters - became flooded. The station commander, Group Captain Evans-Evans, was obviously getting little help from 'Works and Bricks' so ingeniously, he retrieved a rescue dinghy from one of the Forts, put in three WAAFs and floated the lot on one of the ponds which had a road below. The photographs he sent to the Air Ministry did, I believe, bring immediate results.[43]

The squadron's new tenancy was marred by the loss of AN528 on 33 July when 'B-Baker' burst into flames during an engine test on the airfield. Gradually, 12 aircraft were gathered at Polebrook but maintenance problems often reduced the available number of Forts to just three. Meanwhile, bombing practice continued at a pace and by 6 July bomb aimers were deemed to have reached an acceptable standard of proficiency. However, as Roy Boast recalls, practice bombing only took place at low altitude, well below that required for operational bombing. 'We did not do any practice bombing above 25,000 feet during training. I logged the dropping of 33 practice bombs from altitudes between 8,000-20,000 feet.'

Meanwhile, calls were mounting for an operation over Germany and at 15.00 hours on 8 July three Fortress Is, each carrying four 1,000lb ground burst bombs (armour piercing were not yet available) taxied out at Polebrook for the first RAF Fortress operation, to the docks at Wilhelmshaven. The outcome was awaited with great interest by RAF and Air Corps personnel alike. MacDougall piloted AN526 'G-George' with Mick Wood as second pilot. The rest of the crew consisted of Flying Officer Eddie Skelton, the squadron navigation officer, Flying Officer Barnes, the squadron gunnery leader and Sergeants' Tom Danby, Danny 'Mophead' Clifford, both gunners and Tom Imrie, who flew as signaller. Skelton and Barnes had been on MacDougall's crew in Blenheims. Behind them came AN529 'C-Charlie' piloted by Pilot Officer Alexander Mathieson and AN519 'H-Harry' flown by Squadron Leader Andy MacLaren and Pilot Officer Mike Wayman, both ex-Blenheim pilots, with Roy Boast as navigator/bomb aimer. Despite the small size of the operation, crews never questioned whether this and subsequent raids did any good. Roy Boast recalls, 'I had been in single aircraft operations in Whitleys so the attitude was, 'Let's do the job and get out'.'

The loose vic formation cleared the coast and halfway over the North Sea began climbing on 27,000 feet. With light armament and little armour plate, the Fortress Is relied almost entirely on height for protection against Bf 109s and Bf 110s. Roy Boast recalls, 'We started losing oil from the breathers in two engines at 25,000 feet. It streamed back and started freezing on the tail-plane and the aircraft began vibrating very badly. MacLaren was forced to abandon the attack and I aimed our bomb load on an airfield on Nordeney.'

Meanwhile, MacDougall dropped all four demolition bombs on Wilhelmshaven but two of Mathieson's bombs 'hung-up' and were released over the Frisians on the return journey. Both aircraft climbed to 32,000 feet as two Bf 109Es rose to intercept, but the German fighters lost control at such high altitude and failed to close the attack. It was just as well because the RAF gunners reported that all guns and mountings had frozen. Bombing results at Wilhelmshaven could not be determined because the cameras had also failed to function. Tom Imrie was 'pretty relieved to get back'. Condensation trails were a dead giveaway at our height of 28,000+ but fortunately we did not encounter any fighters. We were on oxygen for almost the entire flight.'

On 23 July Winston Churchill the Prime Minister planned to make a speech in the House of Commons to coincide with a raid by 90 Squadron Fortresses on Berlin. Because the Fortresses would be operating at their extreme range, additional fuel tanks were installed in the bomb bay at the expense of two of the bombs, which reduced the high explosive load to just 2,200 lb. Even so, engine and throttle settings would be critical. Meanwhile, a blackout was imposed and crews were confined to camp at Polebrook much to the chagrin of Tom Imrie and the other airmen, who felt 'boot-faced' (fed up) about it.

Despite the grandiose scheme, once again only three Fortresses were available for the raid which began at 09.00 hours. Wing Commander MacDougall was at the controls of AN530 'F-Freddie' with MacLaren in AN523 'D-Dog' and Mathieson in AN529 'C-Charlie'. MacLaren's navigator/bomb aimer, Roy Boast, recalls:

'It was a beautiful summer's day; 'gin-clear' without a cloud in the sky. We had been told to stick to the throttle and engine settings as briefed but we tended to exceed them. Even so, we could not keep up with the other two aircraft and by the time we crossed the Dutch coast we were only at 23,000 feet. Mike Wayman and 'Mac' didn't want our aircraft to arrive over Berlin on our own and at such a low altitude, so after 'Mac' had checked the fuel and found we had used more than we should have and we were making vapour trails anyway, he decided to abort. MacLaren dived for the deck and we flew home at 100 feet (being ex-Blenheim pilots, 'Mac' and Mike were used to this). We were alive but we thought the other two would get their posthumous VCs.'

However, increasingly thick cloud had forced MacDougall and Mathieson to abort. MacDougall instructed Imrie to radio base. Churchill was presumably warned to change his speech in the Commons. All three aircraft returned safely but Sergeant Denny passed out through lack of oxygen and experienced frostbite to the side of his face. The New Zealander was saved by Tom Danby who attached a walk-around oxygen bottle. Generous tots of rum helped completely to revive him and the Kiwi gunner suffered no lasting effect apart from a huge hangover!

The following day the same three crews were required as part of Operation 'Sunrise', an all-out attack by Nos. 5 and 2 Group squadrons on the battle cruisers *Gneisenau* and *Prinz Eugen* which were berthed in harbour at Brest. MacDougall and MacLaren began the attack, dropping their 1,100-pounders from 27,500 feet. Although bursts were seen on the torpedo station and the outer corner of the dry dock, targets of this nature really required armour piercing bombs if they were to cause any lasting damage. Five Bf 109s rose to intercept the Fortresses, but they soon gave up and veered away to attack the incoming stream of 90 lower flying Hampdens and Wellingtons. The Fortress crews had not been briefed that a large RAF formation would be inbound after they came off the target. One of MacLaren's gunners saw the formation at 10,000 feet; mistook the twin-tailed Hampdens for Bf 110s and shouted that 100 Messerschmitts were below them. MacLaren bolted for home. Nine bombers were lost and no hits were made on the ships.

'Great propaganda value attached to the use of the aircraft' wrote Leslie Kark. 'Fortresses meant something in Europe. Broadcast followed broadcast and privileged visitors all but queued up to visit the Wing Commander's Squadron. I escorted some, ranging from a gallant Gaumont British cameraman, who was bowled over by the slipstream, to the Archdukes Robert and Felix of Austria and I did not tire of the task of 'selling' these aircraft to our guests. There was something visionary and almost impossible about flying at a height where the atmosphere is a quarter of its density on earth. Even the most prosaic of the air-crews, I found, were touched and inspired by the sights they saw. Young men who had been bank clerks, wine merchants, assessors, were now looking at the curvature of the earth and watching, unseen, the colours of the world.

'Keen to obtain impressions from these pioneer voyagers into the upper air, immediately after their raids I wrote out accounts from two very different types of men, Mathieson and Pilot Officer Tony Mulligan [one of the bomb aimers]. Mathieson told me it took him less than an hour to climb more than 30,000 feet above ground after his take-off. There was, frankly, he said, considerable pleasure in knowing they were travelling at a greater height than anyone had ever reached before on a bombing raid. The temperature was 75° Fahrenheit below zero and there was white crystalline frost to a depth of about a quarter of an inch on the astro bowls. He had to fly with front windscreens open because the thickness of the rime had rendered them so opaque. Beads of sweat froze into ice on his flying kit and a film of perspiration congealed on the crew's finger-tips and hurt. The mind at that height is slow, but not insensitive to beauty. The colours of the world from a great height are richer and more intense. The sea, he found, had never been so blue - a flamboyant blue of wonderful depth. The physical reason for this of course is that the air itself reflects blue in the sunlight and the more air you look through the bluer things become. By a strange contrast the sky above tends to grow blacker with height because there are fewer particles of air to reflect the sun. There was no line to mark the sea from the sky and he felt he was flying in a ball of space. He discerned at last a smudge below him more than fifty miles to the south, denoting the whole plain of France.

'The Fortress came over its target and the crew saw the *Gneisenau* in the harbour of Brest appearing about the size of an infant caterpillar. Cross-hairs in the automatic bomb-sight centred over her and the bombs curved down. Among the reflections of the sun glancing on glass specks and on the sheet of water they could pick out the pin-points of flame and then the smoke. Even to the hardened Huns below it must have been terrifying to have felt the shattering explosions and then to have looked up into the sky and seen nothing and heard nothing. So the Fortresses flew back, down through the height at which the white vapour coming from their four engines were whipped into a single trail by the slipstream.

'Mulligan gave me these impressions: On your first high ascent you are keenly aware that you are flying in unexplored space and, realising that you live solely by the grace of God and the oxygen in the bottles, you think of the immensity of the almost Wellsian task you have been given. But after a few trips you become accustomed to new colours in the sky and when, from one point only a hundred miles from the English coast, you can see right across Denmark into the Baltic and into Germany by Hamburg and the plain of Holland lies like a check duster-cloth beneath you, you do little more than note the visibility in your log.'

The Brest raid was the last MacDougall flew on 90 Squadron. He handed over his crew to Mick Wood and Wing Commander Peter F. Webster DSO DFC took over as squadron commander. On 26 July Sergeant Mick Wood flew as first pilot on 'F-Freddie' and with 'C-Charlie' flown by newly promoted Squadron Leader Alexander Mathieson headed for Hamburg. Thunderstorms prevented an attack on the primary so Wood dropped his bomb load on Emden. Mathieson returned to base with his bomb load intact, but Wood's aircraft developed engine trouble and he was forced to land at Horsham St. Faith near Norwich. Two days later the squadron's second flying accident occurred and claimed AN534, which crashed at Wilbarston,Northants, after encountering turbulence during a test flight. Flight Sergeant Brook and Lieutenant Laird W. Hendricks USAAC and crew were killed. Once again, Tony Barwood escaped certain death. He was briefed to make the flight but was delayed after an airman on a routine chamber test developed the 'bends' during a session in the mobile pressure chamber and he had to cope with his descent and possible after effects.

On 2 August AN529 'C-Charlie' flown by Squadron Leader Mathieson and AN530 'F-Freddie' flown by Pilot Officer Frank Sturmey took off to attack Kiel. After 20 minutes into the flight Sturmey was forced to abort with engine problems and brought his bombs back to Polebrook, only to burst his tail wheel tyre on landing. Mathieson carried on to the target alone and successfully dropped all four 1,100lb bombs. At 17.15 hours, his tail wheel tyre repaired, Sturmey took off again and this time headed for Bremen. However, thick cloud made bombing impossible and he headed for the seaplane base at Borkum in the Frisian Islands. Roy Boast dropped his bombs from 32,000 feet. On the way home two Bf 109s intercepted the Fortress at about 20,000 feet over the North Sea and one began attacking the nose while the other concentrated on the beam. Roy Boast, who hastily manned the nose gun, recalls: 'I fired one round and the machine-gun jammed. The fighter came round for another head-on attack and I crouched behind the bombsight. Fortunately, he did not fire (probably out of ammo) but kept on doing head-on attacks while the other carried out beam attacks. We had about 20 holes in the fuselage. I think he was trying to put the beam gunners out of action.' Sturmey lost them after some violent evasive action and made it back to Polebrook without sustaining any casualties.

Apprehension was growing about the B-17C's ability to remain immune from attack on high altitude but operations continued. On 6 August Sturmey in AN523 D-Dog and Alexander Mathieson in AN529 'C-Charlie' set off for another crack at Brest where the battle cruisers *Gneisenau* and *Scharnhorst* were in harbour. Aboard 'C-Charlie' the pilots could only wait, hands off the controls, while Roy Boast took over lateral control of the Fortress through the Sperry auto pilot system linked to the bombsight, to place the cross hairs on the target and keep them there while the bombsight calculated the wind velocity. Suddenly, the intercom crackled in his ear. Sturmey said, 'Where are you going?' Boast replied, 'Nicely on the run', only to be interrupted by a shout, 'Look out to starboard!' The bombs were going down into the sea, proving that the bombsight was way off. Mathieson bombed the target from 32,000 feet and claimed hits.

On 12 August four Fortress Is were ordered to take part in diversionary operations to draw Luftwaffe fighters away from Blenheims of 2 Group which would be making an attack on the Knapsack and Quadrath power stations near Cologne. Because of increasing doubts about the proficiency of bomb aimers and/or the bomb sight, both Roy Boast and Pilot Officer Tony Mulligan (who did the setting) flew as bomb aimers with Pilot Officer Sturmey in 'D-Dog'. Sturmey was briefed to bomb De Kooy airfield in Holland but the target was covered by 8/10ths cloud and an airfield at Texel was bombed instead. Mulligan released his bombs from 32,000 feet after Boast had checked his settings. Boast adds: 'The Sperry was a very good bombsight, in advance of its time. Our problems arose because we tried to use it outside its design capabilities. Sperry's preset calculations had not been fully tested and though they worked well in certain wind conditions they did not in others.'

Meanwhile, Pilot Officer Wayman in AN532 'J-Johnny' bombed Cologne through cloud from 34,000 feet and Pilot Officer Taylor in AN536 'M-Mother' also bombed through cloud over Emden from 33,000 feet. Mick Wood in 'C-Charlie' suffered an engine failure over Oxford (to reach altitude before crossing the coast the aircraft had to fly west turning over the Midlands, as a loaded B-17's rate of climb was so slow) and was forced to return to Polebrook after only 27 minutes.'

Flushed with the success of actually getting four B-17Cs into the air, 90 Squadron was assigned two targets on 16 August. Mick Wood and Pilot Officer Taylor were allocated Düsseldorf while two others attached the *Scharnhorst* and *Gneisenau* at Brest again. Bad weather forced Wood and Taylor to abandon their operation and they returned to Polebrook with their bomb loads intact. Frank Sturmey and Pilot Officer Tom Franks in 'D-Dog', together with Pilot Officer Wayman in 'J-Johnny', made a successful attack on Brest but on the return Sturmey's Fortress was intercepted by seven enemy fighters at 32,000 feet. For 25 minutes Sturmey and Franks carried out a series of violent evasive manoeuvres all the way down to 8,000 feet. Tony Mulligan recalled later on the BBC: 'Three minutes after our bombs had gone Flight Sergeant Fred Goldsmith, the fire controller, called out that here were enemy fighters coming up to us from the starboard quarter, 1,000 feet below. They closed in and here was almost no part of the Fortress which was not hit. A petrol tank was punctured, bomb doors were thrown open, flaps ware put out of action, tail tab shot away, tail wheel stuck half-down, brakes not working, only one aileron any good and the rudder almost out of control. The centre of the fuselage had become a tangle of wires and broken cables; square feet of the wings had been shot away.'

Flight Sergeant Fred Goldsmith had been badly wounded by shrapnel during the first attack but he continued to call out the enemy positions to Sturmey so the pilot could take evasive action and even attempted to cross the open bomb bay to give first aid to the gunners. He was prevented from doing so and an attempt by Mulligan also failed. Unfortunately, the gunners were already beyond help. Sergeant Harold Needle the WOp/AG had been hit in the stomach by cannon fire as he tried in vain to fire his frozen dorsal gun. Sergeant Sidney Ambrose the beam gunner had also been killed during the fighter attacks and Sergeant Michael John Leahy the ventral gunner had been mortally wounded and he died later in hospital. The Luftwaffe pilots only broke off the attack as the English coast came into view. Sturmey decided Polebrook was out of the question and put the badly damaged bomber down at Roborough airfield near Plymouth but he overshot, hit a tank trap and the aircraft caught fire. A Marine sentry sheltering behind the tank traps was killed in the crash.

The raid was described by the anonymous wing commander who informed his readers that on the first occasion that a Fortress was intercepted, which was not until 15 August 1941, it was by a standing patrol. This was after another daylight attack on Brest, this time by Fortresses alone. Flying at a great height, but not at their full ceiling, the bombers crossed the Channel. The weather was such that one of the bombers left vapour trails behind it and it is probable that these were seen by the enemy before the Fortresses reached Brest. Near Brest one of the Fortresses got separated from the rest of the detachment; it swerved to the left of a large patch of cloud while the others swerved to the right. After that it flew on, attacked and returned by itself. Three minutes after the Fortress had bombed, the fighting controller, whose task is to direct the fire of the other gunners, who was standing in the astro hatch and watching every part of the sky, saw two Heinkel 113s coming out from light cloud about 1,000 feet below the Fortress and slightly to starboard. They were joined almost at once by five Messerschmitt 109Fs; all the fighters appeared to come from the same quarter of the sky. Their arrival was so prompt that it was obvious they had come from a standing patrol, almost certainly sent up when the vapour trails were first seen over the sea.

The fighters made many attacks from both sides and from dead astern. Two of the Fortress's gunners and the wireless operator were severely wounded. In spite of his wounds, the wireless operator continued to signal to his base. The captain swung the bomber quickly from side to side and dived, now fast, now slow. Down came all the fighters after him, firing all the while. The Fortress's No. 4 petrol tank was punctured and the crew thought the engine had caught fire; as one of them said, 'There seemed to be no part of the bomber which was not hit.' One of the fighters passed in front of the Fortress as it dived and at once the observer fired at it. Then, when the fight had gone on for twenty minutes, the Fortress reached a low patch or cloud and all the enemy fighters broke away. Black smoke was now pouring from the bomber.

As soon as the fighters had left, the fighting controller, wounded himself in hand and leg, made to reach the other wounded men. But to do this he would have had to walk along a gangway which leads from the pilot's cabin to the rear. The gangway was covered with a tangled mass of wires and cables and the guide-ropes alongside it had been shot away. The bomb doors, damaged in the battle, were wide open and the gangway was now a narrow bridge over empty air and sea. To cross this was no task for a wounded man and the fire controller had to be held back. The observer then tried to get across, but half-way over he found that a slip was almost certain; he went back for his parachute and tried again, but this time his parachute was caught and entangled in the wreckage. He had to give up.

When the Fortress reached the English coast the captain, who still thought that his No. 4 engine might be alight, made for the nearest aerodrome. With flaps out of action, tail tabs shot away, bomb doors wide open, tail wheels stuck half up and half down, brakes not working; only one aileron any good and a scarcely controllable rudder, the captain had to land on a small and unfamiliar aerodrome. With his second pilot doing everything he could to help, he made his landing.

This was one of the few occasions when things went wrong with a Fortress. In other attacks it showed how useful a weapon of war it was. The attacks by Fortresses were an extremely interesting experiment, with promise of much more to come. The Boeing Fortress II is now in large-scale production in America; it made its first flight on 6 September 1941. It is a larger machine than the Fortress I with three gun turrets and able to take a greater load of bombs. As this bomber is designed to cruise at 35,000 feet it will presumably be used for work in daylight, when great height is especially useful.'

Düsseldorf was again targeted on 19 August but bad weather, freezing guns and tell-tale contrails forced Pilot Officer Wayman and Sergeant Wood's crews to abort. Pilot Officer Wayman also had trouble with a turbo. Throttling back was critical at higher altitude as the engine exhaust drove the turbo superchargers. If exhaust pressure flow dropped the turbo would 'stall' and could not be restarted. Wayman's signaller alerted 2 Group that they had, in RAF parlance, 'dropped a turbo'. Group radioed back, 'Where did it fall and could it be recovered because it was classified!'

Another attempt was made on Düsseldorf two days later when three crews were despatched. Squadron Leader Alexander Mathieson led the operation with Mick Wood in AN518 'B-Baker', a new aircraft and Pilot Officer Wayman in J-Johnny. Mathieson was defeated by frozen guns in heavy cloud over Flushing and Wayman was forced to jettison his bombs in the North Sea after developing engine trouble. Mick Wood's guns also froze and after producing massive contrails at altitude, he too decided to abandon the operation. Dusseldorf continued to elude 90 Squadron when on 29 August Mick Wood failed to get airborne in AN533 'N-Nan' and AN536 'M-Mother' flown by Flying Officer Wayman took off but returned early after producing heavy contrails at altitude.

On 31 August 90 Squadron opted for individual sorties and three Fortress Is were despatched to Hamburg, Bremen and Kiel. Mick Wood successfully attacked Bremen in AN518 'B-Baker' with four 1,100lb bombs but Mathieson, who bombed Spikerooge and Wayman, who bombed Bremen, returned with oil and turbo-supercharger problems respectively. Operational problems were now developing at an increasing rate and the shortage of trained ground personnel did not help the cause. The biggest let down though, appeared to be the continuing failure of the bomb sights. Mr Vose, an American civilian who had been involved in the design of the Sperry bombsight, had taken to heart RAF jibes about the dubious accuracy of his bombsight. The old First World War veteran donned RAF uniform and acted as bomb aimer for Mathieson on the operation to Bremen on 2 September. Sturmey and Wood returned with intercom and engine failures respectively, but although Mathieson made it to Bremen, Mr Vose unfortunately placed his bombs wide of the target. At Polebrook he was last seen leaving the Mess, heading for the USA - it was said, to modify his bomb sight!

In the back of crew's minds was the fear that now the Luftwaffe could engage them at altitude, something had to give and they thought it would be sooner rather than later. At the beginning of September 90 Squadron was alerted to provide four Fortresses for a raid on the German battleship *Admiral von Scheer*, which was sheltering in Oslo Fiord. On 5 September four Fortresses with Mick Wood, Sturmey, Flying Officer David Albert Alton Romans DFC and Squadron Leader Mathieson as pilots, were bombed up at Polebrook before flying to Kinloss in northern Scotland. The aim was to attack and destroy the *Admiral von Scheer* then berthed in Oslo. Squadron Leader MacLaren, the detachment commander, flew a reserve Fortress, AN535 'O-Orange' with ground personnel and spares on board. An attempt was made on the 6th, but at that time Oslo was under ten-tenths cloud. Next day four Fortresses set out to bomb the *Admiral von Scheer*. 'O-Orange' aborted with supercharger problems and the other three crews were prevented from bombing a heavy layer of cloud and smoke which shielded the battleship from view. All three bomb loads were dropped on targets of opportunity from 30,000 feet. Crews were told to stand by for another raid on 8 September while bombs were brought from Polebrook for another attempt. Alex Mathieson tried to convince his friend Roy Boast that he should fly with him, as he recalls.

'His bomb aimer was older and Alex said, 'Come on Roy, my chap will stand down. It's wonderful over the mountains of Norway.' I said, 'No, I don't think I want to.' At 09.10 Pilot Officer Sturmey took off and headed for Norway. He was followed five minutes' later by Mick Wood. Flying Officer David Romans followed but Squadron Leader Alex Mathieson in 'N-Nan' was delayed. Again he tried to convince Boast that he was 'missing a great experience' but although Boast was 'half tempted' he did not go. Mathieson and his crew were never seen again. Next day Sturmey and Boast carried out a sea search for Mathieson's crew but it was in vain.

Sturmey in 'J-Johnny' carried on to the target but encountered heavy cloud and was forced to return early to Kinloss without dropping his bombs. Romans had flown Hampdens in the early part of the war and had twice ditched in the North Sea in September 1940 and had made it back safely on each occasion but this time there was no happy ending. At 11.27 two Bf 109s from 13./JG.77 intercepted Romans at 27,000 feet. Romans' gunners shot down one fighter before Unteroffizier Alfred Jakobi, whose aircraft was damaged by return fire, shot down the Fortress. It erupted in flames and crashed at Bygland in the Norwegian mountains. There were no survivors. It was the first Fortress to fall in combat in World War Two. Mick Wood in 'O-Orange' was about one mile astern when the attack started. He immediately jettisoned his bomb load and climbed sharply at maximum throttle to 35,000 feet in an effort to out-climb the fighters. Mick Wood recalled:

'The aircraft was attacked soon after at a height of 30,000 feet. Two engines were disabled, one of which caught fire but this went out. The aileron control was destroyed which made a turn difficult. The floor in Harry Sutton's navigator's compartment was holed and his maps and instruments were sucked out. The fighter broke off his attack - it was suspected that his ammunition was exhausted - and came alongside before returning to his base. Previously enemy fighters had difficulty in reaching and staying at the high altitudes at which the Fortresses flew. But, fortuitously for the Luftwaffe, its only operational units with the Me 109T model, having longer wings and better altitude stability, were based in Norway.'

He gave the order for all crew to be prepared to bail out, but in the rarefied atmosphere the pilot's vocal chords failed to vibrate sufficiently. One of the gunners misunderstood the instruction and switched to his emergency oxygen supply and then passed out when it was exhausted. A waist-gunner, who went to help him, disconnected from the aircraft oxygen supply but did not connect to his portable oxygen bottle and he too passed out. Wood, who could not contact his gunners on the intercom, asked his wireless operator to investigate. When he was told of the gunners' plight he immediately dived the aircraft but at 29,000 feet the enemy fighters attacked again and riddled the aircraft with machine-gun fire. Flight Sergeant Tates was hit in the arm and Sergeant Wilkins was mortally wounded. The wireless operator slipped into unconsciousness when his oxygen lead was severed by a piece of shrapnel. The fuel tank was punctured and began streaming heavy smoke. Fortunately for the Fortress crew the enemy pilots probably assumed that the smoke meant that the Fortress was finished and broke off the attack. The bomb bay doors had remained open all this time and now that the fighters had gone one of the gunners attempted to hand crank them up. He soon passed out when he lost his oxygen supply but Dave Hindshaw the second pilot went to his aid and quickly connected him to another supply.

Mick Wood again: 'Harry Sutton had memorized two radio beacon call signs on the Scottish coast and with these and the radio compass, guided the aircraft to a landfall by which time the height had dropped to 1,500 feet. I ordered the navigator and wireless operator to leave by parachute, but this was ignored with the remark, 'We would rather stay with you.'

Wood nursed the ailing Fortress across the North Sea, one engine was out and he had no aileron control, but the Australian managed to reach Scotland only for another engine to fail. Wood told the crew to take up crash positions: 'With one gunner dead and another severely wounded, I decided to attempt a downwind wheels-up landing at Kinloss. The tyres were punctured and the flaps were not expected to be fully operable. At that time Kinloss was grass and the risk of fire was less there than on the sealed strip at Lossiemouth. With much firing of red Very cartridges we made a downwind approach over the bomb dump to be confronted with an OTU Whitley taking off in the opposite direction. Without flaps the Fortress floated longer than usual before settling down in a cloud of dust. The CO_2 bottles had been fired in the engine nacelles and there was no petrol fire on impact. An American Master Sergeant remarked that two hundred thousand dollars had been spread across the grass. It was thought that it was the first ever wheels-up crash landing of a Flying Fortress.

I recommended Harry Sutton for a DFM for his efforts when all seemed lost. This was refused as there was not an officer witness on board at the time.'

Harry Sutton said: 'Mick Wood was magnificent in his handling of our shot-up Fortress, bringing it back and making a superb crash landing. No one had any idea what would happen when we hit the deck; when it was of paramount importance to get the wounded out as quickly as possible in case the whole thing went up in flames. Thus I removed a hatch aft of the cockpit and braced myself ready for the crash. The moment we 'grated' down the runway, I shot out of the hatch and round to the rear of the aircraft. However, the ambulance boys, who had been following us, beat me to it. When Mick emerged and joined me his first remark was: 'You had me worried for a moment, Harry. You got out so quickly I damn near ran over you!'[44]

The substratosphere fliers' reliance on oxygen was brought home to Leslie Kark when he met Tony Mulligan after returning from the raid on Oslo.

'Oxygen supply pipes were shot away and the pilot, to save the lives of his crew, had to dive through 20,000 feet. Mulligan, too, spoke of the strangeness of natural phenomena at 30,000-odd feet. Foamy white cloud, he said after a successful raid on Emden, stretched all over England like the froth on a huge tankard of beer. As he flew to Germany the horizon turned with quite sudden changes from a fantastic purple to green and then from green to yellow. There was a haze, he told me, over Germany but he could see Emden fifty miles away. He called to the pilot in the jargon the British Fortress pilots were using: 'Stand by for bombing. Bombsight in detent, 'George' in. OK, I've got her.' He showed me the drill on the automatic sight. There were eleven knobs, two levers and two switches to operate. On the bombing panel there were five more switches and three levers and in addition the automatic camera to start. The navigator kept his eye down the sighting tube, containing twenty-six prisms and worked the bomb-release with his wrist.

Only four more individual sorties were flown after the Oslo debacle. Of these only Sturmey's attack on Emden on 20 September was successful. His bomb aimer, Tony Mulligan, recalls:

'We lost sight of our aerodrome at 2,000 feet and never saw the ground again until we were off the Dutch islands. Foamy white cloud, like the froth on a huge tankard of beer, stretched all over England and for about 30 miles out to sea. The horizon turned - quite suddenly - from purple to green and from green to yellow. It was hazy but I could see Emden fifty miles away. As the cross hairs centred over a shining pinpoint on which the sun was glinting, the bombs went down. We were still two miles away from Emden when we turned away. Almost a minute later one of the gunners told us through the intercom, 'There you are, bursts in the centre of the target' and back we came through those extraordinary tints of sky. During the whole sortie I only had one thrilling moment. I saw a Messerschmitt coming towards us. It seemed an improved type and I looked again. It was a mosquito which had got stuck on the Perspex in the take-off and had frozen stiff. The windows' frequently were splashed, with refrigerated insects' blood. But this chap seemed the right shape for a Hun.

'Otherwise, it proved a typical trip in a Fortress, with the temperature at minus 30°C.'

The most fascinating factor for Leslie Kark in the Fortress raids remained the remarkable colours. 'Sturmey told that on the Emden raid the tints of the sky were even more extraordinary on the return journey than on the outward. The rainbow kaleidoscope ended, he said, with a shining white horizon - like snow in the sun. Over England the cloud formation below exactly compared with the shape of the land. Every bay and inlet was repeated in the strato-cumulus, appearing like a white canopy over the island.' (Sturmey flew another sortie to Emden five days later but the operation was aborted when his aircraft began producing the tell-tale contrails at 27,000 feet). Mulligan, grinning, told Leslie Kark about the dead mosquito on his window. 'In many ways they were memorable and sometimes amusing months in which the British experimented with Fortresses on operations, worthy of recall now that the Americans have developed to such spectacular limits the aircraft modifications and tactics pioneered, now long ago, by the RAF.'

To all intents and purposes 90 Squadron's brief career on the B-17C Fortress was at an end, although on 26 October four Fortresses each with two bomb-bay tanks flew to the Middle East as 90 Squadron detachment leaving five in England to continue operations on 90 Squadron. The four Fortresses flew to Portreath and then out into the Bay of Biscay, over the Pyrenees and the Mediterranean to Malta. Each aircraft carried one additional man. Squadron Leader Andy MacLaren flew as CO with 'Junior' Jim Taylor as second pilot, Kendrick Cox as spare pilot and Tom Imrie as Fire Controller. Tex O'Camb, the Engineering Officer and his assistant, Crew Chief Flight Sergeant Murray, flew with Pilot Officer Freddie Stokes and Flying Officer Frank Sturmey and Barwood, travelling as the specialist flying doctor, flew with Flight Officer James Stevenson with Flight Sergeant Ken Brailsford as his No. 2 and Flying Officer Struthers RCAF as navigator. The next day they flew on to Fayoum, south of Cairo and later went on to Shallufa after the customary 'flying the flag' over Cairo, on 31 October. Operations began on 8 November when Stevenson and Stokes in AN529 'C-Charlie' carried out a daylight raid on Benghazi from 20,000 feet. As the bomb bay doors were open throughout the bombing run the vented hydraulic fluid from the operation of the auto-pilot: swirled up into the bomb bay and froze the lower bomb releases.

Tony Barwood, who was on board to experience high altitude operations under desert conditions, recalls:

'It was the passenger's job to be ready with two screwdrivers to manually operate the lower releases if the bombs failed to come off. On this occasion manual release under the direction of the bomb aimer over the intercom was necessary. It did not contribute to the accuracy of the bombing! There was some flak, which was a shock as we weren't expecting any. Shortly after turning for home the aircraft progressively ran out of fuel, engines 1, 2 and 3 being feathered in turn. The crew prepared to bail out but a convenient wadi came up and Stevenson effectively crash-landed about 200 miles south east of Tobruk, then under siege by Rommel's army and about 200 miles from the wire at the Libyan-Egyptian border. Apart from some sand in the eyes, nobody was injured. We were not trained in desert survival so we stayed put with the aircraft for about 36 hours. It was extremely cold at night. Struthers, the Canadian navigator, took photographs as we destroyed the Sperry bombsight by machine-gun fire. We then opened 500 rounds of ammunition and, using oil and cordite, set fire to the aircraft and then hurriedly beat it. We walked hard during the next three nights as it was so cold, then laid up best we could during the day. We saw several unidentified patrols but we were not sure whether they were theirs or ours and one patrol actually passed between us as we walked in pairs at distance. We had sufficient water for at least 14 days which could have been extended by more severe rationing. We saw what we thought were Ju 88s approaching but as they came nearer, we identified them as South African Air Force Marylands and fired off a Very signal cartridge. They signalled us to stay put and later returned to drop four canisters, three of which fell away from their parachutes and we arrived in time to see the water being sucked greedily into the desert. They had called for ground rescue and we were later picked up by an armoured unit of the Long Range Desert Group and dumped back on an advance desert strip.'

From about December 1941 the three remaining B-17Cs in the desert operated with the Royal Navy from Fuka satellite on the North African coast between Mersa and Alexandria against shipping in the Mediterranean. A Naval observer was attached to 90 Squadron for ship recognition purposes. One aircraft flown by Freddie Stokes with Flight Lieutenant 'Tiny' Nisbet attacked an Italian cruiser and the fourth bomb in a stick of four very nearly hit the target, but the vessel turned at the last moment. A Bf 110 attacked and badly damaged one of the B-17's engines. Stokes made it back safely to Shallufa where Chief Murray and Tony Barwood, bereft of spares, repaired the inlet manifold with elastoplast and Plaster of Paris!

The second Fortress to suffer a mishap was AN521 on 8 January 1942. Frank Sturmey took 'K-King' aloft for a fuel consumption test but, at 20,000 feet and about six miles northwest of Shallufa oil pressure was lost in the No. 3 engine. Tony Barwood was flying this day with a German oxygen regulator salvaged from a Junkers. He had this Draeger device connected to a single 750-litre oxygen cylinder and had slightly modified his mask to be compatible with the regulator function. After some time at 20,000 feet he saw that the oil pressure on No.3 was zero and immediately informed the captain. No.3 could not be feathered as there was no oil left in the engine sump, due to a broken oil pipe, so it ran away and eventually caught fire. He went aft to warn the rest of the crew who he found playing cards, blissfully unaware of their predicament! Barwood had no sooner said 'We have a problem' when he saw two parachutes floating behind them. He had assumed they were going to land but a look up the catwalk to the cockpit revealed that Sturmey, Franks and Mulligan had bailed out. By now the Fortress was dangerously low. Barwood recalls, 'I picked up a chest parachute and bailed out at 400 feet at 300 knots. My boots flew off and two panels in my 'chute were ripped out but I landed safely. Lieutenant 'Kipper' Baring, a Royal Navy ship recognition expert flying with us on a familiarisation exercise, broke both his ankles on landing. Flight Sergeant Mennie bailed out of the astrodome hatch and was killed when he struck the tail and Sergeant Tuson died after he bailed out too low.'

On 12 February 1942 90 Squadron was disbanded at Polebrook and the Shallufa detachment became part of 220 Squadron serving in that theatre. The two surviving B-17Cs were flown to India complete with ground crews while some of the air crews, including Tom Imrie, embarked on an Imperial Airways Empire flying-boat.

'We boarded *Cameronian* on the Nile on 10 May and made several two-hour hops totalling 17 hours 15 minutes' flying time across the Middle East and Karachi before landing at Pandeshwar, near Assensol in Bengal on 11 May. We never flew any operations, the two B-17Cs being handed over to the USAAF in December 1942 and were used for continuation training.'

So ended an unfortunate period in RAF Bomber Command operations using the Fortress I. It should not be forgotten, however, that many lessons were learned about high altitude flight and these led to improvements in oxygen supply, flying clothing and lubricants while the Fortress design was subsequently improved with the addition of armour plating, self sealing tanks and better armament, all of which were incorporated in the B-17D which followed the 'C' off the production lines. By this time the Americans themselves had also learned the hard way, in combat in the Pacific, that although it was a dependable, immensely strong fighting machine, the B-17 lacked the necessary turrets and tail guns, fire-power and armour plate that were to become a feature of the B-17Fs and Gs used in massed daylight formations of 'Forts' that carried on the offensive from England in the colours of the 8th Air Force during 1942-45. For the time being at least, the RAF Fortress I crews had discovered that high level daylight precision bombing was not the method with which to defeat Nazi Germany.

Endnotes for Chapter Seven

40   Arthur Leslie Kark was born in Johannesburg on 12 July 1910 and was educated at Clayesmore School in Dorset and St John's College, Oxford and was called to the bar in 1932. He became features editor of World's Press News (1933), editor of Photography magazine (1934), public relations officer to the Advertising Association (1935), features editor of the News Review (1936) and news editor at the Ministry of Information (1940), alternating as the New York *Herald Tribune's* London theatre critic. He served in the RAF from 1940 to 1946, and wrote the official Far East air war history. His 1945 novel, Red Rain, was about a bomber crew on an operation from which only one returns. Other novels included *An Owl In The Sun* (1948), *Wings Of The Phoenix* (1949) and *On The Haycock* (1957), all intelligent, middlebrow works with an elegance of style that was seen in *Courier* magazine, which he founded and co-edited (1947-1951). Kark bought the Lucie Clayton College in 1950 from Sylvia Golledge, who had started it in 1928. Socially ambitious parents almost automatically sent their daughters to a Lucie Clayton College. Sylvia Golledge became his second wife. In 1960 he started the dressmaking and design school and five years later the secretarial college. He was fond of listing the syllabus: care for the English language, make-up, deportment, elegance, cookery and art appreciation. At the end of the Sixties, Kark disposed of the model agency, which had earlier cradled such stars as Fiona Campbell-Walter (later Baroness Thyssen), Celia Hammond, Paulene Stone, Jean Shrimpton and Sandra Paul (now Mrs Michael Howard). He died aged 93 on 23 February 2004.

41   The Fortress Is were serial numbered AN518 to AN537. On 11 May the squadron took delivery of two B-17Cs, AN534 and AN529.

42   Apart from those already named, three other men were also killed.

43   Quoted in *Experiences of War: The British Airman* by Roger Freeman (Arms & Armour 1989). On the night of 21/22 February 1945 43-year old Group Captain Anthony Caron 'Tiny' Evans-Evans the Coningsby station commander who at take-off time would insist on waving and even saluting each Lancaster as it took off, had managed to borrow an 83 Squadron Lancaster and get a crew together so that he could make the trip to Gravenhorst. The previous summer this huge 'teddy-bear' of a man had squeezed himself into the pilot's seat of a Lancaster and took a crew on what turned out to be a hair-raising cross-country flight. When he landed the crew had gone to see their Squadron CO and told him that they flatly refused to fly with the station commander ever again. Evans-Evans had not let that worry him and he took a scratch crew on an operation in August to Caen, for which he received a DFC. He believed that this award had too easily been earned when compared to aircrew who flew many ops without recognition, so for his second trip he had rounded up a scratch crew for the 5 Group operation by 165 Lancasters and a dozen Mosquitoes to the Mittelland Canal. Included on the crew was 22-year old Squadron Leader William Geoffrey 'Jock' Wishart DSO DFC* the 97 Squadron Navigation Leader, who had flown 83 trips. Wishart never completed his 84th trip nor Evans-Evans his second; a night fighter shot the Lancaster down over the liberated part of Holland and Pilot Officer E. H. Hansen RAAF was the only man who survived to tell the tale. Bomber Command claimed that the canal was rendered '100 per cent unserviceable'

44   90 Squadron were to get involved with the Admiral Scheer again, as Roy Boast, who shortly after Oslo got his wish to rejoin a Halifax squadron, recalls. 'On 9/10 April 1945 I was bomb aimer in the Deputy Master Bomber aircraft - 405 Squadron RCAF (PFF) - on a raid on Kiel. Part of the job was to mark the target for the Main Force of nearly 600 aircraft including Lancasters on 90 Squadron (then in 3 Group). The Master and Deputy stayed in the target area throughout the raid directing subsequent waves of aircraft. The Admiral Scheer was hit several times and capsized. I like to think that perhaps 90 Squadron had some revenge for Oslo.'

Chapter 8

Strange Assignment

Leslie Kark

On 25 September 1942 the expert low-level raiders on 105 Squadron carried out the longest Mosquito operation thus far when Squadron Leader George Parry (later Wing Commander George Parry OBE DSO DFC*) and three other crews attacked the Gestapo HQ in Oslo, a round-trip of 1,100 miles with an air time of 4 hours 45 minutes. They attacked in two pairs, Parry leading the first pair, with Pilot Officer Rowland close up on his starboard quarter; then came Flying Officer Bristow, with Flight Sergeant Gordon K. Carter and Sergeant William S. Young on his right. During the run up to the target, three FW 190s made a diving attack from the starboard quarter, one going for the leading pair and two for the second. Bristow had to turn a few degrees left to get on to his target and Carter was thus left rather farther astern and was hit; one of Rowland's airscrews was hit by a cannon shell which exploded on the spinner. Parry's aiming was good and Rowland actually saw his bombs strike the roof of the Gestapo building. After being hit, Carter and Young turned left and were last seen, still under control, making towards Sweden with one engine apparently on fire and a fighter on their tail. The Mosquito blew up and crashed in to a lake killing both crew. The post-mortem and camera pictures taken on the raid revealed that at least four bombs had entered the roof of the Gestapo HQ; one had remained inside and failed to detonate and the other three had crashed through the opposite wall before exploding.

A little anxiously, by the fire of the Golden Lion, I made the introduction: 'Squadron Leader Parry, Mr. X; Mr. X, Squadron Leader Parry.'

Mr. X was a distinguished and elderly Norwegian journalist from Oslo. Squadron Leader George Parry was young but equally distinguished as a British pilot who had just bombed Oslo. He had led the formation of Mosquitoes in a low-level attack on the Gestapo Headquarters. Wondering about a man's reactions on encountering a pilot who, with the best will in the world, had dropped a salvo of bombs across the places one had grown used to in the home town, I surveyed doubtfully the possibilities of the encounter.

'Squadron Leader Parry?' began the Norwegian. 'You are the leader of the men who bombed Oslo?'

'Well - er - yes,' said Parry and added, I thought a shade thinly in view of the circumstances. 'There was some smoke going up when we left.'

The Norwegian put his hand to his pocket and drew out pencil and paper: He made a sketch of the streets around the Gestapo Headquarters. 'I used to take my coffee there,' he said, placing an 'X' at a corner and my uncle has a place there. Now, please, where were your bombs?'

'There' said the Squadron Leader, without hesitation marking an 'X' between the two. There was immeasurable emotion in the distinguished Norwegian's eyes when he said, 'Thank you. Thank you, good Squadron Leader Blank.' And they shook hands and fell to yarning about the fir trees Parry had observed in the district where the Norwegian played as a child; how white and lovely Oslo had seemed, stained only by the Swastika over the Gestapo building; about the harvesters who were at work on the sheaves arranged like wind-breaks; and of the sailing yachts in Oslo fjord. It was a moving conversation. Was there ever before so curious a means of a wakening a nostalgic mood in an elderly man by the reminiscence of youth?

It was for me also a means of evoking a considering of the strange role, which, among other things, brought me there to the Golden Lion between the pilot and the reporter.

The assignment was symbolic, for I was, after all, one of a world-wide Air Ministry Directorate pointed to that one aim, to introduce the Air Force to the public through newspapers, radio, films, books, magazines and, where possible, in person.

The official title of the post is that of PRO or Public Relations Officer. Inevitably this gives rise to spontaneously sparkling witticisms among, both air - crews and reporters about public-houses, private relations and so forth and, it can be said with modest pride, the PRO, once inured, laughs these off on each occasion as though they were new to him.

The work of a PRO in the field, attached to a Group Headquarters, is mainly that of an official war correspondent who writes, not immediately for the newspapers or the BBC, but for Air Ministry. From there, after censorship and scrutiny, the material, largely collected from attending interrogations of air-crews on their return from operations, is sent to the Ministry of Information, whence it goes out to the assembled representatives of the broadcast companies and newspapers of the world.

A Public Relations Officer has however, roles other than relating about the Air Force to the public. He brings such of the public as can come to, the Royal Air Force. There he has the duty of explaining to them whatever he can and whatever is open. The office of dominie among the bombers is both enjoyable and flattering; nevertheless learning from visitors, rather than the vanity of teaching, has given me some of the war's best private moments.

This I know is unorthodox procedure for a guide, rather as though the sacristan at the Abbey were to pause in his monologue on the tombs of the knights and turn to his tourists to say, 'Now for a change you tell me some of your own adventures.' But we live remote from town and the stream of visitors is a way of keeping in touch.

Our visitors have ranged from the King and Queen down to all who have been officially 'vetted' and have good reason to come. I have little in the way of Royal anecdotes except to say that, after inspecting an aerodrome, His Majesty attended the races' where he led his horse in after winning the Oaks. It was the first occasion on which he had that honour and the King was in RAF uniform. It wasn't reported at the time, but the horse, not satisfied with winning a classic, bent down to take a nibble at the very

As CO of 107 Squadron, Basil Embry led many raids in the 1940 Belgian campaign during April–May, taking his squadron into battle at Sedan on 14 May. He was shot down on 27 May, escaping from captivity to England and subsequently became involved in night-fighting. After a spell of command posts in Operation 'Crusader' in the Western Desert and in Fighter Command AVM (later ACM Sir Basil Embry) took up the post of AOC 2 Group, Bomber Command at Bylaugh Hall, Norfolk on 27 May 1943 with the task of preparing the Group for invasion support in the run-up to Operation Overlord. He is seen here greeting Polish Major General Stanislav Sosabowski. (*RAF Swanton Morley*)

A Boston turns away after bombing the Emmasingel valve and lamp factory, about 1 mile south of the main Philips works in Eindhoven during Operation 'Oyster' on 6 December 1942; and the target for 88 and 226 Boston Squadrons and 21 Ventura Squadron. The leading aircraft on 88 Squadron attacked at rooftop height with 11-second delay bombs, and the remaining aircraft bombed at 1,000-1,500 feet with HE and incendiary bombs. (RAF)

Sergeant Ted Leaver DFM, Flight Lieutenant 'Yogi' Yates-Earl DFC and Pilot Officer Ken Houghton DFC on 226 Squadron, who crewed AL678/R on the Eindhoven raid, examine a seagull's head that completely penetrated the leading edge of their Boston wing during the operation. *(George Casey)*

Flying Officer 'Jack' Rutherford RNZAF, Squadron Leader J. S. Kennedy and Flight Sergeant Eric Lee on 226 Squadron, who crewed Z2234/X on the Eindhoven raid on Sunday 6 December 1942. *(George Casey)*

A rear facing camera view of the destruction at Eindhoven. *(RAF)*

226 Squadron veterans of the Eindhoven operation, 6 December 1942. Left to right: Flight Sergeant W. H. C. 'Erby' Leavitt RCAF who flew W8287/F; Flying Officer L. P. Frizzle who flew Z2261; Flying Officer Bert Hoskins; and Flight Lieutenant Don T. Smith, who flew W8337. Leavitt was awarded the DFM for the Eindhoven raid.(*RAF*)

(Centre) Wing Commander R. J. P. Pritchard AFC CO of 21 Squadron, pictured beside his Ventura II, AFSS6 'Z-Zebra', in which he led his squadron over Eindhoven. He received the DFC for his action, one of eight awarded to aircrew who took part on the operation. The cartoon duck is entitled (*via Wilf Clutton*)

(Bottom) 226 Squadron (L to R) Jock Rutherford, Squadron Leader Shaw Kennedy, Flying Officer Ken Houghton, Sergeant Eric Lee, Flight Lieutenant Yogi' Yates-Earl, Pilot Officer G. Tolputt, Sergeant Johnny Bicknell, Pilot Officer Don T. Smith, three u/ks, Flight Sergeant Doug Farquhar, u/k, Melhuish, u/k, Flight Sergeant Erby Leavitt DFM, Paddy McKee, u/k, Pilot Officer Bert Hoskins, three u/ks, Sergeant George Currah (KIA 19.1.1943), Pilot Officer Cliff Thomas (KIA 29.1.1943), Flying Officer 'Dickie' Bowyer (KIA 29.1.1943). (*George Casey*)

Smoke rises from several sections of the Philips Emmasingel valve and lamp factory. *(British Official)*

Boston III AL749 'R-Robert' on 88 Squadron flown by Pilot Officer Jack Peppiatt of B' Flight behind Flight Lieutenant Johnny Reeve on the Eindhoven raid (Operation 'Oyster') on Sunday 6 December 1942. AL749, a Boeing-built machine, had a chequered career, serving with 88 and 114 Squadrons and 155 MU before the undercarriage jammed up and the aircraft was belly landed at Setif, Algeria on 24 October 1943 and damaged beyond repair. *(Jack Peppiatt)*

Bombs dropped from 8,000 feet by 226 Squadron Bostons, led by Wing Commander Surplice DSO DFC, fall on Caen-Carpiquet aerodrome on 6 November 1942. *(RAF)*

On 22 September 1942, 18 Bostons on 88, 107 and 226 Squadrons set out to attack power stations and secondary targets in northern France. Flying Officer D. Grundy and his observer Flying Officer E. T. Coxall on 88 Squadron were awarded the DFC for their low-level attack on the Aciéries de France Isergues iron foundry which they left enveloped in flames. *(RAF)*

On 8 August 1943 38 Bostons on 88, 107 and 342 Squadrons carried out a low-level raid on the Naval Stores Depot at Rennes. The first six aircraft on 107 Squadron, led by Wing Commander 'Dickie' England, attacked from 50 feet and the remainder from 1,200-1,500 feet, dropping 5,800 lb of bombs. The target was well hit and the main section was set on fire. Intense flak brought down Pilot Officer W. P. Angus on 88 Squadron and Squadron Leader Spencer on 107 Squadron was forced to crash-land at Hurn. *(RAF)*

Hits can be seen on the Finalens chemical works at Douvrin in this remarkable low-level photograph taken by Sergeant Savage's Boston on 88 Squadron during his attack on 22 September 1942.

The Denain steel and armament works under attack by twelve Bostons on 88 Squadron led by Squadron, Leader Cunningham, on 16 August 1943. (RAF)

A photograph of Comines power station on 8 March 1942 taken by a retreating Boston at 50 feet. *(via Nigel Buswell)*

The first Boston 'Circus' operations (C-112A & B) took place on 8 March 1942 when six aircraft on 107 Squadron attacked the Abbeville marshalling yards and three on 88 and three on 107 attacked the Comines power station. In the afternoon six Bostons on 226 and six on 88 Squadron carried out the first daylight bombing raid of the war on Paris with an attack from 400 feet on the Ford Motor Works at Matford, which is seen here burning after the raid. Wing Commander V. S. Butler DFC, CO 226 Squadron, who led the operation, was killed. *(RAF)*

Fortress I on 90 Squadron in flight. *(RAF Hendon)*

A 90 Squadron Fortress I crew get suited up for high-altitude flight. All crew-members had been sent to Farnborough where they had been exposed to a routine 'bends' test in the decompression chamber, as the Fortress I was expected to fly at heights well in excess of 30,000 feet. At first, electrically heated one-piece suits made by Seibe-Gorman with electrically heated gloves and boots were worn, but they restricted movement, which was so essential for the gunners, were bulky and not very reliable. In August 1941 one-piece 'Taylor' suits, but much more easily donned, with an electrically heated lining, glove lining and socks, became available. The suit also provided built-in flotation, was reliable, and much easier to move in. These were used with fleecy lined flying boots and soft leather gauntlets. *(IWM)*

Sergeant Mick Wood's crew on 90 Squadron (left to right) Danny Clifford, gunner; Tom Danby, gunner; Tom Imrie, WOp/AG; Harry Sutton, navigator/bomb aimer (?) gunner; Mick Wood, captain; Dave Hindshaw, co-pilot. *(Antony Barwood)*

RAF and US personnel after a sortie by 90 Squadron Fortress Is.

Boeing Fortress I (Model 299U) AN530 (40-2066) 'F-Freddie' joined 90 Squadron on 10 July 1941 and operated with them until 12 February 1942 when it joined 220 Squadron (MB-J) in Coastal Command. After service in Egypt and India the aircraft was returned to the USAAF on 2 December 1942 and was destroyed in a ground fire. (Charles E. Brown)

The air and ground crew on 'B-Beer' on 88 Squadron, Wing Commander I. J. Spencer's former aircraft, at Hartford Bridge. Flying Officer Thompson, navigator (who after being shot down, escaped from France and spent six months in a Spanish jail); Squadron Leader Pushman RCAF; Flight Sergeant Mike Cleary DFM; and Sergeant Clarke, under-gunner. *(Mike Cleary via Paul Lincoln)*

(Bottom) The air and ground crew of 'N-Nuts' AVI RYMPERE AVI STIRCVS FACIRE on 88 Squadron at Hartford Bridge late in 1944. Left to right: A. F. W. Valle-Jones; Mike Henry; Wing Commander I. J. Spencer with 'Butch'; and Flying Officer G. E. Ploughman. *(Mike Henry via Roy Brookes)*

Top: 180 Squadron Mitchell IIs at Foulsham, Norfolk in June 1943. The nearest aircraft is FL684/'S', which operated with the squadron from 19 June until 20 March 1944. Behind is FL707/'Z', which served with the squadron from 3 October 1942 and was shot down on 26 November 1943 during a raid on Martinvast. Nos. 180 and 98 Squadrons flew their first operation on 22 January 1943 when six on each squadron bombed oil targets in Belgium. FL684 was SOC on 17 December 1946. *(John Smith-Covington via Theo Boiten)*

(Middle) Squadron Leader Len Trent DFC RNZAF the 487 Squadron RNZAF 'B' Flight Commander, who hailed from Nelson in New Zealand was invested with the Victoria Cross by HM King George VI at a ceremony at Buckingham Palace on 1 March 1946 with Wing Commander Yeo-Thomas RAFVR ('The White Rabbit') who received the George Cross for his secret missions in occupied France. Trent's award was for the action on 3 May 1943 when he led a dozen Venturas in an attack on the Amsterdam Power Station. None returned. Trent's Ventura was the last to go down with two crew trapped inside but he and one other crewmember were hurled from the doomed aircraft and were taken prisoner. It was only after they were repatriated that the full story became known and Trent was awarded the VC for his leadership and gallantry.

Bottom: 320 Squadron personnel clear snow off the wings and fuselage of a Mitchell at Melsbroek, Brussels on 8 January 1943. *(via Jan P. Kloos)*

Flight Lieutenant Victor 'Robbie' Robson DFC* (left) and Squadron Leader (later Group Captain) D. A. G. 'George' Parry DSO DFC* on 105 Squadron who led the highly successful pinpoint raid by four Mosquitoes of 105 Squadron on the Gestapo HQ in Oslo on 25 September 1942 in front of their Mosquito B.IV 'G-George' soon after the raid. *(George Parry)*

shoulder of monarchy. I never saw a man drop a horse quicker in my life. The King handed the lead over and smiled.

I certainly do not intend to imply from this Royal reference that even a small proportion of the people who have come my way in this work have been smiling kings. Indeed the first visitor who comes to mind was a very sad-faced girl who somehow changed for the better the views on Russia of almost an entire bomber squadron.

The girl was a Soviet warrior who on the Odessa front and elsewhere had killed 309 Germans.

Now 309 is a considerable score of Germans and there was inevitable speculation when we were told this fine Russian Amazon was coming to visit a bomber station. I suppose we expected something like Boadicea in Red Army uniform.

When she arrived at the satellite our only surprise was that this blooded little warrior was attractive. She used no make-up. She inspected an aircraft and, through her interpreter, said the usual things and all was going according to plan.

As we talked an aircraft flew across us and we witnessed one of those occasional but inevitable flying accidents. We saw the plane go up in flames. There was not a chance of any of the crew being saved alive. It was then that the girl lieutenant astonished us.

This phenomenal killer of Huns looked at the flames, turned away and unashamedly wept. Then she went into the briefing room and made a fluent speech for the news-reels about the glory of the RAF. But somehow, as I have said, she had affected our ideas about the Soviet Union and women warriors in general. It strangely increased our admiration a hundredfold for her sniper's record.

Most guests have come up to witness daylight operations and those whom I haven't been able to warn have all for one cause or another been up and ready for the break of dawn. When I have gone to meet them at a Christian hour they have already been almost worn-out with the excitement of waiting. I suppose the reason is that if you see enough films on a subject the idea becomes a fixation. Visitors somehow never thought there could be any other type of daylight raid except a 'dawn show'. After a little while I tumbled to this idea and if possible used to warn them the night before that most often there was little reason why they shouldn't have a perfectly normal breakfast. Robert Riskin, who wrote *Mr. Deeds Goes to Town*, was, I remember, a victim of this fixation and at 9 am I found the unfortunate man already exhausted. In a way I thought it a kind of poetic justice for a person who not only sees the films, but writes them.

I must digress to say that from these reminiscences - and I mention only those friends whom I know don't mind my writing of them - you should not imagine that guidance of strangers comprises even the main part of the work of a Bomber Command PRO after he has contributed his account of the day's or the night's bombing. Miscellanea have a habit of swiftly disposing of your odd free day. I refer to such work as the liaison between Forces and Factories, for which purpose we try to organise a succession of operational men from air-crews to visit the workers. This last is comparatively simple because real workers fortunately don't expect Air Force types to be articulate. Factory visits by pilots help the war, but the aircrews don't flatter themselves that the good is done by the power of speech. About the most successful factory visit we had was made by a pilot of some forty Operational trips.

Parry had been to Berlin and places but he'd never faced 400 girls in a canteen. He was on the platform and when he was asked to tell his experiences he went rather grey. He stood up, gaped at the sea of faces and not a word came from him. He looked around for help and the silence was wonderful. Then he straightened his tie and said, 'Good God, have I got to speak?' The girls said yes. 'Well, the only two things I really feel like doing,' he said, 'are to kiss that girl in the second row and get to hell out of here.'

Later he privately observed he would rather go to Berlin again, but they say the graph curve showing the amount of work done in the factory went straight up after that statement and shot through the roof. So you can see the factory part really doesn't require anyone quite as good as Sir Stafford Cripps.

Apart from the writing and the privilege of living among the Squadrons, the spare-time occupation of guiding strangers salts the work with many minor pleasures. It gives one a new view of people outside the Service, even though this view is occasionally one of your visitor doing a cabman's dance on the edge of a flare-path in a vain, effort to keep warm on a freezing night.

But this too has its rewards and after a while one knows the things to point out to distinguished strangers. For instance, I find they like to see the four engines of a Stirling ringed with hot red in the dark when first the bomber begins to race along the runway. And they enjoy watching, from the balcony of the control room, the bombers returning in the early morning, while through the window they can hear the wireless directions from Control to the pilots, telling them when to land.

Recently I was having tea with men of a Mosquito Squadron [105] after they had returned from a daylight [on 20 December 1942 when 11 Mosquitoes on 105 and 139 Squadrons led by Squadron Leader Reggie Reynolds (later Wing Commander 'Reggie' W. Reynolds DSO DFC) with Pilot Officer Ted Sismore (later Flight Lieutenant Ted Sismore DSO DFC) attacked railway targets in the Oldenburg-Bremen area in northwest Germany). One Mosquito came down so low that the crew read the name *Fritz* on a river-tug. The bombers swept over men working on a new barracks and one pilot reported later that 'They were near the end of the work and we finished it off for them'.] 'There was a story,' someone says, 'of a bomber the other night seeing a Stirling in trouble with searchlights. And what does the gallant pilot do but go to the other bloke's assistance and divert the flak!'

'Would you say,' I ask, 'that so crazy an action of sacrifice would be even more unlikely in daylight?'

'Sure. Much more unlikely.'

'Last night I should have agreed with you,' I say, 'but this afternoon I have telephoned a story through to Command about an incident that happened this morning over Oldenburg. A Squadron Leader [Reggie Reynolds] bombed a gas-holder [near Delmenhorst]. As his bombs went, his port engine was hit by an explosive shell. He dived down from 1,000 feet and saw the gas-holder exploding and flames come from the side. [45] But that's by the way. Oil was pouring from his engine; also on the dive he had other troubles from a party of rooks. One cracked a hole in his leading edge and another rook joined him in the cockpit for company. The skipper continued on one engine.

'Now the Squadron Leader had a Number Two [Warrant Officer Arthur Raymond Noesda from Western Australia, who had flown Blenheims on suicidal anti shipping strikes from Malta] who saw he was in trouble; so the Number Two dived down with him and then had to throttle right back to minus-four boost so as not to overshoot his leader. They passed over Wilhelmshaven Bay, where the natives became very hostile. And then you have the picture of these two Mosquitoes doing a David and Jonathan act skimming over Wilhelmshaven Bay, with land guns pooping at them from both sides and Number Two never adding a mile to his Air Speed Indicator in case the one-engined man should be left behind.

'Then a Hun warship tried a little practical joke. Instead of firing at the Mosquitoes they fired shells into the sea, sending up columns of water a hundred-odd feet to catch them. An old trick, but it didn't work. And Number Two never changed from his slow speed until they both got back to base. The Squadron Leader might have had to ditch.[46]

'Now is that or isn't it even a gutsier thing than taking the searchlights from somebody? I don't suppose everyone would do it and maybe it's rare, but it happens. In fact it happened from this Squadron, at this station, this morning.'

'Well, dang me,' says the other chap,' who was the Number Two?'

'Warrant Officer Noseda,' puts in the Wing Commander [Hughie Edwards VC DSO DFC].

'Old Nosey do that? Good old Nosey.'[47]

In this job a task far more difficult than the removal of hyperbole from an account of operations is the discovery of truth from understatement. A Ventura Wing Commander returned from Abbeville to say: 'I go. I come back. Nice day.' The trip had, it appeared, been uneventful.

Once I was with Wing Commander Peter Shand, now regrettably missing, when he was handed an RAF telegram, 'What's it say Peter? Someone asked. 'Oh, it's just a message from an old client,' said Peter. 'Only saying hey, hey.' It was, I knew, official congratulations from the Commander-in-Chief on a particularly daring Mosquito raid which Shand had led.[48]

How is it that you can tell the air-crew type immediately you go into a room? I have met pilots who were grocers, pilots who were going to be monks and whose names in religion were not their names in uniform, a pilot who was a mid-Western sheriff, Jewish pilots, captains of bombers who had been drapers, insurance salesmen, meat middle-men. As the war has continued, the crew-rooms which, once were filled with men from these islands have increased their proportion of Dominion fliers and always the impression has remained - that whatever they did, wherever they are, these are the cream of the world.

Endnotes for Chapter Eight

45   Reynolds' four 500lb GP bombs set the gasometer on fire. The Mosquito took a 40mm cannon shell in the port engine, which made the aircraft lurch drunkenly but Reynolds managed to get the Mosquito on an even keel again. However, the anti-freeze mixture was pouring from the radiator and the cockpit filled with cordite fumes.

46   Reynolds got his crippled Mosquito back to Marham where he landed wheels up. Squadron Leader Jack Houlston DFC AFC and his observer, Warrant Officer James Lloyd Armitage DFC failed to return. They were buried in the Reichswald Forest war cemetery.

47   Noseda and his observer, Sergeant John Watson Urquhart were KIA on 3 January when they were hit by anti aircraft fire in the attack on engine sheds at Rouen.

48   On the night of 20/21 April nine Mosquitoes on 105 Squadron and two from 139 Squadron led by Wing Commander Peter Shand DSO DFC carried out a bombing attack on Berlin. This was a diversion for 339 heavy bombers attacking Stettin and 86 Stirlings bombing the Heinkel factory near Rostock. The Mosquito 'night nuisance' operations were also designed to 'celebrate' Hitler's birthday. Over Berlin it was cloudless with bright moonlight and the Mosquitoes dropped their bombs from 15,000-23,000 feet. Flak was moderate and quite accurate but the biggest danger proved to be night-fighters. One of these was Oberleutnant Lothar Linke, Staffelkapitän 12./NJG1 who the night before had claimed to be the second Nachtjagd pilot to destroy a Mosquito whilst flying a standard Bf 110G. Linke, again led by his night fighter controller Eisbär ('Polar Bear'), overtook Shand's Mosquito at high altitude and at high speed in a power dive, shot the Mosquito down over the northern part of the Ijsselmeer at 0210 hours. Shand and his navigator Pilot Officer Christopher Handley DFM were killed. Shand remains missing while the body of his navigator was washed ashore at Makkum. Linke, with 24 night and 3 day victories was killed on the night of 13/14 May 1943.

Chapter 9

Boston Boys

The use of Bostons instead of Blenheims for daylight operations was the most hopeful sign in the months of December 1941 and January 1942. These American bombers, which Fighter Command has been using for some time as night fighters, were much faster than Blenheims and carried a greater load. But in those winter months there did not seem to be a great deal for them to do. There was not much shipping for them to attack, either because of the rough seas or because, as one may now suspect, the Blenheims had succeeded in warning German shipping off the coastal waters of the West. The Bostons were mostly used to accompany fighter sweeps, where they did useful work in bombing ports, aerodromes and factories in Occupied France. And by going with large fighter sweeps they also induced the enemy fighters to take off and risk combat, a necessary but not a very inspiring role.

At the beginning of 1942 2 Group possessed just five bomber squadrons in East Anglia. On 5 January Wing Commander Alan Lynn DFC took over command of 107 Squadron at Great Massingham, while in Malta, Wing Commander Dunlevie RCAF and what was left of the squadron's Blenheims were waging war in the Mediterranean, where they would remain until the 12th. Training on the Blenheim continued until the first Boston III arrived at Massingham on 5 January. The new role for 107 Squadron (and 88 and 226, which also re equipped with the Boston) was to be high-level, pinpoint bombing with a dozen or more aircraft. For two months 107 and 226 Squadrons converted together, using the range at Brancaster on the Wash for firing practice.

Meanwhile, crews in 105 Squadron, now commanded by Wing Commander Peter H. A. Simmons DFC (later killed flying a Turkish Air Force Mosquito) were kicking their heels at Swanton Morley. Sergeant Mike Carreck DFC was an observer in one of the newest Blenheim crews fresh from 17 OTU Upwood, 2 Group's finishing school. Pilot Officer Ronald Olney, first violinist in the London Philharmonic and crew were one of the half dozen or so posted to 105 Squadron at Swanton Morley. Mike Carreck recalls. [49]

'Waiting there for us were a very few survivors from 105's bloodbath in Malta where fourteen days was the lifetime of a Blenheim squadron. We rightly regarded these battle-scarred veterans with the deepest respect but they made us welcome. Life at Swanton Morley - a hellspot only fifteen miles from Norwich but which might well have been in deepest Siberia - began sedately enough. Now and then we did a Blenheim cross-country as I handed my pilot course, compass and ETAs. Sometimes we ventured as far away as Lincoln. We flew to the range and dropped teeny-weeny bombs and once, special treat and with much trepidation, a 250 pounder. Dullish days but nights were duller still, as for recreation, romance and merriment one had to rely on nearby East Dereham where mothers locked away their daughters after tea and every door slammed tight shut on the dot of 1800hrs. Nothing to do but go shivering to our beds in our freezing Nissen huts. Excitement was somewhat lacking. Except for a nonsense of a rumour going the rounds that we were to be re-equipped with a fabulous new aircraft, the fastest in the world, a day bomber that could out-fly any fighter and leave it wondering where we'd gone, that could fly 5 miles high into the stratosphere and had an incredible range of 1,200 miles. We shrugged our shoulders - we'd believe it when we saw it. Which we very soon did.

'On 15 November it came suddenly out of nowhere inches above the hangars with a crackling thunderclap of twin Merlins. As we watched, bewitched, it was flung about the sky in a beyond belief display for a bomber that could out perform any fighter. Well-bred whisper of a touchdown, a door opened and down the ladder came suede shoes, yellow socks and the rest of Geoffrey de Havilland. We pushed and shoved around this impossible dream of an aircraft. No other word for it, it was beautiful. An arrogant beauty, job to do, get out of my way, slim sleek fuselage, high cocked 'to-hell-with-you' tail, awesome power on the leash in those huge engines, eager on its undercarriage like a sprinter on the starting blocks, couldn't wait to leap up and away.

'Called a Mosquito,' they told us. Mosquito W4064 - it was to be shot down six months later on the squadron's first operation.[50]

During those six months only seven more Mosquitoes joined W4064 so flights were few and far between; indeed we new boys had to wait weeks for our first. For us, back to Blenheims and Arctic nights, not counting a Station exercise when it was pretended that German paratroopers had landed and a batch of us were sent to guard the Sergeants Mess. We stretched out on the carpet, blissfully warm at last until somebody came in to wake us with the astounding news that the Japanese had bombed Pearl Harbour. We turned over to sleep our best night ever, the war was won.

'Another rumour now to scoff at, that the Squadron was going to move to a permanent station, central heating, two to a cosy room, hot baths at the turn of a tap. To our amazement this turned out to be pukka gen and on 10 December here we were, with all four of our Mosquitoes, at Horsham St Faith next door to all the joys of Norwich, mildly puzzled, one must admit, that a tremendously Top Secret aircraft had been put on display on an airfield bound by a busy road, spies galore clicking their cameras. Not for us to worry, warmth and comfort, Mosquitoes to fly and Norwich nearby - who could ask for more?

'Three to a crew in a Blenheim, only two in a Mosquito so sadly some of our navs and WoPs were surplus to requirements. Sadder still they were posted to Blenheim squadrons flying in the 'Sea of Carnage', attacks on North Sea convoys whose escorting flak-ships didn't bother to aim, just fired splash into the sea, a curtain of exploding steel through which the doomed Blenheim crews flew with unmatchable courage. One afternoon one of our pilots had to hop the Station Tiger Moth over to one of these squadrons to deliver something bureaucratic. He went to the Crew Room to ask after an OTU friend. 'Jimmy so-and-so here?' 'There he is,' said someone, pointing to a photograph papered to the wall - a head over heels Blenheim somersaulting into the sea. Small wonder they called us *'Poor Bloody Two Group.'*

At Morley's grass airfield meanwhile 105 Squadron were replaced by 226 Squadron, commanded by Wing Commander Vernon Stanley Butler DFC. They arrived from Wattisham where they had been flying Blenheims. Squadron Leader John Castle, a pilot on 226 Squadron, recalls:

It's difficult to imagine now what a rowdy, rumbustious squadron 226 was when it arrived at Swanton Morley on a grey 9 December 1941. We had come from all over the world: New Zealand, Canada, Australia, the USA, the Argentine, a Catholic from Northern Ireland and a Protestant from the South. The only officer left from the squadron that had been in France in 1940 was our CO, 'Bobbie' Butler. The two flight commanders, MacLancy and I, were two of the five pilots surviving a tour of Malta on 110 on Blenheims; 105 came out from Swanton to take over from us. 226 had led the first low-level daylight raid on Cologne and had taken a fair pasting on shipping strikes.'

Training in their new role took time and the Boston crews on 107 Squadron were not considered ready when Operation 'Fuller' was mounted on 12 February. It was a vain attempt to prevent the 'Channel Dash' by the battle cruisers *Scharnhorst, Gneisenau* and *Prinz Eugen,* which were slipping through the English Channel from their French berths to Germany. Six of 226 Squadron's Bostons and four on 88 were involved (as were nine Blenheims of 118 Squadron, twelve on 82 and sixteen on 110). Only Flight Lieutenant Brian 'Digger' Wheeler and his crew on 226 Squadron found the German ships and they were beaten off by six of the escorting fighters. Wheeler landed at Swanton Morley with two holes in the fuselage and an unexploded 20-mm cannon shell in the starboard wing.

The first Boston operation took place on Sunday 8 March with three raids on targets in France. In the early afternoon six Bostons on 226 Squadron at Swanton Morley, led by Wing Commander 'Bobbie' Butler in Z2209 and six on 88 Squadron at Attlebridge took off to make the first daylight-bombing raid of the war on Paris. The target, the Ford Motor Works at Matford near Poissy on the banks of the Seine was turning out tanks and military vehicles for the Germans. Meanwhile, 107 Squadron provided six crews for a 'Circus' operation to the Abbeville marshalling yards escorted by the Kenley and Biggin Hill Wings in 11 Group. Fighters of 10 Group flew a diversionary operation and six more Bostons, three each from 88 and 107 Squadrons, would attack the Comines power station. The Matford works were at the extreme limit of the Bostons' range, so 88 and 226 Squadrons had to use Thorney Island on the South Coast as a forward re-fuelling base. The Bostons would have to fly at very low level to and from the target without fighter escort, which did not have the range to accompany them.

One of the Bostons taking part, flying No. 2 in the 226 Squadron formation to the Matford Works, was piloted by Pilot Officer W. J. 'Bill' O'Connell, a Canadian, with Pilot Officer Peter Saunders as navigator-observer and Flight Lieutenant Douglas 'Chappie' Chapman, as WOp/AG. Peter Saunders recalls.

'We all felt unusually keyed-up at briefing. The target was an important 'first' that no one had attacked before. We did not know what to expect. We knew that split-second flying and navigation, map-reading and target-recognition would all be vital and we realised that if we failed to achieve swiftness and surprise we would be sitting ducks for the German ack-ack and fighters. The 'Wingco' had warned us to be prepared for 50% losses.

'After take-off we swept low in formation over the airfield and then settled on track for the French coast. The sea crossing was uneventful, save for the half-apprehensive, half-jubilant mood of expectancy that we always felt and always much more strongly because of the 'closeness' of everything when we were crossing at 'naught feet'. Everything below seemed to flash past at breakneck speed. Would we make the coast unobserved, as we hoped, or had they got word of our coming and were waiting, defences alert, to destroy us? The weather was good, the visibility was a little too good but enough haze was rising from the sea to help screen our approach and enough broken cloud above, if it should last, to give us some cover from the enemy fighters.

'The cliffs of Cabourg on the skyline, we corrected five degrees to port.

'No ships around,' called Bill.

'They were always a danger, these little coastal fishing smacks and trawlers, which saw you coming and often radioed word of your approach. 'Squealers' we used to dub them and, a regrettable necessity; shot them up or sank them if the need arose. This time none of them in sight, which was lucky for us as well as for them. The haze and the lowness and swiftness of our approach might get us to the coast before we were seen. We watched the cliffs come nearer and nearer. Not a shot, not a signal! We were up and over. Sea suddenly changed to land. Our engines sounded more vibrant. Startled heads jerked upwards, eyes incredulous and momentarily alarmed but we could detect only the onset of surprise as they flashed beneath us and we overhead.

'The Wingco was turning the formation smoothly on to our new course. Next stop Paris, just 100 miles away to the southeast! We did not pause to dwell on our good luck, or the surprise we had so far achieved, for at low level something happens every second and we were looking out in front. What a fast-moving kaleidoscope it was! Neat, chequered fields, trim, square-cut by green-rimmed ditches, came rushing towards and beneath us like a swift-moving film - so close, it seemed, that we could see the very structure of the soil and might have reached out and touched it. A small airfield in front of us, with a few low buildings: blister hangars and aircraft, all innocuous-looking beneath its expert camouflage. No time to line up for an attack on it - Paris was calling. Four sharp stabs of fire from the Wingco's nose and the rest of us followed suit, taking a target as it came through the sights, then it was past. The ground rose slightly ahead of us. We swept up the slope and as we breasted it a double-track railway line flashed beneath us. Maps and watches checked. Must be the line from Pont l'Eveque south to Lisieux. Ground speed OK. Twenty-four miles to Serquigny; six miles flying, nearer six and a quarter. Crossing a road, hedge-lined we had a split-second glimpse of two Hun soldiers diving headlong and panic-stricken towards a ditch. We hoped fervently that it was full and foul!

'I looked out at the other Bostons on our port and thrilled at the sight. (Six Bostons on 226 Squadron had taken off from Thorney Island but one of the eight Bostons of 88 Squadron had become stuck fast in the mud and four more made a late take off and never found the target.) They were flying along wingtip to wing tip and they looked like the arm of a gigantic flail sweeping across fields and skimming the hedge tops. Each man was taking his own hurdles. It might indeed have been the Grand National but with the jumps spaced unequally for each horse and with tremendously greater thrill and excitement. I felt the nose of our aircraft rise and looked around to see telephone wires straight in front. We leapt up and over a branch of a tree and then we were rushing down ploughed slopes into a miniature valley. A plump-faced girl in a yellow blouse and dark-brown skirt was standing in the garden of a whitewashed farmhouse. She swung round with a look of startled amazement and then she was lost to our view. We seemed to surge up the other side of the little valley. Over the top, a wide clean road and, right beneath us, like a cameo. A French family taking their Sunday stroll! What, I wondered, was racing through their minds as they stood gaping at us? The Dutch had a spirit. They had run, waved, given 'V for Victory' - one could almost see their eyes light up and their lips say, 'We won't give up!' But the French? Sometimes they waved. Further on, a stream and then a grey-stone cottage. I could see right in through a long, open window. An old man with a beard, wearing a light smock, dark trousers and a cap with a slick in his hand was sitting inside. He scrambled from his chair and hobbled to the window. As we shot overhead I had a momentary glimpse of him staring upwards, his old eyes alive with sudden interest.

'Houses and spires on the port bow. Serquigny. We crossed a river. Flying Officer George Sayers, our squadron navigator in the Wingco's plane, is making a great job of the trip. I envy him his chance leading a show like this but I admire his skill and calmness. I can see him in the transparent glass nose of 'G-George' map in hand, placidly sucking his dry pipe, looking out at the ground to either side and ahead, coolly noting the landmarks, sizing them up, checking his map. No room for even a momentary slip-up on a trip like this. The Wingco is giving him every chance. His flying is superb and his leadership quick and decisive. He is putting everything he knows into this, his big bulk crouched behind the stick, his helmeted head looking small and oddly incongruous on huge shoulders and his big hands clamped on the control column, responding to every adjustment that his brain demands. He is flying terrifyingly low. The tips of his airscrews seem to crop the grass and as he pulls over trees in his path, the branches appear to bend and scrape along the underside of the Boston's fuselage. The Bostons were lovely machines, powerful-looking with their big, blunt engines, yet smooth-flying, sleek, graceful - and they were beautiful to watch, racing along side by side, fast and low, rising and falling to the contour of the ground like darting swallows. We were accustomed to low level but this was the very lowest that we had ever flown. As we stuck close to the Wingco's plane in formation, my heart jumped involuntarily from time to time as we swept over hedges and fields, as houses and trees slithered close past our wings and as we pulled ourselves precariously over the lip of gullies and embankments. It seemed at times recklessly and unnecessarily low but the whole success of our mission - and our survival too - hung upon the surprise that we must achieve. Flying low was the best method of ensuring that a gunner would have little time to draw a bead on us or an enemy fighter spot us.

'Where were the Me 109s and Focke-Wulf 190s? Were their defences confused? Another flight of Bostons had been sent over as a decoy, flying some distance north of our track in the hope of attracting the German fighters away from us and then making homewards while we made straight and fast for the French capital. We passed Evreux, a mile to the south and altered course a few degrees to port. George had all the strings in his fingers and was pulling us confidently and surely to our target. In less than ten minutes we should be there. The 'Wingco' had never let up for a moment and was still flying as brilliantly and confident as ever. His daisy-cutting was, if anything, getting better (or worse!) The pattern below us looked more ordered now and everything seemed to be running and pointing in one direction, as if to say, 'Paris, this way to Paris!' We shot over a large building with a huge sign reading, 'DUBO-DUBON-DUBONNET. The words seemed to be shouting 'You must come to Paris - You must come to Paris!' 'Damn it!' I thought. I remembered I would be seeing the city only at a distance, for our target was Poissy. Bearing in mind the object of our mission, I hardly had a feeling of 'Paris in the springtime!'

'We came nearer and could see the Seine, highway to Paris. We crossed the railway line from Bueil to Mantes-Gassincourt in an instant and were flying alongside the great river, skirting its southern bank. It looked muddy and yellow but the sun glistened on its surface, conveying an air of somnolent majesty. Everything breathed peace. It seemed a cruel paradox that we were coming to shatter it.

'Ahead of us, in the hollow of the river bank, stood a factory, its big brick buildings ugly and squat against the beauty of the river, its chimneys rising stark and impressive against the sky. The Wingco did not alter course. He climbed slightly, skimming the factory roof. We vaulted upwards and squeezed between the stacks. Our starboard wing seemed to cut one of them in two. I saw deep down into the black, cavernous mouth of another as it slid beneath us. This was the last lap. In just over two minutes from now we should be on target. Involuntarily, we seemed to have closed formation, tighter than before, as though each crew among us was afraid of being left behind or cheated out of our big moment. 'Bombs fused!' I called. Bill replied tersely (but I could detect the thrill in his voice), 'Yep. Check me on bomb doors.'

'Any moment now. A couple of miles in front?' I yelled back through the mike to Bill and 'Chappie'. Things were happening too fast. We were too tense with watchfulness and excitement to make conversation. There was no time. I had my target map in my hand but we still flying too low to be able to see what lay ahead, beyond a fringe of frees. I felt a momentary panic lest we should miss the target and I prayed fervently that George might spot it. The trees were right in front. They rushed at us. Then the river. We were nearly across and - God, no island! Beyond a wooded island in the river lay Poissy. But George had spotted it and a moment later. So had I. We had come out slightly to the south. It was a couple of hundred yards up the river! The Wingco swung his Boston round and began to climb. We hung on his tail.

"Bomb doors open!' I bawled to Bill.

'He yelled back, 'They're open!'

'We were at bombing height - 400 feet - and levelling out. I had a momentary sight of Paris to the southeast but it was a glimpse only, as we turned. I felt a brief disappointment I could not see more but the Matford Works lay ahead and the Wingco was running in. What a perfect target; a huge, long rectangular building lying close to the river bank and a tower nearby with the name 'MATFORD' on it. How obliging to mount it there, to help make doubly sure this was our target!

'I saw the Wingco's bombs go winging down. As we were going in I saw them land, some smack in the middle of a concentration of lorries alongside the factory, the rest on the factory itself. We swept in behind him. Just as our bombs went down, his exploded. The terrific blast shook us and lifted us bodily upwards. Debris rose high in the air and dust swirled around. Some flak was streaming up towards us from the ground. There was a sharp crunching against our starboard wing and the aircraft shuddered violently, then we were past. The other boys were coming in behind us. Chappie was looking out to watch our bombs burst. He yelled jubilantly, 'Plumb in the middle! Good work!' and we knew our bombs had hit.

'Now we were losing height and turning on our course for home. Chappie was shouting out the score as he watched the others bomb. He was finding it hard to count. The Matford Works was going up in smoke, which almost hid them from view. The flak had been light. The Wingco's leadership had been superb, George's navigation perfect, the attack an obviously outstanding success.

'We were down once more 'on the deck' in formation again, en route for home. We had a long way to go to get there but happy thoughts filled our minds. What a perfect day. What an experience; the target decidedly 'pranged'!' What an achievement for Wingco and for George to have led this show; to have carried it off like this! What a thrill for them. What a feather in their caps. What ragging. What backslapping for them when we get back! They deserve it, they can be proud....

'It was then that we saw that the Wingco was having trouble with his bomb doors, They were still hanging open. He was trying to close them, for we saw them come up, stick and then fall open again. He made two more attempts with no success. Had the flak damaged them or could it be the Wingco was hurt? He was still flying skillfully, holding the course, still terrifyingly low. A stretch of thickly wooded ground loomed ahead of us. We swept up and over it. The Wingco's props seemed to trail on the branches below.

'Without warning it came. His port wing cleaved into a trunk. His aircraft lurched violently. We could not see him clearly but he was trying desperately to hold her up, trying to save George in the glass nose of the plane. It was no good. The Boston tottered, slipped heavily sideways and crashed into the trees. Still on its side, it went hurtling on. Trunks splintered and broke in its path. There was a blinding flash of white-blue flame and then the horror of the scene was cloaked in fierce red fire. [51]

'We could not stop. Our thoughts crowded in on each other. 'Chappie' from his gunner's turret was the only one who could see. He said nothing. Neither could we. We sped homewards.'

All six 226 Squadron Bostons placed their bombs on the factory, though only two crews in 88 Squadron bombed the target but damage to the Matford Works was later estimated at 35-40 million French francs and it was out of commission for three months. [52]

'Circus' operations remained the order of the day and casualties were heavy. In April 107 Squadron alone lost seven aircraft from seventy-eight sorties dispatched and eleven aircrew were killed. On 17 April 88 and 107 Squadrons flew diversionary raids in support of Lancasters attacking Augsburg. Six Bostons from 88 Squadron bombed the Grand Quevilly power station near Rouen, while another six hit the shipyards nearby. Meanwhile, 107 Squadron attempted to bomb an artificial silk factory at Calais but their bombs were dropped on railway lines nearby. One of the Bostons (Z2255) was shot down into the sea by Bf 109s killing Pilot Officer Frederick Herbert Ashton Ashford and his two crew. On 25 April all three Boston squadrons operated in concert with one another with two operations against French ports. 88 Squadron attacked Le Havre, while 107 bombed Cherbourg and six Bostons on 226 bombed the dry docks at Dunkirk from 14,000 feet; buildings on the northern end of the Citadel Quay were hit. On the second raid of the day FW 190s attacked 107 Squadron's Bostons and they also came under a heavy flak barrage. One of the Bostons, badly damaged, nevertheless managed to make it home minus part of its tail.

May followed much the same pattern. On 7 May six Bostons in 226 Squadron attacked a power station in Ostend. The German defenders put up a large flak barrage and Sergeant Goodman's Boston was hit and fell out of control. Sergeant Burt, the rear gunner, thought the aircraft was doomed and promptly bailed out but Goodman wrested back control and crossed the North Sea safely. Burt was later reported to be a PoW. On 17 May twelve Bostons led by Wing Commander W. E. Surplice DFC raided the docks at Boulogne. Six of the aircraft were hit by flak and one pilot was wounded. A week later fourteen Bostons of 226 Squadron took a much-needed break from operations when they left for Thruxton for a week long Army Co-Operation Exercise.

In June 226 Squadron at Swanton Morley hosted the A-20 crews of the 15th Light Bombardment Squadron USAAF, who, being the only American unit in the UK at the time and with Independence Day looming, were needed for a flag-waving curtain-raiser to an American offensive in Europe. Both squadrons found that the other flew the Boston differently, even during take-off. While the RAF leader approached the end of the field still on the ground, the US pilot wingmen would be airborne and flying alongside with their wheels drawing up into the wheel-wells. The RAF mechanics were particularly grateful; damaged nose-gear wheels and struts had become a major headache for them. On 4 June the Americans sat in at a 107 Squadron briefing at West Raynham. The target was a 480-foot tower in the docks at Dunkirk. [53] Next day 24 Bostons bombed Morlaix airfield and power stations at Le Havre and Ostend. A direct hit was achieved at Ostend but bombing from 10,000 feet meant that German flak gunners had fairly easy targets at which to shoot and every Boston was hit by flak during their bomb runs. Still the losses mounted. On 11 June Pilot Officer 'Goolie' Skinner and his crew on 107 Squadron failed to return after they were stalked by an FW 190 five minutes from the English coast after a raid on Lannion airfield. Their Boston was raked by machine gun fire from 800 yards; the tail fell off and they fell into the Channel. All the crew perished.

Raids on French and Belgian ports, airfields and power stations continued. Then, on 25/26 June, when the second '1,000 bomber' raid took place, on Bremen, low-level bombing and strafing attacks were at dusk made on thirteen airfields in Germany. Taking part were sixteen Blenheims, twenty-seven Bostons on 88, 107 and 226 Squadrons (making their first 'Intruder' sorties) and four Mosquitoes of 105 and 139 Squadrons, which attacked Stade. Extra bomb bay tanks were provided, carrying 100 gallons. Overall the raids were a success, though one flight in 226 Squadron bombed a dummy aerodrome. Six Bostons went to Leeuwarden and three more flew to Bergen-Alkmaar but it was darker than anticipated and four aircraft were unable to find their targets. The others attacked at 2230 with eleven-second and thirty-minute delayed-action 500lb bombs and incendiaries. Flight Lieutenant A. F. 'Tony' Carlisle's aircraft was caught in the explosion of one of the bombs, which holed the tail of his Boston. His rear gunner had his guns blown overboard as the aircraft was overturned but Carlisle regained control and managed to return safely, his flying skill earning him a DFC. Light flak prevented Wing Commander Lynn and Pilot Officer Allen from attacking but Flight Lieutenant R. MacLachlan flew low at 75 feet and Pilot Officer Rushden dropped his bombs from 100 feet near a hangar. Both aircraft were damaged by ground fire but they returned to base safely. Wing Commander Lynn, meanwhile, was forced down over the coast.

On Monday 29 June twelve Bostons on 226 Squadron, led by Squadron Leader J. Shaw Kennedy, a popular red-haired ace flyer and attacked the marshalling yards at Hazebrouck, escorted for the first time on a 'Circus' raid by Hawker Typhoons. A US crew, captained by Captain Charles

Kegelman flew one of the Bostons, for the first ever US sortie from England. Bombing from between 12,500 and 13,000 feet, the formation recorded two hits on the railway lines at the eastern end of the yard and one or two were seen to burst on railway lines and sheds at the western end. The rest of the bombs fell on buildings to the south and north. No flak was encountered by the formation while over the target and all the aircraft returned. Not so fortunate were the escorting Spitfires, who encountered German fighters en route to the target, claiming three destroyed for the loss of five of their own.

On Sunday 12 July a 'Circus' of six Bostons of 226 Squadron led by Squadron LeaderJohn Castle and six American-crewed Bostons (in the last of sixteen sorties with the RAF) led by Captain Bill Odell and escorted by fighters, headed for Abbeville-Drucat airfield. There 150 fighters were reportedly dispersed in the woods just north of the runways. The crews bombed from 8,500 feet but owing to 4/10ths cloud over the aiming point the accuracy of the bombing could not be observed. Slight to inaccurate flak was encountered from both heavy and light anti-aircraft guns, with two aircraft receiving hits but all returned safely. (In September the 15th Bomb Squadron flew a few missions before transferring to the 12th Air Force earmarked for North Africa.)

On 16 July 2 Group ordered the first of a series of low-level attacks by Bostons on power stations, marshalling yards and other industrial targets using cloud cover. Each squadron was to send ten aircraft a day when visibility and cloud cover permitted escorted by fighters of 11 Group. Each target was to be bombed by a pair of Bostons, with each squadron being given five targets. On Sunday 19 July twenty Bostons of 88 and 226 Squadrons mounted raids in pairs on ten power stations in the Lille area using low cloud as cover. The Boston flown by Flight Sergeant Matthew G. Johnson on 226 Squadron nose-dived into the ground while making a bomb run on Mazingarbe power station and exploded in a wood east of Boulogne. Johnson, Pilot Officer Leonard S. Stewart, navigator and Sergeant Fred C. Thorogood, gunner were given a military burial in the Cimetière de l'est at Boulogne. A second Boston flown by Pilot Officer Aubrey K. G. Niner of 88 Squadron was also lost. Niner's aircraft and another Boston, flown by Sergeant G. W. 'Ginger' Attenborough, had made for the power station at Lille-Lomme but missed it, so they attacked the aerodrome at Lille-Nord instead. Niner's aircraft was hit in the starboard engine and he had to belly-land on a football pitch in Lille. Niner, his WOp/AG, Sergeant George Lawman and his navigator, Flight Sergeant Philip Jacobs were taken prisoner.

During July the Bostons again intruded after dusk. On the 26/27th, when 403 RAF heavies attacked Hamburg, 226 and 107 intruded over night-fighter airfields at Jever, near Wilhelmshaven and Leeuwarden respectively. AL746/M of 226 Squadron, piloted by Pilot Officer Victor N. Salmon RCAF and which had been flown by Captain Odell of the 15th Bomb Squadron on the 4 July Independence Day raid, was brought down by flak en route and crashed on the edge of Langeoog. All four crew were killed. Among them was Pilot Officer Harold F. Deck, the 29-year-old observer, whose two brothers also lost their lives flying with the RAF.[54] On 28/29 July eighteen

Bostons of 88 and 107 Squadrons intruded over Dutch airfields at Alkmaar and De Kooy. Flight Lieutenant R. MacLachlan on 107 Squadron first eluded a night-fighter and was then fired on by a flak ship but he and his crew made it home safely. 🐝

Early in August the Boston squadrons commenced Army Co-Operation training to become proficient in smoke-laying from low level for the forthcoming Operation 'Jubilee', which would involve British and Canadian landings at Dieppe. Sixteen crews in 107 Squadron and those of 88 Squadron were dispatched to Ford while 226 Squadron crews were sent to Thruxton. On 19 August 107 Squadron carried out 32 sorties over Dieppe without loss but several aircraft were hit. At 0416 hours Wing Commander Alan Lynn and Flight Lieutenant MacLachlan joined four Boston intruders on 418 RCAF [55] and 605 'County of Warwick' Squadrons in trying to nullify coastal batteries as a prelude to the start of the Allied landings at 0500 hours. Light was poor however and results were unobserved. Fire was continuing from the Hitler battery, so 107 Squadron was ordered to send twelve Bostons in to silence it. Lynn led the formation in a bombing run west to east but ground haze reflecting back light from the sun made the target difficult to spot and all bombs overshot. Flak was heavy but none of the Bostons was hit. The last Boston smoke screen action of the Dieppe operation involved four crews on 226 Squadron, led by Squadron Leader Graham 'Digger' Magill and one on 88 Squadron. They flew over the beachhead at 1414 hours, being escorted by 66 Squadron, to conceal the few remaining ships still within gun range of the German batteries.

Magill wrote: 'The trip was in answer to an urgent call for protection of the withdrawing naval forces, which were being severely harassed by fire from the shore. The idea was to put down a curtain of smoke from cliff to cliff either side of the town and down to sea level. I think we can justly claim to have succeeded. It meant running in flat out from the east under the cliff, between the lighthouse and the beginning of the jetty, along the line of the beach and withdrawing under the western cliff. We had quite a view of the waterfront and the shambles on the beach. Unfortunately, we lost Flying Officer R. A. Marks AFM and crew in the process. I have little doubt that he collected the fire aimed at me. He was flying to seaward of me and a bit lower (to give depth to the screen) and should have been hidden to the enemy by the smoke from my aircraft. Hit as he was at nought feet, he had no chance.'

Marks' observer-navigator Pilot Officer Kenneth A. I. Warwood recalls.

'We were actually over the beach at Dieppe when hit by flak and assorted ground fire. Within about twenty seconds we had lost the port engine and the tail and we landed in the Channel. Pilot Officer L. K. Brownson, WOp/AG, Marks and me; all very much alive, were picked up by a German E-Boat. I was not in very good shape and only semi-conscious. A Polish Air Force officer named Landsmann on 303 Squadron and two mechanics, part of the crew of an ASR craft blown up by a FW 190 and us were landed at Fécamp. Brownson, Marks and me were taken to Rouen, thence to Le Bourget aerodrome where we were interrogated by a high-ranking Luftwaffe officer who commented, 'We were expecting you six weeks ago' and later, 'You are a very old man to be flying,' (I was 32). A train took us to Frankfurt-am-Main and from there to Oberussel, where we were put into solitary confinement for about a month. Early in October 1942 the three of us were taken by train to Stalag Luft III at Sagan, to the East Camp.' (All three suffered the privations of prison camp and the forced march in the winter of 1945 when the whole camp was evacuated at very short notice. In 1946 Marks was killed at Farnborough while testing an experimental German aircraft).

A second Boston on 226 Squadron flown by Pilot Officer Robert James Corrigan RCAF, an American, failed to return from the day's operations. Corrigan and Flight Sergeant W. Osselton, gunner were killed. Sergeant Moth, observer, although seriously wounded was rescued by a passing Royal Navy destroyer. Altogether, the Bostons made eleven runs in front of the cliffs from east to west. Squadron Leader Shaw Kennedy's Boston on 88 Squadron was badly damaged by naval fire. Flight Lieutenant Ormiston Galloway Edgar McWilliam, who was riding as a passenger, was killed by the blast from the cannon shell and Flying Officer G. A. Casey, air gunner, was wounded. Flying Officer Arthur Asker, observer was uninjured. Kennedy crash-landed the aircraft at Shoreham. Pilot Officer L. J. Waters, air gunner in Pilot Officer W. R. Gellatly's Boston was also killed. Flying Officer Donald T. Smith received flak hits that shattered his windscreen and embedded shards of Plexiglas in his right eye. Despite his injuries, Smith continued on and laid smoke. On the return flight his left eye filled with powdered perspex which still filled the cockpit but he managed to land safely at Thruxton. Flight Sergeant J. C. Bicknell, air gunner and Pilot Officer G. B. Tolputt, observer were uninjured. Smith was awarded the DFC. Wing Commander W. B. Surplice DFC was awarded the DSO and Kennedy received a bar to his DFC. Asker, Casey and Flying Officers Rutherford and L. J. Longhurst were awarded the DFC also, as was Pilot Officer H. J. Archer on 88 Squadron. The Dieppe operation cost the RAF 108 aircraft; 48 German aircraft were lost and 4,000 army and navy personnel. Two Bostons of 226 Squadron, which flew 28 sorties between 0509 and 1500 hours, failed to return from the day's operations. 88 Squadron flew 32 bombing sorties, losing one Boston. The following message from AOC, HQ No 2 Group, was sent to the Boston stations in Norfolk:

'I CANNOT THANK YOU ENOUGH FOR THE WHOLE HEARTED CO-OPERATION OF YOUR SQUADRONS AND HOPE YOU WILL CONVEY MY CONGRATULATIONS TO THEM ON A VERY FINE PERFORMANCE. LEIGH-MALLORY.

Returning to Great Massingham, 107 Squadron was again on bombing operations on 27 August when twelve aircraft attacked the airfield at Abbeville. The flak was heavy and accurate and Pilot Officer Allen was forced to ditch on the way home. He and two other crew survived but Flight Sergeant Gordon Turnbull Relph, observer, was killed. Three FW 190s also attacked the ASR launch that arrived on the scene while it was picking up the downed crew.

Pilot Officer Arthur Paget Eyton-Jones was a navigator in a recently arrived Boston crew with Frank Swainson, WOp/AG [56] and captained by Pilot Officer R. M. 'Dick' Christie RCAF at Swanton Morley to join 226 Squadron on 4 September. At this stage of the war a tour of daylight operations was counted as twenty. Eyton-Jones reflected that, 'Nobody had done that many to my knowledge but a few lucky ones had got through fifteen and gone for a well-deserved 'rest'. Christie's crew had arrived on the squadron at a bad time. The previous week one of the crews had hit a telegraph pole on a low-level flight and damaged the nose-wheel so that on landing it had collapsed and the navigator had been dragged along the ground on what was left of his legs. He died shortly afterwards. On 15 September Christie's crew carried out a sea-sweep. This was a very unpopular type of operation as it consisted of flying at wave-top height in formation out to a point very close to the enemy coast and then climbing to 500 feet to patrol a given area, keeping in line abreast about a half a mile apart. These trips were equally unpopular for the reason that they only counted as half an operation. [57]

Throughout September and October pairs of Bostons on 88, 107 and 226 Squadrons continued low-level attacks on power stations in northern France. Twenty year old Sergeant (later Warrant Officer) Maurice 'Collie' Collins was a Boston pilot in 226 Squadron much of whose time since joining the squadron at Swanton Morley was spent on formation flying, low level flying and gunnery practice. He recalls.

'2 Group sent aircraft to look for pocket battleships and later to cover the landing at Dieppe but the only raids I went on were ten high-level 'Circuses' and one low level against 'Squealers'. My original navigator, Sergeant 'Butch' Beaumont suffered from claustrophobia and could not fly in a Boston (he had flown in the Blenheim with no problem) and Sergeant Arthur Grounds, my WOp/AG, fell downstairs at Bylaugh Hall and broke his leg. Beaumont and Grounds were replaced by Pilot Officer Harold Milford a 27-year old modern languages master from Wimbledon and Sergeant George Nicholls a 24-year old Londoner who had been a clerk in the General Accident Insurance Company respectively. Evenings were spent in Swanton Morley village, the 'King's Arms' in Dereham or the fleshpots of Norwich until the evening of 21 September 1942. We found ourselves on a battle order for a low-level raid on power stations. Early morning found us in the ops room. Eighteen Bostons would be going in nine pairs. We had Chocques in the Pas de Calais as our target. There was a delay in take-off time but at ten o'clock we started.

'Shortly after passing Orfordness the leader of my pair turned back. Off to North Foreland, two or three minutes and climbing to the clouds to cross between Calais and Dunkirk. Neither George nor I could see the other aircraft detailed to fly with us so we carried on alone. Harold managed to pinpoint our target, which was near Bethune. We hadn't gone far when we ran into a pretty thick rain patch and it was here that the trouble started. The rain obscured all forward vision and made it necessary to climb 200 feet or so to avoid hitting trees and houses. At this height we were an ideal target for the German light ack-ack gunners and they paid us most unwelcome attention. When we finally cleared the rain we were right over the centre of Bethune and we fell for some more light Flak. It was just as I was turning back to head for the target that the 20-mm and 37-mm cannon shells hit us right amidships. Poor old George was working overtime trying to shoot at the Germans whilst I was weaving like the devil. There was a horrible lurch and George shouted to me that a large chunk of the rudder had disappeared and that the starboard engine was on fire. Although it was a cold September day, I was in a sweat and to add to the general unhealthy atmosphere, the other engine began to cough. An oil or fuel line was hit and further flight was out of the question. The next few minutes seemed like years as we hastily jettisoned our bomb load on to a railway line and prepared to crash land. We hit some electricity cables, which caused blue flashes as we went by. Milford said, 'What about the trees?' I looked and saw thirty-forty foot high poplars. I went over them at right angles fortunately.

'My guardian angel was certainly smiling on me that day because just ahead was a newly ploughed field and so I put the remains of 'K-King' to rest as gently as possible. We ploughed along in the soft earth for quite a distance and finished up only six feet from a copse. One wheel was on fire and it rolled towards the trees but I didn't wait to watch the fire. I was scrambling to get out of the cockpit. Harold was the first out and I followed. We rushed round to the tail in time to see George making a hurried exit from the escape hatch. There was nothing more I could do to destroy the aircraft and so we three beat a hasty retreat over a road and into a corn stubble field. We found a ditch along by the hedge and dived in. We scampered along this ditch for about a quarter of a mile and then sat down to hold our first council of war. The first task was to make ourselves as much like civilians as possible and to achieve this we tucked our flying boot tops into our trousers and ripped our badges off our battle dress blouses. George was loath to bury his flying jacket, claiming that the September nights were very cold. However, it was discarded and buried with our Mae Wests under a little bush. Next we had to decide how to travel, for obviously if we stayed in a group we would be captured in a short time. It was finally agreed that George and Harold should travel together and I should go alone. Some distance to the south of us was a small wood. We agreed to rendezvous there later that night. Near the bush under which we were hiding, the ditch forked and I took the right-hand turning. With handshakes and best wishes we took our separate ways.' [58]

Only two 'Circuses' were possible during October 1942. The first was on the 15th when three Bostons on 88 Squadron, eleven from 107 and nine on 226 led by Squadron Leader Magill DFC visited Le Havre. Their intention was to bomb a Neumark Class raider, which was reported to be still in dry dock undergoing repairs following damage sustained in an earlier raid. On arrival, however, the Boston crews discovered that the vessel had sailed, so they unloaded their bombs on a 5,000-ton motor vessel in the Bassin de Marée instead. Next day, 16 October, a formation of six Bostons carried out a 'Circus' attack on the *Neumark* at Le Havre. In the late afternoon of 31 October seventeen Bostons on 88 and 107 Squadrons headed for power stations in the area of Rijsel and Bethune. Four Bostons flew to Mazingarbe, four to Gosnay, six to Pont-à-Vendin and three to Comines. Of the four who had Mazingarbe as a target, only one reached its destination and dropped its bombs. The same happened to the Bostons at Gosnay: not one of the seven aircraft could find the target. Most of the Bostons dropped their bombs on secondary targets and strafed them with their guns. Of the six Bostons on 107 Squadron en route to Pont-à-Vendin over the sea the aircraft of Flight Sergeant Grant had to return after experiencing problems with his guns. The other five continued in heavy rain and reduced visibility. Pilot Officer George Turner and Squadron Leader Philip Rex Barr DFC dropped their loads on Pont-à-Vendin while Flight Sergeant Nicols attacked Comines. In the two remaining Bostons Sergeant Simpson and Pilot Officer Henry Collings headed for Pont-à-Vendin. Simpson could not find his target so he dropped his bombs on an alternative. Collings did the same before, over Jonkershove his Boston was picked up by two incoming FW 190s of 8./JG26 from Wevelgem-Kortrijk. Leutnant Paul Galland (one of two younger brothers of Adolph) was flying the leading fighter and his wingman was probably Oberfeldwebel Johann Edman. They attacked as soon as the Boston came within range. Stanley Nash and Francis Pickering, the two air gunners, returned fire but shells from Galland's guns set the aircraft on fire. The other crewmember was Ronald Tebbutt, the 32-year-old navigator. The Boston touched down, flipped over amongst some willow trees and carried on through a field before exploding. One of the crewmembers was still alive but he died shortly afterwards. The wreckage was spread for hundreds of yards. It was Paul Galland's seventeenth victory and his last. Five hours later he was killed when he was shot down into the sea by a Spitfire while returning from an escort mission for the bombers to Canterbury. Edman, who then dispatched the Spitfire, was himself shot down and killed on 21 March 1944, by which time he had five victories.

At the end of October 1942 the Battle of Alamein resulted in a victory for the Eighth Army over Rommel's 'Afrika Korps' and then it was announced that on 8 November Allied Forces had landed in North Africa. At last it seemed that the tide had turned in the Allies' favour. Better times for 2 Group, too were anticipated. The North American Mitchell II had begun to equip 98 Squadron (which had disbanded in Coastal Command in July 1941) and 180 Squadron, which both reformed at West Raynham in September, though the squadrons would not begin flying operations until after they moved to Foulsham on 15 October. Even then, problems with turrets, guns and other systems would delay them further. In October also the Lockheed Vega Ventura entered the picture. Crews sardonically named it the 'Flying Pig' (a reference to its porcine fuselage). When asked what the Ventura could do that the Hudson couldn't, they answered, 'Consume more petrol!'

Squadron Leader Ray Chance, CO 'A' Flight on 21 Squadron (which had disbanded at Luqa, Malta on 14 March and re-formed at Bodney the same day) remembers:

'We spent the summer converting to Venturas - a larger version of the Hudson! In fact it was a Lodestar passenger aircraft, converted - its civil origins never deserted it. Venturas came in 'penny numbers', sometimes one a week; sometimes two. The manual came with it. As new crews came in (an upper gunner was needed), I taught the young pilots to take off and land and formate, etc. Squadron Leader Peter Shand did the same with 'B' Flight.' Venturas carried a crew of four/five, could carry 2,500 lb of bombs and was armed with two .50 and six .303 inch machine guns. Two other Ventura squadrons, 487 RNZAF and 464 RAAF were formed at Feltwell on 15 August and 9 September respectively, occupying dispersals recently vacated by 75 New Zealand Squadron Wellingtons. 487 were commanded by Wing Commander F. C. 'Frankie' Seavill, who came from a sheep-farming family at Waingaro and had left Hamilton, New Zealand in 1930 for a career in the RAF. 21 Squadron remained at Bodney until October 1942, finally moving to nearby Methwold, where it would remain until April 1943.

Ventura operations began on 3 November 1942 when three crews on 21 Squadron, led by the CO, Wing Commander R. J. P. Pritchard AFC DFC, tried to raid a factory at Hengelo but had to bomb railway lines instead. Further sorties were flown on the 6th for the loss of three Venturas. Squadron Leader Ray Chance remembers:

'I lost two close friends on that foray. Flying Officer Allan Ernest Kench Perry was killed in action and Flying Officer Brown did not return but later we heard that he was a PoW. Another close friend was pilot Warrant Officer2 Victor Roy 'Hank' Henry RCAF, a boy of twenty who had come all the way from Vancouver. He died on his first trip, on 7 November and is now buried at Flushing. My crew of 'S-Sugar' on 7 November was Sergeant 'Steve' Stephens, WOp/AG, Sergeant 'Robbie' Robinson, navigator and Flight Sergeant Edinborough DFM, upper gunner. We took off around midday for Terneuzen to attack oil installations there. The flight over the North Sea at about 100-200 feet was uneventful. It was also called a cloud-cover raid, the met forecast being that there would be a front over the Dutch coast with cloud base at about 800 feet. We saw the Dutch coast approaching and flashed over the sand dunes at fifty feet, to keep below enemy radar. We had been going some while when Robbie called me up on the R/T and said, 'Sorry, sir but I'm lost.'

'I said, 'OK, Robbie, stay on this course for a while and see what turns up. Silence and we skimmed along for another ten minutes when up pops Robbie again and says, 'Sorry, sir but I'm still lost.'

'We were somewhere near the Dutch/Belgian border and could have been heading for Bruges or even Antwerp. As this was totally unsatisfactory I decided, rightly or wrongly, to pull up to 250-300 feet to see if I could pick up a pinpoint position. As soon as we reached that height without warning there was an enormous high-pitched explosion. A shell had gone through the fuselage about 3 feet behind my head and exploded in the fuselage. It should have blown my head off but I found later that I had one of the Venturas with a two-inch steel plate behind the seat. This saved me but unfortunately it caught my wireless operator. I kept a straight face and a straight course. I couldn't see behind me. Then Robbie came through from the navigation section in the nose and looked down the fuselage. In his slow, unemotional Lancashire voice, he said, 'Steve's been hit, sir.'

'I said: 'Then bring him alongside me.'

'The crew, including a Flying Officer who had 'come along for the ride', dragged him and laid him down at the side of me. He was covered in blood from head to foot. I later discovered that he had been blinded by phosphorous burns to the eyes, his elbow joint was smashed and he had thirty bits of small shrapnel in him. His lips were moving.

I said, 'What's he saying?'

'He wants to know if we're going back.'

'Two of the crew said, 'He's bleeding to death. If you turn back now, sir, you might just save his life.'

'This calls for very hard decisions when you have been in the same crew for six months. There is a deep personal friendship and bond that grows up quite regardless of rank. There lay poor Steve in an ever-widening pool of blood. I pulled the 'stick' back and shot up into the clouds at 800 feet, levelled off and let them give him such help as they could. Someone tried a morphine injection. They said again, 'He wants to know if we're going back.'

'I shouted to them, 'Shout in his ear and say we've turned round and we're going back.'

'We had not. We were going straight on.

'After this I descended through the clouds to ground level again. I calculated that it would be ten more minutes to the target (and ten minutes back to at least this point), putting twenty minutes on to Steve's time. When the time was up on that course Robbie and I decided to do a square search of the area and if the oil installations could not be found I was permitted to look for a secondary target.

'I decided to fly NNE, when we should come to the estuaries from the Rhine. Then Flight Sergeant Edinborough called me up from his top turret and said that firing was coming at us from behind. So up again into the clouds for blind flying, as one instrument had gone. After a few minutes I decided to come down again. As I broke cloud I saw to my left a broad estuary and three ships sailing out to the sea in line astern. I said, 'This is it.'

'So we did a diving turn to the left and, pulling out above the masts of the rear ship, did an attack on all three from the rear. Having pressed the bomb button on the wheel, I immediately pulled up straight into the low cloud base and climbed to 800 feet in cloud. Steve wasn't taking any part in all this, though as we dived one way and then the other I saw blood run to one side of the cockpit, then the other.

'After some time flying blind I felt sure we must be over the sea, so I put the nose down and broke cloud again quite low down. I was slap over a harbour. At once flak guns opened up so yet again stick back and up into the clouds. This time we kept the course we had chosen for home. After fifteen minutes we ran out of cloud cover; we had passed through the front and were in clear blue sky at 800 feet. At once the worry was German fighters, so down to sea level and give it all it's got.

'As we approached Great Yarmouth I pulled up to about 1,000 feet so that we could easily be seen and fire off the identification colours of the day. There were three Royal Navy ships parallel to the coast heading north but they were quite unimpressed by our activities and at once opened fire on us! I was just beginning to feel that it just was not my day!

'Poor Steve was again thrown about the bloody cockpit floor. They didn't hit us but as I headed overland into Norfolk a low November mist had settled in the late afternoon. Finally we admitted that we were lost above this low fog, although there was a perfect blue sky above. We stooged around for over half an hour looking for something. At last by the grace of God I saw Swaffham church tower sticking up through the mist. A cheer went up. I knew where I was and the course to fly to Bodney and Methwold.

'One of the crew must have worked the W/T set, for as I came in low over the hedge an ambulance and a fire engine were at the end of the runway and raced down the runway with us. The medics were wonderful. Before the great wheels had stopped they were inside with a stretcher and by the time I reached the perimeter track Steve was already on his way to RAF Hospital, Ely.

'When I got to dispersal I walked slowly over to an elder tree, leaned against it wearily, then bent down and threw up. That evening I stole a gallon of petrol, put it in the Flight Truck and drove to Ely. Steve was propped up and was what is euphemistically called 'comfortable'. Matron told me of his injuries and the thirty little bits of shrapnel they'd got out of him. Thankfully he lived, regained his sight and later demanded to go back again to 21 Squadron and do some more. It is sad that they do not give medals to young men like Steve who showed such quiet but indomitable courage.'

Losses in 2 Group generally were high. For instance, in November 107 Boston Squadron flew eleven sorties for the loss of four Bostons and sixteen aircrew killed - an almost 40% loss rate! On a raid on the marshalling yards at Courtrai on 7 November Squadron Leader Philip Rex Barr DFC hit high-tension cables and crashed near Wevelgem; he and his observer, Flying Officer Walter Barfod DFC were killed. Two 107 Squadron Bostons collided near Le Havre on the 10th with no survivors. There was not even the consolation that the 'tip and run' raids by 2 Group on airfields, power stations and docks, flying low over the sea, so reminiscent of the shipping strikes, were accomplishing much material damage.

Flight Lieutenant George Turner DFC *, a pilot on 107 Squadron, recalls.

'27 November 1942 was a typical November day with grey cloud sheer at about 1,000 feet and visibility of about three miles. It started out as a normal one for us Boston crews on 107 Squadron at Great Massingham, Norfolk. The officers had arrived from West Raynham in the crew bus at about 8.30am and the NCO aircrews had walked up from their billets in Massingham to the airfield. As usual we gathered round the stove in the crew room. Some played cards, some chatted and some read. By 9 o'clock normal training was under way. Sometime during the morning, probably about eleven o'clock, the Flight Commander sent for Warrant Officer A. J. 'Tony' Reid and myself to tell me that we had been detailed for a low-level operation that I was to lead. (The squadron was only sending out a pair of aircraft.) We were to tell our crews to have an early lunch and to report for briefing at 1 o'clock. I was a bit excited (low-level trips in Bostons were exciting) and rather flattered, as this was the first time we had been chosen to lead another aircraft on a raid. Tony Reid was not pleased. He was a much more experienced pilot than me (although his operational experience was about on a par with mine) who had spent nearly a year at Upwood flying observers under training in Ansons and had thus built up twice as many flying hours as I had. With this behind him he felt that he should be the leader and said so to me.

'The Royal Dutch Steelworks at Ijmuiden lay behind and slightly to one side of the town and for some reason we were briefed to come in from the sea, cross the harbour and town, then attack the steelworks. In our ignorance this meant nothing to us (we were still very inexperienced as this was only our fourth low-level trip) but it certainly meant something to the Intelligence Officer, who came out to our aircraft as we were getting in and wished us luck. This was unusual - it had never happened before, nor did it ever happen subsequently!

'We took off, flew to the coast at about 100 feet and set course for the target dropping down to sea level as we did so. The visibility was not very good and, being very conscious of Tony Reid's displeasure, I flew as low and as accurately as I could. We had no aids so accurate compass courses were essential. We had a full load of fuel and four 500lb bombs fused for eleven-second delay. I was flying one of the few aircraft on the squadron (at that time) that incorporated a RAF modification to improve the Boston's range - a 140-gallon fuselage tank fitted over the bomb bay. The normal tankage was one inboard of the engine of 140 gallons and one outboard of sixty gallons, in each wing. For some reason I decided to use the outboard tanks first. I don't know why but it had a bearing on subsequent events.

'We did not say much over the sea. We were never a chatty crew, so it was Arthur Liddle, my navigator, warning me that the enemy coast was five minutes ahead that broke the silence. I changed tanks to inners, went in to rich mixture, pushed the revs to 2,350 and the boost to forty inches of mercury (flat out was 2,400 rpm and 45 inches of mercury). As the speed built up to about 280mph I re-trimmed the aircraft and gave a quick glance over my shoulder to see Tony Reid nicely in position a little to one side and behind. Visibility had improved as we neared the coast and we saw Ijmuiden from about five miles out. Impressions now get a little confused. I remember flying between two breakwaters into the harbour and there was tracer flak from all directions crisscrossing in front, at the side and straight at me from ahead. I was flying as low as I could with the prop tips about a foot or so above the water and most of it seemed to be going over the top of us and then I heard four loud bangs and knew we had been hit. The engine instruments seemed OK although the starboard engine was a bit down on boost but the fuel gauge for the starboard inner tank and the fuselage tank gauge were sinking towards zero. At the time I conned myself that I was trying to check on the damage to the aircraft. I was probably suffering from shock because when I looked out again we were up about 300 feet and a target for every flak gun for miles around, which were having a field day. It seemed to take ages to register that I was the centre of all this attention. But it can only have been a second or two before I pushed the stick forward, shot down to ground level, pushed throttles and pitch levers against the stops and changed to the starboard outer tank, which still had a few gallons in it. I flew in a wide curve to port well behind the town and turned north for a couple of miles or so before taking up a north-westerly heading that Arthur gave me before passing out. In our sweep round I checked on the crew. The gunners were OK but Arthur said he had been hit. The starboard engine was making a horrible clanking noise and was down to about thirty inches boost but it was helping us along at about 270 mph so I kept it going.

'We crossed some sand dunes and headed out to sea. Heavy guns opened up behind us and great spouts of water rose around but that did not last long, as the chances of us being hit were remote. Ron Chatfield, my WOp/AG, now reported a couple of Me 109s behind us, so I pulled up into cloud. After settling down there I switched off the starboard engine (it had done us proud but it did not sound at all well), transferred the remains of the fuel from the outer tank to the port inner and calculated that we had enough to reach England at our reduced airspeed. From time to time I tried to raise Arthur but with no success.

'Just short of the English coast we came out of cloud and as we approached land I fired the colours of the day to identify ourselves. I had decided to land at the nearest airfield to get medical attention for Arthur as soon as possible. I pinpointed our position near Norwich and headed for Horsham St Faith, the nearest airfield. At that time the only R/T the Boston possessed was a set called a TR9 (the following year we were equipped with VHF radios), a very efficient apparatus with a theoretical range of five miles but which in practice rarely worked, so we tended to ignore it. Thus I just flew over the tower at about 800 feet, did a circuit and landed. As a Boston would taxi on one engine I switched off the good engine on touchdown.

'At the end of our landing run we shot out of our cockpits, raced around to the front of the aircraft and started to get Arthur out. He and the nose were a mess. There was blood everywhere and great chunks of the perspex were missing. Arthur was covered in blood, unconscious and very cold. As we were doing this I looked towards the tower but nothing seemed to be happening, so Ron dashed off to wake them up while George and I finished getting Arthur out and laid him on the ground.

'At an operational airfield a twin-engined aircraft landing on one engine would have had a fire tender alongside as it stopped and things would have happened fast. Unknown to us the RAF had left Horsham, leaving a care and maintenance party to hand over to the Americans, whose advanced party had just arrived, so things were very different.

'Ron eventually turned up with a fire truck, having browbeaten the corporal in charge to take action. I went off with Arthur in the truck to SHQ (Station Headquarters) where I made a bit of a nuisance of myself because I thought they were so slow. In fairness to them, we had arrived unannounced and unexpectedly and they were short of men and vehicles. I was a bit overwrought and rather rude. Although it seemed ages it was probably less than ten minutes after landing that Arthur was rushed to the Norfolk & Norwich Hospital in the care of a medical orderly.

'Having seen Arthur away I went back in a truck to the aircraft to pick up Ron and George. This time I had a good look at the machine, which was a sorry sight. All the shells that had hit her had come from ahead and the right. One had burst on the bombsight, flinging fragments of steel (and perspex) into Arthur's leg, arm and face. A second had entered the fuselage a foot or so behind my head and had burst in the fuselage tank. A third had smashed through the leading edge of the wing inboard of the starboard engine and holed the fuel tank there. The fourth had burst against the bottom two cylinders of the starboard engine, making a mess of the cylinder heads and rocker boxes. These were all 20 mm and probably came from one gun.

'It was getting dark by now, so we collected up our flying gear and went to the control tower to report to base and arrange transport home. Eventually, an eight cwt. van with a WAAF driver came from Massingham to pick us up and we got back to our messes about ten o'clock. It had been rather a long day.

'This operation illustrated the part that luck played in these things. We were lucky that the tanks that were hit were full, otherwise they would most likely have exploded and caught fire. Intelligence had given Ron a 16-mm cine camera to take a film of the target. He was using this, not his guns, when 140 gallons of 100-octane swished past his legs and out of the rear hatch. George told me that he was getting ready to fire back when he was doused in petrol and thought it unwise to do so. It was a miracle that we were untouched after bombing when I was stooging along at 300 feet; quite a lot of the stuff was coming from the harbour and town behind us and it was non-deflection shooting for them.

'Conversely, it was our bad luck that our very experienced CO, Wing Commander Lynn, had been replaced by Wing Commander P. H. Dutton, who had come from India and had no experience of European operations. No experienced CO would, at that stage of the war, have allowed any of his crews to fly through a heavily defended harbour to attack a target behind it. I suspect that the instructions came from Group. Dutton, a regular officer, would not question it and the Intelligence Officer, who did know the score, was not senior enough to get it altered. Apart from the normal harbour defences, an E-boat squadron was stationed there and those not out on patrol would grin have joined in the fun. (107 Squadron attacked the steelworks again in 1943. Six aircraft under a very experienced CO, Wing Commander [Richard Grenville] 'Dickie' England, came in from the north and attacked the works, keeping the town between them and the harbour. Although a fighter shot down one aircraft, none were hit by flak.) I guess that our attack was to have an element of surprise - straight in from the sea was the shortest way to the target and it might have worked. We didn't surprise them but they certainly surprised us.

'Tony Reid, who was behind us and theoretically in the more dangerous position, did not get a scratch. (The theory was that gunners aimed at the leading aircraft and did not allow enough deflection to hit the No 2.) However, his luck ran out a week or so later and he was shot down on the Eindhoven operation, as was Wing Commander Dutton, both crews being lost.) We were on this one too with a spare observer but were untouched.'

Endnotes for Chapter Nine

49 MAA The Mossie No.36 September 2004

50 W4064/C FTR on 31 May 1942 when it was hit by flak on the operation to Cologne and was ditched 10 km SW of Antwerp, at Bazel on the bank of the Schelde. P/O William Deryck Kennard and P/O Eric Raymond Johnson were killed.

51 Wing Commander Butler, Flying Officer Basil Mervyn Sayers and Flying Officer Weston James Robertson were killed.

52 Squadron Leader John Castle took temporary charge of 226 Squadron until the appointment of Wing Commander W. E. Surplice DFC.

53 On 4 July six American crews joined six crews from 226 Squadron for Independence Day attacks on De Kooy, Haamstede, Bergen-Alkmaar and Valkenburg airfields in Holland. Three aircraft were lost; two of them crewed by Americans.

54 One had died on 1 November 1941 in the first ever Typhoon crash, at Roudham, Norfolk and the other was killed over Germany flying a Tempest in April 1945.

55 In March 1943 418 Squadron re-equipped with Mosquito FBVIs and in 1944 was adopted by the City of Edmonton. 605 Squadron re-equipped with Mosquito FBVIs in February-March 1944.

56 KIA during a low-level attack on Mazingarbe on 31.10.42.

57 Day Bomber, by Arthur Eyton-Jones, Sutton Publishing Ltd, 1998.

58 'Collie' Collins evaded and eventually returned home nine months later via the French Underground and imprisonment in Spain. (A full account of Maurice Collins' adventures can be found in Low Level From Swanton, by Martin W. Bowman (ARP, 1995). Pilot Officer Harry J. Milford and Sergeant George Nicholls were captured almost immediately and later placed in PoW camps. Milford was sent to at Stalag Luft III, Sagan in Pomerania. He became heavily involved in the 'X' Escape organisation in the British compound and was one of those who took part in the Great Escape on the night of 24 March 1944 when 76 prisoners got out of the camp in an underground tunnel. All except three of the prisoners were recaptured. Furious, Hitler ordered that 50 of the recaptured prisoners were to be shot and Milford was one of those executed by the Gestapo. Collins was awarded the DFM and went on to fly three more tours - over 100 ops - on 226 Squadron, in Mitchells. In 1945 he was awarded the DFC. On 22 September 226 Squadron lost a second Boston, flown by Flight Sergeant Marcel Auguste Henri Demont, which was claimed by Hauptmann Klaus Mietusch, Kommandeur, 7./JG26 who shot his victim down at 1315 hours 3 kms E of Ostend. A career officer who had joined the Geschwader in 1938, it was his 23rd victory. Demont and his crew were killed. Major Mietusch was KIA on 17.9.44 when his FW 190A-8 was shot down by Lieutenant William R. Beyer of the 361st Fighter Group, 8th Air Force who was flying a P-51 Mustang. Mietusch had logged 452 combat sorties and was credited with 75 victories. See The JG26 War Diary, Vol. 2 1943-45, Donald Caldwell (Grub Street 1998).

Chapter 10

Operation 'Oyster'

'...Now that it is all over England about our attack on the Philips Radio Works in Eindhoven, I can say more about my experiences. First of all, we had been on standby for this raid for many days but the weather was bad so it was cancelled each day until last Sunday. We were briefed for this raid about a week ago and were expecting to go the following day but, as I say, the weather was against us. Since that briefing (when we were told the target) we have been confined to camp. The telephones were locked and there was no outgoing mail. We were completely isolated from the outside world! However, the camp cinema had a new film showing each day, which helped. These precautions were, of course, so that there was no leakage of our intended target. Much to our relief, the secret was kept because on Sunday the weather improved and we had another hurried briefing, were issued with rations, escape kits etc and were in the air at about 11.40 on Sunday 6th December. We manoeuvred into our formations along with 464 (RAAF) Squadron who share our airfield.

'Before we reached our coast, we were joined by many other aircraft, I think there were about 100 in all. It was a very impressive sight, I can tell you. We were all flying very low over the sea, it seemed about 10 feet to me! It was not long before Burt [Sergeant W. Lowe] our navigator said, 'Dutch coast ahead'. No sooner had he said this, than we were greeted with a small amount of Ack-Ack, which increased, as we approached the coast. The first thing that struck me after crossing the coast were the sand-hills and pine forests which looked just like those at home - I soon found out the difference though, as these forests were full of machine-gun nests and the sky was filled with tracer. Little blobs of light were whizzing all around our plane, some very fast and others seemed to appear as a slow curve. Our pilot, Bill Lee, excelled himself with violent evasive action, which made it more difficult for the Germans to aim accurately. We were soon out of this area though and by dropping over the treetops, this made a screen, which gave us some protection behind.

'You know Con, when I have read about other aircrew reporting people waving to them whilst flying over occupied countries, I found it hard to believe. I don't now! As we hopped over trees and roofs there were people waving like mad, handkerchiefs, even flags. I suppose, with the leading aircraft having already passed over, it gave more time for them to run out of their homes. After more Ack-Ack and machine-guns we at last reached the target area where we ran into a terrific barrage, again, as we were still so low it proved ineffective so far as we were concerned. Bill, the pilot, rose from about 20ft to about 60 feet and I heard the navigator say 'Bomb doors open'. Then we flew into clouds of smoke and I heard 'Bombs gone'. I saw lots of flashes and sparks rise up as our bombs and incendiaries went into the centre of the target. What a blaze! As I looked back from my turret I saw 2 German machine-gunners still on the roof (this was confirmed later). I think it would have been impossible for them to get down and were most likely blown up by the other planes behind us. S/L 'Digger' Wheeler, our Flight Commander, was in front of us, so one by one we formated on him again, dived down low and belted as fast as we could for home but just before coming to the sea there was more flak which followed us right over the water. I then noticed big splashes of water in front and behind us - boy was I scared. I thought it was aircraft crashing but we later learned that it was German Ack-Ack shells bursting on the water in the hope of us running into one of these 'spouts'. It was about this time I saw a tugboat, towing a string of barges. I let go a few rounds at it but we were soon out of range. I'll bet the tug captain was as scared as I was because he was being shot at from both sides! Anyway, after using more violent evasive action we soon were over the open sea, heading as fast as we could for home.

'I kept a good lookout, especially in the sun (we gunners were told time and time again 'Watch out for the Hun in the Sun!'). All this time we were very thankful not to be attacked by enemy fighters but we were told later that our own fighter escort was having a good time somewhere above us. We eventually sighted England and there were four loud cheers, one after the other, then altogether. Another 40 minutes and we were back at our dispersal, carefully examining our plane for damage. There wasn't a scratch. The only casualty was the remains of a stork, which was struck in the port engine air cooler. I only hope it wasn't carrying a baby cargo at the time. Birds are a menace when flying at low level and many of the other aircraft had broken perspex in the turrets and nose cones. I'm sorry I didn't manage to get you a genuine pair of Dutch clogs Con but we didn't stay very long!

'My pal Pat Stokes and his crew [59] didn't return from this trip. We were so low, I doubt very much if they got away with it. They say that about 11 aircraft didn't return from this trip but if this is an overall estimate, then it's not too bad out of 100. Never worry about me Con, I will be OK and in any case, we won't be flying again for a few weeks as all the planes have to be inspected and repaired where necessary. In case you have forgotten, the planes (we call them kites!) we fly are called Venturas. The full name being Lockheed 'Vega' Ventura. On the side of our 'kite' is the painting of a Maori Tiki. His name is Kia-Ora. Well, that is my life story to date and an impression I have of the destruction of the Philips Radio and Valve works. I did not mention that there are two buildings separated by a playing field and according to how we were briefed some bombed one and some the other, joining up immediately after for the flight home. Much has been reported about this raid and on yesterday's 6 o'clock news a W/C from one of the other Squadrons with us gave his account of the raid - Did you hear it? The Germans say that we hit hospitals, houses etc but that is all baloney as every bomb went right on the target. You could not miss it from that height! The Bostons went in four minutes before us with the H/E bombs; then we came in with the incendiaries and delayed action bombs. You should have seen the photos that were posted in the Mess of the Mess!! Write soon, love to Mum and Dad - Pete xx.'

Letter by Sergeant Peter H. Mallinson, WOp/AG on the 487 Squadron Ventura piloted by Flight Sergeant Bill Lee, written to his sister Connie shortly after he got back to Feltwell. 'Oyster' was his first operation and it had come no more than eight weeks after his eighteenth birthday.

Rain was falling in East Anglia on the morning of Sunday 6th December 1942 but near the outskirts of Eindhoven, sixty miles from the coast of Holland, the weather was clear. Frits Philips and his wife, along with his brother-in-law van Riemsdijk and sister Jetty were visiting a niece who had christened a child. Philips was director-general of the Philips electro-chemical factories in Eindhoven, a built up area of Holland only fifty miles from the Ruhr. Philips was the largest manufacturer of its type in Europe, thought to produce over one-third of the German supply of valves and certain radar equipment. Although some industrial processes had been dispersed to other sites, Eindhoven was still the main centre, especially for research into electronic countermeasures and radar. Production was centered in two factories, the Strijp Group main works and the Emmasingel valve and lamp factory, both in built-up areas within the town. Their destruction, which demanded precision bombing from a very low level to minimize the danger to the local people, was considered by London to be of vital importance. In Philips opinion however, his factory produced only a tiny amount of material for the Germans, a view shared by the Philips family and staff in America. But, in order to satisfy the German commission from Berlin, Philips always prepared graphs showing that production totals were better than they were so that the Germans could return home satisfied. These graphs were seen by a number of employees, some of who were members of the local resistance but Philips' efforts to look less productive were not forwarded to the allies so readily. After the church service Philips, his wife, brother-in-law and sister were drinking the usual cups of coffee, when suddenly they saw a formation of low-flying aircraft approaching in the distance. Their suspicion was that it had to be British machines. Philips' first reaction was, 'Are they going to bomb the Eindhoven railway station?' At the same moment they saw the first bombs being dropped and heard the crashing of the impact. With a feeling of deprivation they realized that their town was being bombed! As fast as they could Philips and his brother-in-law cycled to the De Laak, where fortunately nobody was harmed. At some distance they saw the Demer, the most important shopping-street in Eindhoven, which was already ablaze.

Only now did Frits Philips realize that it had been his factories, which were the target of the bombardment. There was a momentary silence and he thought that the bombardment had finished but cycling to the Emmasingel yet another wave of bombers rushed in to the attack and he had hurriedly seek shelter in a cycle-shop. Meanwhile, he noticed that the office building had been hit several times and it was on fire. Despite this Frits wanted to rescue two portraits of his father and Uncle Gerard, which had been painted by Jan Veth in 1916 at the occasion of the 25th anniversary of the company. Fortunately all the other portraits and valuables had been stowed safely away long ago. The portraits were hanging in the commissioners-room at ground level. Frits climbed in through a window and was able to rescue a silver cigar-box from his desk and Frits distributed a box of good cigars which had been left by his father amongst the fire brigade who had joined him. Philips went into the commissioners-room, opened the door and at that same moment a large piece of ceiling came crashing down. The firemen would not let him enter the room and so sadly he had to leave the portraits to the fire. The building burned out completely.

Unbeknown to Philips preparations for Operation 'Oyster', the most ambitious daylight raid conceived by 2 Group had been given the green light on 9 November 1942. Originally plans called for the Strijp Group main works to be bombed by twenty-four Venturas, twelve Mitchells and twelve Mosquitoes, while twelve

Venturas and thirty-six Bostons would at the same time attack the Emmasingel Lamp and valve works half a mile to the east. The slower Venturas would lead the way at low level with HE and 30lb incendiaries before surprise was lost. On 17 November a full-scale practice was held on a route similar to the one to be used, with the St. Neots power station as the 'target'. Many basic lessons were learned, while other problems associated with a mixed force, such as the differences in bombing techniques and cruising speeds, were exposed. The Mitchells fared particularly badly on this first practice but even worse were the Venturas. Next day thirty of their crews tried again on their own on the same route and a vast improvement was recorded. On 20 November on the third practice, all four aircraft types took part.

Sergeant Stan C. Moss RAAF, a Ventura pilot on 464 Squadron was feeling a bit 'miffed' at not being chosen to participate in the first rehearsals. He consoled himself that his crew were recent arrivals at Feltwell and at age twenty, he was the second youngest on the Squadron. 'Both my observer and wireless air gunner - Sergeants Reg A. Wagner and J. A. Wallis - were Londoners and we had teamed up through unusual circumstances. At OTU I had a 'million to one chance' accident and was sole survivor of a head-on collision with another Blenheim in smog-like conditions over the North Sea. I parachuted into the sea and floated around in a one-man dinghy for fifty hours before being picked up by a passing ship. It took me almost a week to get back to Bicester where my course mates at first greeted me with ghost-like awe. A Court of Enquiry, at which my actions were affirmed, inevitably followed and I was exhorted by the CO to get back to flying as soon as possible. I was given the option of accepting a staff job in Training Command to assuage the memory of those traumatic days. Eventually, I was introduced to another crew whose pilot had been held for further training. The fourth member, Sergeant F. C. Lindsay, an air gunner who hailed from South Australia, joined us at Feltwell. First, we had to become familiar with the Ventura. Vega was a subsidiary of the Lockheed Company, which produced the renowned Hudson to which the Ventura was similar but bigger. In fact, it was a military version of the Lockheed Lodestar, a short haul airliner. This accounted for its undesirable bulk as a warplane, its relative slow response to the touch of control and its rather swanky interior appointments - automatic pilot was a dream. The best features of the Ventura were its powerful Pratt and Whitney engines and exceptionally strong all metal airframe.

'Then came news of my posting to the Middle East. All was approved provided I would name my wireless air gunner. Transferring to the Middle Eastern theatre where Australian troops had long been operating had always been a priority for me but my English WOp/AG adamantly refused to go, understandably, because he was married. So the posting fell through and eight days later I was listed to fly as number two to the Flight Commander in what was to be the third and final rehearsal for the 'big do'. We flew east beyond the English coast then turned north, a tightly packed formation of Venturas at almost nought feet. But the 'tail-gating' effect meant we were flying in each other's slipstream and this caused ones s aircraft to twist and yaw with the fearsome danger of hitting the water or another aircraft. One sweated at the controls like a navvy. At Flamborough Head, where we turned inland to the supposed 'target' we became entangled with Bostons and

Mosquitoes in a frightening shambles, exacerbated by a simulated attack by Spitfires which dived amongst us with amazing daring. Surprisingly, there were no collisions, even though more than 100 aircraft were involved. In the scattering of our formation, I managed to hang on to my number one until reaching base but jibbed at following him under high-tension wires!

'Next day a frank post-mortem took place, which much relieved everyone's anxiety about the slipstream hazard. Then came the announcement: target Philips' Radio Factory at Eindhoven, The Netherlands. Bostons were to go in first and bomb from a medium height, followed by Venturas carrying a mixture of incendiaries and delayed action bombs and finally the Mosquitoes would sweep in to distract the fire fighters. To bluff enemy defences, our fighters would make three diversionary sweeps and there would be top cover for us as well. It all sounded foolproof.'

The three simulated attacks revealed deficiencies that led to the two Mitchell squadrons, 98 and 180, being withdrawn from the starting line-up for the raid, scheduled for Wednesday 3 December. In any event, since converting to Mitchells both squadrons had been plagued with turret and gun, intercom and oxygen problems and were far from operational. It was also anticipated that smoke and fires from the Venturas' incendiaries would obscure the target for the succeeding waves, so they would have to go in last behind the Bostons and Mosquitoes. Consequently, the routes and timings differed between the aircraft, the fastest, the Mosquito; being followed by the Boston, then the slowest, the Ventura. Obviously, it was vital for each squadron to arrive over the targets separately, to avoid confusion, yet it was imperative that the whole attack be completed in the shortest possible time. Therefore it was finally decided that the Bostons would, after all, attack both plants and with eleven-second delayed action bombs. These would hopefully divert attention from the Venturas as they climbed to bombing height.

By 2 December preparations were complete. Altogether, twelve Bostons on 88 Squadron, twelve of n226 Squadron at Swanton Morley and seventeen Venturas on 21 Squadron at Methwold were to bomb the Emmasingel valve factory. Another twelve Bostons on 107 Squadron at Great Massingham, fourteen Venturas on 464 RNZAF and sixteen on 487 RAAF Squadron at Feltwell (who were flying their first full-scale Ventura operation) were to attack the Strijp Group main works. The New Zealand Squadron would take off in two boxes of eight, one led by Seavill and the other by Flying Officer G. W. Brewer DFC from Papatoetoe, New Zealand. All the crews had been instructed to wear steel helmets to protect their heads from being knocked against the insides of the aircraft during evasive action and also to safeguard against flak splinters! Pilots and crews on 487 Squadron were concerned to learn that they were at the end of the bomber stream, behind and to the left of 464 Squadron. Squadron Leader Len Trent DFC the 487 Squadron 'B' Flight Commander, who hailed from Nelson in New Zealand, recalled. 'I thought of the unfortunate troopers in the Charge of the Light Brigade as we prepared our maps and our aircraft were bombed up with heavy incendiary missiles capable of crashing through the factory walls before erupting into flames. We studied photographs of the target, a complex of huge buildings on the edge of the town.... and the biggest building, which was to be my victim, was five storeys high - a bulls-eye impossible to miss.' As they were driven to their Venturas Sergeant John

Bede Cusack RAAF, air gunner on a 464 Squadron Ventura flown by Pilot Officer P. C. Kerr RAAF heard someone say, 'Well, it's something new but I hope those bloody Spits keep close to us. I don't want to tangle with any Focke Wulfs in this bloody crate. I looked at the faces of these young airmen who were about to be blooded. They were serious and generally quiet. As each crew got out the rest wished them luck.' [60]

The American built bombers would be joined by eight Mosquitoes on 105 Squadron, led by Wing Commander Hughie Edwards VC DFC who had returned from Malta to take command of the Squadron on 3 August 1942 and two on 139 Squadron. Squadron Leader Jack Houlston AFC DFC and Warrant Officer James Armitage DFC of 139 Squadron would take off at noon to carry out damage assessment. At Marham the briefings were carried out by Edwards accompanied as usual by his white bulldog 'Sallie'. If she was late Edwards would halt proceedings until she had settled down![61] Edwards and Flight Lieutenant Charles Patterson, who had a black spaniel by the name of 'Jamie', often took their pet dogs aloft in a Mosquito during practice flights. Patterson, who flew the Eindhoven operation with Flying Officer Mills ('armed' with a cine camera) in 'O for Orange' and who had flown a tour on Blenheims on 114 Squadron, recalls.

'Mosquito operations were far more ambitious than Blenheim ops but casualties were lower. For a period from about July-September 1942 the casualties were as high as the low-level daylights in Blenheims a year before. There was even talk of the Mosquito having to be written off after all. In some way we still had such enormous faith in this aeroplane so we just could not believe that it could not be made to operate successfully at an acceptable rate of casualties. Operationally, the Philips works from a Mosquito point of view was regarded as a comparatively straightforward target, nothing to get terribly frightened of. Something we would have taken in our stride as part of routine operations. I flew in the second formation of four Mosquitoes, No.3 to Squadron Leader George Parry and one of our flight commanders, behind six led by Edwards. We were supposed to be so timed that we didn't get involved with either Venturas or Bostons. Our concern was that we would get tangled up with the Venturas or even the Bostons and have to reduce speed, which of course from a Mosquito point of view was very dangerous because we had no defensive armament. We were to fly to somewhere just south of Eindhoven and turn to port and then attack the target. The Mosquitoes were to go up to 1,500 feet just short of the target and shallow dive on to it because it was assumed that some Bostons would have gone over low level before us. We got across the Dutch coast flying at low level. Looking across my port wing tip I saw 190s and 109s [of 4th and 6th Staffeln JG1] literally in line taking off from Woensdrecht to intercept us. They only looked about 200-300 yards away. It was actually about half a mile. They looked so normal; just like Spitfires taking off in England, that it was hard to realise they were coming up to kill you. We had to slow right down. We found ourselves getting involved with some Venturas. We were not far above stalling speed trying to get behind them.'

With great coolness and decisiveness, Squadron Leader George Parry DSO DFC and his No.2, Flight Lieutenant W. C. S. 'Bill' Blessing, an Australian from New South Wales, broke away, at Turnhout, deliberately drawing the 190s on themselves, then let them go chasing as they opened the throttles to full speed.

Parry was later able to rejoin the formation but Blessing's and another Mosquito flown by Pilot Officers Jimmy Bruce DFM and Mike Carreck[62] were forced to return to Marham. Two Bostons had also aborted, while the Mosquito formation, which had departed the coast at Cromer and had flown further north of the main force, had unfortunately got ahead of schedule. Edwards and his navigator Flying Officer Cairns successfully led the way through a 200-foot cloud base over the sea. The Mosquitoes were supposed to rendezvous with the rest of the formation at the target but they now made landfall with the Bostons and Venturas at the Scheldt Estuary. Edwards had to slow the Mosquitoes to just 150 mph and fly at fifty feet in order to stay behind the others when they should have been flying to the Strijp Works at 270 mph, before climbing to 1,500 feet, diving and releasing their bombs from 500 feet.

John Bede Cusack in the Ventura formation continues.

'It was a fine, windless day with a slight mist. As we streamed across the flat Norfolk countryside the field workers stopped to wave to the modern cavalcade that rose the sky so close above their heads. The North Sea was grey and unruffled. We crossed it at zero feet. Our box was tail end of this bomber stream. A box consisted of six aircraft. No.1 the leader had as his supports Nos.2 and 3 on either side. No.4 flew just below No.1 to miss his slipstream and was supported on either side by Nos.5 and 6. Thus No.1 flew at approximately twenty feet so that No.4, which was ourselves, to dodge slipstreams, was down to ten feet. Despite the nervous qualms at the pit of my stomach, I found this new experience exciting. The low-level approach was intended to spoof the enemy radar. The idea was that the island defences would be taken by surprise and we would be across them before they recovered. What someone had omitted to allow for was that the initial beating up by fighters and Mosquitoes who had gone in ten minutes ahead would have the Jerry gunners right on their toes. I heard Jack [Flying Officer B. J. E. Hannah RNZAF, navigator] say, 'Enemy coast coming up' and then the sea beneath us began to churn white as the enemy gunners extended their welcome. Overhead, black smudges lined with red appeared as if by magic. Luckily the heavies could not depress far enough to get our range but the concentration of Bofors, 20 mm and light flak was terrific.[63]

In the leading 464 Squadron Ventura flown by the CO, Wing Commander R. H. 'Bob' Young AFC navigator Flight Lieutenant E. F. 'Hawker' Hart observed that 'the whole formation of forty-eight Venturas looked a very impressive armada' as they flew just over the surface of the sea. Pilot Officer George M. 'Jock' Shinnie, a veteran of Blenheim operations and the WOp/AG was positioned at the astro hatch. Shinnie's first priority was to keep Young, a pre-war Qualified Flying Instructor, who initially had given dual instruction to many of the young inexperienced pilots, informed of the overall state of the Ventura formations.

'At times we reduced speed slightly to allow sections at the rear to catch up. Flying at tree top level and having to take evasive action individually to avoid trees, power pylons etc made formation flying difficult at times but overall formation keeping was excellent. We were not very impressed by the size and shape of the Ventura. Neither were we impressed by its performance compared to the known performance of the Boston and Mosquito. To its credit it had two superb 2,000 hp Pratt & Whitney Double Wasp engines. The engineering staff adored them, as they were almost trouble free. So did the pilots but what a dreadful cumbersome airframe they had to drag around the air. Because of their power, large 'paddle' propellers were needed. These proved during formation flying to cause considerable turbulence to following aircraft within large formations. Again not a popular aspect particularly when flying at tree top level. My secondary role and the role of Pilot Officer J. M. Quinlan RAAF the other WOp/AG who was also positioned at the astro hatch, as there was no need for the lower rear firing guns to be manned at such low-level, was scanning the sky for possible fighter attacks. We were fortunate as most of the fighters were elsewhere but we experienced considerable light flak from crossing the Dutch coast and en-route to Eindhoven. After my Blenheim days of 1940-41, it was a new experience to me to have the flak coming from higher than we were flying.'

Sergeant John Bede Cusack continues.[64]

'Two tremendous splashes that tossed water over our heads marked the passing of two crews.[65] Then we were over the defenders. A little to our right a plane plunged into the earth, skidded into a strongpoint and exploded in a burst of flame and debris. It suddenly struck me that in this sort of flying, parachutes were useless. If you went in there were no survivors. I sweated across those islands and anyone who says they were never afraid on ops is a bloody liar. Suddenly we were flying across the mainland. A few black smudges chased us but it looked as if we had passed the strongly defended coastal area. As we roared over the flat Dutch countryside the inhabitants out on their Sunday strolls waved frantically and jumped with joy. These Dutchies let it be known whose side they were on. Bill [Sergeant W. Kirk RAAF] had his head stuck out of the astrodome until the latter was blown away coming in over the coast, without giving him anything worse than a scare. He returned to the front of the kite. Suddenly Jack said, 'That's an aerodrome' and the next moment we were skipping across an excellently laid out drome. This was a costly blue on someone's part because two more planes ploughed in a smother of dust a, flame and smoke. Probably this place had taken a beating earlier and was out for revenge. A cannon shell blew the perspex out on the starboard side of the cockpit, giving Bill his second fright but doing no damage. The gunners poured a fusillade back without much apparent effect. A little further on we passed another Ventura burning fiercely. Four figures scrambling awkwardly in their flying boots away from it showed they at least had escaped. As we swept over them they turned and gave a forlorn wave.'

Fellow Australian Sergeant Stan C. Moss RAAF and his 464 Squadron crew had been hit over Walcheren. Moss recalled.

'Suddenly a muffled explosion sounded behind my seat. 'Sorry, Skip,' said the WOp/AG Sergeant J. A. Wallis, 'I mistakenly pushed the IFF button.' He must have known something, for shortly after a puff of black smoke appeared in the air directly ahead of us about 500 feet above the very flat shoreline some miles away. We had obviously been detected and our landfall was not an undefended shore somewhere up 'de Schelde' estuary as planned but directly over the coastline. As we were almost crossing the coast, the Squadron Leader's aircraft began to gently weave and I was about to follow suit when, like a flash of lightning, the right side cabin-window exploded almost noiselessly below the roar of the engines. Instantly and involuntarily I doubled up in my seat in reaction at being hit by pieces of exploding flak shell. My distress was immediate and my sudden movement had lifted the aircraft several hundred feet. One thought dominated my mind, namely, that I must get the machine on the deck before blacking out.

'In a haze, I saw a tiny ploughed field to the left in a tree surrounded area and pulling back throttles and pitch, I pushed down undercarriage and flaps. As I came down over the treetops, making for the edge of the field, some interior prompting told me to lift the undercarriage lever. The plane touched down smoothly [at Vrouwenpolder] and sheared across the field at right angles to the furrow ending up about a cricket pitch length from a belt of trees. The observer, Sergeant Reg A. Wagner, sitting unharnessed on the bench seat next to me, was immediately thrown forward on impact into the bombing hatch, yet fortunately unhurt by the fall.

'From some unrealised reserves of energy and determination, I forced myself out of the aircraft and collapsed to the ground about ten yards away. Three of us had been wounded by shells bursting inside the cabin of the machine slightly above and behind my right shoulder. The observer received pieces of shrapnel into his left shoulder, narrowly missing his vertebrae and aorta, whilst the WOp/AG had perspex splinters in his face, upper chest, side, back, ribs and arm and I had also been well peppered by about a dozen smaller pieces. Bleeding profusely, a crewmember thoughtfully shot a capsule of morphine into me and a welcome calm descended. I remember looking up at the rolling cumulus clouds, which seemed so large and so near and thinking to myself, 'So this is how one dies'.

By contrast Flying Officer S. B. 'Rusty' Perryman a New Zealander from Christchurch flying a Ventura on 487 Squadron, saw three small children waving and waved back at them. Perryman would return from this operation but others in his squadron were not so lucky. He and the remainder of the formation headed inland where twenty-three Bostons and Venturas failed to avoid a huge flock of ducks that smashed windscreens, splattered the cockpits with blood and feathers and damaged wing surfaces. Over the Colijnsplaat two seagulls came through the nose of Flying Officer Philip Burley's aircraft injuring his navigator, Flying Officer Herbert L. Besford in the legs while at the same time the draught whisked his maps away. Besford directed his pilot from then on by memory. Twenty minutes later their Ventura was attacked by a Bf 109 when over Oost at fifty feet. The enemy fighter made four separate attacks from the stern but no strikes were scored and the Bf 109 was claimed as damaged by a five second burst from Flight Sergeant T. Smith, the rear gunner at 400 yards range.

Pilot Officer Jack Peppiatt, skipper of a Boston on 'B' Flight, 88 Squadron recalls:

'The journey cross-country was a 'Circus' really. We slid about, keeping sight of our leader and watching to avoid airfields. The other hazard was overhead cables, etc and the trick was to look out to the sides ahead so that you could spot the lines of pylons, which could reveal where the invisible cables might be. Although there was a lot of apprehension, there was also a great thrill in it. Talk over the intercom went on the whole time between the navigator and myself, discussing where we were, where the leader was going and did you see that railway or canal, etc? I saw the landscape flying by with brief flashes of recognition; a house, some people, vehicles and every now and then a blink as I thought we had gone too near an airfield. As we neared the turning point near Eindhoven [at Oostmalle, SSW of Turnhout] it did get taut. We all knew that if the target were missed there would be no way of recovering. In front I had glimpses of the leading Bostons and we began to pack in as we saw the buildings of the factory way ahead. The first two went in low and we then sailed up to 1,500 feet, which felt very vulnerable! We seemed to suddenly stand still and hang about waiting to be shot at.'

As the Venturas passed near to Woensdrecht the formation was bracketed by heavy flak. A 20-mm shell from the airfield flak defences hit the starboard engine of a 464 Squadron Ventura flown by Squadron Leader Tony Carlisle but he continued to the target. Sergeant Smock RCAF had more than five feet of his wing torn away when he hit a chimney. However, he was able to nurse the aircraft back to Norfolk safely. The Ventura flown by 32-year old Wing Commander Frankie C. Seavill RNZAF, 487 Squadron CO was hit by flak and crashed at Schaapskooi on the airfield at Woensdrecht; all four crew were killed. Like almost everyone else in the Venturas, Seavill was flying his first operational sortie and he had refused a Group Captain post to stay on 487 Squadron (which was taken over by Wing Commander G. J. Grindell shortly after). Squadron Leader Len Trent DFC pressed the firing button on his control column and sprayed a flak gun position with .50 and .303 machine gun fire. At the Strijp target Trent climbed to 250 feet to clear the parapets and let loose his stick of two 250lb GP bombs and forty 30lb incendiaries on his high target building, holing it from basement to roof-top. As his aircraft cleared the top of the flaming and smoking target he glimpsed on the left hand corner of the building, a German machine gunner stubbornly sticking to his post and pouring a steady stream of fire at him. None of the bullets damaged the Ventura but 'There,' said Trent, 'was in my book, a damn good soldier.'

A 21 Squadron Ventura flown by Pilot Officer H. T. Bichard was attacked by Unteroffizier Rudolf Rauhaus, one of the pilots in II./JG1 returning from combat with the American attacks in France and was shot down. Bichard belly-landed the Ventura at Rilland-Bath in Zeeland and he and two of his crew survived to be taken prisoner. Sergeant Roy Lamerton, the 30-year old navigator was killed.

Twelve Bostons on 107 Squadron dropped their loads on the Strijp Group main works. First over the target was Squadron Leader R. J. N. MacLachlan's crew. They encountered a flak gun on one of the factory buildings and one of his gunners opened fire on it, forcing the German crew to abandon their exposed gun position and flee into the factory building just as MacLachlan's bombs scored a direct hit and destroyed the structure. This feat would earn MacLachlan the DFC. Meanwhile, the Bostons on 226 Squadron, led by Squadron Leader J. S. Kennedy and Squadron Leader G. R. 'Digger' Magill, released their delayed-action bombs on the Emmasingel valve factory before the Mosquitoes came in behind at 1,000 feet with high-explosive and incendiary bombs.

Charles Patterson continues.

'Ahead of me I saw the front formation of Mosquitoes in the distance already climbing up to 1,500 feet so I immediately took my formation up as fast as I could to 1,500 feet to catch Edwards' formation. We caught up about two-three miles south of Eindhoven. He banked over to port and started to dive down on the Philips works in the centre of the town. The moment I turned to port I could see this factory standing out unmistakably, very prominently, right in the centre of Eindhoven. We all went down in this shallow dive, full throttle and at the appropriate moment, dropped the bombs. As I went across the Philips works the whole factory seemed to erupt in a cloud of smoke and flashes. It looked as though the whole thing was completely eliminated.' Squadron Leader George Parry and Flying Officer Victor 'Robbie' Robson, Canadian Flying Officers Spencer Kimmel and Harry Kirkland, Warrant Officer Ray Noseda DFC and Sergeant John Urquhart and Flight Sergeants K. L. Monaghan and A. W. Dean also bombed the target from 1,000 feet. Two FW 190s intercepted Noseda and Urquhart on the return in the Overflakee area. Although damaged by cannon fire, they managed to return safely. Mosquito 'A-Apple' on 139 Squadron flown by Canadian Flying Officer John 'Junior' O'Grady and Sergeant George Lewis was hit in the engine and, trailing smoke and flames pulled away to head back towards England. They made it only as far as thirty miles off Den Helder, where they crashed into the sea. Their bodies were never found.

Last in were the Venturas, flying four minutes behind the Bostons and carrying their incendiaries and delayed-action bombs. In the space of just seven minutes, four of the Venturas were shot down by flak. The 21 Squadron Ventura flown by Flight Lieutenant Kenneth S. Smith was hit by flak directly over the target. It ran in with a stream of flame from a punctured fuel tank crashed into Nieuwe Dijk Street just north of the Emmasingel works and blew up on impact. All four crew including Flight Lieutenant Wallace Martin RAAF DFC, from Murrurundi, New South Wales, Bombing Leader on 464 Squadron, who had volunteered to navigate for 21 Squadron were killed. The Ventura piloted by Flight Sergeant Beverly M. Harvey RCAF on 464 Squadron at the rear of the formation was hit by flak and crashed with the loss of all the crew in the so-called 'Fitterij' on the Strijp complex.

Another 464 Squadron machine, piloted by Flying Officer Maurice G. Moor, stalled and dived out of control before crashing into a square in the Schoolstraat, north of the target, demolishing and setting fire to a row of houses. Pilot Officer 'Jock' Shinnie, WOp/AG in the leading 464 Squadron Ventura flown by Wing Commander 'Bob' Young, saw both Venturas crash. 'It appeared that his [Harvey's] target was so obscured by smoke the pilot could not see the top of the building and tragically flew into it. Some minutes later I was shocked to see our number two aircraft [Moor] on our port side suddenly completely enveloped in flames. The aircraft dipped, flew into the side of a house and then appeared at the other side. It was all over in seconds. We successfully attacked our respective targets but the buildings appeared to be far taller than expected and they were well protected by flak batteries on the roofs. Although flying so low we did get over the buildings in our cumbersome Venturas, albeit with little room to spare.'

Sergeant John Bede Cusack RAAF on the 464 Squadron Ventura flown by Pilot Officer Kerr, recalled.

'In all the excitement I had completely forgotten about the target. Wilbur's voice, 'Target coming up' brought me back to reality. It would be hard to give my impression over the next minute for the area was a nightmare of burning buildings, smokestacks and high tension wires. Jerry gunners still manned their weapons on rooftops even though the windows belched smoke and flame. We went through so fast that it was hard to pick a target so I put my finger on the teat and sprayed the entire area. How we missed the stacks and wires I'll never know. I saw a Vent veer crazily and hit a smokestack plumb in the centre and plunge downward in a welter of dust, bricks and flame. Jack screamed 'Bombs Away' and we swung violently to the left. The clusters of incendiaries flew off at a tangent, travelling almost horizontally to smash into the front of the building in such a welter of explosion and fire that it really shook me. I knew why the place was so thoroughly alight. We straightened up and missed a set of high-tension wires by inches. I saw a burning Ventura [Moor] that had smashed into a row of tenement houses. The next moment we were doing a split-arse left turn as we went for home. It was only then that I noticed I still had my fingers on the teat and that neither gun was firing. Around us in the air dogfights were going on everywhere but enemy fighters appeared to have their hands full…We came out along a canal about three-quarters of a mile wide. Guns placed on either side turned in and churned the water white below us. Bill who had gone to man the lower guns, had this third life when a shell hit both of them, curled them up in a 'V' but failed to explode. Miraculously, no direct hits were scored on this fleeing target. A mile astern we saw a plane, which turned out to be a Canadian 'Pete' [66] limping home. The German gunners concentrated on this inviting target but again, despite a hail of shell, the crew came through. We came out over a marshy flat area without a shot being fired which later prompted the thought, Why the hell didn't we go in that way?…'

The Ventura flown by 26-year old Flight Sergeant John L. Greening on 487 Squadron cleared the rooftops and was believed to have collided with another aircraft over the target area before crashing into the Veemgebouw on the Strijp complex. Both crews were killed.

After the bombing the aircraft streaked for home at low level, desperately avoiding high-tension cables, flak and flocks of birds again and fighters, before they reached the sanctuary of the open sea. Just before they reached the Zeider Zee the Venturas were bracketed by flak. Sergeant A. V. Ricketts' Ventura on 21 Squadron, the ninth and last overall, ditched seven miles off Bawdsey after a piece of flak severed a fuel pipe and he finally ran out of fuel. Their aircraft sank in about fifty seconds. ASR from Felixstowe rescued all four crew twenty minutes later. Another 21 Squadron survivor was Pilot Officer Arthur E. C. Wheeler who recounted that the raid was 'an exhilarating experience rather than a frightening one, seeing gunners on the flat roof of some of the buildings swiveling round as we flew over and dropped our incendiaries. We were at zero feet as I saw ahead of us a line of electrical pylons, which I knew we could not climb over. However, I breathed a sigh of relief when I realised that fortunately for us somebody had been there first and there were no power lines between them.' After debriefing, the operation was immediately hailed as a great success though, from 21 Squadron's viewpoint, it was tempered somewhat by the casualties they had suffered. The worrying statistic was that the three Ventura squadrons had suffered at least twenty per cent losses on the raid.

Pilot Officer Gordon A. Park on 487 Squadron put his failing Ventura down just outside Long Stratton village after oil pipes or the starboard engine was damaged by a bird strike. Others in his squadron also had lucky escapes. Flight Sergeant Ron W. Secord, WOp/AG was grateful to his pilot, Flying Officer Brewer

DFC for ordering him to leave the astrodome and take up his gun position while flying over the coast for when Secord returned later to his hatch his found the dome punctured by flak. In the same aircraft, Sergeant R. F. 'Bob' Edmonds a Maori air gunner from Auckland, had his steel helmet knocked off his head by flak but was miraculously unharmed. The nose of the Ventura flown by Flight Sergeant Ian Baynton also of Auckland was broken when the Ventura struck a treetop but the aircraft returned safely. Boston 'D-Donald' piloted by Flight Sergeant G. E. T. 'Nick' Nicholls on 107 Squadron, crash-landed at Great Massingham on one engine and his wheels up and overshot the airfield. The aircraft went through a gun position and a hedge and finally came to rest in a slit trench. 'D-Donald' was written off but the crew escaped relatively unharmed; Nicholls was awarded the DFM for his exploits. Sergeant W. E. Burns, meanwhile, put down at Ipswich. Sergeant Chas Tyler's Boston (Z2211) on 88 Squadron had been hit in the starboard engine and they had a very anxious flight across the North Sea, as Bob Gallup, the observer, recalls:

'Shortly after we had released the bombs we were hit by flak in the starboard engine. We lost contact with the rest of the squadron as we began to slow down. We were unable to gain height and the prospect of covering the 150-mile North Sea return flight looked remote, so it was decided to force-land in Holland and give ourselves up. After turning back inland, however, we conferred once more and decided to 'have another go'. We turned for the Dutch coast once more and as we crossed out again every gun in Holland seemed to be firing at us. The tracers seemed to be like hailstones in reverse. Over the sea we tried to gain a little height but were unable to do so. After about fifty minutes we recognized Lowestoft ahead. We crossed the coast and force-landed immediately, finishing wheels-up in a ploughed field at Brewhouse farm, Carlton Colville. My feet were buried in soil and I had a problem getting out through the top escape hatch. As we hit the ground the strap of Chas Tyler's seat harness broke and he hit his head on the gun sight. Apart from that we were unhurt. Chas was taken to Lowestoft hospital while Stuart and I were taken home by the farmer for a lovely meal. After we had been to see Chas in hospital, we were taken to the local pub, where we were allowed to win every game of darts. We spent that night at the farm near the aircraft, with clean sheets and pillow. Life was great until next morning, when transport arrived to take us back to camp.'

Flying Officer Kerr's Ventura got back to Feltwell although many did not, as Australian gunner John Bede Cusack recalled.

'It was a badly mauled Squadron that limped home. Because of the absence of runways, planes all pleading various emergencies landed everywhere. The place was a shambles. Our petrol indicators showed empty five miles from the station and we landed, like everyone else, straight into the wind, with another plane on our tail and, while taxi-ing back on the tarmac, ground to a stop completely out of petrol. At interrogation I found the six bombers gunners had come through, which was almost a miracle…A young gunner said, 'Well, that wasn't so bad.' 'Not bad, said 'Hally' dryly. Another three ops like that and we will have completed our tour.' The young fellow looked at him open-mouthed and said, 'But it's thirty ops for a tour isn't it? 'That's right, said 'Art' patting him paternally on the head. 'Only we won't have to go that far.' [68]

In Eindhoven over sixty tons of bombs hit the factory buildings, which were devastated, essential supplies destroyed and the rail network disrupted. Fourteen aircraft - nine Venturas, one Mosquito and four Bostons - had been shot down. Photographs taken after the raid showed that both factories had been very badly damaged, fully justifying the decision to make the attack in daylight from low level. The Germans reported that 'Damage was caused to nearly all the work buildings'. The factory was in the middle of Eindhoven, so a considerable number of homes were also destroyed or damaged. Frits Philips recalls.

'The destruction was enormous. The time of the bombardment, on a Sunday morning, was chosen because the factories were closed but the death toll was over one hundred civilians. The hospitals were crowded with injured people and part of Eindhoven was destroyed by fire. My wife and my sister Jetty visited the wounded. They told us that not one of them blamed the allies! There was one man who had lost his wife and three of his seven children. Still no complaints could be heard from him. [69] The morale of the population during that bombardment had been exemplary. Personally the bombardment caused very deep emotions. To see the factories that had been erected with such devotion and offered jobs to thousands of people going up in flames was a terrible reality of war, though I realized that this war against the Germans had to be fought hard if they were to be conquered. This thought reconciled me to this hellish scene. The following morning I had visitors from The Hague. Our commissioner Mr. Woltersom, Mr. Hirschfeld and Dr. Ringers, the government commissioner for reconstruction, came to see the results of the bombardment themselves. Ringers and myself were on good terms and it was his help we needed the most. He did not disappoint us. My immediate concern was to commence repairs of our factories on short term, utilizing all our personnel to prevent them being deported to Germany. In the first months all the effort went into clearing away the debris. There was no way to make good the production capacity but it might have been worse. The heavy machinery could be repaired. Despite the never ending allied bombardment, the German war industry had suffered less than expected but the damage was substantial.'

Wing Commanders Hughie Edwards VC DFC, James Pelly-Fry and R. H. Young AFC were awarded the DSO. Eight DFCs were also awarded. Recipients included Wing Commander R. J. P. Pritchard AFC of Squadron, Pilot Officer J. M. Rankin of 107 Squadron, Flight Lieutenants 'Hawker' Hart and T. H. J. 'Jock' Cairns DFM and Flying Officer C. A. 'Buster' Evans DFM (Pelley-Fry's air gunner). Two DFMs, including one to Sergeant pilot W. H. C. Leavitt RCAF of 226 Squadron, were also awarded.

What of the others who took part in the Eindhoven raid? Sergeant Stan Moss, who was peppered with pieces of shrapnel, had survived. 'Other members of the crew were in state of shock and panic. Attempts to fire the aircraft failed and there was no real opportunity to escape. Glancing back across the field, I noticed how the four bombs had detached themselves from their racks and were lying forlornly on the surface of the field one after the other along the line of our crash path. Obviously, the retracting undercarriage had provided a cushioning effect. Whilst lying there, I heard a formation of low flying aircraft roaring back in the direction of England. 'Not many minutes later, some steel-helmeted German soldiers appeared running towards us from an adjacent field. When they reached us, they detached a wooden farm gate from its fittings and lifted me onto it. They carried me quite a distance but I don't remember any conversation. Still sedated and somewhat detached under the influence of the morphine, I was taken to a small wooden hut - a command post of some kind - and placed on soft material, maybe blankets. The other wounded crewmembers were seated and an officer at a desk rang for an ambulance.

'As the effects of the morphine withdrew, I recall feeling terribly weak and sticky as the blood on my saturated jacket began to congeal on the skin of my right shoulder, chest and arm and the pain re-surged. When the ambulance arrived, the three of us, on stretchers, were slotted into it like sardines in a can. We had no clue as to where we were going but later ascertained that we were brought down on the island of Walcheren. At one point, we travelled very slowly across a causeway and, on reaching a town, were carried into a hospital and almost immediately out again, without explanation. We ended up at a German Army Hospital at Goes on Zuid-Beveland. Their X-ray equipment much impressed me and I was given a thorough examination. I soon gathered there was concern about internal bleeding, later confirmed when a group of immaculately uniformed medical officers came around my stretcher, talking earnestly to one another. There was a hush as one bent down to me with a pocket dictionary in one hand, questioning in guttural tones *Belly gut? Belly gut?*

'Taken immediately to the operating theatre, an electric clock on the wall indicated that it was 7pm, seven hours after being shot down. As I lay on the table, before proceedings commenced, several Dutch sisters came across surreptitiously encouraging by touching me and whispering, *Englander gut*. Eventually the chloroform was dropped on to the mask and in a mind-blowing crescendo of screaming sound and flashing lights; I willingly went into oblivion, knowing that this was the only way to recovery. Feelings of regret in my misfortune at being captured came later with the return of health and strength. Subsequent passage of time has brought a wider realisation of what could have happened to me and my abiding response remains - one of immense gratitude that the Providential Hand from above was overruling all things for good.'

Others like Squadron Leader Jack Houlston AFC DFC on 139 Squadron, who with Armitage carried out two runs over Eindhoven, who survived the 'Oyster' operation, went missing on subsequent operations over enemy territory. Though their Mosquito was attacked by two Bf 109s and was shot at by flak Houlston and Armitage got back to report that 'the Philips works was a mass of smoke and fire, explosions were still in progress and some buildings were completely gutted'. Both men were killed in action attacking railway targets in northwest Germany on 20 December. Warrant Officer Ray Noseda DFC and Sergeant John Urquhart on 105 Squadron were KIA on an operation to bomb rail sheds at Rouen on 9 January 1943. Sergeant W. E. Burns who had put down at Ipswich was KIA on 11 February 1943. Four of the pilots on 487 Squadron were all killed on 3 May 1943. One of these was Pilot Officer Stanley Coshall of Auckland who on the Eindhoven raid had flown so close to the Ventura piloted by Sergeant C. J. J. Baker a New Zealander from New Plymouth, that the wings of both aircraft had actually touched 'with a tearing sound'. However, as both had been flying at the same speed no damage was caused. Another was Flight Sergeant Andy E. Coutts of Whakatane, whose Ventura was hit on the Eindhoven raid by an explosive cannon shell which set a Very light on fire, filling the aircraft with smoke. It was finally subdued by Sergeant W. D. L. Goodfellow an air gunner from Takapuna with the aid of a fire extinguisher. (Goodfellow was killed flying with Coutts on 3 May). Pilot Officer 'Rusty' Perryman and Flight Sergeant T. J. Baynton were the other two pilots who died on 3 May while Flight Sergeant T. L. B. 'Terry' Taylor who reached the Strijp target but was unable to release his bombs also failed to return that day.

To the vanquished, death or glory - to the victor the spoils. Hughie Edwards was later promoted to Group Captain and he finished the war as Senior Air Staff Officer, Air Command Far East Asia. Pelly-Fry, who when his crews were billeted at Blickling Hall was nicknamed 'Baron Fry of Blickling', was surprised to be appointed in 1943, Air Equerry to HM King George VI - the first RAF officer to be so honored. Several months later Pelly-Fry managed to discreetly arrange a move from Buckingham Palace and now a group captain, took command of Holme on Spalding Moor, a Halifax bomber station. In 1945 he was posted to Australia to take command of RAAF Camden near Sydney. Pelly-Fry retired from the RAF in 1958 and acted as civil air attaché for Australia and New Zealand until 1962.

Endnotes for Chapter Ten

59 23-year-old Sergeant Patrick. I. Stokes, his pilot, 23-year-old Canadian Flight Sergeant Alexander Gordon Paterson from Saskatchewan, and the two other crewmembers were KIA.

60 *They Hosed Them Out* by 'John Bede'.

61 see *Mosquito Thunder* by Stuart R. Scott (Sutton 1999).

62 Eindhoven was Mike Carreck's final op on 105 Squadron. His tour over he was posted to 17 OTU 'on rest' as an instructor.

63 *They Hosed Them Out* by 'John Bede'

64 *They Hosed Them Out* by 'John Bede'

65 Flight Sergeant Alex G. Paterson RCAF of 487 Squadron, which was hit and crashed off Oostkapelle with the loss of the whole crew.

66 Most likely Sergeant A. M. Swan of 464 Squadron who had about 7 feet of his port wing shot away by light flak.

67 *They Hosed Them Out* by 'John Bede'

68 *They Hosed Them Out* by 'John Bede'

69 107 houses and 96 shops were completely destroyed and 107 Dutch workers and civilians living around the factory were killed and 161 wounded. Among the dead were Joanna van den Broek, wife of H. Bongaarts and their daughters Catharina, Margaretha, Wilhelmina, and son Hendrik who all died at Lijmbeekstraat 404. Lamert A. Raaijmakers, husband of M. S. Elbers and their daughters Albertina, Elisabeth, Geradina, Joanna and Sibeylla, all died at Harmoniestraat 30. Seven German soldiers were killed and eighteen wounded.

Chapter 11

When Frenchmen Bombed Paris

Paul Lambermont

We're flying binding Bostons, at 250 binding feet,
Doing night intruders just to see who we might meet.
And when the daylight dawns again and when we can take a peek,
We find we've made our landfall - Up the Clacton binding Creek.'

A shock awaited the 342 Squadron navigators listed in battle orders when they got into the briefing room. On the large map hanging from the Nissen hut's rear wall, the thread of red wool starting from their airfield, Hartford Bridge, stopped at Chevilly Larue, right at the gates of Paris! The details of the target were briefly summarised: Target No. S 1565 Latitude 48° 46' N Longitude 02° 22' E Height 260 feet. A photograph of the target showed Route Nationale No. 7, the main road from Paris to the Riviera, with at its edge huge electrical transformers from which swarms of cables ran out on to heavy pylons.

So, for Sunday, 3 October 1943 the target was Paris - Paris, where most of 342 Squadron crews had enjoyed their childhood, and spent their youth; Paris, which most of them had last seen three or four years earlier, when they left behind a mother, a wife, a sweetheart and friends. Flight Lieutenant Bond summed up the general feeling: 'It'll be a bloody good show!'

Nobody quite believed it would happen. The past three weeks had gone by without a single operational flight. The station had been permanently on standby. Operations were posted, and then indefinitely postponed. True, during September, the whole of September, the weather had been atrocious. But on this October Sunday morning, it seemed set fair.

On their charts, the navigators carefully marked in their route: 'Hartford Bridge - across the Channel - the French coast at Biville - across the Seine at Mantes - then flight towards Paris.' Attack on the target. Back by quite a different route, over northern France. Red pencils pinpointed the danger spots: enemy airfields, flak batteries, etc; blue pencils circled the church spires on the way, and the high voltage lines likely to be met, for the whole operation was to take place at only a few feet above ground level.

When the navigators had finished with their pencils, computers, their calculations for course, ground speed, ETA etc., the pilots, wireless operators and gunners came into the briefing room. The 342 Squadron CO, Squadron Leader de Rancourt, who was to lead the twelve aircraft, immediately spoke:

'Since the target we shall shortly be attacking is very small, we shall go in at very low altitude. We shall fly in three boxes, each of four aircraft. The first box, which I shall lead, will remain at low level throughout. The two other boxes will be led by the crew of Boston 'N' i.e. Langer and Pierre Mendes France. When these two boxes are about 8 miles from the target, they will climb to 1,500 feet and will drop their bombs on to the explosions caused by the bombs from the first box, and then they will come down and continue flying at low level. So, except for a few minutes, we shall be daisy-cutting throughout the whole operation. At 13.30 hours we shall cross the French coast; at 13.50 we shall be over the target. As the power station is heavily defended by flak, it's possible that one of our aircraft may be hit. If that happens and the aircraft cannot keep flying, the pilot must do everything possible to avoid crashing on dwelling houses. He must try and crash-land his aircraft on the Vincennes artillery ground, or better still, dive it straight into the Seine.'

Before the air crews had time to say a word, the Intelligence Officer started his piece: 'You are one of three squadrons which will today attack three power stations in France supplying the Paris-Orleans railway network, the Paris Ceinture, outer circle, railway, and also providing some of the electricity supply for Paris, the suburbs of Paris and Bordeaux. For the operation to succeed, the three power stations must be destroyed together. The Free French crews of 342 Squadron will have the honour of attacking the trickiest target: Chevilly Larue. 107 Squadron will bomb Chaigny power station near Orleans, and 88 Squadron a power station near Tours. The three squadrons will fly together as far as Essarts-le-Roi and will then separate and make their way singly to their respective targets. This is intended to put the enemy's observer corps off the scent. The whole operation will be carried out at very low level, without fighter cover, except on the way back, where you will be met by eight squadrons of Spitfires between Poix and Beauvais, two airfields occupied by German fighters.'

The Intelligence Officer was followed by the Met. Officer, who said in tones of perfect conviction: 'This is the weather you'll have over the Channel and the Continent: Cumulus, base at 9,000 feet, covering 2/10 to 3/10... visibility will be roughly 12 to 15 miles.'

Then came the finale to the preparations: the ritual of setting the watches: 'In thirty seconds, it will be 11.48...15 seconds...10 seconds...5 seconds...Top!'

All the air crews then had the same time. Briefing was over. Just one hour till take off.

At the dispersal point, de Rancourt personally gave a last word of advice to each air crew: 'Quite close to the target are the working-class districts of Chemin Vert. It is essential that not even the smallest bomb splinter should hit them. Bring your load back, if you're not absolutely sure of yourselves. You can always drop it into the Channel on the way back.'

Some people kept on asking themselves the everlasting question: 'Are we entitled to bomb Frenchmen like ourselves?' Pierre Mendes France, later to become French Prime Minister in a post-war Government, had the answer to those scruples: 'In the last war our fathers bombed Lille and if we won't go to France, then other Allied airmen will go instead of us. Will they aim at their targets with as much care, as much anxious precision as we do? No matter how great may be their desire to spare French lives, we have one more reason than they have to act with the least possible care for ourselves, even if that means running additional risk.'

At 12.55 the twelve Lorraine Squadron Bostons passed with ear-splitting din above the main runway of Hartford Bridge (now renamed Blackbushe) as they headed south. At 13.25 the French coast could be made out in the distance. Seven minutes later, Biville-sur-Mer. Slight pressure on the stick and the aircraft crossed the coast and, led by de Rancourt's group, continued their breakneck flight.

Mere feet below them, in a speedy whirligig jumble, flashed villages, hamlets, tree-lined roads. The countryside rushed past at 250 mph. In the meadows, startled cows ran madly till they crashed into the hedges.

Suddenly a gigantic pylon loomed up straight ahead. In their perspex noses, the navigators crouched low. As the enormous metal structure came closer, they shut their eyes. But the Bostons swung sideways, skimmed the high voltage cables and, with their bellies almost on the ground, kept on going.

After the Normandy houses with their exposed brown and white wooden beams came the large Lyons forest. The Seine was crossed at Mantes and the formation forged on towards the Etang d'Essarts. People out for a walk waved handkerchiefs at the aircraft casting shadows on the ground.

The Bostons went up the Chevreuse valley. Not a sign of flak. Visibility was perfect. In the background, the Eiffel Tower, the Sacre Coeur and other landmarks were already visible. In the foreground was Orly.

At Saint Remy the formation split into two. The box of the four leading aircraft remained at very low level, the eight other Bostons started to climb. In perfect line, as if on parade, the first four Bostons passed 6 feet plumb over the target and dropped their bombs. Just eleven seconds later - delayed action to give the aircraft time to get clear - huge sparks erupted, followed by thick smoke. Then the flak opened up. The aircrafts' heavy machine guns fired downwards raking the target, making a wall of fire.

'We bomb in a few seconds.' It was Flight Lieutenant Mendes France speaking on the intercom, as he adjusted his sight. Followed by the seven other aircraft, he was now at 1,500 feet.

'Left, left...right...steady...steady...Go!'

Into the smoke of the first explosions crashed thirty-two more 500-pounders.

The first round was won! What about the return journey? Course 42 degrees. The bomb-rack doors closed and the aircraft resumed very low level flight. Then the game of leapfrog over the roofs of Paris started. The flak opened up, and evasive action followed evasive action. At Vincennes, the formation zoomed over a game of football.

Course: 'Crepy-en-Valois.' One Boston was limping. Its pilot, Flying Officer Lucchesi, called on the wireless:

'My right engine's packed up. Direct hit by flak. Can you wait for me?'

The ten remaining aircraft (over Paris, one of them had broken formation; and not till the next day did news about it come through on Radio Paris) lowered speed to 170 mph. But it was no good. Lucchesi had to be left behind. The German fighters were out for the kill. The lives of ten air crews could not be risked for one straggler.

12.45. Crevecoeur. Almost a quarter of an hour late for the rendezvous with the fighters! Where had they got to?

Suddenly, a babel of shouts could be heard on the Bostons' wireless sets:

'Hello, Yellow One, look out at four o'clock.'

'Bandits at six o'clock.'

'Roger.' While the crew's gunner was propping d'Astier up against a tree, a loud 'Heraus! was repeated several times. Two German officers, who were out hunting, approached the wreckage of the aircraft with rifles in their hands. Seeing d'Astier and the gunner, they took them prisoner. Fortunately, Lucchesi and Marulli kept their heads and flattened themselves on the ground. The Germans were so pleased with their capture they made no further search. A few hours later, the two who got away were drinking Calvados - the local brand of applejack - to get their strength back. They were hidden by peasants and a month later embarked for England at Austerlitz.

News of what had happened to the other Boston, 'H' piloted by Flying Officer Lamy, came through a day later. Paris Radio, broadcasting a commentary taken from a daily newspaper, said in its midday news:

'A week after an American bomber crashed into the Louvre department store, another plane hit by flak early yesterday afternoon came down in the very heart of Paris 100 yards from the Pont National.

'When the alert sounded, a group of Anglo-American planes was making for the southern suburbs of Paris. Their dirty work done, the pilots turned north towards Ivry. Above Ivry, one of the bombers went out of control, lost height but kept on its course. It skimmed a clump of trees a few hundred yards from the Pont National and then flew just above a pedestrian footpath. When it passed above the railway bridge, one of its wings struck a signal post. The plane was then violently knocked off course and 200 yards further on it exploded in the Seine, not far from Austerlitz Station.

'Rescue workers succeeded in removing the half-dead survivors from the metal body. One of them was burnt to death.'

When he ditched, Flying Officer Lamy had carried out to the letter de Rancourt's final orders: 'At all costs avoid the slightest harm to civilians. Rather than that, ditch into the Seine.'

Every day now thousands of air passengers go from Orly Airport to the Paris terminal at the Invalides station and on the way pass the brand new Chevilly power station. How many of them realise that the power station was not brought fully back into operation until 1948? A full five years after the 342 Squadron bombing!

The attack, which lasted but a few seconds, in fact had incalculable consequences. Chevilly Larue, linked by 220,000 voltage cables to Chaigny, which was simultaneously bombed by 107 Squadron and also drawing on the hydro-electric power sources of the Alps and the Rhine, at that time supplied almost one thousand million kilowatts per year to the Paris district. When it was put out of action, all the local thermal stations had to be pushed to their utmost capacity, but the railways bringing coal from the mines in northern France were then being bombed nonstop.

Twelve aircraft sufficed to disorganise completely the complex organisation supplying electricity to Paris and the railways. Most of the crews later returned to live in Paris, and during 1945 and 1946 had to put up with many annoying power cuts and lighting restrictions. Poetic justice?[70]

Endnotes for Chapter Eleven

70 *When Frenchmen Bombed Paris* by Paul Lambermont, writing in *RAF Flying Review*, June 1957.

Chapter 12

Invasion Days

'On 5 June 1944 at Hartford Bridge' recalls Flight Sergeant Jack Parker 'there began to develop, by mid-afternoon, some sort of a 'flap'. We had been up in 'our' Mitchell II, FV900 in 'C Flight, 226 Squadron, on an exercise involving air-to-sea firing at patches of aluminium powder in the sea just off the Isle of Wight. I was the navigator/bomb-aimer. On looking back, the mentality of those responsible for sending us off on such an exercise in that area at that time must seriously be called into question. However, possibly even they may have been having second thoughts, for it was just after George 'Junior' Kozoriz, our Canadian mid-upper gunner, remarked, 'Jeez, look at all them ships out there', that we had a very panicky 'Return to base' message sent to us personally on VHF We returned...

'On our return we were amazed to find all and sundry being press-ganged into grabbing cans of paint and suitable brushes and painting broad black and white stripes, later to be known as 'invasion stripes', on the wings and fuselages of our Mitchells. Being now somewhat experienced, we ourselves, by methods known only to professional aircrew, managed to skive out of this. However, we did not think of invasion, but rumour-spreaders had been at work, and had accounted for the stripes by saying that we were going to Iceland to protect the Atlantic convoys and the stripes were to help our shipping identify us (partly right, anyway, but hadn't they heard of Coastal Command?). Another faction had us going to the Middle East, but this did seem a bit unlikely in spite of a claim to have seen 'a hangar full of tropical kit'.

'I had just finished an early supper, unwisely as it proved, washing it down with several cups of strong tea, when my Aussie skipper, Flying Officer Grant Crawford Suttie, a pre-war regular RAAF, appeared on the scene. Old 'Sut' told me with some urgency to report to the Operations Room for briefing, as we were to be 'on' that night. I grabbed my kit, mounted my squadron bike and on the 1½-mile ride to the 'Ops' Room, visualised a course either to Prestwick, Reykjavik or St Eval, and ditching in the Bay of Biscay if Gib' didn't come up on ETA. Or were we to bomb Berlin, Berchtesgaden or whatever? No, that's the heavies' job, thank God.

'With such thoughts I entered the Ops Room, having saluted as was de rigueur, and was there amazed to see our route already displayed - 'from HARTFORD to POINT OF AIR to POINT OF AYRE, Isle of Man, to TREVOSE HEAD to STURMINSTER NEWTON to BASINGSTOKE' - thence back to base.I asked, as respectfully as I could, 'What the hell.. .?' The Briefing Officer told me that, as far as I was concerned, it was a VHF calibration trip. What it was as far as he was concerned he didn't say, nor did I press the point, being much too relieved by this 'non-op' operational route being presented.

'(Our flight was, in fact, to test specialist communications equipment, although we did not know this at the time. 'C' Flight was code-named the 'Ginger' Mitchell Flight, a very special and secret Flight under the direct operational orders of SHAEF. From early summer, Mitchells were sent out at night over France, ostensibly on 'Nickelling' - leaflet dropping sorties - but really as a cover for picking up transmissions from agents. To the normal Mitchell crews were added a number of French radio operators. Later, ours was Andre Bernheim, who had been a French film producer and was a personal friend of Charles Boyer. Another was Joseph Kassel, the writer. The special operators' task was to receive transmissions on the 'quarter wave' voice system from agents in Occupied France who were equipped with special radio equipment for the purpose. The normal slow Morse transmission was too dangerous because it could easily be picked up and 'homed' on to by Gestapo direction-finding vans. Quarter wave transmissions, on the other hand, were very difficult to detect at ground level, but they could easily be picked up by an aircraft at 20,000 feet or above by a special operator using 'Ginger' equipment.)

'I prepared the flight plan with some trepidation, for the met forecast was terrible. Cloud base was 1,000 feet, tops 2,000 or above, Icing Index high. I therefore spent more time than usual on the flight plan. I was to be glad of this. At about 2230 we clambered into dear old FV900, by then fully refuelled, but without stripes as I recall. We had not been airborne long before the forecast proved only too accurate. We climbed up through ever-thickening cloud and at one stage, when lumps of ice hurled off the prop were striking the fuselage, I suggested the possibility of a return to base. Young George - he was all of 18 - made the same suggestion, but in more forceful terms. 'Sut', however, was the 'press on' type, so we pressed on. In fact, old 'Sut' really deserved a medal for this trip, for he was on instruments all the way round.

'We saw neither the Point of Air, nor of Ayre. We passed our VHF messages, but got no reply. All I do recall was a broad North Country voice from time to time saying 'Turret to turret, over'. This meant nothing to us. We were now at 20,000 feet, oxygen full on. The oxygen did make one feel just a little intoxicated, at any rate sufficient to take the rough edges off. The cold was fearful. Cabin heating? Don't make me laugh. I was, in fact, far from laughing, for about half-way between Point of Ayre and Trevose Head my excessive tea-drinking earlier now led to an anti-social accident, the stuff freezing on the floor of the kite and costing me a quid later that day to have the long-suffering ground crew mop up.

'No sign of Trevose Head. We were in and out of solid cotton wool cloud. No Gee -that packed up very early on, so we had to rely solely on the flight plan. We got no messages, and no response to our transmissions. We were now heading in the general direction, hopefully, of Basingstoke, and I felt that we were at least sufficiently clear of the hills - we were in awe of these - to start our let-down. I informed 'Sut' accordingly, so down we let through the clag. As the altimeter unwound, I recalled the old joke about 'If this altimeter's correct, we're in a ruddy submarine', and as it went off the scale at zero, I prepared for one big bang and oblivion -1 had a ring-side seat in the nose of the Mitch. But just then the cloud mercifully broke and there, below, perhaps 200 feet, perhaps more, was a broad, winding river meandering through a built-up area. It couldn't be the Rhine, nor the Seine, but. .. 'OK, Sut, two-six-zero Magnetic - sharpish!'

I think 'Sut' put our port wing tip into the Thames somewhere east of Putney Bridge. We whipped round in a split-arse turn - to quote the jargon of the day - and headed in the general direction of Hartford. Continuing our previous course might have led to an even greater anti-social accident, costing more than a quid to clear up, for we were headed for Big Ben and the Houses of Parliament!

'Ten minutes or so later, we were thankfully in the good old Hartford circuit, 'Downwind, cleared to finals'. We landed, cleared the runway, and finally got back to dispersal. We did our post-flight checks - 'IFF off, Petrol off, Switches off - and went off to debriefing. In the mess later we were able to obtain our 'operational' eggs and bacon. The kitchen staff believed that we had been on some daring mission over the invasion beaches. We did not disillusion them, but ate to a background of Mairzy Doats alternating with Lili Marlene. It was only at about 05.30 on 6 June that we even heard of the invasion.

'Now, if anyone mentions D-Day to me, I cannot help laughing. Privately, I picture myself in a pool of urine trying to avoid a too-close encounter with the Mother of Parliaments. A strange sequel to this was that on 28 July 1945 a USAAF B 25 Mitchell similar to ours did collide with the Empire State Building in New York. We might have made a similar spectacular impact.'

'It is D-Day today.' The announcement, made in matter-of-fact tones, brought to an end the weeks of speculation for the squadrons based at Hartford Bridge in Kent. Aircrew of three squadrons, 88, 226 and 342, the Free French Squadron with which Paul Lambermont flew, were gathered for the briefing. 'The time was 0100 hours on 6 June 1944. In front of us were two maps of Europe. Threads of wool, showing the course, stopped at the coast of France. Then the officer who had come from the 2nd TAF to brief us began to explain. Speculation was finally ended when we learned that we were to form the aerial vanguard of the biggest and most important operation of World War II. Ever since the turn of the year we had felt the tempo of things quickening. Then, in late April, Eisenhower himself had come to visit us. 'Hello, boys,' he had said in a familiar way. Then he signalled the aircrew to make a circle round him, and spoke to us in an easy manner. 'I know the good work your crews have done but now you'll have to do twice as much, and keep it up day and night. You will be called on to your last ounce of strength.' The first tangible result of Eisenhower's visit was a long white sheet of paper pinned up on the mess door. It read: 'Second Front Sweepstake. Tickets One Shilling. All Takings will be paid on the Day after the Opening of the Second Front to the Person or Persons Guessing the Right Date.' A footnote added: 'General Eisenhower is not allowed to take part.' There was a brisk sale of tickets, and almost every date in the calendar was picked by someone or other.

April came to an end; May passed; but there was still no Second Front. But there was no rest at Hartford Bridge. In addition to operations, mainly against V1 launching sites, aerodromes and marshalling yards in Northern France, we were put through a very stiff training course. We practised dropping dummy bombs on to the Isle of Wight during combined exercises with Commandos, or we laid smoke screens along the edge of woods, at tree-top height. For this task, the Bostons' normal load of four 500lb bombs was replaced by smoke containers, a cylinder about eight feet long with exhaust pipes hanging down. The smoke escaped from four openings to make up the screen.

At last June came. Operations were virtually at a standstill. There was nothing to do; Hartford Bridge was, in fact, at actions stations. Group Captain McDonald, the new CO, had issued very strict orders. Everybody confined to quarters. No one to leave the station, not even to go to the pub barely two hundred yards from the main entrance. No telephone calls, no telegrams. Aircrew to remain in the crew room or in their quarters. Ground crews to continue with their usual duties.

On 5 June, in the afternoon, I went to the dispersal point. There I got my first hint of things to come. The mechanics were painting white bands on each wing and on the body of the Bostons. 'Yes,' said my mechanic, 'same treatment for all the Bostons and the Mitchells on the station: make them into a fine target for the Heinies' flak. We've also been ordered to keep all aircraft in readiness with smoke containers aboard.' I jumped on my bike and made record time to the officers' mess. Battle orders were posted. There were two of them: one for 88, and one for my squadron, 342. Twelve crews in each squadron were to 'stand by.' On the 342 list, I read: 'A/C Q. Pilot P/O J. Clement. Navigator F/O P. Lambermont.' Briefing was midnight on the night of 5/6 June.

At midnight, after a hurried breakfast, served by WAAFs still half-asleep, the stand-by crews made for the navigation room. There was not a sound to be heard as the officer who had come especially from 2nd TAF HQ explained the part our Bostons were to play in the landing. 'As I'm speaking to you now,' he said, 'the Royal Navy and the United States Navy are already on their way to the Continent; some of the vessels will already be at their destination before daybreak... *Warspite, Rodney, Duke of York* and other vessels will be between the mouth of the Orne and the northern part of Bayeux. To hide them from firing by German coastal batteries, 88 Squadron will lay a smoke screen between the vessels and the famous Atlantic Wall. To make the screen last longer, aircraft will operate in pairs, following each other at ten minutes intervals. . . .

'The Free French in 342 Squadron will be responsible for laying a screen in front of the American invasion fleet off the Cotentin peninsula, between Ste. Marcouf Island and Barfleur Point. Everything quite clear? Right, then,

I'll hand you over to your respective squadron commanders.' Then came endless practical advice. 'To be effective, the screen must start at the level of the waves. As the wind is blowing from the south-west, you won't have any trouble.'

'When you lay the screen, turn your oxygen on full. It's unwise to breathe in any of the smoke that might get forced back into the aircraft. That could happen aft, at the wireless operator's post. Avoid breathing in even the smallest whiff of the smoke. It might seriously damage your lungs.' At 3 am I was completely ready. I went back to my Nissen hut, going over the various points in the briefing. I didn't sleep a wink. What was the use? In two hours I'd be off.

5.45 am. I got into my parachute kit more slowly than usual. I checked my Mae West, tested my mike, made sure that the oxygen supply to my mask worked properly. Sitting on my dinghy and with my safety belt fastened, I spread out my charts and my log. The two 1,800hp engines were already running. The mechanic lifted his thumbs into the air. Our Boston reached the entrance to the runway. Then at full power we took off and the tricycle landing gear disappeared from view. Over countryside still fast asleep, we flew at more than 230 mph. In 20 minutes we reached the sea. As far as eye could see, there was nothing but craft of every kind, an incredible criss-cross of funnels, masts, and tiny balloons kissing the clouds. Suddenly we saw France, right ahead, standing out of the water. The land came at us at full speed. I was only 20 feet above sea level. I looked at the time: 0644 hours. We made one last turn. Every gun in every battery on the Atlantic Wall was firing all-out. The American vessels facing them followed suit. Visibility - roughly eight miles - was better than our briefing had led us to expect. In a few minutes, we'd have to get in between the two opposing sides. I adjusted my oxygen mask. I heard the intercom: 'Everyone OK? Oxygen on full!' Without warning - we were literally skimming the waves - huge columns of water shot up in front of us. The Boston shook to its last rivet. A shell aimed - by the Germans or the Allies had landed a few yards from our aircraft.

The time had come. I pressed the bomb release button, and a miracle happened. An endless stream of thick, whitish smoke belched out behind my Boston, now doing 260 mph. The wireless operator aft shouted, 'Bang on!' We made a perfect run. For a few moments the screen, eight miles long, hid the American armada. When the four containers were empty, I gave the pilot the route back and let out a long 'phew' of content.

At 0730 my Boston touched down at Hartford Bridge and by eight o'clock all the station's aircraft should have been back. There were some casualties. One aircraft in 342 Squadron was missing. It had exploded at sea, very close to an Allied cruiser - a huge sheet of flames rapidly extinguished by the sea water. Another Boston, in 88 Squadron, safely laid its smoke screen ahead of the Royal Navy, and then crashed at its own home base. It smashed into the runway at Hartford Bridge and in no time was on fire. On D-Day the sky was burdened with more than 6,000 aircraft. Of that 6,000, a mere 24 formed the advance guard of the gigantic landing

Armada. Of the 24, 12 were flown by the Free French in 342 Squadron. And I was there with them.'[71]

'On 10 June 1944' recalls Squadron Leader Malcolm Scott DFC 'Flying Officer 'Butch' O'Halloran RAAF's crew had taken part in an evening operation involving 71 Mitchells in a spectacular raid on the Chateau La Caine which Intelligence had established was the headquarters of Panzer Group West. The raid was preceded by 40 Typhoons from 83 Group going in at low level with rockets and bombs, whilst the Mitchells from 98,180,226 and 320 Squadrons attacked from 12,000' using Gee-H with extreme accuracy and concentration. The General Chief of Staff was killed in the bombing along with all his retinue who were dining with him. This necessitated withdrawing the HQ to Paris which seriously delayed the organising of a Panzer counter attack. The raid was described by Viscount Trenchard as an attack of major importance, and proved a turning point in the Allied offensive in Normandy. Night operations followed this raid on 10/11 June and on 11/12 June, but in the late afternoon of the 12th orders came through calling for yet another maximum effort from all six squadrons in 137 and 139 Wings.

'Flight Sergeant (later Flying Officer) Jim Jennison DFC RAAF was on his first tour and the story continues in his own words:

'We were listed as one of the reserve crews on the Battle Order and not called for briefing to the Ops Room. I was standing around in the Flight Office when the crews came out from the briefing. The Squadron CO, Wing Commander R. N. Goodwin, grabbed me and said I was to fly 'upfront' in his aircraft to release the bombs as the met forecast was 8/10ths cloud and bombing would be by 'Gee-H' which his own navigator would operate. As we taxied out I looked round the airfield, and it seemed every Mitchell from the three squadrons was on the move converging towards the end of the runway. Once airborne, I crawled along the tunnel between the cockpit and the bomb aimer's position as we climbed through the murk. Above the cloud, the sky appeared full of aircraft; nine boxes of 139 Wing's Mitchells were joined by six boxes of Mitchells and Bostons from 137 Wing and very soon after a huge escort of Spitfires providing medium and high cover took up position.

'It was a little after 8 pm, still very light, and I was happily sitting in the glazed nose admiring the view of this aerial armada, when I noticed the bank of cloud suddenly come to an end and beyond the edge I could see the Channel and the distant shores of France. I wasn't the only one who'd witnessed this sudden change in the weather conditions. My tranquil existence was shattered when the Wing Commander's voice came through my headphones, 'Jennison, we'll bomb visually!' Shaken, I tried to point out I hadn't attended the briefing, that I didn't know where we were heading exactly, and certainly hadn't a clue as to the actual target. The next moment a target map was hurled down the tunnel and I was told to get on with it! 'Anyone got a bombing wind?' I called out plaintively. The navigator yelled out the wind direction and speed which I inserted into the bomb sight. 'Target height and bomb TV?' More figures came over the intercom which I fed into the computer box. I checked that everything was working correctly on the bomb sight and then tried to sort out the navigation. We were not leading the whole show, thank goodness, but we were leading the squadron's three boxes and all 18 aircraft would bomb on my say-so. Despite the traumas and anxieties, it turned out to be a very successful prang and I sat back afterwards resting on my laurels. The cloud was still over Dunsfold when we got back to base. Subsequently, I learnt at the de-briefing, we'd well and truly plastered a huge concentration of 21st Panzer Group tanks in the Fôret de Grimbocq.'

It was the largest raid carried out by the two Wings since D-Day. Ninety Mitchells and Bostons took part and only two Mitchells from 320 Squadron were lost. One to flak over the target, the other ditched in the Channel, the Dutch crew being picked up later by a British destroyer.'[72]

In March 1945 David J. W. Vickery and his crew were members of 297 Squadron, 38 Group, 2nd TAF stationed at Earls Colne, in Essex and flying Halifax Mk.III's. 'My log book reminds me of the practices: 'MTO (Mass take-off) and formation glider lift' held in mid-March. On the afternoon of the 23rd we had a pre-briefing for pilots, navigators and air bombers for Operation 'Varsity' - a glider lift across the Rhine involving our two squadrons, 296 & 297 and, no doubt, the other squadrons in the group. 17,000 men, with 600 tons of ammunition and 800 vehicles and guns were to be carried in 1,500 aircraft and 1,300 gliders in support of ground forces' big push to cross the last great natural frontier of Nazi Germany. The camp was sealed. I remember being awakened on the morning of 24 March very early (5.30?) and eating a massive breakfast. The Air Minister, Sir Archibald Sinclair, was present at the squadron briefing, standing beside our squadron commander 'Dixie' Dean and after delivering a brief exhortation, he moved along us, no doubt absorbing our feelings of mass excitement and pre-op tension. Walking out to the crew wagons I recognised the novelist, Ernest Hemmingway - a large, genial man with a large hat - intent on being in on the action. The Horsa gliders, containing troops of VI Airborne Division, were positioned at the end of the main runway in close formation, whilst our aircraft were parked further up, on either side, facing inwards and angled like modern cars in a car park. Each crew was deposited by its own kite and we were completing pre-flight checks when the first Halifax taxied out, turned to face the runway, the tow rope was attached and it trundled slowly forward until the rope tightened and the Horsa started rolling.

'The organisation was admirable. The atmosphere taut and purposeful. The Halifax on our left taxied out to the centre of the runway, the trolley ac. was plugged in to our kite and the engines run up as we watched another glider go from stationary to 60 knots in a few tenths of a second and follow its tug before leaving the concrete. The aircraft opposite us taxied out and the process was repeated. Then it was our turn. Flying control ordered us (N Nan) out. We taxied out, turned 90° port, Pinky from the tail turret called 'Tow line attached', and we were off. As our glider, piloted by 'Baldy' of the Glider Pilot Regiment, became airborne and went into high tow, I could see the combination preceding us about two miles ahead and climbing.

'The first Halifax to take off had to fly almost up to Bury St. Edmunds and back, the second to a point a few miles less, and so on; so that the last aircraft to take off turned directly onto course - almost exactly 090°, I remember - as the squadron, with its gliders, formated into a tight box. As we approached the coast we were joined by more and more squadrons of tug aircraft, more Halifaxes, Stirlings and some Albermarles, and by the time we had crossed the coast, south of Harwich, I, from my vantage point in the nose, could see aircraft ahead of us, tightly packed, aircraft above, aircraft below and to port and starboard, each with its attendant Horsa or Hamilcar. Ahead were the formations of Commandos and C47s and Dakotas carrying the paratroops. Over the sea, I went up to have a look out of the astrodome and, looking aft, could see hundreds and hundreds of kites in a huge phalanx, stretching back about forty miles. It really was indescribably impressive. Returning to the nose, I observed squadrons of fighters overtaking our formation at about angels five, whilst other members of the crew who could see switched on their mikes and excitedly remarked on the hundreds of our bombers. Lanes, Mitchells and Bostons returning from their task of softening up targets on the east bank of the Rhine. Somewhere between Rotterdam and Antwerp we were joined by a huge formation of Dakotas towing Waco gliders flying beneath us at 500 feet.

'The landing zone selected for our gliders was east of a wooded area about six miles north of Wesel, and the release point over an elongated lake three miles before the LZ. We made a 10° starboard turn south of Goch and I got a pinpoint over Udem (I still have, in my nav. bag, the Essen sheet I used then). Then I saw the Rhine ahead. I was struck by its width - truly, a big river! Five minutes to the RP. A Stirling, down on our starboard bow, about seventy yards away, received a direct hit, probably from an 88. It disintegrated (apparently slowly) and its glider disengaged smartly. I vividly remember watching the air bomber come out through the shattered nose, doubled up and turning over and over in the air, and thinking 'My God! He hasn't got his chute on'. Then the big river was below us. there was masses of activity on the ground. Flashes of gunfire. Lots of smoke. I counted many burned and broken Messerschmitts. I learned later that the 51st Highland Division and Guards' Armoured had crossed earlier in the day at Xanten and were then engaged on the east bank of the Rhine, I called to Pinky, in the tail, 'Stand by' and then 'Release' and he flashed the signal to our glider pilot. We all felt the effect of the glider's release and Baldy put the Horsa into a steep dive - a lesson learned on D-Day! The Skipper, Reg Langtry, came on the intercom and asked for a course for the rope dropping area. The flak was lighter on the starboard side so, without hesitation, I said 'Diving turn starboard and we'll drop the ruddy thing in the river'. Jack Tipper, the wireless op, remarked that there was enough nylon in the tow rope to make two thousand pairs of nylon stockings. He would! You could hear which way his mind worked. Then we emerged from the chaos and set course for base. I remember thinking to myself triumphantly, 'Well, we've as good as won now - it's all over, bar the shouting'. It felt good to be alive. Six weeks later a newspaper placard appeared outside the mess bearing the legend: 'Latest war result - Allies 1: Germany nil'.[73]

'For more than a week during March 1945' recalls Squadron Leader Malcolm Scott DFC 'the Mitchells and Bostons of 2 Group had been pounding targets in the Rhineland in close support of the 21st Army Group fighting its way to the great river barrier; 22,000 British, Canadian and American casualties had been suffered in clearing the area between the Maas and the Rhine. Xanten, one of 2 Group's earlier targets and more recently the recipient of a devastating night raid by Bomber Command, was now occupied by British and Canadian troops. The last strong bastion of the German troops on the west side had fallen and within a few days the rest of the territory was cleared and the Allied armies stood on the west bank looking at the remains of the Wesel bridge blown up by the retreating Germans.

'For the six squadrons of 137 and 139 Wings in 2 Group (I was a Mitchell navigator in 180 Squadron) the targets now shifted to the east side of the Rhine. At least two, occasionally three, raids were made each day on marshalling yards, communication centres and bridges, oil dumps, billeting areas and barracks, artillery emplacements and troop concentrations. Some penetrations were deeper to important rail centres, but mostly attacks were concentrated in the Weser-Emmerich-Munster area where 'Plunder', the code name for the overall operation covering the Rhine crossing, was to take place. Maximum effort had been ordered, and quite often up to 15 aircraft per squadron took part instead of the usual dozen aircraft in two boxes of six.

'Montgomery's preparations for the Rhine crossing were, as always, massive and painstaking: troops being ferried to the rear echelons to practice 'boat drill' and the handling of small craft up and down the muddy banks of the River Maas at night in preparation for the real thing. There could be no misleading or attempted feints this time. Within a mile or two, the Germans could estimate where the Allied crossing would be made. As Kesselring wrote, 'The enemy's operations in a clearly limited area, bombing raids on headquarters and the smoke-screening and assembly of bridging materials, indicated their intention to attack between Emmerich and Dinslaken with the point of the main effort on either side of Rees.'

'The only questions facing the enemy were when and how. Always before, the Allies had launched a parachute and glider attack as a prelude to the full force of the main assault. Kesselring could but wait to see where the paras dropped, or so he thought.

'In the meantime, RAF medium bombers and Typhoons and the 9th US Air Force Marauders and Thunderbolts carried on with their now familiar role of 'softening up' the area around the chosen points of the great river and the hinterland of the proposed bridgeheads on the east bank. One important road and rail junction town and troop-billeting area was Bocholt, which became the object of almost daily attacks and quickly gained a reputation for providing a very warm reception. On 18 March it was bombed and again two days later. We all got back but with our aircraft and a few aircrew heavily peppered by shrapnel.

'The next morning, 21 March, Bocholt was again listed as the target. On the bombing run No 1 in the box was badly damaged and an air gunner's leg was almost shot away, but the pilot retained control and made an emergency landing at Eindhoven. No 2 in the box received a direct hit as the bombs fell away and virtually disintegrated, taking down No 3, an all-Australian crew, from which one parachute was seen to emerge. This belonged to an air gunner, who, although captured on landing, was freed eight days later by advancing British troops. The pilot of No 4 was severely injured, shrapnel smashing through his right thigh bone, but he managed to retain consciousness long enough to get his aircraft back over friendly territory after bombing, before passing out. The mid-upper gunner then took over the controls and managed, under the pilot's guidance, to crash-land at the first airfield en route without further casualties. The leading aircraft of the second box was seriously damaged by flak, wounding an air gunner, but the pilot pressed on, bombed and led his formation back over the Rhine before breaking away to force-land at Eindhoven. Bocholt deserved its thick red ring on the map as a place to be avoided if possible!

'Of the twelve 180 Squadron Mitchells that had left Melsbroek earlier, only seven returned to base, all with varying degrees of flak damage and some with wounded aboard. Only six aircraft took part in the afternoon show, but the other two squadrons operated 24. The next day they were joined by eleven aircraft on 180 Squadron, attacking an enemy strongpoint near Dingden in the morning and Isselburg in the afternoon. Notification was received of an immediate award of the DSO to the wounded pilot, Pilot Officer Perkins, a CGM to his air gunner, Flight Sergeant J. Hall, who carried out the emergency landing, and a DFC to the leading pilot of the second box, Flight Lieutenant G. Howard-Jones.

'On 23 March the Mitchells and Bostons bombed strong-points near Wesel in the morning and, on return from a second visit to Isselburg in the late afternoon, we were told at debriefing that this was 'R-Day' and that British, Canadian and American troops would be crossing the Rhine that evening at various points on either side of Wesel and Rees. An early night was suggested, and while we slept Bomber Command put in a heavy attack on Wesel.

'Long before dawn on the 24th, R Day plus 1, we were called to attend briefing at 05.30. The target was set for the forest of Diersfordterwald, north west of Hamminkeln where we would be making the final bombing raid before the airborne assault (coded operation Varsity) came in. Our bomb load was six clusters of 20lb AP's. These clusters, large tubular containers, hexagonal in circumference opened at a predetermined height, releasing 15 fragmentation bombs. In turn, these, dropping on parachutes, exploded approximately 50 feet above the ground - very unpleasant. Bombing was to be under MRCP instructions. The Mobile Radar Control Point ground controller, operating in a caravan a few miles from the target, guided the formations when within range of the release point where the bombs were dropped on his instructions. Bombing by this method was extremely accurate producing an average error of only 40 yards. The bombing height was to be between 11,000 and 12,000 feet, approximate heading on bombing run 075, turning right off target after bombing. A mass of information was available and old hands among the navigators had a log sheet already partly completed with all the headings and just filled in the details except the flight plan itself. By 07.35 we were checking over our individual equipment in the aircraft and half an hour later we took off leading 'Grey' Box whilst 'Brown' Box tucked in behind as we set course. We picked up our Spitfire escort as we set course for Xanten where we contacted 'Cosycoat', the MRCP controller. Within minutes we crossed the Rhine but the flak was minimal and not particularly accurate. Bomb doors were opened as the pilots followed 'Cosycoat's' instructions on the run in to the target and the 6 clusters dropped clumsily away from each bomber. Flak was now more accurate but, judged by earlier standards, only moderate. 'Cosycoat' signed us off and took control of another box running in. It all seemed very impersonal as the bombing details were noted in the log and the pilot was given the new course and it was not until we'd made our right turn off the target that I became aware of all the activity taking place below. Even during the Ardennes breakthrough in the snow of the previous December and January I saw nothing to match the scene below us.

'On either side of the river we could see the ripple of flashes from gun batteries and tanks and the occasional puff of dust and smoke as a flurry of shells landed. The little boats (from our height) handled by the Navy were ploughing back and forth across the river and we could see the spans of the demolished bridges lying in the water. Already pontoon bridges were being thrown across the great waterway looking like threads of cotton. We knew, although we couldn't see them, that the Army and Marine Commandos alongside various infantry units were fighting around Rees and Wesel and our tanks were already in action on the east bank, having 'swum' across during the night and early morning. Smoke was still drifting about and we could see Tempests, Typhoons, Mustangs and Thunderbolts diving in to attack enemy positions. We learned afterwards that Churchill was there on a high vantage point with Alan Brooke, Eisenhower and Tedder, but I don't think they got the marvellous view we did.

'As we left the Rhine behind us we could see, coming in from the west, several thousand feet below, the vanguard of the Airborne Divisions. Dakotas, C-46 Commandos and C-47s loaded with paratroopers and their equipment occupied the first waves of the assault, heading three great columns stretching back as far as the eye could see. Following the paratroops came the gliders towed by Halifax, Stirling and Albermarle tugs, and, of course, the ubiquitous Dakotas. Our south-westerly course was gradually taking us away from this awe-inspiring sight. We hoped our bombing had been of support and had reduced in some measure the opposition that the Airborne were bound to encounter.

'Our fighter escort left us over Goch and we were all back at base by

10.10. There was the inevitable 'turn round' call; the bomb trolleys were waiting to fill the empty bellies of our aircraft as we taxied in. Another briefing was on at 10.45 and the Squadron was airborne again by 12.50, attacking another strong-point near Brunen. The great colonnade had gone. All that remained of it were masses of 'broken' gliders and splashes of discarded parachutes. Smoke and gunfire were still in evidence, but it was not the same. The morning of 'R-Day + 1' was the only time that I really appreciated to the full our true role in tactical air support'.

Endnotes for Chapter Twelve

71   *I Laid The D-Day Smoke Screen* by Paul Lambermont, writing in *RAF Flying Review,* August 1958.

72   *How to Succeed Without Really Trying* by Malcolm Scott writing in *Intercom* magazine, winter 1986.

73   *Intercom* magazine winter 1986.

Chapter 13

They Flew Mosquitoes

No praise is too high for the gallant Mosquito and the team of designers, led by Captain Sir Geoffrey de Havilland, who produced it. In the 1914-18 war it was the de Havilland DH.4 which turned the tide of aerial warfare. In WWII the DH.98 - the Mosquito - won the same laurels: the fastest aircraft then in service in the world. Commercial aviation virtually died when World War II started. A year later, invasion barges filled Continental ports, Britain s cities were being bombed, submarines cut supplies. But Geoffrey de Havilland looked past the threat of invasion and set to work to design the tools of victory. He whipped out an extraordinary twin-engined fighter-bomber, the Mosquito, built of wood. The Mosquito became the sensation of the RAF and over seven thousand of them helped to save Britain in the years to come. It was incredibly fast: when de Havilland's son Geoffrey, test pilot for the Company, flew it, he hit 420 mph. De Havilland was knighted and his name evoked respect and gratitude from his countrymen. Then, at this high point, the treacherous air hit back. His second son, John, also a company test pilot, was killed in a Mosquito collision. Thousands were dying for their country, but Sir Geoffrey could not forget that John died in a D.H. plane, flying under D.H. orders. And yet another disaster was in the making. In 1946 de Havilland built the experimental D.H.108, and released it to 36-year-old Geoffrey for test. In the first cautious trials the new plane behaved beautifully, but as Geoffrey stepped up the speed he unsuspectingly drew closer to an invisible wall in the sky - the Sound Barrier. One evening he went still faster and his plane disintegrated. Young Geoffrey's body was not found for ten days. De Havilland was unable to go near the factory for two weeks. Lady de Havilland, hard hit, died three years later. There was one son left, not a test-pilot, and he and his father took up their lives again with a dreadful sense of having paid too much to the air.

Geoffrey de Havilland; the unconquerable pioneer of the air by Francis Vivian Drake, writing in RAF Flying Review in 1959.

Berlin, January 30th, 1943...Berlin, the heart of Hitler's Germany at the height of the war... Berlin on the tenth anniversary of the German Army. A big military parade has been planned to celebrate the occasion and from early dawn Nazi troops have been assembling in the capital ready to stage a mighty demonstration of their omnipotence. It is announced that Reichsmarschall Goering will broadcast at 11 am, to be followed at 4 pm by Propaganda Minister Goebbels. It should be a big day for the Nazis. But the anniversary has not gone unnoticed in England. In the chilly air of early morning three Mosquito aircraft are warming up their engines on the runway at Marham airfield. Shortly after half-past eight Reggie Reynolds (later Wing Commander

'Reggie' W. Reynolds DSO DFC) strides up to the leading plane with his navigator, Pilot Officer E. B. 'Ted' Sismore (later Flight Lieutenant Ted Sismore DSO DFC). A last-minute check on the Met report - it seems OK - and then Reynolds turns to the two other crews of 105 Squadron. 'All right, chaps,' he says. 'Let's go.' The RAF is off to drop its own highly individual birthday present on the Reich. This is the first raid on Berlin ever made in daylight and no one knows quite what to expect. Reynolds is relying on the high speed of the Mosquito to keep him out of trouble from German fighters but on the five-hour round trip there will not be much fuel to spare for evasive tactics. The plan is to drop the bombs dead on eleven o'clock to coincide with the beginning of Goering's speech and this will require some pretty accurate navigation. Sismore is confident that he can do the job: he is the squadron's ace navigator and is later to lead the Pathfinders in some of the war's most devastating raids.

Germany basks in brilliant sunshine on this January morning. The three Mossies have flown at low-level over the North Sea, then high, higher into the heart of Germany. A few minutes before eleven o'clock the tell-tale lakes around Berlin show up as bright white patches as they glint in the sunshine. Dead on target come the Mossies and at eleven o'clock precisely Sismore says 'Bombs away.' There are no enemy fighters, very little flak. The Germans have been taken completely by surprise. The timing could not have been better. At eleven o'clock listeners to the German radio are told by the announcer to stand by for an important speech by Goering. At one minute past eleven, accompanied by the explosion of bombs around the broadcasting studio, the programme fades out. There is a long pause. Then, 'There will be some delay' apologises the announcer. Gramophone records fill the gap. It is not until an hour later that the voice of Goering, plainly harassed and angry, comes on the air. By then the three Mosquitoes are winging their way safely back home. Opposition has been practically negligible: only Flight Lieutenant John 'Flash' Gordon DFC and Flying Officer Ralph G. Hayes DFC, flying back over Bremen in error, receives the violent reception from the ground defences that is his due.

But the RAF has not finished yet. Herr Goebbels is to speak at 4pm and there is a birthday surprise for him, too. At 1.25 pm three more Mosquitoes, this time from 139 Squadron, take off from Marham. Led by by Squadron Leader Donald F. W. Darling DFC and Flying Officer William Wright, they fly at wave-top height over the North Sea to a point north of Heligoland, then inland towards Lübeck. By now the weather has deteriorated and it is squally and raining all the way. By now, too, the German defences are on the alert and there are indications that the intruders will meet with stiff opposition. As the Mossies turn on to the climbing leg to 20,000 feet, Sergeant R. C. 'Lofty' Fletcher, observer in the second plane flown by Sergeant J. Massey, shouts out a warning of bandits. A bunch of Me 109s have spotted the Mossies and are giving chase. Sergeant Massey takes violent evasive action and manages to give them the slip. The third pilot, Flight Sergeant Peter John Dixon McGeehan and Flying Officer Reginald Charles Morris, throws them off too. But two of the Jerries have fastened on to the tail of Squadron Leader Darling and he dives down out of control; he fails to return from the mission.[74]

The two remaining Mosquitoes continue on their course - over Scherm and then above cloud. At ten minutes to four they are over Berlin and Sergeant Massey drops his bombs. The flak is intense, determined to avenge this slight to German power. It is another eight minutes before McGeehan can get into position to let his bombs away and they are seen to burst some half mile south of the city centre. The German radio this time continues without interruption and Goebbels' speech goes out as planned, but listeners note that he has obviously taken the precaution of speaking from an underground studio. There is no time for more observation. McGeehan and Massey turn their Mosquitoes wildly to avoid the flak and some FW 190s which have come upon the scene. The speed of the Mossies gives them the advantage of the subsequent encounters and they soon drop down to low level for the long flight back to the Dutch coast. Over the Frisian Islands the AA guns bark again, but ineffectually. At half-past six the operation is over, as the two Mosquitoes come in to land at Marham. They have carried out the most audacious raid yet. They have proved that from henceforth even the German capital is not immune from attack in daylight as well as at night.[75]

The story of the Mosquito in the annals of British air warfare is packed with incidents like these. De Havilland's 'Wooden Wonder' (its structure was almost entirely of plywood and balsa sandwich) served in every operational command of the RAF and revolutionised the concept of aerial attack. Built around two Rolls Royce Merlin 21 engines, its high speed (408 mph for the Mark IX bomber version) made it almost impossible to intercept and Mosquito bombers carried no defensive armament at all. They did not need it. The prototype flew for the first time on 25 November 1940 and Air Ministry tests began in February of the following year. Then, on 31 May 1942 four Mosquitoes of 105 Squadron struck their first blow against the enemy. It was an auspicious and noteworthy date, for this dawn attack by the Mossies followed the first thousand-bomber raid on Cologne on 30 May. The Mosquitoes' bombs created more havoc in the ravaged city, but their main task was to take photographs of the destruction.

Thereafter the Mosquitoes were at first used mainly for their nuisance value and for some particularly daring intruder raids against enemy-occupied territory. A typical operation was that led by Wing Commander Hughie Edwards VC on 27 January 1943 when nine Mosquitoes from 105 and 139 Squadrons attacked the submarine Diesel engine works in the shipbuilding yards of Burmeister and Wain at Copenhagen. The 1,400-mile round trip strained the Mossies' endurance to the utmost, loaded as they were with 500lb bombs and for two hours it was heavy going through banks of cloud and rain over the North Sea. There was one early casualty. Shortly after crossing the enemy coast, ack-ack guns began belching out at the intruders and making things unpleasant with some pretty accurate fire. Suddenly Flight Lieutenant Gordon called out, 'I've been hit!' Blue smoke was pouring from his starboard wing and he naturally jumped to the conclusion that flak had caused some radical damage. In fact it wasn't flak, but at the speed things were going now it was easy enough to misjudge. Turning on his tracks and weaving violently at low level to avoid the hail of shells from the ground, Gordon roared at roof-top height over the enemy countryside. For one moment it looked as though he would make it and get away, but then, by a cruel mischance, his port wing caught in some telegraph wires below. The raid was over for Gordon - though he got back to take part in the Berlin raid three days later. Eight Mossies left now.[76]

Over the target the weather improved and conditions were perfect as, with dusk falling, Hughie Edwards led his crews in over the Danish capital. Speeding in between 50 and 300 feet up the pilots dodged the chimneys and many spires of Copenhagen making for the island east of the city, where the shipbuilding yards stand. There was intense flak now, both from shore batteries and ships in the harbour and the Mosquitoes were so low that they had to dodge the tops of the vessels' masts. At five minutes past five the first bombs were away: they had delays ranging from 11 seconds to 36 hours and all the bombers managed to hit the target area. As they turned away they noticed a huge fire and the flames shot 100 feet up into the air.

Enemy fighters were on the alert now, but, with their bomb loads gone, the Mosquitoes were too quick for them. It was an unlucky shell from an ack-ack gun on the Danish mainland that sent Sergeant Dawson crashing into the ground with a terrific explosion. There was another casualty, too. Damaged by flak, the Mossie piloted by Sergeant Clare managed to struggle back to make an emergency landing near Shipdham but crashed as it hit the ground. Six Mosquitoes of the original nine landed safely at Marham at twenty minutes to eight. They had been in the air for five hours and 13 minutes.

Perhaps the most spectacular of all Mosquito operations were those against individual, pin-pointed targets of special significance. The famous raid on Amiens jail in February 1944 when the outer walls were blasted to allow over 200 political prisoners to escape is so well-known as to need no repetition here. But there were other similar exploits. There was for instance, the raid by Mosquitoes of 613 Squadron on a Gestapo headquarters at The Hague in April 1944. To avoid casualties among Dutch civilians the raid had to be meticulously planned and executed. The Gestapo HQ was situated in a house in the Scheveningsche Weg, near its junction with Carnegie Plein. Its value as a target lay in the fact that the house contained many thousands of documents, collected laboriously over a period of years - documents relating to the activities of the Dutch resistance movement and black-lists of suspected 'traitors.'

Preparations for the raid went on for weeks beforehand in conditions of strict secrecy. A scale model of the house was built to familiarise the crews with the look of the building from the air and reconnaissance photographs and maps were pored over until every detail was imprinted on the pilots' minds. Success would be measured not in yards but in feet and inches. Leading the half-dozen Mosquitoes was Wing Commander R. N. 'Bob' Bateson DFC and his navigator Flying Officer B. J. Standish. Splitting his small force up into three sections, Bateson's plan was for the three pairs to come in at two-minute intervals, dropping high-explosive and incendiary bombs. The high degree of accuracy required necessitated run-ins at the lowest possible level. For some time the pilots circled behind The Hague, then Bateson led the first pair in, skimming the housetops and making straight for the target building. A German sentry stood on duty at the front entrance of the house and screamed with horror as he saw the Mosquitoes streaking towards him. Throwing away his rifle, he ran for his life. Nearer, nearer... then 'Bombs Away!' Flight Lieutenant Peter C. Cobley, in the second plane, saw his leader's bombs going 'right in at the front door.' A parade was going on in the yard behind the building and some other off-duty soldiers were playing football. No further goals were scored that day, for Cobley's machine came in over their heads and scattered the troops in all directions. More bombs, dead on target.

Squadron Leader Charles W. M. Newman led in the next pair two minutes later. The house was now partly obscured by smoke, but he and his colleague dropped incendiaries across it. Last in were Flight Lieutenant Vic A. Hester and Flying Officer Ray Birkett and a Dutch pilot, Rob Cohen, an ex student at the Delft Technical University who had escaped to England by canoe. Hester attacked with more incendiaries and delayed-action HEs, but the Dutchman had bad luck as his bombs hung up. Despite two circuits and two runs over the target he could not get them away and had to return home without scoring.[77] It was only at the end of the attack that any flak came from the town and it was spasmodic and inaccurate. The Germans had been taken completely by surprise. Reconnaissance photographs later showed that the target building had been reduced to rubble while neighbouring houses were untouched. The only bomb which overshot landed in a German barracks. An Air Ministry bulletin at the time described this as 'probably the most brilliant feat of low-level precision bombing of the war.'

A similar attack took place at the end of October the same year when the target was the Gestapo Headquarters at Aarhus in Denmark. Led again by Reggie Reynolds (a Wing Commander now), aircraft from three squadrons took part in the raid - Nos. 21, 464 and 487 Squadrons - twenty five Mossies altogether. The Gestapo headquarters were housed in two adjoining buildings which had previously been part of the University of Aarhus and it was necessary to come in low and pinpoint the target to avoid the possibility of destroying other Danish buildings of no military value. The Mosquitoes roared off from Thorney Island shortly after 7am for their long flight across the North Sea. They were loaded with thirty-five 500lb bombs with 11-second delays and were escorted by eight Mustangs. On the way across enemy territory the fighters beat up trains and scattered troop concentrations, then the Mosquitoes swept in over the Gestapo building, dropping their bombs dead in the centre of the target and leaving it a smoking ruin. Over 200 Gestapo Officials were killed and all the records were destroyed. The attack was carried out so low that one aircraft actually hit the roof of the building and the port half of its tailplane was wrenched off, together with the tail wheel. In spite of this and in spite of the heavy flak that surrounded the target area, all the planes landed safely.

There were two 'Casualties' not due to enemy action, however: collisions with birds in the air. This was a common occurrence with Mosquitoes, due to their high speed. On many occasions sea birds intercepted the Mosquitoes far more successfully than did the enemy. During an attack on Tours, Flying Officer Dean experienced the devastating effect of such a collision. The bomb aimer's perspex was shattered, the starboard mainplane was badly holed and a bird was found protruding from the port mainplane. Dean himself received a cut over the eye and a mouthful of feathers!

By virtue of their speed and manoeuvrability the Mosquitoes were often at the spearhead of attacks carried out by other aircraft. Their role as Pathfinders for the 'heavies at night became familiar towards the end of 1943.

Devastating as the Mosquito was with its ' sting' administered by four machine-guns, the advent of the six-pounder cannon, slung underneath the aircraft's fuselage and firing in quick succession as the Mossie dived to attack, proved more deadly still. The cannon was first fitted to three Mosquitoes which became a detachment of a secret experimental squadron at the end of 1943. The first major success was achieved on 25 March 1944 for which Flying Officer D. J. Turner and his navigator Flying Officer Des Curtis were awarded the DFC. Escorted by four fighters, Turner and another Mosquito pilot were on patrol off the French western coast, near the Ile de Ré, when they flew slap-bang into a hail of shells flung up by an enemy destroyer. The flak caught the British pilots by surprise and momentarily broke up their formation. Two minutes later Turner was flying over a coastal minesweeper when he saw ahead of him... could it be? Yes, a fully-surfaced U-boat! The target was too good to miss. Roaring in over the minesweeper and weaving violently to evade the flak, Turner attacked the U-boat with his six-pounder and scored numerous hits. While he was doing this, the other Mosquito roared in and raked the decks of the surface vessels with machine-gun fire and cannon. The U-boat disappeared into the sea and a large oil patch on the surface was all that was left.

In all, 6,700 Mosquitoes of all types were built and delivered during the war years. In Bomber Command, Mosquitoes were responsible for dropping 26,867 tons of bombs on enemy targets. From 20 February 1945 Mosquitoes bombed Berlin for 36 consecutive nights and the last bombs on Berlin during the war were dropped by Mosquitoes. In Fighter Command, Mosquitoes defended Britain by night for three years, during which period they shot down 600 enemy aircraft and destroyed 600 flying bombs in 60 nights. Mosquitoes did the major part of the photographic work in Europe, Burma and the South Pacific.[78]

Endnotes for Chapter Thirteen

74 Darling and Wright were buried in Berlin's 1939-45 war cemetery.

75 Flight Sergeant Peter J. D. McGeehan DFM and Flying Officer Reginald C. Morris DFC were killed on the 16 March raid by sixteen Mosquitoes of 105 and 139 Squadrons led by Squadron Leader John Berggren DFC on roundhouses and engine sheds at Paderborn and are buried at Den Burg, Texel.

76 On the night of 5/6 November 1943 26 Mosquitoes carried out small-scale raids on Bochum, Dortmund, Düsseldorf, Hamburg and Hanover. Flight Lieutenant John 'Flash' Gordon DFC and Flying Officer Ralph Gamble Hayes DFM in a 105 Squadron Mosquito were returning over Norfolk. They tried to land at Hardwick, an American Liberator base when at 21.10 hours they crashed into a field at Road Green Farm, Hempnall, about ten miles south of Norwich. Both men were killed.

77 Cohen was killed later that summer on a sortie over France.

78 Peter Williams, writing in *RAF Flying Review*, April 1956.

Index